YOUNG KING

YOUNG KING

THE MAKING OF
MARTIN LUTHER KING JR.

LERONE MARTIN

AMISTAD

An Imprint of HarperCollins*Publishers*

HarperCollins books may be purchased for educational, business, or sales promotional use. For information, please email the Special Markets Department at SPsales @harpercollins.com.

hc.com

FIRST EDITION

Designed by Jason Kayser

Library of Congress Cataloging-in-Publication Data has been applied for.

ISBN 978-0-06-334094-7

Printed in the United States of America

26 27 28 29 30 LBC 5 4 3 2 1

For Bishop, Benjamin, Livingston,
and all the Young Kings . . .

Contents

Part Three: Finding God

Part Four: Finding a Life

Part Five: Finding a Wife

Introduction

I n February of 1948, nineteen-year-old Martin Luther King Jr. decided to apply to seminary.

While filling out the application, one section nagged him: "Give your personal reasons for the decision to study for the Gospel Ministry." This was a complicated question.

He had long ago sworn off the ministry, pledging to become a physician, maybe a lawyer; some profession that could contribute to society. He considered ministry backward. It lacked intellectual respectability. Besides, his overbearing father was a minister. The young King traveled the traditional rebellious road of opposing dad. Yet now as a college senior he had changed his mind and decided to pursue formal ministerial training.

"My call to the ministry was quite different from most explanations I've heard," he sheepishly wrote in cursive. He had not experienced any of the miraculous signs that often accompany divine calls. No angels had appeared before him. No burning bushes. No voice from heaven directed his journey. And yet, he remained confident he had found his calling.[1]

King grounded his blessed assurance in the summer he spent working on a tobacco farm in Connecticut's Farmington Valley. "[My] dicision [sic] came about in the summer of 1944," he wrote.[2]

That fateful season, the then fifteen-year-old made the journey from his home in Atlanta, Georgia, to the Farmington Valley to participate in Morehouse College's annual work program. He went to earn funds for college tuition, but reaped so much more.

During the three months he spent on the Cullman Brothers' shade tobacco farm in Simsbury, Connecticut, King freely explored the nearby Northern cities of New York, Hartford, and Boston. For the first time, he saw life beyond the bounds of the Jim Crow South. No signs berating him with Whites Only or Colored Only. He ate where he wanted; he spoke to whomever he wanted. He shopped where he pleased and had his choice of seats at the movie theater. He was also elected the religious leader by his coworkers. In that role, he preached his first sermons in the farm's ramshackle barns.

Connecticut was not paradise. He was also stopped by the police for the first time, swept up in a Northern whirlwind of antiblack policing.

But he had seen a path toward service and racial equality. The summer, he wrote on his application, caused him to be gripped by "an inescapable urge to serve society . . . a sense of responsibility which I could not escape."

The summer of 1944 would forever stalk King. Throughout his life, he pinpointed his time in Connecticut as the light that illuminated his path and fueled his unshakable commitment to God and humanity. "I came to see that God had placed a responsibility upon my shoulders," he later reflected, "and the more I tried to escape it the more frustrated I would become." On this farm, far from home, King found the key that unlocked his freedom dreams.

The growing list of King biographies and media have virtually ignored the importance of the words King wrote about his journey to the ministry—how he transformed from a kid who swore off the ministry to one of the world's most iconic clergymen. King biographers have taught us much about the man and his ministry, but too often his path is treated as a foregone conclusion. Narratives of his life rush through his adolescence to get to his momentous adult years in the civil rights movement. This oversight gives us a King who arrives in our consciousness and public memory as a determined superhero with no backstory.

However, King was not born a hero. Like all heroes, he was shaped; and it is only by attending to our hero's background that we can truly understand the origins of his strengths, weaknesses, and the moral compass that guides him. There would be no visionary without the quotidian ingredients of his childhood and adolescence. As his sister Christine King Farris liked to say, "Every now and then I have to chuckle as I realize there are people who actually believe ML just appeared. They think he simply happened, and that he appeared fully formed, without context, ready to change the world. Take it from his big sister, that's simply not the case."[3]

The man, the minister, the political theorist, and the activist that Reverend Martin Luther King Jr. became was not inevitable. He was shaped; and he was shaped, in part, in the Connecticut River Valley.

"He always referred back to the summers he spent in the tobacco fields," close friend and aide Andrew Young remarked. "If it hadn't been for . . . the tobacco fields, we might never have gotten the Martin Luther King we got."[4]

This book chronicles how that overlooked summer in the life of Reverend Martin Luther King Jr., as well as the neglected years that preceded and succeeded that moment—his birth, his family, Ebenezer, junior high, a school shooting, high school, Morehouse, seminary, and, finally, meeting and marrying the experienced activist Coretta Scott—all coalesced to produce a man, a minister, and a dreamer who changed the world.

This journey requires many things of us. It asks us to strip Reverend Dr. King of the iconic status that adorns him today and allow him to simply be an adolescent. This vantage point has been rare in popular assessments of adolescent King, and Black youth more broadly. Black childhood is scarcely granted the measure of innocence and grace that should accompany it. Instead, modern social scientists have argued, Black children are consistently portrayed and treated as older and bigger; not as children, but as adults. The moral failings of Black youth are then treated as character flaws, as opposed to the folly of youth.[5] This book departs from that vice. It provides space for the young King to be young.

It allows us to see him as a toddler with the innocent dream of being a fireman. It invites us to witness a preteen renounce his faith, only to find it again. It allows us to see a student whose academic struggles are interspersed with flashes of brilliance. It summons us to see a kid with the audacious ambition to enroll in college at the age of fifteen with a dream to become a world-changing lawyer. It bids us to see an adolescent scarred by white supremacist violence, leaving him drowning in the hatred and resentment of white people and turning to agnosticism for answers. It permits us to see a teenager draped in all the fits and starts that hallmark those strange, all-too-familiar years: thoughtfulness and selfishness; passionate infatuation and aggressive apathy; extrovert and introvert; growth and immaturity; excellence and mediocrity; confidence and insecurity; insightfulness and ignorance; jubilance and depression. It forces us to witness the roller-coaster ride that is young love. And it enables us to behold the humility of humanity, the sinner and the saint.

He was extraordinary, ordinary, and everything in between.

The book then beckons us to allow King the opportunity to make discoveries and missteps along the way: We get to walk with him as he searches for an identity, as he tries to find God, as he attempts to discern a vocation and a calling, and finally, find love and a life partner.

In this little-known story we get to see a King of flesh and blood, one seeking direction and meaning in life. In return, we receive the privilege of witnessing how a vacillating soul became an anchor of the country's spiritual and democratic life.

Part One

FINDING A NAME

1
LITTLE MIKE

Noon. Tuesday, January 15, 1929. The mood in the family's up-stairs bedroom at 501 Auburn Avenue was as overcast as the gray sky in Atlanta.[1]

Death seemed to loiter. Mrs. Alberta Christine King was in pain-ful labor with her second child. Everyone in the room knew the stakes. In interwar America, Black mothers and their children died during childbirth at more than twice the rate of white women. It was an inequity *Time* magazine would label the "Number 1 public health problem" of the era. Alberta was particularly in danger of becoming another statistic. It had been only sixteen months since the difficult birth of her daughter, Willie Christine.

That pregnancy had drained Alberta. The Reverend Michael King believed his twenty-five-year-old wife quietly suffered from an-gina. The reduced blood flow to the heart, often triggered by exer-tion or stress, caused her severe chest pain, sometimes spreading to her neck, shoulders, and arms. Left unattended, it could even cause a heart attack. Pregnancy made it worse, putting extra strain on an already strained heart. The firstborn, whom everyone called Chris-tine, arrived early. But she seemed to inherit her mother's pain. She suffered from an abiding fever and bouts of violent seizures. Doctors were clueless and helpless. The family's church, led by Alberta's dad Reverend A. D. Williams, prayed for the child's deliverance. Until one day, the illness simply went away. Now it seemed the laboring Alberta would need a second miracle to give birth to her second child.

As she came in and out of consciousness, the room was covered in prayers and the smell of chemical disinfectants. The flu pandemic, which had begun seven weeks earlier, had spread quickly, killing more than twenty-six thousand souls across the nation. Seven thousand cases of the flu were reported in Atlanta alone. The virus even visited the Governor's Mansion, infecting Governor Lamartine Hardman, a practicing physician. The Kings hoped sickness and death would skip their door.[2]

Fears rose when the second born entered the world completely motionless. Eyes closed. No crying. Not even a breath.

Everyone in the family's upstairs bedroom—Alberta's midwives, and Dr. Charles Johnson—took their cue from the newborn, holding their breath. The anxious father—Michael King had married his bride on Thanksgiving Day 1926 and moved into that very bedroom in his in-laws home—paced in the hallway.

Was the child dead?

The doctor dangled the motionless newborn by his tiny ankles. He tapped the brown, wrinkled skin on the baby's naked bottom, looking for signs of life. The pat elicited only a loud silence. The baby did not move. The only sound was the gasps of the adults in the room.

The doctor tried once again. Making a viselike grip on the baby's ankles, he coiled his hand back even farther, hoping a harder smack would impart life into the lifeless, dangling body.

Whack!

The baby boy slowly opened his eyes, expanded his tiny chest, and spit out a weak cry. His trickle of tears broke the dam of pent-up emotion in the room. The first sound from the child's vocal chords elicited joy and tears. It was a harbinger of the life to come.[3]

A slumped but smiling Alberta held the child who would tease her for years about his challenging birth: "I hear that I was a burden to you in the period before I was born," he would say. "Was I worth it?"

The same smile would flash across her face as she promised the child named after his father that she would do it all over again.[4]

And she did. A year and a half later, she would give birth to another boy. Alfred Daniel, known as AD, arrived on June 30, 1930.

Three children: born in less than three years.

But there was something special about the firstborn male. When Daddy King heard the cries of his first son, he could not contain himself. He leapt with delight, slapping the ceiling, as if giving the heavens a high five for the gift of a boy. Father and son would respectively be known as Michael and Little Mike.[5]

Christine and Little Mike, 1931.
Lillian Watkins, Daddy King's secretary and the children's
Sunday school teacher, met Little Mike around this time.
She was immediately taken with "the fat normal child,"
occasionally serving as a babysitter.

2
501 AUBURN AVENUE

Little Mike was born on Black Atlanta's main street.

"Sweet Auburn," as locals called it, was a stretch of two blocks, comprising the commercial, cultural, and civic heart of Black Atlanta. It intersected with the city's main commercial district, Peachtree Street. But in the Jim Crow South, the citizens of these thoroughfares did not converge, rather they existed on parallel planes. One Black. One white. In 1956, *Fortune* magazine labeled Auburn Avenue the "Black Peachtree" Street, the "Richest Negro Street in the World," and with good reason. The avenue was home to two towering institutions of Black business: Citizens Trust Bank opened on the avenue in 1921, becoming the first Black-owned bank to join the Federal Reserve. The Atlanta Life Insurance Company, founded in 1905, quickly became a leading Black enterprise. At its height, it was the second-largest African American insurance company in the country.

Alongside these monuments to Black capitalism were the Black-owned businesses and organizations they financed, insured, and patronized. The *Atlanta Daily World*—the first Black daily newspaper in the country—was headquartered on Auburn Avenue, as well as the local offices of the NAACP, the Odd Fellows, the Masons, and the

National Urban League. The Top Hat Club hosted celebrity musicians including Bessie Smith, Cab Calloway, Louis Armstrong, Dizzy
Gillespie, and Duke Ellington. Barred from staying in white hotels,
these stars lodged at Sweet Auburn's Savoy Hotel.

Segregation made it a common sight to see celebrities dining
alongside everyday folk at Henry's Grill, or weighing in on the famous fried chicken and barbecue ribs at Ma Sutton's Restaurant. Local giants such as John W. Dobbs, the Grand Master of the Prince
Hall Masons of Georgia who was dubbed "the mayor" of the avenue, and Reverend J. M. Gates—bestselling phonograph preacher,
made news in the Atlanta Daily World for sporting new cars, wardrobes, or race philosophies on "The Ave." Between clips at the Silver
Moon Barber Shop, locals weighed in on everything, trading gossip
and verbal sparring alongside civic strategies and the latest in Negro
Leagues Baseball. Yates and Milton Drug Store was home to a soda
fountain, milkshakes, and soapbox pulpits, while parishioners filed
into Big Bethel African Methodist Episcopal Church and Ebenezer
Baptist Church to hear the professional pulpiteers. Black Atlantans
were sandwiched between these commercial and cultural spaces all
along the Ave. Jim Crow segregation forced Black residents of all
classes to live together. Large houses shared the avenue with small,
narrow shacks, known as shotgun houses, and boarding rooms.[1]

To take a summer stroll along Little Mike King's street was to
journey through this Black world in all its overcrowded abundance
and scarcity. It was to hear the ring of cash registers spilling from the
stores, the rev of fancy cars and the sputter of old ones, the latest
jazz and blues, the constant chatter of street gossip and street gospel;
all amid whiffs of cologned men, perfumed women, alcohol, and
soul food. It was the cacophony and aroma of Black accomplishment and striving, joy and struggle.[2]

The family home at 501 Auburn Avenue taught Little Mike his

first and most valuable lessons in navigating this fast-paced segregated world. Despite the grinding poverty of the Great Depression, the family enjoyed economic security. By 1931, King Sr. was the well-paid senior pastor of Ebenezer Baptist Church, one of the largest churches in the city. The family's spacious, twelve-room, Queen Anne–style home housed Michael and Alberta King, the three children, their maternal grandmother, great-aunt, hired domestic help, and Mikey, the family dog. The family was not rich, an adult King would later recall of his childhood. They were, he liked to say, "Negro wealthy." Indeed, the family possessed what many Black Atlantans could only wish to have. The reality of this Black class privilege helped to form some of Little Mike's earliest memories. He remembered consistently thinking, and eventually asking his parents, "Why do we have more than all our playmates?"[3]

Mrs. Jennie Celeste Parks Williams, Little Mike's maternal grandmother, was the first of many Black women who helped him answer such questions about the world. Mama, as the children called her, was born in Atlanta in April 1873. Married to Reverend A. D. Williams, pastor of Ebenezer Baptist Church, she was widowed in 1931. A political veteran of Black church politics, she directed the church trustees to appoint a novice, her son-in-law Big Mike, the new pastor. The trustees were not convinced Reverend Michael King was up to the task. But the trustees were not up to the task of collectively opposing Mrs. Jennie Williams, so Reverend Michael King was appointed pastor of Ebenezer Baptist Church. She remained in the house and cared for the growing children while her daughter Alberta tended to her duties as a full-time church musician and the new first lady of Ebenezer Baptist Church. Mrs. Williams, whom Little Mike remembered as "saintly," was the matriarch. She was a stylish, college-educated woman who never went anywhere without her gloves, hats, furs, pearls, and black purses. She always looked as if she had just stepped out of a fashion magazine spread. The motivation for grandma's fashionable ways went beyond a mere love of clothes. Her style was also a key weapon in her arsenal of protest. She was president of the church's missionary society and of the 5th District of the Georgia State Baptist Convention. She was also a member of the executive board of the National Baptist Women's Auxiliary (WA). The evangelism of the WA espoused a culture of racial uplift; with the motto "Lift as we climb," they believed Black women could combat racist ideas and images of Black inferiority by embodying Western bourgeois culture, while serving and educating the less fortunate. Black women had to scale the heights of purity, respectability, thrift, chastity, and tasteful fashion if the race had any hopes of climbing out of the mire of Jim Crow. Mrs. Williams, as she was respectfully addressed in the Black community, looked like a fashion model so she could model the fight for equality.[4]

She led the domestic affairs of the King household—assisted by her sister, Ida Worthem, known to the children as Aunt Ida—ushering the kids through their rigid schedule: The day began and ended with prayers and Bible reading. After a hearty breakfast of cheese and eggs, bacon, and toast, she saw the children off to school. When they returned, their educated grandmother assisted with their homework. She loved all the children, but Little Mike was her favorite. She tried to hide it, but it was a losing battle. "She was *very* dear to each of us," her favorite recalled, "but especially to me. . . . I was her favorite grandchild."[5]

Alberta, whom Little Mike called Mother Dear, also showered the children with loving care and education. She had received diplomas from leading Black institutions. With no public Black high school in the state, she attended high school at Spelman Seminary, gained her teaching certificate from Hampton Normal and Industrial Institute, and finally received her bachelor's degree in 1938 from

Morris Brown College. She was an acclaimed musician, playing the piano and organ at Ebenezer, eventually serving as the organist for the WA, and passing along her love of music to her children. She was quiet, slow to speak, but ever present at school events, special church services, and sporting events. Little Mike remembered her as always "behind the scenes setting forth those motherly cares, the lack of which leaves a missing link in life." He loved to go shopping with his mother, pestering her with the ruminations of his imagination or playing hide-and-seek in the aisles, and playing the role of sous-chef in the kitchen. It made dinner take twice as long, but Alberta was endowed with the virtue of patience, especially when it came to her children.[6]

Daddy King, however, did not possess this virtue. He seemed perpetually clenched in bouts with his temper, causing even his affection for his children to be prickly. He was the son of a sharecropper and laundress in rural Stockbridge, Georgia, a sturdy man of some 220 pounds even in his youth. He ran off to Atlanta when he was fourteen years old, armed with an elementary school education and a burning desire to rise—a flame that was fueled by a yearning to become more than his abusive, alcoholic father, and a hope to become everything his church-going mother prayed for. He joined the ministry and married Alberta after a six-year courtship, during which he labored in the church and the railroad to save up money, establishing himself as a self-made man, a fact he never let his children forget. Alberta encouraged him further, directing him to professionalize his ministry by enrolling at Morehouse College, the all-male sibling school of her beloved Spelman. He obtained a bachelor of arts degree in theology in 1930. The church grew rapidly under his leadership and penny-pinching fund raising. Soon, he became the highest-paid Black minister in the city. He made certain his children had every material possession they needed: comfortable housing, full meals, and education—the very things he had lacked in Stockbridge. "I have never experienced the feeling of not having the basic necessities of life," King reminisced years later. "These things were always provided by a father who always put his family first." In addition to being a provider, the father was also the unquestioned authority in all family matters. He was a fundamentalist minister and man. He did not question the authority of the Bible, and he did not tolerate anyone questioning his authority. He was the family disciplinarian, running the house like a military barracks. "My father was very strict," Christine told one interviewer in 2010, "a very strict father." An adult King was slightly more measured in surmising his father's regime. "It was relatively strict," he said. "I faced the discipline that you would face in . . . a fervent religious background."[7]

Childhood letters and cards the son sent to his father attest to the spiked, orderly affection of their relationship. Little Mike would use a child's typewriter to peck out letters to his father whenever Daddy King was away preaching or attending church conventions. The very act of writing his father hints at the affection. Little Mike missed him, but the words do not say so. The word "love" does not appear either. Rather, these childhood billets focus on behavioral assessments. "I am being a good boy while you are away," Little Mike wrote on more than one occasion to his dad. In another letter he touted his academic achievements, ironically writing, "I am doing fine in my scool [sic] work."[8]

His emphasis on his behavior was due in part to his father's belief in physical punishment. Daddy King dished out spankings whenever he believed his children failed to meet his standards. Years later, he compared his children to "three impatient weeds, each one curving in a different direction." He believed whipping his children, especially his sons, was the best way to get them to change course. "My impatience made it very hard for me to sit down with the boys and quietly explain to them the way I wanted things done," he confessed years later. "I found that a switch was usually quicker and more persuasive." Accordingly, he called the boys' butts their "seat of understanding."[9]

Discipline and decree were his love language. He believed it was the best way to instill toughness and resilience, prerequisites for Black survival in Jim Crow society—a world that imposed all limitations on Black skin. It was, he believed, a Black father's job to "prepare a child for a world where death and violence are always near." The job produced an inward parental rage. "Inside you, there is always a fist balled up to protect them," he lamented. That rage often spilled out, lashing the children. But he would explain with the clarifying distance of time, "It was only because I wanted them to be strong and able to be happy."[10]

All of this—loving care, education, and discipline—came together every night at the dinner table. "In our home," Christine joyfully recalled, "sit-down dinners were not optional. They were *mandatory*." The family dinner seating arrangements were as ironclad as Daddy King's rules. "Daddy sat at the head of the table—no exceptions," Christine noted. Alberta sat at the opposite end. Grandmother and Aunt Ida sat to his right. Little Mike, AD, and then Christine sat to his left in that order, with the oldest son seated closest to his father's throne. "Each time when we sat for dinner, that's the way we sat," Christine fondly remembered. Fitting the family's regal last name, every meal—Sunday through Saturday—was served on the family's finest place settings.[11]

Mama, Alberta, and Aunt Ida fed the family a steady diet of Black Southern cooking: pork chops, fried chicken, glazed ham, fresh collard greens from the garden, macaroni and cheese, black-eyed peas, bread pudding, and an assortment of pies and cobblers, day in and day out. AD, who was fast surpassing Little Mike in size and stature, could never get enough of her cooking, but Mama made sure her favorite had his fill.[12]

The meals were filled with the kind of joy and laughter that accompany home-cooked meals. They were also filled with lessons. Politics was discussed, who was running for which office, which politician would best serve the Black community. They were instructed to stand up for what they believed in. Christine recalled her dad, always donning a necktie—but sleeves rolled up for dinner—dispensing decrees from his ceremonial chair. It was the same decree seemingly day after day, Christine remembered, but every time her father said it, he did so like it was a fresh revelation: "If you stand up for what you believe in, and what's just, God will always be on your side."

Jennie, Alberta, and Aunt Ida policed language. "No, ma'am" and "Yes, sir" were required. If one of the children ended a sentence with a preposition—"Where's that at?"—one of the educated trio would launch into a lesson on the use of prepositions. "These lessons stuck so well," Christine noted, that even in the absence of the adults, the children "took to correcting each other's use of the English language."[13]

The lessons continued after dinner. As soon as the children were physically able, they were assigned chores. They were expected to help clear the table, package the leftovers, and assist in washing the dishes. The latter chore rotated, and Little Mike did his best to avoid his turn. He used a rotation of excuses—sickness, more homework, forgetting, or even hiding in the bathroom—to avoid housework. The latter was his favorite excuse. Christine recalled that every time it was his turn, he suddenly had an unstoppable urge to use the bathroom. His ruse, as well as the doting affection of his grandmother, freed Little Mike from his date with the dishes. AD developed his own roster of excuses. "They were typical boys," Christine confessed to an interviewer years later. "They'd try to get out of it any way that they could. . . . So it fell on me most of the time."[14]

Little Mike was slothful in his chores, but, to his grandmother's delight, he excelled in his required Bible memorization. A photographic memory enabled him to recite Scripture verses, a family requirement at dinnertime, before he could even actually read. Every evening, after the children completed their to-do list, they would gather around Mama and Aunt Ida to hear stories of "Little Boy Blue," "Little Miss Muffet," and Mother Goose. Aunt Ida eventually graduated the children from listening to fairy tales to history and current events. "She spent hours reading to us from newspapers, books, and encyclopedias," Christine remembered. She used maps to show the children the world, taking their minds and imaginations across the globe. "We learned lots of history that way," Christine recalled. Little Mike cherished these moments. "I can remember very vividly how she spent many evenings telling us interesting stories," he remembered as an adult. Christine traced the origin of her brother's curiosity and love of books to these sweet, routine moments. "The things he heard from her whetted his curiosity about the world around him. It helped him develop into an inquisitive child and an avid reader," she noted years later.[15]

Life at 501 Auburn Avenue was simple and beautiful. It was, King plainly described years later in a school assignment, "very congenial."[16]

3
CHURCH

Ebenezer Baptist Church was like an annex of the King home.

The Late Gothic Revival–style church was just a block away at 407 Auburn Avenue, squatting on the corner of Auburn and Jackson Streets. The bright red bricks made it appear as if it had been baptized in Georgia clay soil.

Founded in 1886, it moved to several locations, including a shack on Airline Street. The small working-class congregation never boasted more than fifty members. The church began to grow rapidly in 1894 when the second pastor, Reverend A. D. Williams, Little Mike's maternal grandfather, took the helm. Over the next decade, the native of Greene County, Georgia, grew the church to more than 400 members, and his second decade of leadership brought the church to 750 members.

The *Atlanta Independent*, a local newspaper, praised the preacher's leadership, noting in 1913 that "few churches in the city have made strides more rapidly, nor have contributed more to the moral and intellectual growth of the city." That same year the church purchased property on the southwest corner of Auburn and Jackson Streets for $5,750, or $1.2 million in 2024 dollars. The cornerstone of their permanent home on the Ave was laid the following year. Construction was gradual, reaching completion in 1922 at an estimated cost of $40,000, or $5 million today. Reverend A. D. Williams, a charter member of the Atlanta branch of the NAACP, led the church until his death on March 21, 1931.[1]

When Reverend King took over, he ran the church like he ran his house. Everything was regimented and scripted. "As far back as I can remember I was in church every Sunday," King Jr. noted. On a typical Sunday, the children were expected to be in the church basement for Sunday school at 9:00 a.m. sharp. Around 10:45, the deacons gathered in the newly carpeted sanctuary, sat down on the backless, hard wooden benches—eventually replaced by modern cushioned pews—and began "prayer service," offering up prayers and hymns. Worship began precisely at 11:00. The children were expected to be seated with their grandmother, while Alberta sat down at the old mechanical pump organ. Service commenced when Alberta pressed the peddles on the organ, leading the choir to belt out the great Protestant standards, including "Amazing Grace," "I Need Thee Every Hour," and "My Faith Looks Up to Thee." When the old pump organ was replaced with a grand Wurlitzer pipe organ, it seemed Alberta could make the whole church quake to the melodies of the great hymns.

The worship was spirited. "People were moved," Christine remembered. "They would literally get up and shout." After rounds of moving singing, Scripture was read. And then Reverend King mandated a time of meditation. Alberta would play the organ, no singing, just music to prepare one's heart and mind to receive Reverend King's sermon. His preaching always encouraged the faithful to trust God, stay away from dancing and alcohol, and resist white supremacy at every turn. After filling their spirits, the faithful could fill their stomachs at the feeding kitchen or nourish their physical ailments at the medical clinic Reverend King established. Seeing his father call

all the shots while his mother assisted led Little Mike to remember church functioning as "a second home for me."[2]

Little Mike adored the church, not so much for the spiritual, but for social reasons. Black churches were the first autonomous institutions in African American life. They were political, social, cultural, and spiritual centers, organizing for freedom and broader societal changes such as equal access to voting, fair wages, housing, and public accommodation. Black religious leaders also understood that "politics" went beyond formal participation in explicitly political activities, but included the everyday practices that enabled Black folk to live as human beings amid the daily dehumanization of Jim Crow.

Black churches provided sanctuary from the harshness and distortions of a segregated society that demanded the erasure of Black humanity. At church, ministers proclaimed that Black flesh was made in the image of God. Black men who spent their days being haunted by taunts of "boy" and "nigger" could be granted the respectful distinction of "Reverend," "Minister," "Deacon," "Mister," and "Sir." Black women who were denied the courtesies of their white counterparts—chivalry, protection, and dignity—were recognized as the paragons and custodians of virtue.

The Black church was not free from the flaws that accompany any human institution. Hypermasculine egos, sexism, and personal jealousies were ever-present. But Black churches offered a society within broader society, an institution that taught people how to live together, not according to the color of their skin, but by recognizing their shared humanity.

In this space, African Americans could enjoy normal social relations. King said he met some of his closes friends in Sunday school. It was church, he reckoned, that cultivated within him the "capacity for getting along with people." It provided him with the space and structure to engage in healthy friendships. There, he could be a child like any other: running, laughing, teasing, sharing, learning, and getting in trouble. In church, unlike in broader society, he was free simply to be a child, nothing more, nothing less.[3]

In this free environment, he was taught a fundamentalist version of the faith. "The lessons which I was taught in Sunday School were quite in the fundamentalist line," King recalled. "None of my teachers ever doubted the infallibility of the Scriptures. Most of them were unlettered and had never heard of Biblical criticism. Naturally I accepted the teachings as they were being given to me. I never felt any need to doubt them, at least at that time I didn't."[4]

Even when Little Mike could not quite read the Bible nor church hymns, he memorized and sung its words. With his mother providing accompaniment on the piano, at four years old he began moving congregations across the city and Baptist Church conventions with his rendition of "More Like Jesus." The little boy would bellow,

> I want to be more like Jesus,
> And follow him day by day;
> I want to be true and faithful,
> And ev'ry command obey.
>
> More and more like Jesus,
> I would ever be;
> More and more like Jesus,
> My Savior who died for me.

Congregations would stand and clap; and some, his father remembered, would simply weep. Christine recalled, "People would just, you know, marvel at him." Throughout King's adolescence, Alberta fielded requests for the little boy with the big voice, even taking him to large Baptist gatherings to perform. In 1934, Little Mike

amazed the audience at the annual meeting of the General Missionary Baptist Convention of Georgia in Newnan, Georgia. Among the
chronicle of sermons, resolutions, and financial statements, the organization's journal noted, "Master M.L. King, age five, accompanied by his mother, sang for the convention and was given a rising
vote of thanks."[5] From a young age, King had the ability to move
people with his voice. And he learned it and honed it at Ebenezer
Baptist Church.

4
PLAY

But Little Mike was not an angel.

He was a social butterfly, always having friends over for play-dates. "When he was a little boy," Alberta remembered, "he used to keep my house so full of children sometimes, seem like I was running a nursery or a playground or something."[1]

But his siblings were his closest friends. So close in age, the children grew up like triplets. The three children quickly moved from toys and innocuous games of tag (Christine was the fastest), to mischief. And when there was no mischief to be found, they invented it. As the oldest, Christine was expected to be in charge, to keep the younger two in line. "That was supposed to be my role," an adult Christine admitted, "but I wasn't really a disciplinarian cause a lot of times I would be with them." They were a triumvirate of boundless energy. The gang loved to "borrow" one of Mama's fancy fox furs and attach it to a stick; with glistening glass eyes and tiny feet, it looked alive. At twilight, they would hide behind the bushes in front of their house. When unsuspecting pedestrians walked by, the children made their furry apparatus emerge from the bushes, wiggling and flailing—women and men would scream, holler, some even ran. The gang's preferred victims were couples; they loved to see terrified men pretend to be tough in front of a romantic interest. "It was a lot of fun to see those people jumping in awe," Christine remembered joyously. "That was our creative way of having fun. . . . It was hilarious."[2]

The joy abruptly ended when one man failed to see the humor. "He passed by us and went in the house and found my father and told him what we were doing," Christine recalled. "And, of course, that stopped that because my father took care of us. . . . And so we didn't do that anymore."[3]

The trio spared no one in their hijinks, not even the piano teacher. Mother Dear wanted her children to learn the instrument. Christine submitted without a fight, but Little Mike and AD had other plans. The rough-and-tumble boys considered piano lessons soft, something meant for girls. Their instructor, Mr. Mann, was a serious taskmaster who would smack the children's hands with a ruler anytime they made a mistake. One day, around age seven, AD became fed up and took a hammer to the piano, determined to destroy the instrument of his tormentor. Little Mike stopped his brother, convincing him there was a better way to exact revenge. Prior to their next lesson, the boys loosened the legs of the piano bench and swore their sister to secrecy, or else. When Mr. Mann arrived, he sat down on the bench only to find himself, his notes, and his menacing ruler crashing to the floor. The children swore ignorance, but Daddy King knew better. The three met their fate in the form of their father's leather belt on their seat of understanding.[4]

Sometimes Little Mike and AD would join forces to terrorize Christine. They regularly beheaded her dolls—and, as if that gruesome fate was not enough, they would proceed to dismember the entire doll and then scatter the body parts: a head in the bathroom, a leg under the bed, an arm thrown to the weeds in the backyard. Christine despised the prank, hurling insults in retaliation, calling them "bullheaded boys."[5]

And of course, the children, particularly the boys, fought one another. "I was always bigger than ML as long as I can remember," AD told a reporter in 1957, comparing his 195-pound adult frame to Mike's 165 pounds. "And maybe I did take advantage of it." There was no doubt in King's memory. He said, "AD used to beat me up." But AD's penchant for dominating his smaller older brother often came at a price that Daddy King exacted. "I know that the worst beating I ever got," AD ruefully recalled, "was for giving ML a bloody nose. I don't remember exactly what it was all about but Daddy really gave it to me."[6]

The two brothers.

5
BIG WORDS

Y ou just wait and see," Alberta remembered four-year-old Little
Mike telling her, "I'm going to get me some big words."[1]

The child seemed born with a fascination for the power of language. Grandma and Aunt Ida spent hours talking and reading with
the middle child, and it seemed that he could never get enough.
Books became his constant companion—more so even than stuffed
animals and teddy bears. "Even before he could read, he kept books
around him, he just liked the idea of having them," his father recalled. He loved words, especially when they were performed in the
Black preaching tradition. "When anybody of standing was going to
speak," his father remembered, "he'd want to go." Little Mike was
mesmerized by the talent of his dad and the roster of visiting preachers who gave new life to old biblical words; the way they stretched
short-syllable words into long, sonic flurries—"The wages-sssssss
of sinnnnn is death-ahhhhhhhhhh!" He admired their ability to give
meaning and melody to multisyllable words, ending in crescendos—
"Community-eeeeeeeee." He craved their gift to transform words
into powerful phrases and sentences that seemed to take flight in
song and become real, making a word like "salvation" feel like shelter in the time of a storm or "grace" feel like a hug. And he admired

how the Black preaching tradition possessed the ability to rally the emotions and bodies of listeners, moving them to shout "Aaaaaaaa-man," in agreement, or to weep, and even dance. After church, his father recalled, Little Mike would issue his assessment of the speaker of the hour. If he approved, he would say, "That man had some big words." Words the child was desperate to copy.[2]

He made Christine his earliest audience and competitor. The two were always challenging each other with their knowledge of big words. Little Mike could not compete with his younger brother's physical prowess, but he was convinced he could keep up with his older sister's academic abilities. The two spent hours flipping through the dictionaries and encyclopedias Aunt Ida read to them, challenging one another to discover, define, and spell multisyllable words. They competed, Christine recalled, to see who could learn "the biggest ones." Decades later, one word challenge still stuck out in her mind: "concatenation," or the act of linking together in a chain.[3]

Their rivalry naturally led to a desire for academic achievement. When six-year-old Christine went off to school in the fall of 1933, four-year-old Little Mike begged his parents to let him follow her. Six was the state age requirement for enrollment, but the precocious four-year-old laid out his case to his mother. He did not want to stay home and play with AD, nor suffer another bloody nose. He wanted to go to school, get some big words, and keep up with his sister.

Alberta relented, while the father saw the boy's desire as a sign of maturity and ambition. Despite the age gap with his peers, the child performed well in the first grade at the Yonge Street Elementary School. He kept pace with his big sister throughout the fall as the two grew to become more than just siblings, but close friends, playing together at recess and doing homework together. However, their shared school days were short-lived. Following Little Mike's fifth birthday on January 15, 1934, a teacher heard the boy bragging to his peers about his big birthday cake and the large "five candles on it." Five candles? The teacher spoke with his parents to confirm the child's age. Little Mike was immediately expelled.[4]

The taste of formal education whetted his appetite for more. He returned to school one year later, on January 28, 1935, less than two weeks after turning six, but with a different name. In 1934, Big Mike, who was born without being issued a birth certificate, changed his name and his son's name too. He was inspired to do so by his dying father, who begged Big Mike to officially change his name to Martin Luther, the first names of Big Mike's paternal uncles. He found the necessary conviction to carry out his father's final wish when he traveled to Germany with the Baptist World Alliance in 1934. He found himself walking where Martin Luther, the great religious reformer, had walked centuries before. The grieving pastor believed it was divine confirmation. Michael King would forever more be known as Martin Luther King Sr., and Little Mike as Martin Luther King Jr., affectionately known to his family and friends as ML.[5]

ML spent half the year in first grade, when his natural curiosity helped promote him to the second grade on September 11, 1935. He continued to sail through school, receiving satisfactory marks in behavior and academic performance, except in spelling and math, where he teetered on "satisfactory" and "unsatisfactory." His difficulty with spelling did not spoil his appetite for big words. He fed his quest with visits to the public library. "He was unusual for boys his age," noted Mrs. Leathers, a librarian at the Auburn Avenue Library. "He would always come in to read." But ML bypassed the well-stocked children's books at the Carnegie Corporation branch library. Instead, he made a habit of requesting that Mrs. Leathers get him, what he called, "serious books," meaning books for adults.[6]

Annie L. McPheeters, the head of the library and its adult education programs, noticed the young fixture in the adult section. "He came to the library many times during the week," she remembered. "He loved to read." During his visits, he would often make a beeline for her desk to show off his newly acquired knowledge. She did not realize ML was drafting her into his word game. More than fifty years later, she vividly recalled how their regular exchanges took shape.[7]

"He would walk up to the desk. He would stand, and I could always tell when he wanted to say something. . . . He would look me straight in the eye, and I would say: 'Hello Martin Luther, what's on your mind?'"

"Oh, nothing particularly," ML once replied nonchalantly.

"Well, what did you do today at school?" she inquired.

"Oh, nothing particularly—we didn't do very much particularly," he repeated.

As McPheeters continued to talk with ML, she noticed that he kept finding ways to say "particularly." The head librarian soon recognized the youngster was challenging her, inviting her on his word quest. "I noticed then that Martin Luther learned a new word; and that was 'particularly.'" McPheeters then joined in, showing the youngster the various ways the word could be used.[8]

The pattern was set.

ML continued to challenge her throughout his time in elementary school. "Each time he would learn 'a big word' as we [both] called them then, he would come and try it out on me; and we would play this game," McPheeters recalled.[9]

He did the same thing with poetry. "I would ask him what was on his mind or how he was feeling," she said. Occasionally, ML would respond with a line of poetry he had committed to memory. "For I dipped into the future, far as human eye could see," ML once responded. He then paused in midsentence, inviting and testing the librarian to finish the stanza from Alfred Lord Tennyson's "Locksley Hall," a poem about a rejected lover who becomes disillusioned with the societal championing of wealth and scientific advancement. "Every time Martin Luther would learn a memory gem," McPheeters reminisced, "he would come to the library and he would start the verse, and then I would complete it. And we played that game down through the years."[10]

Whether through challenging his older sister, immersing himself in "serious books," or issuing word challenges with the librarian, ML was determined to get some big words.

6
SAVED

ML's competition with his older sister led him to get saved.

"I well remember how this event occurred," ML recalled in a divinity school assignment. It was a memorable experience not because it reflected his heartfelt decision to follow Jesus, but rather his determination, once more, to follow and compete with his older sister.[1]

On May 1, 1936, during Ebenezer's two-week spring revival, guest evangelist Reverend H. H. Coleman of Detroit visited ML and Christine's 9:00 a.m. Sunday school class to talk to the students about salvation. In the Baptist tradition, accepting Christ is a cosmic event. One's soul is "born again," cleansed of past sins and empowered to live a pious life. The soul is promised upon death to be "saved" from an eternity in hell, but instead to live with Christ in heaven forever. The ritual of conversion via baptism symbolizes this rebirth and one's membership in the universal church. Yet the seven-year-old's conversion experience was more social than cosmic. At the conclusion of the children's homily, Reverend Coleman invited the young souls to accept Christ, and Christine was the first to do so. "After seeing her," ML reflected, "I decided that I would not let her get ahead of me, so I was the next." The competitive ML accepted Christ as his savior.

He was not concerned with the eternal fate of his soul, nor with joining the Christian community, when he was baptized two days later. "I had never given this matter a thought," he admitted, "even at the time of baptism I was unaware of what was taking place." He confessed it was "quite clear I joined the church not out of any dynamic conviction, but out of a childhood desire to keep up with my sister."[2]

ML's faith continued in this manner throughout his childhood, rooted in familial relationships rather than metaphysical transformation. The youngster's experience of conversion never reached the heights of religious ecstasy that is common in the evangelical tradition. Rather, ML was nurtured into the faith. Christian nurture, an established tradition in liberal Protestantism, attests that a soul fostered in a Christian home and church has no need for a singular, dramatic religious experience. "Conversion for me was never an abrupt something," ML noted in the assignment. "I have never experienced the so-called 'crisis moment.' Religion has just been something that I grew up in." His commitment to Christianity was simply "the gradual intaking of the noble [ideals] set forth in my family and my environment." And for the most part, he admitted, up to that point, his acceptance of the faith was "largely unconscious." Like oxygen, it was something he absorbed, but rarely considered.[3]

7
THE TALK

M other Dear," ML cried out, "why do white people treat colored people so mean?"

As school brought about the beautiful adventure of big words, it also introduced ML to the word "racism."

When ML was six years old, his parents had to have "the talk" with him, the difficult but necessary conversation that millions of Black parents and guardians had and continue to have with the Black children under their care, often before the precious offspring are ready and capable of fully understanding. The conversation lurks like storm clouds over Black childhood. The deluge of inferiority and terror are unleashed whenever and wherever white supremacy decides it is time.[1]

Reverend ML King Sr. and Alberta King had tried their best to build a fortress around their children. It was a doomed but understandable attempt to protect them from the persistent scourge of racism. But with one terse question from their middle child, the citadel had collapsed.

The mother of two of ML's friends had just told him that her sons could no longer be his playmates, because he was "colored"

ML, age six.

and her children were "white." The revelation of the color line was a shock to ML. The boys were the children of a local grocer. The families lived one block apart. The children had grown up together; for over three years ML, Christine, and AD, and the two white boys were inseparable, an interracial battalion of childhood joy. "None of us seriously thought anything about those white boys being different," ML recalled during a 1957 interview. "We played with them all the time." Auburn Avenue was their playground, and they were all equal on the field of play. They had scraped their knees together playing stickball in the backyard, tussled together while playing basketball on the Kings' homemade hoop, chased one another with glee during games of tag, and even enjoyed field trips of their own making to nearby grocery stores, the firehouse, and soda fountain.[2]

And then, almost overnight, the white boys' parents began to make up excuses for why their children could not play with the King trio. When it was time for the youngsters to go to school, the parents drew the color line. ML recalled that the faces of the parents, which had once welcomed him with a warm smile, had turned cold. He was crushed. "I cried," he remembered. "I rushed home and asked mother about it." The six-year-old wanted—or rather, demanded—answers.[3]

With both Christine and AD looking on, Alberta hesitated as she began to explain the inexplicable. Like countless Black parents before and after her, she tried to render the complex simplicity of racism in terms accessible to a child. How to make evil intelligible to an innocent soul? How to equip and protect her babies without scaring them, without making the color of their skin a blot of shame? She had to instill in her children a sense of "somebody-ness" in a world that was designed to tell them that they were less than human.[4]

Alberta did that and more. She led her children on a journey, an excursion through slavery, the Civil War, and Jim Crow—the segregation of schools, restaurants, shops, theaters, housing, and bathrooms. She knew the history. She had been educated at the best Black schools in the country, and she had been employed as a schoolteacher before a state law restricting married women from full-time teaching terminated her job. The "marriage bar" forced Alberta from the classroom, but she never stopped teaching: Her children became her sole pupils. (The marriage bar law was not fully overturned until the passage of the 1964 Civil Rights Bill, legislation that her son ML would help to get passed.[5])

She explained why the family avoided buses and streetcars; why they could not ride the whites-only elevators at Atlanta's city hall; why they could not visit some of the museums and parks around town; and why some white parents would not let their children play with "negroes." Mother Dear was thorough and unflinching in her description of how segregation touched all parts of life, though she was careful to preserve the self-image of her children. Racism was a social system, she told them, not a natural order. And no matter what the social system said, she told her children they were as good as anybody.

As King remembered the moment: "She said the words that almost every Negro hears before he can yet understand the injustice that makes them necessary." She told her children, "The law might say that we had to go different places from them but the law was wrong." He remembered his mother repeating, "You must always feel that you are somebody."[6]

The conversation continued over the dinner table that evening. The parents shared their own experiences of racism. Their testimonies of hope and dignity did little to comfort ML. The world of a six-year-old is small, fragile, and easily broken. Through the loss of his friends, ML was made aware of race and racism for the first time. Despite his parents' insistence that it was his "Christian duty" to love white people, no matter what they thought of him, the boy began to harbor hate in his heart. He purposed to hate every white person. How, he wondered, could he love a race of people that hated him and were responsible for separating him from his best friends? Christine recalled that ML left the familial lesson committed not to love, but to revolt. "Mama," he pledged, "I'm going to turn this world upside down!"[7]

Losing his white childhood playmates was the first scar, but certainly not the last. Other wounds were inflicted during what should have been innocent daily errands, trips that too often turned ugly and violent. On shopping trips with his mother, excursions ML loved, he would often make friends with white children who were also accompanying their parents. Alberta remembered, he would play hide-and-seek in the aisles, exchanging giggles and smiles, only to be interrupted by an indignant white parent shouting about the encounter, just like the parents of his neighborhood best friends.

ML would run to his mother and ask, "Why do they do that to me? What's wrong?" The hurt would subside, revealing an abiding anger. "He'd be hurt and angry every time," Alberta said. Despite the repeated hurt, ML kept trying to befriend white children. It was natural. And virtually every time, he was disappointed and enraged, only to hope that next time things would be different. Alberta kept hoping too, trying to balance her inclination to protect her child from himself, while also allowing him to be curious. And she was there each time Jim Crow hurt her baby. "I managed to quiet him down each time," she recalled. But even her soft words could not completely heal the child's wounds. His world was becoming eclipsed by racism. "You could see it was worrying him," she said years later, "he was thinking about it even that early."[8]

One shopping trip resulted in ML becoming the victim of violence. He was slapped in the face by a white woman, a mild violent act by Jim Crow standards, but it provided further fuel for ML's developing hatred. He was standing in front of the store, holding some of his mother's purchased goods while she went to retrieve the car. Suddenly, a white woman attacked him, shouting, "You're the little nigger that stepped on my foot!" The brazen physical assault and her prideful departure happened so quickly that ML did not have the chance to inform her that he was not the culprit. It would not have mattered, though, the color of his skin made him guilty by default. He told his mother when she swung the car around. Once again, the kind, helpless mother did her best to comfort and calm her inconsolable child. Her son was angry, huffing and puffing, but as he would remember later, she found consolation in the fact that at least her son was still breathing.[9]

White supremacist violence seemed ever-present, even on the Ave. As a child, ML earned money as a delivery boy for the *Atlanta Daily World*. Around the same time, robed Ku Klux Klansmen unexpectedly held a parade down Auburn Avenue. On the front page of the newspaper, the march was dubbed "a cowardly form of intimidation to frighten the progress of Negroes on Auburn Avenue." Accompanied by a police escort and more than fifty carloads of Klansmen, the show of force reminded ML and all those on Atlanta's Black main street that their economic, civic, and social strivings, and even their physical safety, were subject to the whims of white supremacist rule and violence. And when that racism decided to lash out, not even the police could be trusted to deal with it justly.[10]

Not even Daddy King and his physically imposing frame could protect ML from the dangers and affronts of white supremacy. Daddy King was a fighter. He persisted in his battle to reform society and protest all its ills. He refused to ride Atlanta's segregated buses and streetcars, and he led the fight for equal pay for the city's Black public school teachers. Local white clergy told him fighting for equal pay was too dangerous. They called the house, begging him to give up the protest. When the telephone rang, at times interrupting the family's dinner, what often emerged from the receiver was an anonymous chorus of tirades, promising Daddy King that he would be murdered for his stance. The postman brought a steady stream of insulting and threatening letters. Drawings of Daddy King in a coffin were a favorite, second only to detailed sketches of him being hanged, with bulging eyes and a strangulated neck. Through it all, ML watched his father stay the course. Daddy King could not protect his children from racism, but he tried to model a steadfast somebody-ness and commitment to equality.

But there was only so much a father could do in the face of such entrenched and pervasive bigotry. Around the same time Jim Crow severed the bonds with his two white friends, ML accompanied his father downtown to purchase new shoes. His excitement quickly turned into horrific embarrassment. They arrived at the shoe store and took seats in the front. "I'll be happy to wait on you if you'll just move back there to those seats in the rear," a white clerk politely told them. "Nothing wrong with these seats," the preacher barked back. "We're quite comfortable here!"[11]

The comfort of negroes was not the clerk's concern. His face began to turn red as he explained that all Black customers knew the rules and were happy to follow them. "You'll have to go back there," he insisted. "You take it like everybody else, and stop being so high and mighty." Furious, Daddy King shouted, "We'll either buy shoes sitting right here, or we won't by any shoes at all!" As if in one motion, he grabbed his son and stomped his 220-pound frame out of the store. It was the first time ML had witnessed his father reach this level of anger, spewing curses and muttering a personal pep talk under his breath: "I don't care how long I have to live with this system, I am never going to accept it." What should have been a simple moment of father-son bonding, Daddy King remembered, gave way to a car ride home full of a father's angry cursing and a son's tears and confusion.[12]

The furious father managed to calm himself long enough to answer ML's questions. The father stripped his responses of venom and attempted to explain his actions to his child. "I'm never going to accept the stupidity and cruelty of segregation, not as long as I live! I am going to fight against it in some way or other as long as there is breath in me."[13]

The child was still puzzled. He did not understand why one's skin color determined where they could try on shoes or buy shoes. But he was not confused about the morality of the issues. He knew it was wrong, and that his father was right. "If you are against it," he told his dad, "I will help you fight it in whatever way I can." His dad smiled at the child and told him how much he appreciated the child's commitment. "He was such a little fellow then, but sitting there next to me in the car, ML seemed so thoughtful and determined on this matter that I felt certain he wouldn't forget his promise to help."[14] On that day, Daddy King had no idea of the power of that promise.

Even ML's attempts to get a job promotion were capped by racism. After working for the *Daily World*, ML switched to *The Atlanta Journal*, the city's white daily. The industrious youngster was promoted to assistant depot station manager. He was the youngest person to hold that position in the paper's history. After the delivery trucks dropped off the hundreds of newspapers for his district, ML was responsible for making certain that the three dozen or so newsboys, many his age, got the papers for their respective routes. He handled all emergencies, including an absent delivery boy or a customer complaint, and if the station manager failed to show up, ML took over. Despite his gifts, ML was barred from becoming a station manager; those top-paying positions, even in Black neighborhoods, were reserved for white men.[15]

These were just a few of his known adolescent experiences of Jim Crow segregation. But there were plenty more. ML repeatedly described his adolescence as hallmarked by Jim Crow segregation. "I can remember as a little boy passing by parks and playgrounds, waiting to play, but having to face the fact that I couldn't go there because of segregation, I can remember the time that I went through the Fox and Roxy theaters in Atlanta as I walked there it was made plain that the Negro had to go around the back alley and up some back steps and go up to what we call the buzzards roof and there we had to face the humiliation of segregation. I can remember being downtown with my mother then the moment came when I wanted a hotdog or a hamburger, or a Coca-Cola and I would ask my mother because we were standing close to a lunch counter and mother had to say to me that I couldn't eat there." Jim Crow violence was also a constant, lurking facet of his childhood. "I had passed spots where Negroes had been savagely lynched and had watched the Ku Klux Klan on its rides at night. I had seen police brutality with my own eyes, and watched Negroes receive the most tragic injustice in the courts."[16]

The experiences gnawed at ML, leaving him scarred. King told television journalist Mike Wallace in 1961 that his early experiences with Jim Crow did "something to my growing personality." Jim Crow America was so psychologically taxing, in part, because US law and culture implied that African Americans deserved their plight. The landmark 1896 US Supreme Court case *Plessy v. Ferguson* ruled that racial segregation laws did not violate the equal protection clause of the US Constitution. The court's justification for the "separate but equal" doctrine stated that the equal protection under the law clause of the Fourteenth Amendment did not eliminate "distinctions based upon color" nor was it meant to "enforce social . . . equality." If African Americans believed that segregation stamped them as an inferior race, "it is not by reason of anything found in the act," the court claimed, "but solely because the colored race chooses to put that construction on it." According to the court, inferior accommodations—schools, waiting rooms, train cars, drinking fountains—and inferior services were not the result of unequal tax distribution and enforced white supremacy; they were the result of Black malpractice and perception. This frame allowed Jim Crow segregation to masquerade as natural, an inevitable occurrence because Blackness was innately inferior. White preachers, politicians, judges, political pundits, and everyday people discussed racial segregation as something ordained by God; its most ardent supporters and defenders believed it sacred, an unspoken eleventh commandment. African Americans who desired equality under the law were seen as fighting against God's natural order. They were a problem to be tamed or extinguished. This feeling of being a problem, and the anger that comes with it, W. E. B. Du Bois warned in *The Souls of Black Folk*, can easily lead Black Americans to carry a "silent hatred of the pale world about them and mocking distrust of everything white."[17] That certainly was ML's experience. His adolescent experience of racism, King noted, made him "perilously close to resenting all white people."[18] And every time he was denied entrance into Atlanta's public swimming pools, parks, schools, theaters, and lunch counters, or witnessed the Ku Klux Klan or the police assaulting an African American, the seeds of rancor were watered anew.

But such hate can also turn against its host, leading to self-hatred. "As I look back over those early days, I did have something of an inner tension," ML noted. "On the one hand my mother taught me that I should feel a sense of somebody-ness. . . . On the other hand, I had to go out and face the system, which stared me in the face every day saying, 'You are less than,' 'You are not equal to.' So this was a real tension within."[19] The internal strain led ML, like so many other Black children, to experience bouts of self-hatred and anxiety. King would confide to a journalist that he had experienced moments in his childhood—fleeting, but reoccurring—when he wished he were white. He yearned to be free from the burden that was blackness to experience a glimpse of the freedom that accompanied whiteness: food service at any restaurant, courteous treatment at stores, the ability to use a public pool or park, and the ever-evasive meritocracy.[20]

This was very common among Black youth of the day. In 1939, when ML was ten years old, trailblazing psychologists Kenneth Clark and Mamie Clark began publishing studies arguing that Black adolescents who experienced prejudice, racism, and discrimination developed a sense of inferiority and self-hatred. Their studies found that many children sought to resolve the inner conflict through escapism, wishing to be white.[21] The Clarks did not know it at the time, but their studies were describing the life of young King.

ML, thanks in part to his parents, would eventually put the tension to rest. Modern developmental scientists have argued that parental messages about faith, family, and cultural heritage promote positive psychic and social adjustment. A steady diet of "the talk" can equip adolescents with the tools to combat the negative effects of racism.[22] The parental messages ML received—particularly those from Mama, Mother Dear, and Aunt Ida—helped to inoculate him against ultimate hatred and despair. They refused to let the white world turn their baby into a receptacle of hate, corroding him from the inside. They reminded him of his "somebody-ness," that his humanity, not his personal accomplishments, made him just as good as anybody else. Thanks to their vigilance, ML became a man who never succumbed to the tension. Every time racism interrupted his life, and every time it threatened his existence, King could recall "Don't you be ashamed. You're as good as any white child. . . . Don't let this get you down. . . . Never lose your sense of somebody-ness." The maxims would become a constant in his ministry.

Young King had several bouts with self-hate and hatred of white people throughout his adolescence—winning some battles, losing others. But ultimately, he would win the war within and without. When he was an adult, friends and loved ones would marvel that he did not seem scarred by the constant barrage of racism. James Baldwin concurred, writing in *Harper's Magazine* in February 1961, "He came through it all unscarred. He never went around fighting with himself."[23]

Baldwin was able to pen those lines because young King was a constant recipient of "the talk."[24]

8
FIGHT

Talking was good, but words had limitations, especially in a violent world. All the talking left Daddy King believing his namesake was too sensitive to survive the terrorizing world that awaited.

Father and son shared the same name, but not the same temperament. The King men, the father boasted to one journalist, were notorious for their rage and anger, lashing out at the simplest slight, perceived or real. "We always had a lot of temper. Me, my father, my whole family, and AD too," he confessed with a sense of pride. But ML broke the King mold. He was a sensitive child: kind, slow to anger, quick to cry, and hated to fight.[1] ML could certainly be adventurous and mischievous—like the time when he and AD discovered their dad had left the car keys in the ignition. Nine-year-old ML started the car, only to watch it plunge through the back of the inclined garage. But when it came to plunging into fights, he was completely reserved.[2]

He preferred to reach resolutions by talking. On more than one occasion he tried to talk AD out of fights. "We always had to get AD home from school for fighting somebody." AD was notorious for arming himself with a rock, brick, bottle, or whatever was at hand during the smallest disagreements. Whenever the hot-tempered youth found himself in a street quarrel of his own making, his older brother would show up and do his best to calmly resolve the conflict. "I don't know why, but I never liked to fight," ML reflected years later, "even when I was provoked." Religion had nothing to do with it. "I don't think it was because of religious scruples," ML remembered, "because I didn't have many when I was little, even though I grew up in a church-minded family . . . It's always been a part of me, I guess."[3]

As a child and preteen, ML was a punching bag. When he was in elementary school, Black Billy, the school bully, expected everyone to move out of his way when passing on the stairwell. ML did not know this. One day, his arms full of books, he accidently brushed against Billy. "Excuse me," Christine remembered ML telling the bully as he walked along his merry way. Black Billy followed ML, taunting him. "I'm going to take care of you," he said, but ML kept on walking, trying to ignore him. The bully ran ahead of ML and confronted him.

"What do you want?" ML asked.

Black Billy laughed.

A crowd began to gather around the two boys, daring them to fight.

"What do you want to fight about," ML said, trying to remain calm. According to family lore, ML told the bully, "In the first place I haven't done anything to you. I brushed into you accidently. I asked you to pardon me. Now why do you want to tear up our clothes or cause us to get hurt? What will hurting each other prove?"

Black Billy responded with a flurry of fists and kicks. ML refused to retaliate. Black Billy, King bashfully recalled, beat "me down the steps, but I didn't retaliate." It was the first but certainly not the last time, he would sacrifice his body for the cause of nonviolence.[4]

But as a child these nonviolent stands embarrassed his father.

"He just didn't see sense in fighting and that was strange in my fam-ily." The child needed to be tougher if he was going to be a King, let alone survive Jim Crow. The prideful minister refused to be known as the dad of the neighborhood whipping boy. He admitted that he was "ashamed of ML's refusal to fight" and disappointed that ML "was always one to negotiate a dispute." Exasperated, King Sr. re-membered, "I used to threaten to whip him if he let the other boys beat him and run him home." If ML ran home fleeing a fight, there was no conversation: He would have to face his father, who treated him to the switch—or sometimes an old razor strap for more conse-quential infractions.[5]

Every time Daddy King set out to spank ML, grandma would attempt to run interference, begging her son-in-law to spare the child. When he brushed her aside, she would plead, "The child looks so pitiful." But behind the façade was a brave, determined soul who was different than his siblings. Christine, the doting daughter, was rarely on the receiving end of the switch. Christine, Daddy King recalled, "was the exceptionally well-behaved, serious, and studious member of the trio." The boys were different. AD did his best to rebel, then cry out for mercy or help. Junior chose his own path, a third way.

"He was the most peculiar child whenever you whipped him," his father remembered. Unlike AD, ML did not resist, run, or scream. Rather, "he'd stand there, and the tears would run," but he refused to give his dad the satisfaction of hearing him whimper or holler. Only silent tears.[6]

Occasionally, Daddy King would make the children put the switch or the strap on one another, instructing them to strike the offending sibling on the hands or buttocks. He believed his regime of harsh peer punishment helped his children understand that discipline was impersonal, a simple result of cause and effect: You disobey, you get punished. ML passively accepted lashings from his siblings, but he refused to return the punishment. He was a conscientious objector of his father's regime of punishment.[7] ML's third way became a pattern in his life. He was always respectful to his dad, but then he did what he wanted to do. As an adult, he revealed what he believed were the results of these strategies, confiding to Andrew Young that the compliant Christine and rebellious AD were "destroyed" under the weight of their father's overbearing ways. But not ML. His strategy prevented him from forming what he called "any personality conflicts." It helped him "develop certain disciplinary principles," enabling him to evolve his own personality and to grow into the man he wanted to be, not the man his father thought he should be.[8]

But parenting does not come with a crystal ball. All Daddy King could see in front of him was a son with a failing masculinity, a child who loved books and singing but hated fighting. Daddy King was a father like so many fathers before and since, befuddled by his offspring. He saw all his children, but especially his firstborn son, as an extension of himself. He struggled, as he put it, "to understand where the parent ends and the child begins." He wanted his children "to be strong and able and happy." But, he reasoned, happiness required strength to survive "a world where death and violence are always near." He found ML terrifyingly ill-prepared for that world.

He was not worried about Christine. She was smart, gentle, and quiet—a proper lady who would find shelter behind a strong husband. AD's emerging masculinity was also not cause for concern. Anger was the one safe masculine emotion. His hot temper would keep him warm in a cold world. But he was frustrated by ML being perpetually "sensitive in his responses to even the most casual matters" and refusing to stand and fight. Daddy King could not reconcile ML's temperament with masculinity. Eventually, he forfeited the idea of understanding the delicate child, leaving the burden largely to his wife. "ML came along with sensitivities only she could investigate and soothe," he admitted years later. ML would eventually teach his father that sensitivity was not the opposite of bravery. There was more than one way to fight. But as a youngster, the father could not see how his son's empathic, sensitive heart could be a strength, one that would enable the son to rise above the very racialized and violent limitations that so concerned the father.[9]

9
A DREAMER

M L learned to fight with the language of dreams.

In the fall of 1940, he enrolled in the seventh grade at the Atlanta University Laboratory School. Founded in 1930, the small private school was housed on the city's two Black college campuses: the 162 elementary school students met on the campus of Atlanta University, while 211 junior and senior high students comprised the upper school at Giles Hall at Spelman College. In 1940, the cost of attendance at the upper school was more than $85 a year for day students. Residential students from across the South paid an additional $225 for room and board. Both were significant expenditures. The average annual income of Black families was around $700. The cost made the school more than just a place of learning. Attendance was a conspicuous marker of economic status, and a rite of passage for the scions of Black Atlanta. It was the school for the children of the city's Black elite, including the children of John W. Dobbs, the Grand Master of the Prince Hall Masons of Georgia; and Samuel Garrett Sellers, the prominent owner of Sellers Brothers Funeral Directors and Morticians.[1]

The school was a laboratory of democracy. The curriculum

emphasized the skills and comportment necessary for resisting and repairing America's broken democracy. Principal William A. Robinson was the mastermind. The former president of the National Association of Teachers in Colored Schools took leadership of the upper school in 1931. He outlined his progressive approach to pedagogy in a 1936 report for the state's Black teachers. "The Georgia Program for the Improvement of Instruction" called for Black schoolteachers to abandon "teaching subjects or textbooks to children, with no particular regard of children's interests, needs, and experiences." Lesson plans should be guided by social problems and student interests, rather than state curriculums and textbooks. Students should choose which topics to study and help make lesson plans. They should learn how African Americans solved difficulties and look to apply these lessons to their own challenges. Learning, then, could not be measured by the number of textbook pages or chapters that were covered, nor by a letter grade. Rather, Robinson believed all courses should be graded pass or fail, based on a qualitative assessment of the pupil's civic and moral development. "I think we learn to take responsibilities here," an upper school student noted in a 1940 national assessment of the school. "We learn how to discuss in our classes and we also learn how to plan work together. When we get out of school into life, we will have to be able to plan our own affairs. So while we are in school we ought to learn to plan for ourselves." This was Robinson's vision.[2]

It was the perfect educational environment for a curious eleven-year-old to foster dreams of solving America's racial nightmares. And ML seemed to know it. The previous summer he had petitioned his parents to allow him to attend the school. When Alberta was attending a church convention in Richmond, Virginia, ML was busy preparing for school and collecting important dates for registration.

On June 20, 1940, the precocious child wrote his mother. "Listen mother dear . . . If I am going to Lab [School] I will have to register by Monday."[3] The child who loved big words was excited about attending the cutting-edge institution.

His first teacher there, Miss Elizabeth Elaine Lemon, did not disappoint. The thirty-six-year-old with bobbed hair and a smooth, round brown face became his favorite instructor. She was a Ball State– and Columbia University–trained educator who served as the school's teaching principal. She instilled racial pride in the rambunctious children under her care. Every morning her seventh-grade students sang "Lift Every Voice and Sing" a poem by African American writer James Weldon Johnson, which was turned into song by his brother John Rosamond Johnson. The song would be dubbed the Negro national anthem.[4]

She adorned her classroom with pictures of famous African Americans, such as Johnson, a leader in the NAACP, making her class an oasis of dignity and pride. Remarkably, one day ML's face would decorate elementary classrooms across the country, but he could not have imagined that.[5] At the time he was just an inquisitive student, in a hurry to learn big words.

Miss Lemon encouraged her students to use their voices to challenge anyone who said they could not thrive. In her thinking, according to one biographer, she was not just teaching students, she was nurturing adults. She believed her job was to prepare her students for a world that she knew did not love them and saw them only as growing "things" that needed to be periodically cut down.[6]

Her students and colleagues recalled that she was always ready with a maxim to instruct or inspire:

"Hold your head up and walk straight!"

"You do not have to fight with people to show that you do not like what they are doing to you."

"You can rebel inside, and find quiet ways to show your discontent."

"You can rebel and still maintain your dignity."[7]

According to her biographer, her directives were music to ML's ears.

Miss Lemon also taught her students the importance of democratic participation. She organized her classroom like the executive branch of the US government. She was the president and her students the cabinet, allowing them to take some ownership of the classroom. It was her way of teaching the children something they had never witnessed nor experienced: a true representative democracy.[8]

At the time, about 95 percent of African American adults across the South were legally prevented from voting. African American men gained the right to vote in 1870 with the passage of the Fifteenth Amendment, and all women in 1920 with the passage of the Nineteenth Amendment. However, beginning in the late 1800s, Southern states began passing Jim Crow laws and exercising extrajudicial measures—grandfather clauses, poll taxes, literacy tests, white primaries, economic reprisals, and outright violence—that made voting perilous or impossible for African Americans. As a result, in 1940, only 3 percent of voting-age African Americans were registered to vote in the old Confederacy. Miss Lemon's classroom gave her students the dignity and purpose that broader society had stripped from them. "Without you, this government cannot be run properly," she liked to tell them.[9]

Self-governance included self-punishment. Students who erred were required to march to the front of the room and punish themselves by whacking their own hand with a ruler as their classmates watched. Each student determined the number of smacks needed to reform their ways. "If you do not punish yourself well, I will have to do it myself," she politely threatened students. It was the most embarrassing and effective system of accountability.[10]

ML was caught horseplaying—the contagious virus that afflicts every elementary school. Miss Lemon recalled his acute embarrassment as he slogged his way to the front of the room. Even then, he exhibited a tendency to take self-blame to the highest level. He proceeded to inflict and receive the punishment for his classroom transgression without a sound, save the thwack of the ruler. He gave himself ten hard smacks, the maximum allowed under classroom governance—usually reserved for the most egregious actions, such as fighting or name calling—not foolish antics.[11] But it was all the same to ML's sensitive soul. He did everything as if his life depended on it.

Every day was Black History Month in Miss Lemon's class. She made sure her lessons on American history and literature featured African Americans. She did not teach about George Washington or the Revolutionary War without introducing Crispus Attucks, the first person killed by the British in that war. Frederick Douglass received as much attention, if not more, than Abraham Lincoln. The students centered the writings of Ida B. Wells, Paul Laurance Dunbar, and Nannie Helen Burroughs, allowing white novelists such as F. Scott Fitzgerald and Ernest Hemingway to fade into the background of American letters.[12]

Her lesson plans centered on social problems. ML, using his paper-route wages to purchase extra books, did reports and presentations to the class, including one on the history of Black education in Atlanta. But Miss Lemon, true to the school's pedagogy, always coupled such assignments with high-impact learning experiences such as field trips across the city. ML's report included a tour of the city's Black colleges.[13]

Classroom lessons were also filled with dramatizations. Radio was the most advanced communication technology of the day, and her students conducted pretend historical radio interviews, retelling prominent moments and accomplishments in Black history. Students imagined Crispus Attucks reporting from the Boston Massacre. They became Benjamin Banneker, a Black farmer and scholar who helped survey the nation's capital and capitol building; or Matthew Henson, the explorer, talking about venturing to the North Pole. They embodied Harriet Tubman escorting the enslaved along the Underground Railroad. They relived the experiences of Black musicians such as opera singer Marian Anderson and classical tenor Roland Hayes.[14]

ML's favorite role-play was performing the poetry of Langston Hughes. Miss Lemon introduced him to Hughes's 1932 seminal children's book, *The Dream Keeper*, an illustrated book that contained many of Hughes's noted poems. In whimsical style, the stanzas emphasized Black creative genius, survival, and joy even in the face of white opposition, misunderstanding, and ridicule. It was one of ML's earliest opportunities to perform Black orality, to mimic what he saw in church; to make his voice and body an instrument meant not just to communicate, but to give life and color to words. He was especially drawn to perform Hughes's "Negro Dancers." The youngster with amazing recall adored performing the poem from memory. It was a statement of Black affirmation, and the words about doing the Charleston dance rolled off his tongue with delight and activated his limbs.

ML would break out into the dance made famous in the 1920s, his stout legs and arms swinging back and forth as if walking in place, his right arm and left leg rushing forward and then retreating backward as his left arm and right leg began their rush forward, leather shoes smacking the carpet. "Da, da . . ." Without fail, according to Miss Lemon, his classmates showered him with applause and laughter, affirming ML's ability to move people with his oratorical and dramatic performances.[15]

In the child's more pensive moments, he took flight on Hughes's dream poems, teleporting him far from Jim Crow. ML was never shy about telling others of his desire to change the world. But when Miss Lemon introduced ML to Hughes's poems, it was one of his earliest encounters utilizing the dream metaphor in speech. Hughes, the man whose poetic prowess gained him the nickname "the king of words," taught ML how to position and pitch his dream of turning the world upside down.

A wide-eyed ML was greeted with the opening lines of the eponymous first poem, "The Dream Keeper," and another poem, "Dreams." The poems encouraged ML to remain steadfast in his dreams, as Hughes reminded readers that, if their dreams died, life became a bird with broken wings.

The book established Hughes as ML's favorite poet. He repeated, riffed, and sampled Hughes in his sermons and speeches for the rest of his life.[16]

As an adult, ML wrote to Hughes: "My admiration for your works is not only expressed in my personal conversations, but I can no longer count the number of times and places, all over the nation, in my addresses and sermons in which I have read your poems. I know of no better way to express in beauty the heartbeat and struggle of our people."[17]

The church whetted ML's desire for big words and oratory. The classrooms of the Atlanta Lab School satisfied that hunger, encouraging him to embody and relay the drama, genius, and tragedy of Black life. There, under the guidance of Miss Lemon, ML imbibed the words of Langston Hughes, and learned to be a dreamer.

Part Two

FINDING HIMSELF

10
MAMA

S ometimes dreams come with nightmares.

In King's young life, the only incident that rivaled the sting of racism was the death of Mama—his grandmother—when he was twelve years old. Many adolescents experience the crushing loss of a grandparent, but for ML it was a life-altering experience. He had what he called "extreme love" for Mama, and her death caused him to react in extreme fashion.[1]

In 1938, three years before her death, ML thought Mama had been killed because of AD's perpetual horseplaying. The incident occurred when AD slid down the banister, something his parents forbade, and struck Mama with his full weight. Her aging body was sent tumbling down the stairs until she came to a motionless halt. She was knocked unconscious, but ML believed his beloved grandmother was dead, and he decided he would join her.[2]

While the family was tending to Mama, a distraught and sobbing nine-year-old ML climbed the stairs to the second story of the house. Downstairs, a scene of confused commotion unfolded, but ML felt a profound sense of clarity. His father had long complained that ML was "always a little sensitive," and ML proved him right:

the boy opened the window, mounted the ledge, and flung himself into the air.[3] It's unclear if ML was attempting suicide. Recent King biographers have downplayed the incident or overlooked it altogether. But psychologists have found that Black youth who experience significant racial stress and trauma are more likely to deal with post-traumatic stress disorder (PTSD) and have a higher risk of suicide. Given all the racist violence he had seen and endured, it is very probable that at some point the youngster dealt with suicidal ideation. News of his grandmother's death could have pushed him over the edge.[4]

Thankfully, nobody died—not Mama nor ML. Their respective plunges left them both battered, bruised, and bedraggled, but still breathing.

Three years later, on Sunday May 18, 1941, Mama suffered a heart attack while sitting in a pew at church. She slumped over while awaiting her introduction as the keynote speaker at the Mount Olivet Baptist Church Women's Day Program. Rushed from the sanctuary to the hospital, she was pronounced dead on arrival. The fashionable and pious woman died just a month after her sixty-eighth birthday. ML was nowhere to be found. He told his parents he needed to stay home from evening worship to do some homework, but instead, he ducked off downtown to watch a parade, a revelry that his fundamentalist father strictly forbade on a Sunday. When a friend informed ML that his grandmother had suffered a heart attack and had been rushed to the hospital, he headed home as fast as he could.[5]

The youngster, panting incredulously, arrived at 501 Auburn to find everyone—Daddy, Mother Dear, Christine, and AD—mourning. The rumor was true: The woman who read to him, fed him, cried when he received whippings, and unashamedly loved him as her favorite grandchild was dead. And instead of doing as he was told or even being by her side as she suffered, he was frolicking on the avenue. ML was convinced her death was God's punishment for disobeying his father.[6] Never had his father's fundamentalist preaching seemed so true: As it says in Romans 6:23, "the wages of sin is death."

He was inconsolable. He marched upstairs once more, threw open the window, and jumped. And once more, the fall left him scraped up but alive. Once again his plans to join Mama in the great hereafter had been thwarted.[7]

Aunt Ida shared the child's pain. "Right after mama died, Aunt Ida seemed to lose the will to live," Christine later said. After holding forth at her sister's standing-room-only funeral, she quickly deteriorated. The lover of books and storytelling stopped reading and stopped talking. And she slowly stopped eating, starving herself. She just sat in her room, like she was waiting for death to come get her. It arrived, just short of the four-month anniversary of her sister's passing.[8]

ML was grief-stricken. To make a new start, the family moved a few blocks away, to a large, two-story yellow brick house that sat high on a grassy knoll at 193 Boulevard Street. It had always been Daddy King's dream to own a large brick house. The new home on the stretch of street known for large Black-owned mansions did nothing for ML's ailing heart. The change of scenery—removed from the familiar scents, sounds, and rooms that contained memories of his grandmother and Aunt Ida—made them both seem even further away. "It took ML months to come to terms with Mama's loss," Christine remembered.[9]

King Sr. recalled his sensitive son "cried off and on" and was "unable to sleep at night." Seeking to put an end to the sleepless nights and tear-soaked days, the father tried to comfort his son. He reminded ML of the Christian idea of immortality, that his grandmother's body was dead, but her soul was still alive and would spend eternity with God. Then he tried to alleviate the child's guilt. "I sat in the bedroom he and AD shared, explaining for nearly all of an afternoon that God wasn't *that* angry about ML neglecting a little homework or going to see a parade," he recalled telling his son. "Don't blame what has happened to your grandmother on anything you've done," he told the heartbroken child. "God has His own plan and His own way, and we cannot change or interfere with the time He chooses to call any of us back to Him." This sense of Christian immortality and fatalism—what the fundamentalist Reverend King Sr. referred to as God's sovereignty and providence—provided ML with little comfort at the time.[10]

As an adult, ML would came to embrace this idea. During his early days of activism, facing repeated death threats, he began to adopt a version of his father's words to process the reality of his own future death, inserting them into his sermons and casual conversations. Clarence Jones, King's attorney, recalled a stinging remark King made to him in 1963 following the assassination of President Kennedy. Jones had been urging King to take security measures to protect himself. King told Jones that the president's death showed the futility of such actions. God was his appointed bodyguard and undertaker. The idea that he could alter his divinely orchestrated date with death, King told Jones, was nothing more than a "fantasy."[11]

The teenage King had not yet embraced such Christian assurances. The death of his grandmother—the first close loved one he had lost—threw his world into disarray. All his life, his father had preached sin resulted in death. But now, his father was trying to convince him that the equation was not always true. Instead, the sting of death was random, striking sinners and saints alike. If the wages of his sin did not result in his grandmother's death, what other Scriptures were not true? As a graduate student, ML would pinpoint his grandmother's death as having "a tremendous effect on my religious development." Indeed, the ground of his religious understanding was shaken, his religious world was rocked. Nothing was as it seemed. So he launched an attack on everything he had been taught, starting with the foundation: faith.[12]

11
AGNOSTIC

M L began to rebel.

The trauma of his grandma's passing awakened his critical thinking, commencing a period of skepticism about everything in his world—a period otherwise known as being a teenager. He remembered it as "a normal rebellion of any young man at that time." But ML's teenage rebellion was particular—it was a revolt that only a child who feels they have been lied to all their life can summon. "I started raising questions . . . anything I could think of . . . about . . . what I'd been taught," he confided to a journalist in 1967. He launched a personal inquisition against the Bible and the Black Baptist faith.

He began to question the "truths" he had received in Sunday school. "Doubts began to spring forth unrelentingly," he remembered. Within months of his grandmother's death, ML publicly questioned one of the seminal doctrines of fundamentalist Protestant Christianity: The Resurrection of Jesus Christ. "I shocked my Sunday School class by denying the bodily resurrection of Jesus," King remembered. Death was death, he argued. There was no coming back. The still-grieving teenager knew this firsthand: Grandmother—with all her kisses, hugs, cooking, stories, and the very safety of her arms—was gone forever.[1]

Sunday school teacher and church secretary Lillian Watkins was scandalized theologically and personally. How could the cute, chubby child she babysat so many times, the son of the senior pastor, toss aside a literal interpretation of the Bible? The Resurrection of Christ was a foundational belief not only to his father, but the very doctrine of Ebenezer Baptist Church. It was the reason Protestants embraced the empty cross as a symbol of faith and central relic of church buildings, Christian homes, and a favorite fashion symbol of parishioners. But it did not matter to ML; he no longer believed.

The fundamental Christian stories and truths ML had been taught—the goodness and sovereignty of God, the divine inspiration of the Scriptures, the immortal soul, and the return of Christ— were no longer sources of comfort. They became subjects that he ridiculed as fairy tales.[2]

His behavior at church reflected his growing disbelief. ML had always sat with his grandmother in or near the front row of the church during worship service. After her death, he and his younger brother began sitting in the balcony, laughing, talking, and joking with other preteens and teens. Occasionally, Reverend King would stop his sermon mid-sentence to chastise his increasingly wayward son. Christine remembered her dad's booming voice over the microphone, "ML, you and AD come down here and sit," the pastor would say, pointing at the front row.[3]

The collapse of his religious world also led him to question the harshness of the broader world. "I was grappling with evil. If God was really as all-powerful and as good as they said, why was there so much evil on the face of the earth?" he began to wonder. "I continued

to go to church, but I became an agnostic," King confessed to a journalist. The man who would lead America with a stalwart faith in God
once doubted God's very existence.[4]

The death of his grandmother, the ultimate personal tragedy in
ML's world, made all other atrocities seem even more urgent. The
warmth of his grandmother's love was gone, leaving him unable to
see anything but the coldness of the world. It was as if Mama's death
evicted him from the safety of childhood, leaving him in search of
a meaningful adulthood, one that could address the evils of the
world. "After this experience," Christine recalled, ML "seemed to
have grown more mature." He began to consider his future occupation, and how he could make the world—a world without his grandmother, a world less loving and warm—a better place.[5] Daddy King
wanted his firstborn son to follow in his footsteps and become a
minister. But ML was not interested. He recognized his father's personal courage and ministerial activism. Daddy King rode the "whites
only" elevator at City Hall to reach the voter registration office. He
served as chairman of the Committee on the Equalization of Teachers' Salaries, which resulted in salary gains for Black teachers. He
was president of the Atlanta Baptist Ministers Union, the Sunday
School convention, and the Atlanta Ministers Council. He also held
leadership positions in the Atlanta Civic and Political League and
the local chapter of the NAACP, leading a massive voter registration
drive and march on city hall. ML witnessed all this, and honored his
father's courage, but as an agnostic teenager, he wanted nothing to
do with religion and its backwardness.

Like his father and mother, he wanted to serve the race. "Because of the influence of my mother and father," he reflected years
later, "I always had a deep urge to serve humanity, but I didn't start
out with an interest to enter the ministry. I thought I could probably
do it better as a lawyer or doctor."[6] He loved the oratorical style of

Black preaching, but not the subject matter. "I had doubts that religion was intellectually respectable," King remembered. How could a faith that relied on the supernatural address problems rooted in the natural world? As he told *Time* magazine in 1957, as a teenager he came to doubt that the ministry "could serve as a vehicle to modern thinking." Christ was not going to return to right all wrongs. That was the responsibility of professional men, not clergy—they were just heralds of biblical fairy tales.[7]

ML wanted a profession that was respectable, one that would empower him to refute everything the white world said about him and tried to take from him. W. E. B. Du Bois noted in 1903 that the experience of white supremacy made him and countless other young Black Americans desire to reach for the heights of professional accomplishment, not simply for the joy of a profession, but also to prove the white world wrong. "Just how I would do it I could never decide," Du Bois recalled of his youth, "by reading law, by healing the sick . . . some way."[8]

ML followed suit. In an act of maturation and teenage rebellion, he started telling people he wanted to be a physician. The job of a physician was intellectually respectable, grounded in the perceived exactness of science, unlike his dad's profession. The pain of loss was inevitable, but at least as a physician he could treat the bodies that were racked by racism.

Like a young Du Bois, he also considered law as a possible path. It was as respectable as medicine, grounded in cold logic, and could directly address the conditions of Black suffering, attacking the laws that upheld segregated public accommodations and white immunity. The daydreaming teenager imagined himself a lawyer "breaking down the legal barriers to Negroes." He began practicing his courtroom monologues in the mirror, picturing himself channeling the oratorical pizzazz of his father's preaching in the pulpit into the courtroom, moving jurists, instead of parishioners, to verdicts instead of amens.[9]

ML decided he would change the world from the operating room, or perhaps the courtroom. But it would definitely not be from the prayer room, the preteen King was certain of that.

12
A TOUGH GUY

M L decided he would become a tough guy.

The moments that marked the first decade of his life—refusing to engage in schoolyard fights, experiencing segregation and racist violence, losing his grandmother, abandoning his faith, and harboring a growing resentment of white people—all seemed to coalesce when ML officially became a teenager. What had started as a religious rebellion of a twelve-year-old grieving the death of his grandmother morphed into what ML later called a "general rebellion." He would tell a group of students at Coppin State University in 1965 that he became a bit "devilish." But he refused to internalize the violence the world had inflicted upon him. Instead, he externalized it, commencing a dramatic change: The boy who was "too sensitive," the child who refused to strike others, became a tough guy ready to fight. [1]

Becoming a fighter may have been a form of angry rebellion, or perhaps survival, a shield to protect him from a world that seemed increasingly violent and unpredictable. Whatever the cause, one thing was for certain: ML had changed.

Mr. E. R. Thomas, ML's physical education teacher at the Lab School, noticed the change in the newly minted teenager. In a January 23, 1942, evaluation, just eight days after ML's thirteenth birthday, Thomas noted that ML was not as cooperative as he had been. To make matters worse, Thomas noted, the once kindhearted boy had developed a habit of "mak[ing] unkind remarks" to his classmates.[2]

ML's sensitive heart—the soul that outright refused to harm others—was lost for a time, giving way to a weathered, tough teenager.

• • •

In the fall of 1942, ML was forced out of the private confines of the Lab School, and into the overcrowded local public school. The Lab School closed its high school during ML's freshmen year, leaving him no choice but to enroll at Booker T. Washington High School. ML and Christine both went. Both children were promoted to the next grade: ML in the tenth grade and Christine in the eleventh.[3]

Every day, the hardening of his heart began during his daily city bus ride across town to his new school. It was the first time ML had to use the city buses. His father had forbidden the family from doing so, shielding them from the humiliations of Jim Crow transportation. But for some reason, ML began riding the bus. Perhaps it was an act of independence from his father, another expression of his general rebellion.

The experience stuck with ML. He recalled what it felt like to be treated as a second-class citizen. Black passengers were greeted with signs directing them to sit in the back while whites were seated in the front in the designated "whites only" section. Even if the white section was empty, Black passengers could not sit there. Rather they were expected to stand over the empty seats. And if the white section was full, Black passengers were forced to give up their designated seats and move farther back. The trip to school taunted him daily, challenging him to maintain a sense of dignity and calm.

"I went through that experience going to Booker T. Washington High School," King reflected years later, "but my parents taught me something very early . . . they instilled in me a feeling of somebody-ness and they would say to me over and over again that you're just as good as any child in Atlanta." He recalled rehearsing this lesson every day on his way to high school. Surrounded by dehumanizing and infuriating circumstances, he tried to psychologically construct a sense of hope amid despair. "I would get on that bus day after day. I would end up having to go to the back of that bus with my body, but every time I got on that bus, I left my mind up on the front seat. And I said to myself, one of these days I'm gonna put my body up there where my mind is."[4]

The overcrowded public high school magnified the anger and rebellion brewing inside ML. His private high school had an enrollment of just 206 students. Washington High, the only public high school for African Americans in the city of Atlanta, had 4,343 students, the result of white local and state officials refusing to legalize integrated public education or allocate funds for more Black high schools. The school opened in 1924, thanks in part to the advocacy of ML's grandfather Reverend A. D. Williams, and remained the only Black public high school in the city until 1947. The difference in scale and resources must have been staggering to ML. Starting in a new high school is a common fear for a teenager. The difference in class size and instruction certainly would have compounded the teenage nightmare.[5]

The school also had a reputation for being exceptionally rough. "In that time," AD's girlfriend Naomi remembered, "you had little gangs and violence" in the hallways. The violence made June Dobbs, a classmate of ML, hate going to school. "It was dangerous, people would be in fights and people would get mauled," she ruefully remembered.[6]

ML became a target in this rough environment. He showed up to the public high school dressed more like a lawyer than a student. The teenager, like so many teens then and now, became very focused on his appearance. Every day became a dress rehearsal for adulthood. When he completed the eighth grade, Alberta rewarded him with a brown tweed suit, a symbol of accomplishment, as it resembled the uniform of British royalty and estate men. But ML's suit blended the posh fabric with modern American styling. It was a draped suit, going against wartime fabric rationing, featuring a longer loose jacket with wide-notch lapels and suspenders to hold up the baggy trousers that tapered to a tight cuff at the ankle. ML styled his suit with wide-collared shirts, starched flat like cardboard, the pleats of his pants creased to a razor's edge, and two-tone wingtip shoes shined just right. His family recalled that he could not leave the house without a long gander in the mirror, making sure everything was immaculate. "He loved that suit," Christine teased years later. "He wore it every-where he could, every chance he got." Including high school.[7] His adolescent crew—a cast of characters with nicknames to match: Rial "Rooster" Cash, Joe "Shag" Roberts, Oliver "Sack" Jones, Howard "Mole" Everett, and Emmett "Weasel" Proctor—quickly assigned ML a nickname as well. "He liked good clothes from as early as I can remember," Emmett Proctor told a journalist in 1957. "But where the rest of us would say 'My papa is going to buy me a new suit,' he'd say 'my daddy's going to buy me a tweed.' He said it so much that we just named him Tweed, and he's Tweed to us to this day."[8]

The suit made him a conspicuous private school transfer, a bull's-eye for the school bullies. Mattiwilda Dobbs, a Lab School alumna, remembered her younger sister June and the other Lab School transfers to Washington High "didn't have a very good time being received there."[9] ML's youth and stature made matters worse. As a thirteen-year-old sophomore, he was even younger than the average freshman. And standing at five six and 140 pounds, he was heckled with calls of "Shrimp." All of this put him in the crosshairs of a few upperclassmen. "Because Tweed was such a dude," one classmate remembered, a group of "boys decided one day they were going to haze him." Six students hatched a juvenile plan to embarrass him: Hold Tweed down long enough to rip off his razor-creased tweed trousers to reveal the "the long drawers" he was rumored to wear underneath. The ambush succeeded. "We finally pinned him down and stripped him," an unnamed culprit admitted years later, but not before ML put up a fight with elbows, fists, and kicks. The boys suffered bloody noses, sore jaws, and bruised egos. "I know," the unnamed culprit confessed, "because mine was one of them."[10]

ML did not have any problems at school after that. His willingness to go down swinging put the teasing and the threats of violence to rest. Gone were the days of allowing bullies to beat him down. It began the process of solidifying his schoolyard reputation as a well-dressed tough guy.

He also stopped being AD's punching bag. Once, he even backhanded his younger brother. The shocking blow occurred while they played a board game. When the Kings moved to Boulevard in 1941, they became fast friends with the Dobbs family, and the three King children and sisters Mattiwilda and June Dobbs formed a crew. They routinely met to play board games. The relatively new game of Monopoly, invented in 1935, became the favorite. The game rotated houses and the hostess provided the food. Their fathers—King Sr. and John W. Dobbs—welcomed the activities. They did not permit their young teenagers to attend recreations that were segregated due to Jim Crow laws. As June Dobbs, six months older than ML, recalled, the two fathers spoke with one voice, telling their children: "You have to ride the street car, but you don't have to pay good money for a movie or a concert downtown where you'll be discriminated against." Entertaining at home was the safest, most dignified option.[11]

"We'd do our little chores in the morning and then we'd play Monopoly in the afternoon," June remembered. That summer, AD told June he wanted to "spice up the game." She remembered AD telling her, "I can make you the Monopolist, we have an old set I found, of money and stuff, and I'm just going to slip you a couple of hundreds every now and then, don't ever let them know." AD kept his word. "AD was just a nuisance, he was impetuous, and funny, and always stealing something, or doing something," June recalled. "As others puzzled over my 'luck' in becoming 'the Monopolist,' A.D. and I chuckled."

June's "luck" made ML suspicious. He eventually discovered the embezzlement. He flew into a rage. "Now, all this took place long before Martin adopted the doctrine of nonviolence," June hedged when retelling the story. As Christine and AD laughed, ML, hands full of Monopoly money, backhanded his brother. "He was just so outraged he cuffed his brother . . . hit him across the face." June recalled ML screaming, "How could you do such a thing? Cheating! You cheated!" June became fearful that ML's anger would spill over given her involvement in the scheme. She braced herself to be the next victim. "I was taller than he was, but I still thought he was going to hit me . . . I was really afraid he was going to hit me but he didn't . . . I held my breath but nothing happened to me." She tried to make penance to ML, offering profuse tears and apologies. But nothing could atone. He quit Monopoly. The routine gatherings came to an abrupt end.

ML's willingness to use physical force during his early teen years became part of his teenage identity.

"He was always the roughest one in our whole gang," Rial Cash told a journalist in 1957 as King was set to receive an NAACP award for his nonviolent activism. "What are they trying to do? Make a plaster saint or a sissy out of Tweed?" he complained, conflating masculinity with violence.

ML began looking for opportunities to display his newly discovered toughness. "He could outwrestle anybody in our gang and he knew it," Joe Roberts chimed in. "And he was always challenging one of us to wrestle." ML, ever a lover of words, invented a phrase to issue a wrestling challenge. He would look his potential opponent in the eye and say, "Let's go to the grass!"

ML never publicly spoke about the violent, aggression-filled phase of his teenage years. However, as an adult he did express blanket remorse. Reminiscing on his adolescence, he told a journalist that every time he engaged in physical violence, "I always regretted it."[12]

13
BASKETBALL

When ML's challenge to "go to the grass" was rebuffed, he looked to sports to display his dominance. "You could skip such a challenge," his friend Joe said, "but you were in for it if you tried to play against him in any other sport."[1]

Oliver Jones bore witness. "You could not hurt that guy with anything from the very start. It wasn't a matter of hurting him; it was a question of keeping from getting hurt. You took a chance of getting hurt even when you were playing football or basketball for fun against him."[2]

Wallace "Pickles" Coombs, captain of ML's youth basketball team, also knew this to be true. "He was a tiger on the basketball court. He was aggressive," Pickles remembered. "He would run over you if you let him."[3]

ML loved basketball. Though his five-six frame meant he was better suited for the football field, he had hoop dreams he refused to relinquish. It was a lifelong love. As an adult, ML would organize basketball games following dinner at staff retreats. The losers had to do the dishes.[4]

As a youngster, ML did not make the high school varsity team. Instead, he made a name for himself playing club basketball with the Adelphi Junior Club, a church-affiliated organization founded in 1930. The traveling club, known as the Purple and Gold Dragons, had three divisions. "Varsity," "Intermediate," and the lowest division, the "Midgets."[5] ML played on the Midgets with Coombs and Emmett Proctor.

Prior to the days of integrated basketball, the Purple and Gold Dragons competed exclusively against other Black club teams across the South. They became the most dominant junior basketball club in Dixie, netting a ten-year record of 165 wins and only 24 loses. Word of their Southern prominence reached Harlem, New York City. In 1940, the Harlem Young Men's Christian Association (YMCA) Junior Basketball Club, purportedly the best in the North, invited the Adelphi Junior Club Dragons to Harlem to play for the imaginary title of national junior club basketball champion. A lack of funding prevented the national standoff being played in the Big Apple. Instead, ML and the Dragons became legends while playing at Atlanta's Butler Street YMCA, the segregated facility for the city's African Americans.[6]

ML established a reputation as "real scrappy," coach Lucius Jones told reporters during the 1942 season. The founder, director, and longtime coach of the club praised ML as "rated second to none in sheer aggressiveness and fight." ML's aggressiveness not only got him into foul trouble, it also caused him to run afoul of his teammates. Leading with physical force, he had very poor shot selection. Every time ML got his hands on the ball—no matter where he was on the court—he was determined to find a way to shoot the ball. "He loved to dribble," Coombs smirked, until he found just enough space to shoot the ball. His "shoot at all cost" attitude gained Tweed another moniker: Teammates labeled the pugnacious guard "Will Shoot" because any time ML got his hands on the ball, he "will shoot," they complained.

His penchant for hogging the ball made him notorious on his two-time championship team. It did not matter if leading scorers Coombs or Lincoln Crittenden were open or near the basket, ML was going to show off the jump shot he honed on the homemade court in his backyard. "He was one of the subs on our team," an unnamed teammate told a journalist, "and we kept him as a sub because he didn't know what teamwork was." His teammates would routinely "give him hell" about his shoot-first mentality. Undeterred, after the game ML would just shrug off their disapproving grumblings. "Look, I just felt like shooting," he routinely explained.[7]

"What more could [we] say," one teammate acknowledged, since most of the time ML "actually made the basket!" In a few games, King even managed to get hot, coming off the bench and ending the game as the team's second-leading scorer. Every year at tryouts, ML's shooting ability guaranteed him a spot on the team, but his shot selection assured he would be coming off the bench. And every time he entered the game, he had *that feeling*, ready to let it fly.[8]

14
DATING

M L's assertiveness on the basketball court carried over to courting: He was never afraid to take his shot at winning a girl's
heart. "I can't remember when he began being interested in girls,"
AD recalled of his brother, "neither can I remember when he
wasn't." Christine, the watchful older sibling, remembers ML's first
crush came when he was seven. She said it was on ML's classmate
Emma Lyons. His parents told interviewers that ML began talking
about marriage when he was "very young." "When he was a small
kid, he would talk about the family he hoped to raise," his father
noted. "Who he was going to marry. What kind of girl. How many
children he would have."[1]

By the time he entered high school he was, like many teenagers, consumed by romantic matters. His life became a whirlwind of
first dates, dances, parties, outings, and breakups. When it came to
carousing, ML was every bit a teenager, and his entire family knew
it. Every time Christine's friends came to visit, ML would linger
around, chatting up the older girls and convincing his sister to set
him up with a few of her friends.[2]

In truth, ML had little need for a matchmaker. He played the gentleman, while his peers counted flirting as synonymous with teasing

and pranks. He would chastise them for their lack of manners. "He was already making time with that low voice and smooth approach of his when the rest of us were still thinking you could get a girl's attention by pulling her hair," a classmate remembered.

ML's skills on the dance floor also caught the girls' attention. The jitterbug was the dance of the day, and ML mastered it quickly, gaining a reputation as the best jitterbugger in town. His ability to glide across the floor with his partner, swing her through the air, and bring her back down with ease kept his dance card full, wounding the egos of competitors. "Boy, he could really cut a rug," AD reminisced. Christine was more demure in her assessment: "He was quite a dancer." His Baptist clergyman father adamantly opposed dancing, but that meant virtually nothing to his oldest son. According to Christine, all three of the King children dismissed their father's prohibitions. His concerns were not religious commandments. They were, the children agreed years later, nothing more than "the generational conflict that every family with teen-aged children goes through."[3]

ML also used his tough-guy image to impress girls at dances. When he saw certain young men—those he was confident he could outwrestle—pushing up on girls, dancing too close, or making unwanted advances, he would intervene as if he was protecting his mother. First, he would interject a lighthearted comment, encouraging the guy to take it easy. If the young man persisted, one culprit remembered, "He'd tell you flatly to stop it." If that didn't work, ML would knuckle up, issuing his infamous challenge, "Let's go to the grass!" It was a successful strategy. "Nobody ever called his hand as far as I remember," the classmate confessed.

Rial Cash sensed something else afoot. "You know, I always thought that policing business was part of Tweed's line with the girls," he stated. "He was always a big hit with each individual dame after he put one of us in our place."

AD tried to emulate his older brother, but he soon came to realize there was no competition. They tried double-dating, but AD could not keep up; ML's social calendar was too full. AD went in the other direction. He met Naomi Ruth Barber when both were twelve. The two became steady teenage lovebirds. "We were . . . serious," Naomi recalled years later, "we were just inseparable." They married in 1950, at the age of nineteen. Not so for ML. "He kept flitting from chick to chick," AD joked.

ML in a tweed suit after winning the local speech competition. *Atlanta Daily World*, Sunday, April 16, 1944.

15
SCHOOL SHOOTING

M L, like too many kids then and now, had his school day—classes, flirtations, and teenage daydreams—interrupted by a shooting at school.

• • •

Joseph Livingston was a nice kid. The seventeen-year-old was studious, placing third in the school's 1943 social science quiz bowl. He had a small job at the *Atlanta Daily World*, nothing major, but a job perfect for a teenager. He donated a portion of his income to the NAACP and the Red Cross. He was considered one of the most promising kids in the senior class.

But even nice kids can be pushed too far.

In the fall of 1943, ML's junior year, Joseph Livingston began shooting in a classroom in the middle of the school day. The prior week, the *Atlanta Daily World* had published his opinion piece decrying racial inequity in public school funding. But on November 2, the published writer put down his pen and picked up a gun.

Livingston testified that he had been the victim of daily schoolyard bullying from Milton Williams, whom Livingston referred to as "the big bully of the school." Williams intensified his threats against Livingston on November 1, flashing a knife in the middle of class, promising to cut Livingston. Fearful for his life, Livingston brought his father's .38-caliber revolver to school the next day. Livingston and Williams shared a 10:00 a.m. class. The course convened inside Portable Number 10, one of the many detached trailers the school used to accommodate overcrowding. The class did not have an instructor for the day, leaving the kids idle and unsupervised. Williams approached Livingston and again brandished his knife. Without hesitation, Livingston fired two shots, striking Williams and an innocent bystander. As the blood of the victims oozed onto the floor, Livingston gave the gun to a quick-witted classmate, who raced to hide the weapon under wooden planks near the football field. Responding to reports of gunshots, police arrived and apprehended Livingston, who confessed to the crime. He was later indicted by a Fulton County Grand Jury and charged with assault with intent to murder.[1]

An unnamed eyewitness expressed despair to the local press. When asked by a reporter why Livingston did not report the bullying to school officials, the student replied, "It wouldn't have done any good." The underpaid and understaffed administration was simply too overwhelmed to discipline menacing students like Williams or ensure the protection of bookish pupils like Livingston.[2]

ML's relationship to the shooter and the victims is not known. But surely, a shooting in the middle of the school day would have shaken most everyone, even tough guy ML.

16
THE BUS

D espite the overcrowding, the fighting, the dating, and the shooting, ML did his best to stay focused in the classroom. As a
fourteen-year-old junior, he put up solid academic marks: B's across
the board—English, Geometry, Chemistry, History, and Citizenship.
But he struggled in his vocational courses. He received a D in Au-
tomotive Mechanics, perhaps one of the greatest indications of his
professional white-collar path.[1]

By the spring of his junior year, the now fifteen-year-old maintained steady grades, just above average. But his ambitions were anything but average. Completely settled on being a lawyer, he began
practicing his oratory in the mirror: the choreographed placement of
his hands, the pacing of his voice, and volume modulation to emphasize certain phrases.[2] It was his goal to use his intelligence and
the skills of the Black pulpit to move juries and crowds for the cause
of racial equality.

"The Negro and the Constitution" was the teenager's earliest
known public oration on race and the law. ML delivered his speech
on Thursday, April 13, 1944, at 10:30 a.m. in a speech competition
sponsored by the Improved Benevolent and Protective Order of
Elks of the World (IBPOEW). The African American fraternal order

was founded in 1897, borrowing part of their name from the all-white Benevolent Protective Order of Elks. The latter was neither benevolent nor protective toward African Americans, barring them from membership since its founding in 1868. The bylaws prohibiting Black members were not amended until 1972, something ML would not live to see. The IBPOEW dubbed itself the "Improved" version because it did not practice racial segregation.

The IBPOEW established the annual oratorical contest in 1926 to encourage young adults to study the US Constitution and prepare public compositions addressing universal equal rights. High school students were generally given the option to choose from three themes pertaining to the intersection of the African American experience and the US Constitution. Students were then challenged to research their chosen theme, draft an address, and recite it from memory at the competition. Students were judged on their content and delivery. In 1944, the general themes were "The Negro and the Constitution," "The Constitution and Slavery," and "Booker T. Washington and the Constitution." ML was coached by his English teacher, Ms. Sarah Grace Bradley. She had begun teaching at the school in 1923, and quickly became one of the most popular teachers. She served as the faculty adviser to the student newspaper and as the state education director and state deputy of the Black Elks. The previous year she victoriously guided William Tunstall, also a student at Booker T. Washington High, through the local, state, regional, and national competitions, landing second place in the nation. Bradley and ML hoped they would achieve the same outcome. Later, ML would credit her guidance with being his first public-speaking coach. "She coached me," King told an interviewer in 1963, a few months after his momentous "I Have a Dream," address, "and that was . . . the beginning of my training in public speaking."[3]

ML won the high school title. He and runner-up Hiram Ken-
dall, a senior at Washington High, qualified for the statewide contest, which would be held on April 17 at the First Baptist Church in
Dublin, Georgia, approximately 140 miles southeast of Atlanta. His
victory was heralded in the *Atlanta Daily World*. For his first press
appearance, ML sported his beloved tweed suit and a mustache that
was as nascent as his jurist dreams.[4]

ML was optimistic heading into the statewide competition. Tunstall had won the 1943 state contest focusing on the same theme. It is
unclear if his coach shared Tunstall's remarks with ML. But the 1943
contest was held at Ebenezer Baptist Church, so it is very likely ML,
a lover of words, was present.[5]

The speech ML gave for the competition was drenched in
hope. Like a closing argument from a trial lawyer, ML weaved legal documents and famous quotes into an oratorical performance.
He hoped it would be the first of many orations that would leave
audiences spellbound while attempting to win a verdict for Black
equality.

His speech outlined the discrepancy between the nation's pro-
fessed Christian faith and constitutional values with the experience of
legalized discrimination. He began by reviewing the evidence of his
case. Africans were enslaved and brought to America to labor; they
were treated as property, denied human rights and citizenship. Despite the Civil War, Reconstruction, and constitutional amendments
outlawing discrimination based on race, "Black America," ML thundered, "still wears chains." Then, deploying the oratorical flair of the
Black Baptist preaching he had absorbed all his life, ML unleashed a
flurry of charges. America claimed to be a Christian nation, yet it ignored Jesus's "Golden Rule," to treat others as we want to be treated.
Accomplished Black performers, like famed opera singer Marian
Anderson, were praised for their talents but barred from public ac-

commodations on account of their race. The nation claimed to be the land of opportunity, but Jim Crow placed a severe limit on African American achievement.

He closed by offering his dream for white people. "My heart throbs anew in the hope that, inspired by the example of Lincoln, imbued with the spirit of Christ, they will cast down the last barrier to perfect freedom," he declared. "And I with my brother of blackest hue possessing at last my rightful heritage and holding my head erect, may stand beside the Saxon—a Negro—and yet a man!"

It was like a dress rehearsal and a blueprint for his famous "I Have a Dream" address that he would give nineteen years later, using the same formula to articulate his hope for America.[6]

But in 1944, the budding lawyer's dream did not move the audience. ML failed to place at the contest. First place and a portion of the $1,000 scholarship (enough to cover tuition for four years at most historic Black colleges and universities at the time) went to Miss Euris Smith, a junior from Beach High School in Savannah, described by the Black press as possessing "histrionic ability." (Smith would go on to win the national competition the following year. She used the scholarship money to obtain degrees from Bennett College in Greensboro, North Carolina, and New York University. She worked for the Ford Foundation studying juvenile delinquency, and later became a middle and high school teacher, specializing in deaf education.) ML's schoolmate—the tall and lean Hiram Kendall—split runner-up with Miss Alice Freeman.[7]

King may have failed to place because his performance paled in comparison to the dramatics of Euris Smith. ML was still opposed to the melodrama of Black orality. Or perhaps it was the content of the speech, some of which was borrowed. He reworked a speech by Henry F. Coleman called "The Philosophy of the Race Problem (From a Negro's Point of View)." That speech by the Cornell College (Iowa) student was reprinted in a 1928 book titled *Fifty Orations That Have Won Prizes in Speaking Contests*, which ML may have come across in the library during his quest for big words. Remixing and repurposing words and phrases without attribution was and remains very common in the Black preaching tradition. ML would have heard reorchestrations among the Black Baptist preachers—the big wordsmiths—he desperately tried to imitate and emulate. He did his best to rearrange Coleman's speech, adding in relevant historical and current events. But he copied most of the dramatic ending word for word.[8] Like a jazz musician, his improvisation was original, but most of the words were not.

Nevertheless, the following month, the speech was published in the Booker T. Washington High School yearbook, *The Cornellian*. It was his first of many publications. But his dreams of being a celebrated orator were deferred. He had to make the long trip home alongside his victorious classmate and coach.

During the trip, ML was painfully reminded of the limits of the US Constitution for Black Americans. After leaving Dublin, the nearly empty bus stopped in Macon, where several white passengers boarded. Jim Crow mandated that Black riders immediately give up their seats and move to the back of the bus. ML's classmate followed the law. Ms. Sarah Grace Bradley, ML's coach and chaperone, reluctantly stood and moved to the rear. As a civically engaged citizen she was aware of her constitutional rights and the joys that came with public dignity while she was a student at Harvard and the University of Chicago. But the Athens, Georgia, native knew things were different in the South. She begrudgingly suffered the indignity.[9]

She turned to see that ML had not moved. She beckoned him to follow her lead. "It's the law," she ruefully whispered to ML.

But ML refused to move.

It was his first time openly opposing the ravages of racism. Just hours earlier he had told a packed Black church that his heart was pulsating with the hope that Black equality was in reach. Here was the moment to prove to himself and others that his speech was more than just empty, improvised rhetoric.

He had done nothing when racism caused him to lose his best child playmates. He had stood idle when he and his father were refused service at a shoe store, and he had not resisted when a white woman physically and verbally assaulted him outside a department store. And every day during the school year, Monday through Friday, he complied with Jim Crow rules on the bus on the way to his segregated high school. But those days were over. Tweed, the dapper tough guy, was done being pushed around. He had been telling himself that one day he was going to stand up to bus segregation. While riding on the bus back to Atlanta, he decided that the day had arrived.[10]

The white bus driver grew irate. King remembered the bus driver's pursed lips quivering with venom. Then he showered down curses on the teen and his teacher, berating them, calling them "niggers" and "black sons of bitches."[11]

Some Black passengers tried their best to look away from what was surely an impending catastrophe. They wanted no association with the brave but naive youth, for fear that they would be implicated in his lawless act. Others, including Ms. Bradley, urged ML to give up his seat, with good reason. They were old enough to know that those who chose to travel along the path to bravery were almost always broken. Ms. Bradley was particularly aware; as a staff writer for the *Atlanta Daily World* and member of the Associated Negro Press (ANP), she was very acquainted with the tragic stories of what befell those who refused to comply with Jim Crow on the bus.

One month prior to ML's singular protest, the ANP was ablaze with front-page reports of what it called "the latest outrage": the killing of Private Edward Green. The twenty-three-year-old Black soldier from New York was shot and killed in Alexandria, Louisiana, on March 13, 1944, for refusing to forfeit his seat in the largely empty white section of the bus and move to the crowded "colored" section, where there was standing room only. The Associated Negro Press noted that eyewitnesses recalled that a few Black passengers encouraged Green to move. Some say Green refused, others say he reluctantly began to move. But all agreed that Odell Lachney, the thirty-five-year-old white bus driver employed by the city of Alexandria, was not pleased. He left his seat at the wheel, drew his revolver, and confronted the soldier, prompting a white passenger to demand, "Don't kill him on the bus."

Lachney, careful to cater to his white passengers, exited the bus and marched to the rear, swinging the door open. "Now you nigger! Come on out of there!" An unnamed white passenger pushed Green in the back, causing the serviceman to fall out the back door of the bus as he pleaded for his life. "Please don't kill me! I'll get off if you promise not to shoot me!" As Green arose from his fall, still begging for his life, Lachney shouted to the white passengers, "Keep the other niggers on the bus!" The doors were closed. Lachney shot the pleading serviceman twice in the heart at close range. He then dragged Private Green's lifeless body off the street into the gutter. The bus driver opened the bus doors. A white passenger then tossed a knife next to the servicemen's body before telling police officers Lachney shot Private Green after the servicemen drew a knife. Police "escorted" Lachney to police headquarters "in hero style," while helping him rehearse his story. No local criminal charges were filed. The NAACP, led by legal counsel Thurgood Marshall, pressed the US Department of War to look into the matter. The subsequent Army investigation concluded there was no "moral or legal" justification for the murder. Nevertheless, the US Department of Justice declared it would take no action. Odell was reinstated to his job.[12] Not even those Black soldiers who defended their nation in war abroad could expect their nation to defend them at home. Black newspapers, church bulletins, the NAACP, as well as barbershop and beauty salon grapevines, were inundated with stories about Green's murder. White supremacy—whether in the form of a bus driver, police officer, or everyday citizen—was unforgiving.

And now, one month later, ML was beginning to reenact the tragic front-page news. "I intended to stay right in that seat," he remembered. Ms. Bradley continued to plead, desperate to prevent a child from being harmed on her watch. Her logic was as simple as it was pervasive: The indignities of curse words and racial epithets were preferable to death. Embarrassment would end; tired feet and bruised egos would heal; but death was forever.

Eventually, ML was moved by her sincere pleas. He was taught always to listen to his teachers, and so he finally relented, forfeiting his seat.

He had to stand for the nearly ninety-mile trip home. "It was the angriest I have ever been in my life," he later wrote of the incident. "That night will never leave my memory."[13]

ML had been riding high, proud to represent Georgia's largest Black high school in a statewide competition. By all accounts, he was a promising young man. And then—"suddenly," as he observed—he was pierced with the insults and daily reminders that he did not "count." He was made to feel like "a nobody." Years later, he recounted, "I decided right then, that someday I would do something about those daily pinpricks and insults."[14]

King reflected on this moment throughout his life, careful to convey how much it inspired him to labor for change. However, he never mentioned how the experience may have inspired his teacher and speaking coach. Later that summer, Miss Bradley, along with her sister, protested treatment on a bus trip scheduled from Atlanta to

Athens. Bradley, suffering from a fracture from a fall at a recent Elks Convention, was physically forced off a bus on account of her race. Bradley testified in court that the bus driver was "indignant," calling her and her sister "niggers." When the two women made claim to their civil rights, arguing with the bus driver, he threatened their lives. The bus driver and dispatcher called the Atlanta police. The women, for the first time in their lives, were arrested, held in jail, and found guilty of disorderly conduct. Adding insult to Miss Bradley's physical injury, she and her sister were fined. The Jim Crow court fined her $10, plus court costs, stealing from her already paltry state-mandated Black teacher salary of $400 a year.[15]

Miss Bradley may have been the first person ML stirred to protest racial discrimination against all odds, but she would certainly not be the last.

ML returned home exhausted from standing, but too restless to rest. It was time to start his future. In an act of audacious ambition, he decided he would skip his senior year of high school and apply for early admission to Morehouse College. With so many college-age Black men fighting abroad in the Second World War, Morehouse began an early admissions program to maintain enrollment. A student only needed to pass an early admissions test. ML took the test. Senior year of high school may have been important to some. But not to ML. The significance of high school games, dances, homecoming, and graduation melted under the heat of his anger. He was in a rush to do something about the legal condition of white supremacy.

Morehouse was the perfect educational institution for an aspiring lawyer. It was founded in 1867 in Augusta. The Augusta Institute, as it was named, was established to educate the formerly enslaved. In 1885, the school moved to Atlanta, later changing its name to Morehouse, named after prominent white Baptist Henry L. Morehouse. It would become the premiere all-male private liberal arts college for Black men. Its liberal arts focus made it unique among the bevy of Southern Black private schools founded during the Civil War and Reconstruction era. Schools such as Tuskegee Normal and Industrial Institute (now Tuskegee University) and Hampton Normal and Agricultural Institute (now Hampton University) focused on training elementary school teachers, as well as agriculture and industrial education. Morehouse aimed to train the freedmen in the liberal arts, to expose them to theology, literature, history, philosophy, and languages.

ML also had sentimental connections to Morehouse. "There's a tradition in our family to go to Morehouse," King told a journalist in 1967. "And I never wanted to go anywhere else. I never considered anywhere else or applied anywhere else." His grandfather and father had graduated from the college. His grandmother and mother attended Spelman College, the women's counterpart to Morehouse. His sister, Christine, always a source of competition, was graduating from Washington High School and was headed to Spelman that fall, giving ML an extra dose of motivation. "Of course, he [was] you know, trying to keep up with me," Christine said years later. June Dobbs, his neighborhood Monopoly buddy turned foe, was also taking the early admissions test to Spelman.

June recalled that after being at the private Lab School, she and ML had a challenging time adjusting to the packed, rough accommodations of Booker T. Washington High School. The place "was terribly overcrowded," Dobbs recalled. And the shootings, fights, and teacher shortages made it "an impossible . . . very lamentable place to try to get an education." When the opportunity to skip the twelfth grade became available, she and ML "were glad to get out of there, she remembered. Attending Morehouse would please ML's parents, it would pay honor to Mama, and it would allow him to keep pace with his big sister, all while gaining ground on his destiny.[16]

As summer arrived ML still had not been told if he had passed
the Morehouse early admission test. But he acted like he did. He
enlisted in Morehouse's summer work program to pick tobacco in
the Connecticut Valley. Since the program began around the First
World War, one third to half of the student body annually went to
Simsbury, Connecticut, and the surrounding areas to harvest shade
tobacco.[17]

ML had plenty of reasons to sign up for the program. He wanted
to get out of Atlanta, out of the South, and away from those telling
him to slow down and learn to live with Jim Crow racism. And after
losing the speech contest, he wanted to make money to pay his tuition. ML could net about $150 to $200 over the summer. It would go a
long way toward paying the $50 tuition for the first semester, plus $28
in annual fees (including registration, $5, wear and tear, $5, medical,
$6, student activity, $12) for a total of $78. Room, board, and laundry
were an estimated additional $121.50 per semester.[18]

But his parents were, to put it mildly, resistant to his plans to go
to Connecticut. Tuition was not an issue. It was a bill his parents,
who lived on his father's annual salary of more than $2,500, could
afford.[19] The family lived comfortably in their two-story brick house,
with a housekeeper, and owned their own automobile. Daddy King
was happy to financially support ML's college dreams—to a point.
When ML requested to live on campus, his father nixed the idea.
"It's a waste of money!" Daddy King remembered dismissing his
son. But King Sr. committed to paying ML's tuition. He loved the
idea of his son going to college early. It was a show of manly, audacious ambition. "My pride swelled," the senior King recalled of
the moment, "because ML's confidence simply left no room in our
house for uncertainty. He was going to take the step that told him
what nothing else could: where he was going."[20]

But they resisted Connecticut being one of those places. Daddy

King hated the idea of his children working for white people, especially on a farm. It was reminiscent of slavery, a life he himself had barely escaped in rural Stockbridge, Georgia. He would be damned if he saw all the striving he had done to give his family a good life result in his first son returning to the fields. Mother Dear had her own reasons for opposing ML's proposal: Her baby was too small to do farm labor, and he was too young to be a thousand miles away from home by himself. Her concerns were valid. A Morehouse student had mysteriously drowned in Connecticut during a previous summer with no explanation. It was front-page news in Black Atlanta.[21]

But ML continually solicited his parents, assuring them of his safety and the benefits of the program. A rotation of esteemed Morehouse faculty accompanied the group every year. Professor Claude B. Dansby was assigned the duty in 1944. The Morehouse- and University of Chicago–educated mathematician enjoyed a reputation as a steady, trustful hand. He was a fixture in the Mathematics Department, serving as chairman from 1927 until his retirement in 1967, when the Mathematics building was named in his honor. He began chaperoning the trip in 1923, the year he joined the faculty. He told the Atlanta Daily World heartwarming stories of educating Morehouse men on the utility of mathematics as they labored in the tobacco fields. "Pop," as the students called the aging professor, was known for having a "prodigious memory for figures," helping him to compute equations while also maintaining a tally of student behavior in his head. Pop was notorious for keeping his thick-framed spectacles focused on the conduct of Morehouse men—from taking attendance at required chapel services on campus, or surveilling behavior in the Connecticut tobacco fields. Under the careful supervision of the trusted Professor Dansby, ML explained to his parents that he would be safe, and earn more money than he could working for the newspaper. And he would be around other Morehouse men, including his friend Emmett Proctor. Proctor, a Morehouse man who had gone to Simsbury the previous summer, assured the Kings that the money was good—"It defrayed my tuition," Proctor recalled of his earnings, "and I had some to spare." And he assured the Kings that ML would be safe.[22]

ML told Weasel that his steady campaign convinced his parents to take "a long look" at the program. Eventually they consented. Next, the eager teen petitioned the Morehouse Dean's office for permission to join the year's cohort of "Tobacco Boys," as they were called. But it was not "an elite situation," one Morehouse farmhand recalled, "most anyone could go." The criteria was minimal: a solid reputation—"Those that could be trusted to behave properly"—and a stated desire to work.[23]

ML received permission to be a 1944 Tobacco Boy. He would take the train, bound for Connecticut.

This was an important step in the life of ML. It would be his first long trip without his parents. The journey would force ML to summon every ounce of somebody-ness to shield himself from the onslaught of dehumanization during his Northern excursion. As Benjamin Elijah Mays, president of Morehouse College from 1940 to 1967, warned: "Buying a ticket at a segregated window in a segregated waiting room in Atlanta and riding in a segregated coach on a train out of Atlanta was a most humiliating experience. . . . Everything was done to degrade Negroes."[24] It was an experience teenage ML would come to know all too well.

Part Three

FINDING GOD

17
TERMINAL STATION

In Black America, the train was more than just a means of travel. It was a vehicle and symbol of change and freedom, becoming a dominant metaphor in Black cultural expression. The secret network of passages and safehouses that helped enslaved African Americans escape slavery was known as the Underground Railroad. Preachers appropriated train travel in religious expressions of piety and deliverance. The fame and celebrity of Atlanta's Baptist pastor J. M. Gates began with his 1926 recorded sermon, "Death's Black Train Is Coming." Gates arrived in Atlanta from the countryside around the same time as Daddy King; they even took classes together. His bestselling sermon used the train as a metaphor, warning listeners to repent and get their soul in order before the arrival of Christ. "If you want to go home and live in peace," the celebrity preacher and his congregation sang, "you'd better have your ticket in your hand. Be standing at the station with your ticket in your hand."

And the King family was steeped in this Black Baptist tradition. "Git on Board, Little Children" was a Black Baptist standard beginning in the late nineteenth century. "Git on board, little children . . . De Gospel train's a comin . . . De Fare is chap an' all can go . . . No second class a board dis train / No diff'rence in de fare."[1] For ML and his family, the train was more than just a mode of travel; it was a stage, a hub in which the drama of life, both real and hoped for, played out.

For ML, the trip held out the promise of transformation—from high school student to Morehouse man—and hope that he would make enough money to pay for tuition to establish himself as an independent man.

But faith and hope collided with fear and trepidation in Southern train travel, where Jim Crow regulations were guarded and enforced with a fierce passion. In Atlanta, the policing began at the Atlanta Terminal Station.

• • •

In late May 1944, the King family headed to Terminal Station to meet up with Pop Dansby and the Morehouse cohort.[2] "Travel," one Morehouse professor recalled of the several train trips he took from Atlanta to Connecticut and beyond, "was always very unpleasant and the atmosphere was usually tense." The stress began at Atlanta's state-of-the-art main train depot.

The national press praised Atlanta's new station as "the most beautiful station in the south." But for Black patrons it was too often a site of the ugliness of race prejudice.

The Kings, along with other Black Atlantans were still in horrific shock from the latest brutal beating, stripping, and arrest of ML's sixteen-year-old high school classmate by Terminal Station police. Earlier in the year, Hattie Mae Bell was at the station bidding farewell to her uncle, a soldier fighting in World War II to, as the US government framed the conflict with Germany, "make the world safe for democracy." There was no such safety for Hattie. Officers S. E. Smith and W. A. Jones falsely claimed Hattie "was drunk," using "profane language," and displaying behavior that "was generally

disorderly . . . loud, [and] boisterous." When they attempted to arrest her, Officer Smith claimed, she spat in his face and "grabbed at
the collar of his uniform." Enraged, the officer handcuffed her and
admitted to beating her "unmercifully." When she fell to the ground
from the force of the grown man's blows, he proceeded to kick her,
ripping her bloodstained dress, revealing her naked, broken Black
flesh for all to see. A concerned white woman tried to cover Bell's
"nakedness," but an officer chased her off, barking "get back" and
"attend to your own business." He deemed himself completely "jus-
tified" for pummeling Hattie while she was handcuffed and prone.
He tossed her exposed and bleeding body into the patrol wagon and
charged her with assault and resisting arrest. Black Atlantans flooded
the courtroom, protesting her treatment, only to hear the "burly"
officer testify that he was shocked, not at his actions, but that such
a citywide fuss was being made over the beating and arrest of a
"nigger" girl.[3]

The local branch of the NAACP provided legal defense, led by
A. T. Walden, past president of the branch and legal counsel for Citizens Trust Bank. He called nine Black terminal employees to the
witness stand. Their eyewitness accounts countered the officer's version of events. They testified one by one to the packed-out courtroom that the hefty officer first questioned and then accosted the
high school girl without provocation, and then proceeded to assault
her. An all-white jury took just forty-five minutes to find the bruised
girl guilty of assault and battery of a police officer. For the crime of
bruising the officer's fist and scuffing his shoes, Judge Jesse M. Wood
sentenced Hattie to a $50 fine ($1,600 today) and a year of probation. Judge Wood, in a warning to Black families like the Kings, told
the charged courtroom that Hattie had to be convicted, otherwise
"members of the police force would not be free from a succession of
attacks at the hands of you nigra' girls."[4]

Hattie Mae was the latest victim in a long roll of Black passengers and patrons who were unjustly brutalized by police at Atlanta's Terminal Station. In less than two years, Second Lieutenant Warren Cornelius, Jerry Davis, and Herschel Holmes were all beaten and thrown in jail for the vague charge of disorderly conduct.[5]

The King family did not want ML's name to be added to that growing list. The previous month he had shown his willingness to protest racist treatment on the bus. He had been lucky to escape physical harm, but Black patrons did not have a history of being lucky at Terminal Station.

One wonders if ML was the slightest bit bothered by the danger. He did recognize the dehumanizing dangers of Jim Crow travel. He faced it every weekday on his way to school, and he experienced it on his way home from Dublin, Georgia. But these ever-present fears likely competed with his excitement over his impending trip and the thrill of being thousands of miles away from his parents' watchful eyes.

The exact number of students who joined ML on the trip is unclear. However, Atlanta native William Garfield Pickens, a fifteen-year-old who was also preparing to enter Morehouse in the fall of 1944, remembered that about half of the Morehouse contingent—about forty to fifty boys—began the journey from Terminal Station, while the other approximately forty to fifty Morehouse men made other travel arrangements.[6]

The cohort stood amid some of the South's most impressive architecture. Twin minarets framing the ornamented stone and brick façade of the station rose more than one hundred feet above Mitchell Street and Madison Avenue (now Spring Street). The terminal's Art Deco murals were modeled after New York's Grand Central Station. In the sunlight, the red-tiled roof shone bright, the color of Georgia red soil. The tobacco boys, saddled with their luggage and college

Atlanta Terminal Station, 1940.

The Arcade of Porticos at Atlanta Terminal Station, 1948.

Heavyweight boxing celebrity and former champion Jack Dempsey arrives at Atlanta Terminal Station, 1940. The Art Deco design of the main entrance is on full display along with the racially segregated greeting line.

dreams, met in the Beaux Arts–style arcade for passenger drop-offs and pickups. It was likely crowded. More than ten thousand people passed through the station every day during the war years.[7]

Inside the terminal, the families could view the city's commercial progress. The grand waiting room, also modeled after Grand Central Station, consisted of ten thousand square feet of marble flooring, providing "every luxury and convenience known to the modern railroad." Art Deco design covered the lofty ceilings as well as the ticket office windows. As a hub of modern communication technology, the station boasted booths for Western Union, phones, an information bureau, a newsstand, and a post office substation.

A bevy of "royal restrooms," waiting rooms, and parlors catered to respective genders, while men also enjoyed a barbershop and a cigar stand. A purveyor of flowers and candies served the needs of romantic suitors. For physical nourishment there were several cafés, a lunchroom capable of seating two hundred people, an upscale restaurant with imported linen tablecloths and fine dinnerware, and a soda stand.[8]

But the monument to American commercial progress was not meant for Black Americans. The grand waiting room had WHITES ONLY signs hanging from the entrances to restaurants, bathrooms, and waiting areas.

Black passengers were prohibited from entering the white waiting room; only Black servants and railroad employees were permitted. All other people of color, regardless of fame or notoriety, risked life and limb at the hands of Terminal police. In 1940, world-famous singer Marian Anderson was denied entrance to the grand waiting room. When she walked into the main entrance, the train caller on duty ordered her to exit and walk around to the colored waiting room. During the 1940s, a police officer threatened to shoot Atlanta University President Dr. Rufus E. Clement for walking *through* the white waiting room. "You can't go in there," he told the college president as he approached the main entrance. Dr. Clement informed the officer he had no intentions of fraternizing with white passengers or protesting their racism, he was simply using the main entrance to avoid the rain. He promised to go directly to his train. But in ML's Atlanta, Black common sense was considered dangerous ambition. "You can't go through there," the menacing officer repeated. "If you do, you'll get shot!"[9]

White patrons dubbed "race traitors" received similar treatment. Florence Read, the white president of the historically black Spelman College, was prevented from using the white facilities.[10]

ML and his fellow Morehouse hopefuls had to go to the "colored entrance" more than one hundred feet from the main entrance. It was a small, nondescript, side door on Mitchell Street. The Black entry did not have a canopy, making Black passengers susceptible to Atlanta's unforgiving elements: the blistering summer sun, the driving rain and mud of spring's torrential downpours, and the winter's gusting winds.[11] The city promoted the state-of-the-art depot as a place "for all," but Black passengers knew better.

The configuration of the waiting rooms, lounge areas, and food service was similarly unequal. The grand waiting room was flanked on the right by a ladies' private parlor and lady's café, where white women and children could sit or lounge on rose-colored rocking chairs. The soft blue-and-rose-painted room with rose-colored marble trim was attended by Black maids to service the needs of passengers. To the left was the gentleman's reading and smoking lounge, adorned in rich oak and green marble trim, with leather chairs and loungers to match.[12]

However, the King family and fellow Black travelers were quarantined to "the colored waiting room." It was the only waiting room for Black passengers, regardless of gender, and the room was the smallest of all, dwarfed by the size of the grand waiting rooms for whites, separated by gender. At the grand opening event of the depot, the white press assured white readers that the Black waiting room was "quite separate and secluded . . . with never a chance for the mixing of the two races." Yet, to preserve the idea of separate but equal, *The Atlanta Constitution* promised its readers that the colored waiting room was "*almost* as luxurious" as the white waiting rooms, affording "*much* the same facilities," and providing "comfort . . . *practically* . . . the same as those for white people."[13]

The words "almost," "much," and "practically" were, at best, approximate.

In keeping with the practice of Jim Crow, "the colored waiting room" was constructed with fewer comforts. There were no leather chairs upon which to relax, nor any plush pillows or cushions upon which to lounge. There were no maids assigned to cater to the family's needs, no one assigned to greet the family with a comforting smile, no one designated to bring the parents a cold drink. Instead, they were offered wooden pews. There was no concern for indoor climate control. It was normal for the room to have virtually no heat in the winter and no cooling ventilation in the summer. The small, wooden room was prone to feel more like a sauna than a waiting area in the summer, and a cold cave in the winter. Yet, when construction was completed, the railroad industry congratulated itself, calling the "colored" facilities, "the best to be found in the United States."[14]

To make matters worse, the room was deliberately left unattended and perpetually dirty, while the white waiting rooms were eternally spotless. Benjamin Mays inquired about the discrepancy during a trip departing from Atlanta in the 1920s. He asked a Black janitor, "Why the difference?" The janitor promptly told him that the white supervisors made the staff keep the white waiting room immaculate, while also making sure the Black waiting room lagged far behind in cleanliness.[15]

By 1944, the deficient waiting room that greeted ML was caked with decades of disregard. It was, according to the *Atlanta Daily World*, a victim of "studied neglect." In graphic detail, the Black daily chronicled everything ML would have seen while awaiting his train. The newspaper wrote that visiting the "colored" waiting room was like being herded into a cave. "One has a sinking feeling of disgust as soon as he enters it." The entrance to the cave had "tile walls made alternatively grey and black with thick greasy soot; dirty windows opening to a dirtier lunch counter and 'dining room'; a floor littered with peanut shells and fruit hulls; a can for refuse in the corner, half empty; the sweepings, perhaps of days, piled on the floor behind it; a light receptacle in the ceiling with no light to relieve the darkness made gloomy by the dirty walls." The three-hundred-person seating area was even worse. It was "poorly lighted and worse ventilated . . . the walls, dirtier (if that were possible) than the one in the entrance; the smudgy windows; the sockets without lights; the lack of adequate and sanitary toilet arrangements for either sex; the utter lack of decent facilities for the purchase of lunch, light refreshments, candles or souvenirs or for the sending of telegrams or the securing of information."[16]

The "colored" waiting area, like the larger segregated society, completely removed the Kings and their fellow Black travelers from all the promise that surrounded them. It was a deliberate microcosm of America. Black passengers were completely cut off from the benefits of other paying customers, simply because of their race.

If young King wanted to send one last telegram from the Western Union window or the telegram office, Jim Crow said no. Use of one of the "royal restrooms" was also prohibited. The crowded Black waiting area had one bathroom for men and women. And Black men could only dream of receiving a new haircut or a fresh shave prior to their departure. The hungry Black traveler could never expect a cup of fresh coffee or a meal at the tables with imported linen tabletops. They had to suffer with the cold, moldy, and undercooked fare that was typically offered in the filthy colored dining room. Middle-class families like the Kings usually avoided the lunchroom. "No Negro goes to the lunch-room in the station who can help it," a prominent Black Atlanta resident noted."[17]

The assault upon Black dignity was constant. Jim Crow weaponized every quotidian experience to establish and reestablish a sense of Black inferiority. And at every turn ML bristled. With every step— from the waiting room, to the lunch counter, to the bathroom—he nursed an inward defiance, trying to maintain a sense of somebody-ness. "I could never adjust," he recalled of his teenage journey, "to the separate waiting rooms, separate eating places, separate rest rooms, partly because the separate was always unequal, and partly because the very idea of separation did something to my sense of dignity and self-respect."[18]

The visit to the Terminal Station was yet another occasion for ML to nurture a maladjustment to Jim Crow, to remind himself that despite the surroundings he was forced to endure: He was somebody.

The luxurious "Gentlemen's Waiting Room," Atlanta Terminal Station, May 14, 1905.

The spacious "Ladies' private parlor," Atlanta Terminal Station, May 14, 1905.

The bare-bones "Colored Waiting Room," Atlanta Terminal Station shortly after completion, May 14, 1905.

18
THE PRICE OF THE TICKET

T he train ticket to Connecticut cost more than just money; Jim Crow accommodations exacted the heftier price of dignity and self-respect.

Atlanta's Art Deco ticket counter sat between the two waiting rooms, with several windows dedicated to white customers and only one for Black patrons. Black patrons, no matter how long the line was, were not served as long as there were whites in their cue. There was no way to predict how long it would take to buy a ticket, which could range anywhere from a few minutes to hours.

Black time was subordinate to white desire.

When African Americans were served, ticket sellers were routinely rude and discourteous. No kind greetings were offered. There was no "Hello, Ma'am" or "Mrs. King." Reverend King was not addressed as "Mr.," "Reverend," nor "Sir." Those salutations were reserved for humans of equal standing.

Atlanta's white tellers were known for shortchanging Black passengers. They would accuse Black customers of lying or not knowing how to count, so they could pocket the change for themselves. Or sometimes Black customers were simply ignored. Often the process took so long, African Americans were faced with two choices: miss the train and wait for the next one to arrive, or purchase their tickets on the train. Black passengers were guaranteed they would be able to buy a ticket once aboard—riding for free was out of the question—but point-of-service tickets were more expensive than advance purchase. On board, conductors were just as harsh, barking at Black passengers for not buying their tickets in advance. The whole process was an organized attack on ML's dignity, a drama designed to degrade him. As Atlanta University Professor W. E. B. Du Bois noted, buying a train ticket was simply "torture."[1] It was a torture that provided plenty of fuel for ML's smoldering resentment of white people.

When Black patrons were finally served, according to Mays and Du Bois, Atlanta ticket agents and conductors typically greeted them not as paying customers, but as nuisances. There was no "How may I help you?" Instead, Du Bois noted, Black customers were met with belittling yells of "What d'y'e want?"[2]

A ticket for a Pullman sleeping car was the logical answer for ML's thirty-hour journey. For the price of a first-class ticket, plus the Pullman sleeping car surcharge of 30 to 70 percent, ML would be set to enjoy the "hotel on wheels" all the way to Connecticut. The car's pull-down shelflike beds would allow him to sleep. The Pullman car resembled ML's home life: the mattresses were filled with horsehair—the bedding material of European royalty. The carpet and drapes were elegant. The chairs had padded backs for extra comfort. The bathrooms were private and came with clean towels and high-end soap. And an attentive staff of Black porters and maids would cater to his every need.[3]

But logic did not prevail; Georgia state law did. Georgia State Act 369, passed on December 20, 1899, prohibited "white and colored passengers" from occupying the same sleeping car. Only "colored nurses or servants traveling with their employers" were permitted across the threshold of first class.

The law also noted, "nothing in this Act shall be construed to compel sleeping-car companies or railroads . . . to carry persons of color in sleeping or parlor-cars." The law deputized railroad employees with "full police power" to enforce the law. The law even encouraged the physical, violent removal of violators. Black passengers who managed to somehow violate the law—by passing as white, or claiming to buy the ticket for a white superior—were "guilty of and punished for a misdemeanor." Railroad employees who "fail[ed] or refuse[d]" to enforce the law were also charged with a misdemeanor. It was against the law for ML to ride in a sleeping car, and it was the legal duty of railroad employees to stop him if he tried.[4]

Other states followed suit throughout the twentieth century, viewing such laws as preserving white supremacy and racial purity. Sleeping in the same car brought about fears of miscegenation. An NAACP investigation noted as much. In 1916, a Black physician was denied the opportunity to purchase a Pullman car ticket from Virginia to Alabama because, the ticket agent barked, "You know damn well we don't put any niggers to sleep with white people." Benjamin Mays was also routinely the victim of rude refusals when inquiring about space in a Pullman car. Once, a white ticket agent at Terminal Station snarled, "There's space available, but not for niggers."[5]

The practice continued, albeit in a different form, after the 1941 US Supreme Court case *Mitchell v. United States*. Congressman Arthur W. Mitchell from Chicago was denied the Pullman car accommodations in Arkansas. Just days before ML's trip, the court ruled that racial discrimination in interstate travel was a violation of the

Interstate Commerce Act. African Americans who purchased first-class tickets had to be furnished separate "accommodations equal in comforts and conveniences to those afforded to first class white passengers."

Yet railroad companies evaded the law of the land by refusing to designate any sleeping cars for Black passengers. Following the ruling, Atlanta ticket agents became more courteous in their language—the word "nigger" was not used as frequently—but the expanded gentility and vocabulary was not accompanied by an expansion of Black rights. Ticket agents simply assured Black passengers that there was no space available in the Black Pullman car. It was often a lie.[6] It was an evil, simplistic logic: No separate accommodations meant no space; if Black passengers did not have a Pullman ticket, there could be no constitutional violation.

No matter how much money the Kings had, no matter how sharp his tweed suit was, and no matter what the US Supreme Court ruled, ML was relegated to a coach-class ticket along with the other young men bound for Connecticut, and every single other Black passenger. "It made no difference how important the person was," Mays noted, "if he was black he had no right to sleep on the train at night."[7]

Black celebrities used their power and wealth to evade sleepless nights on the train. Throughout the early twentieth century, Booker T. Washington rented his own Pullman car during speaking tours across the South. Blues great Bessie Smith had a lavish, custom-made railroad car for touring, complete with two stories, seven staterooms that slept four, a full kitchen, and a bathroom. It was a touring vehicle and hotel when Jim Crow laws denied her local accommodations. Both Washington and Smith simply paid the railroad a ride-along fee. It was the only way African Americans could guarantee first-class train travel. However, fame and notoriety were years away for

ML. In the summer of 1944, he was just another "colored boy" trying to purchase a train ticket that would enable him to sleep during
his East Coast journey. The Pullman company advertised, "Travel in
a Pullman sleeping car means repose, and comfort—the direct opposite to a night's journey in a day coach."[8] But because of Jim Crow,
such comfort would evade ML during his nearly two-day journey.
He was bound to the Jim Crow car.

19
THE JIM CROW CAR

All the way to the front!" Southern train conductors routinely shouted at Black passengers.

"Every pig to his pen!"

Black passengers knew the routine. ML and his fellow summer hands joined the sea of Black passengers emerging from the hot segregated waiting room to the train, where they were finally met with the calming kiss of the cool air-conditioning of the Southern Railway's "best travel accommodations ever offered between North and South." But they knew the modern conveniences were not for them. The Black sleeping car porters were not there to serve them. The maids billed as being "in constant attendance to wait on ladies throughout the train . . . [willing to] go to any section or room of any woman passenger for such service as may be desired," did not apply to Black women. The porcelain sinks and tubs of the bathrooms—complete with hot and cold running water, soap, locking doors, and clean towels—were not for the relief and refreshment of their Black bodies. The Pullman car berths would not birth any sleep or dreams for tired Black souls.[1]

Black passengers, regardless of the class of ticket they purchased, were herded to the Jim Crow car.

The Jim Crow car was a mainspring of Black discontent through-out the first half of the twentieth century. At the turn of the century, a journalistic survey noted that "no other point of race contact is so much and so bitterly discussed among Negroes as the Jim Crow car." Almost fifty years later, a 1944 national study of American rac-ism sponsored by the Carnegie Corporation of New York found that "the Jim Crow car is resented more bitterly among Negroes than most other forms of segregation."[2]

ML and his fellow Black passengers boarded the state-of-the-art accommodations of the Southern Railway Company's train number 38: the Crescent, bound for their racially assigned seats in the Jim Crow car. They waved goodbye to their loved ones, as they passed by the lavish accommodations of the glossy Virginia green-and-gold-accented train, brushing past seats that were not there to welcome them, but rather to taunt them, on their way to the dilapidated quar-ters of the Jim Crow car.[3]

The sea of elbows, hats, arms, legs, handbags, and purses could be glimpsed by those waiting to wave goodbye as their loved ones scooted through coaches named after distinguished white Southern gentlemen. The names of white supremacists—such as Confederate General P. G. T. Beauregard, known for starting the Civil War by ordering the bombardment of Fort Sumter, and Confederate Presi-dent Jefferson Davis—were painted on the sides of the cars. It was a source of comfort to many white Southern passengers, a reminder of the proper social order of the "good ole days." But for Black pas-sengers like ML, it served as an enduring sign of America's racial caste system, continuing the trauma and dehumanization of slavery and white supremacism.[4]

This humiliating experience of being rounded up like cattle amid abundance only to be sequestered to the Jim Crow car was, Du Bois argued, a quintessential aspect of "being black."[5]

The Jim Crow car was a fact of Black life. It was, at times, a physical death sentence for Black riders; and a constant physical, psychic, and spiritual assault on Black humanity.

When ML walked into the Jim Crow car, it was very clear whose life mattered and whose life did not. Southern Railway, like other railroad corporations, reserved their oldest coaches for their Black patrons. When they purchased new cars, they did not designate a Jim Crow car from their new stock. Spending money on Black accommodations was out of the question. Withholding funds from Black accommodations was the best way to invest in Jim Crow. The Interstate Commerce Commission (ICC) repeatedly alerted railroad companies that segregation was allowed, but "like accommodations" were required for Black passengers. However, the federal agency had no power to enforce its dictums. The ICC left the implementation of separate but equal in the hands of railroad companies, ensuring accommodations were surely separate, but never equal. When railroads adopted safer metal coaches beginning in the early twentieth century, they did not completely discard their outdated wooden coaches. Instead, they utilized them for their Jim Crow accommodations. These wooden cars on otherwise all-metal trains were extremely dangerous. The wooden Jim Crow car was placed at the front of the train, crammed between massive metal locomotive engines and steel coaches for white passengers. In the event of a collision or derailing, the steel cars were fire resistant and able to avoid being crushed. But they would smash into the decaying, fire-prone wooden Jim Crow cars. In train wrecks, Jim Crow cars were often smashed together "like an accordion," according to one Black publication. It became very common for the only deaths in train crashes to be in the Jim Crow car. It was so commonplace during the first half of the twentieth century that the Black press dubbed them "Jim Crow Wrecks."[6]

White America had long acknowledged this deliberate devaluation of Black life. In a 1913 study of race relations on interstate train travel, University of Louisiana Professor W. O. Scroggs noted the "untoward conditions" of Black travel. White passengers were safely seated in a steel coach, while "negro patrons [rode] in a coach of wood." Scroggs was a segregationist, but even he was alarmed by the arrangement. The Southern professor wrote in his report that he commented on the practice to another white passenger. He was told, "Well, I guess it costs the [rail]road more to kill a white man than a nigger, and so it takes extra precautions for us."[7] Black life was not considered valuable on the train.

Even when wooden Jim Crow cars were put out of rotation, the accommodations were still inferior. Jim Crow cars, situated right behind the engine, would catch all the soot and fumes. The Jim Crow car, Benjamin Mays noted, was always "the dirtiest, sootiest, nosiest, roughest location on the entire train." The settees were dilapidated—caked with dirt and coal dust. The non-air-conditioned car was simmering in hot weather, making clothing stick to sweaty skin. There was no decorative floor, only a grounding of grease and grime. There were no window curtains. Instead, the windows were shielded from the outside by layers of dirt caused by neglect and the emissions from the rusty iron stove used to heat the car in the winter.

An African American porter was assigned to the car but, as with the staff in the Black waiting room, he was instructed to virtually ignore the conditions of the car. Instead he was directed to pay more attention to cleaning the conductor's dirty boots and soiled clothes than the Jim Crow car. Collectively, the dirt, the grimy film, and the heat created a peculiar rancid odor. It was nothing short of an insect's paradise, according to an NAACP report.[8] It was a very unfamiliar and degrading surrounding for a teenager known for his tidiness. The notoriously immaculate Tweed had to confront the infamous filth of the Jim Crow car.

There were no porcelain bathrooms for separate genders. The Jim Crow car had one "filthy toilet" for Black passengers. White passengers stricken with dysentery or vomiting were directed to use the bathroom in the Jim Crow car. With the lack of dedicated staff, it resembled a neglected outhouse more than a modern facility. The bathroom rarely had running water. Soap and towels were not provided. And privacy did not exist as the bathroom lacked a lock. A passenger could easily walk in on another passenger, causing an embarrassing moment. Du Bois offered Black passengers one word of advice regarding the Jim Crow bathroom: "Don't!"[9]

The Jim Crow car undermined Tweed's humanity. Many Black travelers carried brushes and brooms to clean their seats as much as possible. Wrapping one's self in an old blanket was also popular, or wearing old clothes. ML had been bequeathed the politics of respectability, which demanded that he dress his best in public, especially when interacting with whites. However, the reality of the train had its own demands. Reverend Joseph K. Bowler, for example, vowed never to wear good clothes while traveling. The debonair preacher told the *Chicago Defender* he could not afford nor dare to

Political cartoon of a white coach and Jim Crow car, 1904.

wear "a decent looking suit while riding amid such filthy surround-ings." He religiously donned "a pair of soiled overalls" he purchased from a mechanic. "Well-oiled and greased to the limit," he boasted to the Black press. The year-old overalls protected his "best clothes when riding in the dirty Jim Crow coaches."[10] It was a strategic and sartorial dilemma. Was it better to dress respectably in defiance of the disrespect of the Jim Crow car, or to dress in a disreputable way to preserve the fine fabric of one's closet and humanity? Under the strain of Jim Crow, quotidian activities demanded dramatic strate-gies to preserve dignity.

ML's clothing was one challenge, finding a seat was another. Jim Crow cars were "combination" cars, a single coach divided into mul-tiple sections. The divisions were created by shabby curtains hang-ing from a series of parallel metal rods, extending from the back of the seats to the ceiling. These dividing rods—for the purpose of segregation—usually possessed more metal than the entire Jim Crow car itself. Protecting segregation was more important than protecting Black life.[11]

The front section of the car was reserved for undesirable white passengers, including convicts and drunkards, who would still remain separate from their second-class counterparts. The next section was reserved for the conductor, members of the baggage crew, and the newspaper boy. They used the Jim Crow car as their workspace, lounge, and gossip mainline. Typically, the conductor often took up several seats; one for his work tools and another for his personal items and clothes. Members of the baggage crew used as many seats as needed to accommodate overflow baggage and to relax. Ordinarily, the newspaper boy sat in one seat and used an-other to store his stockpile of books—indecent and otherwise—as well as candy, soda, and unwrapped fruit, making it a landing spot for flies.[12]

The designated section for Black passengers existed behind a set of curtains and bars in the rear of the car, occupying roughly half or a third of the car. There was no separation for male and female, adult and children, or smoker and nonsmoker. Blackness determined one's seat assignment. And while the car was used to store the luggage of white passengers, there were no luggage racks for Black riders. They had to hold their suitcases or place them on the grimy floor of the car, cramming their luggage around their feet in an already crowded car. Black soldiers were also relegated to the Jim Crow car. The parade of Black soldiers huddled in the Jim Crow car was always the height of irony: these men were denied the very rights at home for which they were preparing to die abroad in World War II. And if livestock needed to be transported, the animals were always put in the Jim Crow car. Little wonder the overall-wearing Reverend Bowler called the Jim Crow car "the hog train."[13]

The Morehouse crew filled the Jim Crow car to capacity. Partitioned Jim Crow cars usually had forty to fifty seats at most. William G. Pickens remembered that the segregated car was "full of us guys."[14] Crowded Jim Crow cars were a constant during the war years, especially from major stations like Atlanta. Even if seats were available in the adjacent "white" section or the conductor's section, Black passengers were not permitted to sit in front of whites. No matter how long the journey, no matter what Black passengers had with them—a crying child, massive luggage, an ill loved one, a soldier, or a dream of equality—Black passengers had to stand if the Black section was full.[15] It was an experience reminiscent of ML's traumatic bus trip from Dublin, Georgia.

It all made for a charged environment. "Many Negros [sic]," Mays remembered, "were beaten or put off trains because they protested the conductor's using four seats and the [newsboys] using four seats while Negros [sic] who had paid their fares had to stand; or because they protested Negro passengers having to stand while there was space in an adjacent white coach."[16]

Morehouse Professor Hugh Gloster was beaten, arrested, and charged for disorderly conduct and attempting to "break Jim Crow laws" during a fateful trip from Atlanta to Memphis in 1942. The Black section of the Jim Crow Car had been standing room only. The remainder of the three-part coach was empty except for the conductor and newsboy. Dr. Gloster, who later served as Morehouse president from 1967 to 1987, complained to the conductor about the Jim Crow accommodations, demanding that women and children be given access to the empty "whites only" section of the train. The conductor replied, "That's what's wrong now. Too many niggers trying to run the train."

The conductor called ahead to the next station, informing the police. When the train made its stop, the police boarded the train shouting, "Where's the nigger who's trying to run the train?" Gloster recalled the conductor "squeezed" into the crowded Black passenger section of the Jim Crow car and identified him. The police threw him off the train, and beat and mauled him on the platform. "Bruises and contusions . . . literally covered my entire body," he remembered. The attack concluded when a 250-pound policeman deliberately kicked him in the groin, causing the professor "excruciating agony" that remained with him for the remainder of his life. The beating reverberated throughout Black Atlanta and beyond, becoming front-page news in several nationally circulated Black newspapers.[17] If ML considered protesting the crowded conditions, the experience of Professor Gloster warned him otherwise.

Once ML and crew were settled in the Jim Crow car, whether seated or standing, they were likely exposed to some of the sins—cursing, drinking, smoking, and tobacco sputum—that Reverend King thundered against and Morehouse prohibited. An NAACP investigation uncovered that the Jim Crow car was often utilized as a safe space for a "Southern gentleman" to engage in behaviors that were unfit for white women and children to witness. Black patrons, especially children like ML, were not so lucky. As one Morehouse professor noted during a train trip in the 1940s, the conductor and baggage man seemed perpetually "engaged in their *usual* occupation of smoking, spitting, cursing, and drinking."[18]

A Black Southern rider of the era summarized the Jim Crow car experience: "A well fitted Jim Crow car in the south carries all the Race people . . . and the conductor, the [news] boy and his boxes . . . the deputy sheriff with five or six prisoners, all in handcuffs enroute for the state convict farm, and all the chickens, baskets, bags and acting suitcases that weary travelers may claim."[19]

Everything ML despised—segregation, enforced white supremacy, police brutality, and the all-out assault on Black humanity—was embodied in the Jim Crow car. He and his fellow travelers knew the accommodations of the Jim Crow car were intended to inflict some measure of spiritual and psychic death upon them. But they also knew that challenging the rules almost assured physical death as well. ML did his best to comply with Jim Crow while resisting its intended effects. "As a teenager," he reflected years later, "I had never been able to accept the fact of having to go . . . sit in the segregated section of a train."[20] As he and his fellow travelers alternatively stood or sat for their 40-hour, 1,350-mile journey, he did what he tried to do during his high school bus trips: He placed his body in the segregated car, but put his mind in the first-class car.[21] And he thought, just as he told himself during those trips, "One of these days I'm gonna put my body up there where my mind is."[22]

20
THE CURTAIN

At some point during ML's trip, the hungry, rambunctious teenager went to the state-of-the-art dining car to enjoy Southern Railway's fine dining on wheels. He had no idea what was awaiting him.

The tagline of the Southern Railway Company was "Southern serves the South." The company motto referred to more than just geography, but also the "Southern way of life." The Crescent offered the first dining cars on trains departing Atlanta beginning in the nineteenth century. And the company had no plans to change its nineteenth-century segregationist roots. The observation and dining cars were designed to resemble a hotel tavern-lounge, inviting passengers to relax and enjoy complimentary coffee and orange juice, or alcoholic beverages for purchase. Usually, a crew of twelve workers handled the wood-fired kitchens and table service. They served traditional Southern cuisine and traditional Southern mores.[1] African American men often labored in these environments—as servers or cooks—but African American passengers like ML were not welcome.

Access to these spaces was heavily policed. Black passengers could procure food on board but, as Du Bois summed up for readers in *The New Republic*, "it is difficult." William Pickens, the NAACP director of branches and assistant field secretary, chronicled how difficult it was even to purchase decent food and beverages during an interstate Southern train excursion. He was "gruffly informed by the trainmen" there were "no sanitary drinking cups" offered in the Jim Crow car. When the car made intermittent stops at train stations so passengers who were, as Pickens noted, "too stingy to pay the dining car prices and the tips" could get food, Black passengers discovered that station lunchrooms across the South only served white passengers. "As if fate had conspired with the devil," Pickens noted, "the Jim Crow car stopped right in front of this lunchroom, so that the starving colored traveler could see the white passengers go in and out and observe their backs as they sit

This 1941 publicity photo features the Southern Railway's brand-new tavern-lounge observation car. It was a salon for social gatherings for white passengers. White passengers could relax, smoke, visit with fellow passengers, and purchase a beverage. African Americans, as seen here, were permitted to work in such luxury cars as porters and valets to assure white passengers were served and comforted, but were not permitted as passengers.

at the counter and drink their hot teas and cold milk and eat their warm food."

And worse, these white customers were nearly always "served by black hands." Pickens noted the mind-blowing hypocrisy: White passengers could "eat food out of black hands," but would not "eat their own food out of their own hands if a black man at the other end of the counter is eating his own food out of his own hands." To add "indigestion to insult," a few minutes before the train resumed its journey, without fail "a Negro servant is sent out from the lunchroom with a basketful of cold food, which could never be sold to white customers, in an endeavor to get rid of it among the colored passengers." Indeed, while "white passengers in the lunchroom may get a hot drink or a warm egg sandwich for a few cents," Black passengers were offered "impenetrable" chicken that had been "fried day-before-yesterday, old bread, and a slice of musty pie actually cut days ago" for seventy-five cents. If one dared to purchase such disposable fare, there was no way to consume the offensive food with dignity. If African American passengers requested utensils or a napkin they were told "No!" Railroad employees were not permitted to "bring dishes into the Jim Crow car." It is evident, the NAACP concluded, if you are a Negro, there are "practically" no accommodations made for dining on the train.[2]

The violence employed to police these spaces was legendary in the national Black press, especially in ML's hometown. Atlanta's Reverend Martin L. Harvey, who served as Dean of Men at Atlanta's Clark College, was severely beaten for lounging in a tavern car in 1943. As his train from Chicago approached Atlanta, the train conductor shouted at the African Methodist Episcopal Zion national youth director, "Go back to the place where you belong." The minister told the conductor his ticket class entitled him to access. But that all changed once the train entered the South. The conductor was incensed. With all his might, he rained down curses and punches upon the minister. When that proved insufficiently destructive, he grabbed a metal ashtray stand and preceded to beat the bespectacled Harvey. Black passengers and Black citizens were horrified by the measures railroad officials were willing to employ to maintain Jim Crow.[3]

For this very reason, many African American travelers adopted "Jim Crow travel kits." This repertoire of items included clothes as well as food, beverages, and utensils, enabling Black travelers to approximate humane travel. For decades, Black passengers exchanged suggestions and warnings via word of mouth in barbershops, beauty parlors, train depots, churches, and even the Black press. In 1922, Reverend Bowler took to the pages of the national *Chicago Defender* to advise Black passengers to leave nothing to chance or the whims of railroad employees or law enforcement when traveling the rails. His Jim Crow traveling kit kept him prepared for anything the Jim Crow car threw at him. In addition to a pair of overalls, he also carried a miniature gas stove and tabletop. He explained, "the dining car is a closed corporation as far as our people are concerned because white people below the Mason Dixon line maintain that we are animals, virtually camels, and can go without food or water for several days." He continued, "I cannot force myself to sneak to the back of some depot kitchen like a little poodle and ask for food; neither can I take a chance of being shot to death for attempting to invade a dining car to secure my meals." Therefore, Reverend Bowler stocked his luggage with salmon and canned goods, using his stove to prepare meals during his journey. Reverend Bowler's Jim Crow traveling kit served several purposes: It helped him "ward off hunger," while also helping him to maintain a semblance of dignity, and ultimately protect his life from the vicious vigilance of white supremacy. And the small tabletop brought a sense of dignity and propriety to the meal. Animals do not dine at tabletops. Human beings do.[4]

In 1943, *The New York Amsterdam News* gave Black readers an upgraded approach: shoeboxes. Black passengers could carry their food aboard in shoeboxes, giving Black passengers the urbane appearance of a boxed lunch, the kind many railroads and train depots sold.[5] King Hayes, a Morehouse student, recalled doing just that for his trip from Georgia to Simsbury, "ration[ing]" his food for the entire trip north.[6] Such Jim Crow "hacks" increased the chances of survival, but did little toward achieving legal equality.

ML's mother probably equipped him with a "shoebox" meal filled with his favorites—soul food to fill his stomach and protect his body and soul from the ravages of white supremacy.

But something led her son to try the dining car. Maybe the simple basic urge of hunger led him there; he was, after all, on a twenty-four-hour trip. Maybe curiosity led him there. It could have been a combination of desires. Whatever his reasons, as he made his way through the aisles and cars, he had no idea of the absurdity that awaited him.

In addition to violence, Southern Railway began deploying innovative ways to maintain separate and unequal dining service across its Southern routes. In 1942, Southern Railway issued new dining regulations to ensure separate and unequal dining experiences. The railroad was experiencing unprecedented demand for food as the number of train passengers swelled with the war effort. At the outbreak of war, the railroad served a total of 70,000 meals a month. When ML boarded the train in 1944, that number had increased to 350,000 meals a month, making it extremely inconvenient to host racially segregated mealtimes. Southern's new policy instituted segregation curtains in their dining cars. One or two tables nearest the kitchen were designated for Black passengers with a "Reserved" placard, enclosed by a heavy, thick blue curtain, while the remaining eight to ten tables were set aside for white passengers. The slim veil symbolized the gulf that existed between Black and white in America. Like the Jim Crow combination cars, these curtains kept the dining car segregated, while also thinly veiling America's commitment to separate and unequal.[7]

The opaque curtain was a gift to white passengers. Some claimed the sight of Black untouchable diners made them "nauseated."[8] The separation pampered white prejudices and soothed white conscience and stomachs. White comfort required Black dehumanization. It is easier to dehumanize flesh and bone, soul and spirit, when it is rendered invisible. Those on the outside cast their worst and wildest dreams and fantasies about the "things" dining behind the veil; while those inside the veil had to muster all their soul force not to believe what was forced upon them at every turn. The very human desire to eat required Black riders to dehumanize themselves. And if Black passengers dared to pull the curtain aside, the dining car steward would hurriedly pull the curtain closed, or worse. Protecting the sense of superiority of white passengers was the top priority.

The company's new rules also made sure that their Southern cuisine overwhelmingly went to white passengers. Before the start of each meal, the porters pulled the curtains into "service position," enclosing the "reserved" seats. White passengers were served first. If the white diners took all the "white" tables, "the curtain [was] pushed back, cards removed, and white passengers were served at those tables" formerly reserved for Black customers. This was inevitable on crowded war-era trains. If white travelers "fully or partially occupied" the table, "colored passengers" were "advised that they will be served just as soon as those compartments [were] vacated." Or, if food was available, "colored passengers" would be served at their seats "using a portable table, without the extra charge," as soon as staff were available. This rarely happened. Southern Railway testified in court that 85 percent of the company's white diners were served at least two helpings before Black consumers could even place their first order.[9]

The Southern Railroad Company utilized circular logic to justify the policy. They reasoned that "relatively few Negro passengers" desired to eat in the dining car, making it pointless to reserve significant tables for the "exclusive use" of Black passengers. The proof was in the data they cooked up. Over a ten-day period, they conducted a study of 639 serving periods on all Southern Railway trains, which revealed "about 4% of the total meals served were served to Negro passengers." The railroad did not acknowledge that their policy, not the lack of Black hunger, contributed to the low rate of Black patronage. Nevertheless, in a lawsuit accusing them of discrimination, they maintained they were being falsely criticized. Southern was not racist nor lawless, they argued, but generous by reserving 10 percent of their dining-room seating (four seats out of forty) to "Negroes," even though Black customers rarely patronized the dining car.[10]

A few months before ML boarded the Crescent, a Black lawyer, Elmer W. Henderson, filed a complaint with the ICC regarding the train's racist dining policies. Henderson had been denied seating in the dining car of the Crescent because white patrons were using one of the two tables "reserved" for Black patrons. Henderson was promised he would be informed when the negro table became available. He was never informed. The ICC did nothing to change the policy, declaring that Henderson was the victim of a subpar employee, not a racist dining policy.[11] The company, with seemingly no federal accountability, deployed anything and everything—from violence to self-fulfilling studies—to continue to starve Black passengers of food and a sense of "somebody-ness."

The policy had its intended effect on ML. He managed to get

food while on board, but the cost was beyond anything he intended to pay. When the train staff issued the "negro call" for the dining car, ML began his journey from the dilapidated settees of the Jim Crow car to the plush seats of the dining car; from the stench of the Jim Crow car to the culinary aromas of the dining car. Surely keeping his parents advice in mind, ML probably kept to the racial etiquette of day: No sudden movements. Step aside for all white people. Make yourself small. Do not stare. Do not linger. Walk deliberately, but not too fast. Refer to all white people as Mr. or Mrs. Be sure to remove your hat. Don't stand in the white line. Do not expect reciprocity. With all the boxes checked, ML arrived in the dining car.

Yet, the teenager who had been raised to believe that he was as good as any other human being was quarantined behind the veil of the dining car. "The first time that I was seated behind a curtain in a dining car," he remembered, "I felt as if the curtain had been dropped on my selfhood."[12] The system of segregation robbed him of his dignity and humanity. The curtain made him feel like he was simply a thing.

And his failure to protest the system also chipped away at his sense of selfhood. ML found himself complicit with white supremacy. He endured humiliation and degradation just for a meal. No matter how good the food may have been, one can't feel satisfied when one has to forfeit their own humanity.

It is easy to imagine the teenager, once again saying to himself, "One of these days I'm gonna put my body up there where my mind is."

But no one, especially not Southern Railway, took note of the internal yearning of the fifteen-year-old. The train, like life, continued to roll along the tracks of Jim Crow America.

But ML did manage to lift his mind. Through the windows of the Jim Crow car and the dining car, he took note of the things that amazed him, allowing the reader to see the world through his young, astonished eyes. The Crescent took him through the Southern cotton fields his father had escaped. He found himself in awe when the train stopped in Spartanburg, South Carolina. The city had a population of only thirty thousand, much smaller than Atlanta, but as a central hub for the railroad, it bustled. ML wrote to his parents that he was amazed by the "large" city. The train passed through the majestic haze of the Blue Ridge Mountains, covering hundreds of miles of Piedmont tobacco fields and forest, as well as Civil War battlefields where blood was shed for his supposed freedom, and then up the Eastern Seaboard. Passing through Virginia and Maryland, he marveled at "the many airplanes" he saw, and the size of the navy ships. Lost for words, he compared the military might to the massive structures he knew best. "We saw many large ships," he wrote home, "some as large as the Bethel Church and larger."[13]

The next major stop was the nation's capital, the very seat of American democracy, where an original copy of ML's beloved US Constitution resided: A Constitution that seemed meaningless in the Jim Crow car.

But when ML and crew changed to the Pennsylvania Railroad at Washington's Union Station, their citizenship status also changed. Once the Southern Crescent pulled into the station, all trains bound north were emancipated from Jim Crow laws. ML and crew were sprung from the soul-suffocating stench of the Jim Crow car, to await their train to New York City. The clean, fresh air of freedom invigorated their spirits, as they stretched their cramped legs and souls. "It was a different experience altogether," ML's classmate and Atlanta native William G. Pickens recalled, "because the Pennsylvania Railroad was not segregated and we could sit any place we wanted to on the trains."[14]

Some of the students were so overjoyed, they extended their

freedom excursion beyond schedule. According to *The Maroon Tiger*, the Morehouse student newspaper, several of the young men—the "wise guys," the student paper noted—claimed they had "accidentally" got "lost from the group in Washington and New York City."[15] There is no record of whether ML "accidentally" got lost on a freedom excursion in the nation's capital or the Big Apple. But he was in the midst of an admitted "general" rebellion.

One can only imagine the reaction of the otherwise vigilant Professor Dansby. True to form, he ordered the remaining Morehouse cohort to wait for the wanderlust contingent in DC. He wanted everyone to travel together. The delay caused the entire Morehouse cohort to miss their connecting train. Their arrival at the farm would be delayed costing everyone at least two days' worth of wages.[16] But for many on the journey, freedom from the Jim Crow car was priceless.

21

SIMSBURY

The New Haven Railroad dropped ML and crew off at the train station in Hartford, Connecticut. There they boarded a bus for the twelve-mile journey to Simsbury.[1]

ML and crew, a report in the school newspaper noted, "strode into the boarding house (very cool indeed) saying that they were two days late because—'Oh, well, I just missed the train,' an unnamed boy said—which was an excellent excuse, indeed," the school newspaper editorialized.[2]

ML quickly dispatched a letter to his parents. He made no mention of getting separated from the cohort or arriving late. The very mention would have increased the anxiety of his already anxious parents. But he did hint to his mother that he saw more than just the train station in New York City. The city, he jotted down to Alberta, "is the largest place I have ever seen in my life." ML did not offer any further details: no national monuments, no Times Square attractions.[3] Instead, his letters were filled with the social wonders of the North. "After we passed Washington," he told his dad in one letter, "the[re] was no discrimination at all." ML was spellbound. "[I] saw some things I had never antiscipated [sic] to see," the enthralled teenager wrote in another letter. [4]

It was not the rural agricultural environs of the Northeast that shocked him. Atlanta was surrounded by farmland. Rather, it was the work, the people, and the customs that made the Connecticut Valley seem out of this world. ML felt like a welcomed stranger in a foreign land. And he loved it.

He arrived, admittedly, on the verge of hating all white people, harboring a violent aggression. He was reeling from the wounds of racism. He had been slapped by a white woman for no reason; cursed and threatened for daring to assert his humanity on the bus; and witnessed the Klan marching in his neighborhood. And on the train to Connecticut he was forced into being sequestered in the Jim Crow car.

He arrived in Connecticut with a simple plan: Get through the summer. Make money for tuition. Remain true to his cold, calculating agnosticism. Hold on to his resentment of the white world and use it as fuel to matriculate at Morehouse College, and jump-start his legal career.

Yet when he departed Simsbury after three months, things had changed. Unbelief had yielded to faith; and resentment of all things white began to shift to compassion. The experience caused the strange land of the Connecticut Valley to morph into a spiritual home, a place he began to call "God's country."[5]

• • •

The Connecticut River Valley has long been a place of hope and divine purpose. For centuries, the longest river in New England and the surrounding fertile soil has inspired inhabitants to worship and dream. The Algonquian Native Americans were the earliest inhabitants of the region, and they named the four-hundred-mile-long river, the Great River. It was a sacred place; they established rulers and houses of worship throughout the valley, offering thanks for the fertile soil and the gift of broad-leaf, sun-grown tobacco. When European settlers colonized the area, they constructed Fort House of Hope in 1633 at the site of modern-day Hartford. Puritans seeking to worship freely fled communities in Plymouth and Cambridge, Massachusetts, and gravitated to the House of Hope. They chose to settle in the valley and gave the area the same name the Algonquian gave the Great River. Quinnehtukqut, meaning "beside the long tidal river," became the name Connecticut. Even the state's first constitution provided hope. The Fundamental Orders of 1638–1639 was considered the blueprint for the US Constitution, gaining Connecticut its official nickname, "The Constitution State."

Like so many before him, ML came to the land of hope full of faith. But ML placed his faith in himself, not in God nor American democracy. He arrived in the Constitution State in the summer of 1944 disabused of his hope in God and the US Constitution and its drafters—white people. He was, he admitted to *Time* in 1957, "Ready to resent all the white race." His only hope was his admission to Morehouse.[6]

The partnership between Morehouse and the tobacco farms of the Connecticut Valley began in the early twentieth century with the invention of Connecticut shade tobacco. As distinct from tobacco grown in direct sunlight, shade tobacco produced thinner, more elastic leaves. Customers loved the shade tobacco wrapping paper, which was lighter in color, smoother, and neutral in taste, carrying an air of refinement. Traditionally the crop was limited to Cuba and Sumatra, where the humid climate, combined with consistent overcast skies, created the ideal conditions to grow the crop. In the late nineteenth century, high tariffs and high demand for the rarified product put the American cigar industry in a bind. Leading companies pleaded their case with the Department of Agriculture. In 1901, the private-public venture implemented a plan to create the conditions in which the valuable crop could flourish in the fertile soil of the Connecticut tobacco valley.[7] Large tents made of cheesecloth, the loose-woven, gauze-like cotton cloth originally used to make and wrap cheese, brought tropical conditions to New England; the tents became clouds, shielding leaves from the sun while boosting humidity under the cover. Shade tobacco was several times more expensive to grow than field tobacco. The extra expense of special equipment and labor privileged corporate growers over small farmers. A little more than a decade into the shade tobacco boom corporate growers received a blow when the Great War limited European migration, creating a labor shortage. Farmers looked to Southern Blacks to fill the void.[8]

Morehouse gladly obliged, using the arrangement as a recruitment tool. The elite college was not cheap, but it provided its students—young Black men, who were the primary targets of employment discrimination in the South—the opportunity to make money for tuition. "There were no other alternatives," one student remembered. "We were either Pullman porters or we worked in the fields. The (industrial) unions wouldn't let us in. Nobody would let us in." The Connecticut Valley welcomed them; apart from the Depression years, the college annually provided a battalion of 30 to 150 students and college applicants to the region's tobacco farms each summer.[9]

Come June 1944, ML along with a good number of the school's expected 344 enrolled students descended upon the Connecticut River Valley's 8,700 acres of billowing cheesecloth clouds. The first-timers in the crew felt shock, *The Maroon Tiger* noted, due to "the harsh reality" of knowing "the long stretches of land covered by white waving nets" would be their home for the next three months.[10]

The white canvassed fields resembled a massive cocoon, running along the Farmington River for what seemed like eternity. They were interspaced with clusters of flora and foliage, and the picturesque horizon past the river was punctuated by Talcott Mountain. With an apex of 950 feet, the 13-mile mountain ridge formed a continuous line of perfectly exposed cliffs, knobs, and peaks that seemed to hug the tobacco valley.[11]

The Morehouse crew was assigned to the more than 200-acre to-bacco farm of the Cullman Brothers, Inc. Founded in 1892 as a to-bacco brokerage house, Cullman helped lead the popularization of cigars in the United States, growing to be one of the largest cigar to-bacco producers in the country. Following the Great Depression, the industry attempted to attract more customers by changing the image of cigars from the vice of Depression-era gangsters to the accoutre-ment of middle-class businessmen and tycoons. The light color, ver-satility, and smoothness of shade tobacco wrappers helped coax this market turn, so Cullman purchased more than 1,800 acres of land in the Connecticut River Valley to capitalize on it.[12]

The farm was isolated from the trappings of modern life. The nearest store was three miles away and the Hartford bus line five miles away. William Pickens called the farm "a society unto itself." He recalled that all the Morehouse hired hands were housed on a hillside in three-story barracks, lined with rows of crude cots and bunk beds. This would be the summer home of Morehouse students and hopefuls like ML, as well as other Black laborers from Georgia. The accommodations offered no plumbing; just a bathhouse and an outhouse about fifteen yards from the dorm. It was a far cry from ML's comfortable childhood home. The mess hall, recreation room, a kitchen, and a storage space occupied the ground floor. The two upper floors housed sleeping quarters, cots, and bunk beds for more than one hundred workers and Professor Dansby. ML slept alongside prospective and returning Morehouse students, dreaming, hoping, he would join them on campus in the fall.[13]

In his hillside bunk, he scribbled letters home asking about the results of his early admission exam to Morehouse. He reached out to his mother on June 11, 1944, just a few days after he arrived to ask her to contact the principal of Booker T. Washington High School, who oversaw the exam. "Don't forget to see Mr. Cornell about the test as soon as possible!" he pleaded. A week passed. Anxiety bubbled over. He sent off another letter, soliciting all hands on deck, and telling his mother that if she was unable to reach Mr. Cornell, she should draft his college-admitted sister into the effort. "Tell Christine [to] write me and tell me about the test."[14]

The reality of the crude tobacco barns constantly interrupted ML's dream of the majestic heights of higher learning. The long and narrow barns were approximately 30 by 200 feet, with vertical-board siding; the wider, shorter barns measured 40 by 100 feet with horizontal-board siding. Large batten doors on both ends of the barns allowed the workers to easily haul in the crop. The tobacco leaves hung on the post-and-beam interior framing, from waist height to the roof of the barn, to be cured. The siding boards could be opened for ventilation. There was seemingly endless tobacco that needed to be cured. Unlike field tobacco, shade tobacco plants had to be harvested on a nearly continual basis. Shade plants grew throughout the harvest season.[15]

Each day, the Herculean task began with a 6:00 a.m. wake-up call. Breakfast, consisting of a plain but hearty serving of sausage and grits, was served at 7:00 sharp. Shortly before 8:00, trucks rounded up the men and transported them to their specified workstations where they were expected to be ready for the hard, hot, dirty work of picking tobacco. They wore long-sleeve shirts, overalls, and hats to protect their skin from the sun that seemed to perpetually beat down on them. In temperatures nearing 120 degrees under the tents, the young men fought the twin enemies of sweat and insects—

ranging from tiny thrips to healthy grasshoppers. The students had to nurse the delicate leaves by hand, taking care not to rip them. At the beginning of the summer the leaves started at the bottom of the stalk, only about four to six inches from the ground. They forced the students to sit in the dirt to retrieve the crop, scooting on their bottoms from stalk to stalk. "To do this nursing job," *The Maroon Tiger* warned readers, "the 'disillusioned ones' had to bring forth undaunted courage and adjust themselves to the 110 and 120 temperature, backaches, and a social hermitage which can only be found on a tobacco farm." And sometimes, these nascent plants had to be hoed. "But this was easy," *The Maroon Tiger* instructed, all one had to do was "remove their shoes (if they were wearing any), grab a hoe, pick a row and simply hoe—all day." If the tedious process was done properly, by August or September the delicate plants would grow into "trees" seven to ten feet high, with leaf spans of eighteen to twenty-four inches.[16]

The picked leaves were left on the ground as they moved to the next plant. Other Morehouse students retrieved the leaves and placed them in a canvas basket as quickly as possible. The full, heavy baskets were set at the end of the row, then picked up and slogged over to the curing barns.[17]

Noon brought joy in the form of bag lunches of fruit and a trinity of sandwiches: bologna, peanut butter, and cheese. At 1:00 p.m., it was back to work. A water boy, equipped with a fresh pail, would make the rounds, helping the boys stay hydrated and make the final push through the blistering afternoon heat. At 5:00, they were transported back to their quarters. They scrubbed their sticky tobacco-stained hands and peeled their tobacco and dirt-blemished overhauls and shirts from their sweat-drenched bodies, in exchange for the ice-cold waters of the bathhouse. With no hot water available, the Morehouse men described it as "fifteen degree water fresh from a

Connecticut hillside." For many, this was their favorite part of the day. "The nicotine was all over you," William Pickens recalled. It was a relief to scrub themselves clean. Next they dragged their weary bodies into the mess hall for a dinner cooked on the wood-fired stoves. Afterward, the exhausted workers enjoyed a few hours of free time, ending the day at the 10:00 bedtime, with lights out for weary limbs and backaches. They would be approximately five dollars richer—minus four cents social security tax—from the daily travail.[18]

Despite the heat and the strenuous schedule, ML assured his parents that he was managing just fine. Every week, he sent at least twenty-five dollars of his thirty-dollar weekly pay to his parents, while assuring them of his determination and assuaging their worries. "The sun has begun to get pretty hot," he wrote to his mother in the middle of June. "But that is not the beginning they [say] it is going to be so hot here in July that you can hardly [sic] take it but I am going to take in some day how," he promised her. "We are really having a fine time here and the work is very easy," he wrote to his father the same month.[19]

ML was able to make these lighthearted assurances because he was not engaged in the most demanding labor. As the youngest and smallest farmhand, he was the ideal worker to retrieve the low-hanging leaves. Yet despite his physical advantages, and though he had worked urban jobs delivering and packing newspapers, ML had never performed such intensive manual labor. It became obvious to him and everyone else that he was not cut out for it.[20]

ML and Emmett spent their time in the field shooting the breeze. Tweed and Weasel were paired because they were both slow workers, as Proctor noted years later, so they "would not slow other workers down." They spent their time occasionally working, while constantly talking about college life at Morehouse, and the coeds at Spelman—while picking as slowly as possible. As if their leisurely pace was not flagrant enough, they often stopped to make time for horseplay. They were not alone in this. "It was very very hot there," Pickens confessed years later. "But even so we tried to make it fun. We developed camaraderie, singing songs, telling jokes."[21]

But Pickens and other men knew their priorities: work, then play. But not ML. He did more pranking than working. In letters home, he hid this fact, pledging that he was being serious and industrious. Nothing could have been further from the truth. Even from a thousand miles away, ML engaged his dad in his normal pattern, telling the elder King what he knew the patriarch wanted to hear, while he did as he pleased. He told his dad the line almost every parent hears from their teen and wants to believe, but knows is rarely true: "I am not doing any thing that I would not doing [sic] front of you."

ML was one of the chief pranksters on the farm. "He liked to play jokes a lot," one worker remembered, "but he didn't like, really, to injure anyone." One of his antics became legendary, bordering on the kind of harm that only youths who have yet to grasp the concept of mortality could find funny. ML called the signature prank "giving the hot foot." Pickens recalled the caper: "He would pour kerosene on a sleeping fellow's foot and then light it." The hijinks elicited gales of laughter from ML and his audience, but consternation, to say the least, for the victim of the joke. "That kind of joke may sound deadly," Pickens admitted, "however, all of us would be standing around or lying around or sitting around and we would see it . . . so when ML did that and started laughing . . . we would tend to laugh with him but then we would also be on the alert to make sure that nobody was injured because the kerosene would burn off very fast." Another tobacco boy was more measured in his memory. "The practice wasn't *usually* harmful."

ML's congenial nature and general likability shielded him from any retribution, and the supervisors looked the other way. "Supervisors had a way of turning their head when someone would be disciplined by the rest of us," Pickens admitted. What was a joke to ML was seen by supervisors as a disciplinary measure to keep workers awake.[22]

Tweed and Weasel eventually ran afoul of their seasoned foreman, a man of Polish decent who simply went by "Walt." After a few consecutive days during which ML and his friend were the last pickers to complete their respective rows, the foreman—and the white supervisors to whom he reported—had seen enough. "The boss finally said he was going to take us out of the rows," Weasel remembered. He removed Tweed and Weasel from picking and assigned them the less demanding job of raising and lowering the cheesecloth clouds.[23]

The nets were supported by wooden poles, roughly twelve feet high and set at thirty-three-foot intervals. Wire was strewn across the poles and stapled for stability, and cheesecloth measuring roughly thirty-three feet wide was manually cast over the wires and attached, creating the artificial overcast conditions. Each acre required about five thousand square yards of the man-made clouds. The job of maneuvering the nets was not as physically demanding as picking the leaves, and it did not require consistent attention, but it was no less important. The clouds created the shelter that birthed millions of dollars' worth of product; there was no shade tobacco without the shade.

The critical nature of the job did not cure ML and Weasel's laziness. The lethargic duo enjoyed the intervals of rest between lifting and lowering the cloth clouds a little too much. As the shrubs grew to stalks, the leaves provided shade under the shade tents. It was the closest thing ML could find to air-conditioning. It became sacred lore whispered among the Morehouse hands: The makeshift air-conditioning was, one worker fondly remembered, "perfect for hiding . . . catching a few Zs."[24]

One late afternoon the two fell asleep in the field and slept through dinner. Their colleagues and supervisors labeled them a lost cause and left them slumbering among the rows. The youngsters were awakened by strange noises in the darkness. As the sounds grew closer and clearer, the boys believed they were being stalked by "hulking" beasts. Feeling themselves surrounded, they ran all the way from the field to the bunkhouse, screaming, Proctor recalled. It was the fastest they had ever moved on the farm.[25]

When they awoke the next morning, the light of day revealed that the night's menacing beasts were just grazing cattle. The city boys were hopeless on the farm.

"We were so sorry," Weasel confessed. And it was no secret. In a straw poll, coworkers voted ML and Weasel the "laziest workers."[26]

• • •

ML was slothful, in part, because he was so taken with his new social world.

He was exuberant about experiencing equal accommodations and encountering white citizens who treated him as an equal. "We go to any place *we* want to and sit any where [*sic*] we want to," he wrote to his dad. "The white people here are very nice."[27]

As his letters indicated, ML's psychological and spiritual transformation likely began as soon as he stepped off the New Haven Railroad and touched Hartford soil. After the roughly twenty-four-hour journey, the boys were hungry. Pickens remembers they went to a restaurant directly across the street from the Hartford Union Station. Ravenous, but careful to be on their best behavior, the boys entered the restaurant to inquire if they served African Americans—a nagging but necessary inquiry in Jim Crow America. "We found we could be served with no difficulty whatsoever," Pickens joyously recalled more than fifty years later. "For us that was a new experience . . . it seemed like we were as well accepted as anyone was, so that was quite a novel experience for us and quite an enjoyable experience for us which happened right away upon our arrival in the city of Hartford."[28]

After that initial experience, many of the Morehouse men took whatever chance they got to get off the farm and travel to Hartford. The city was booming during the war years and had reached its all-time peak population at that time of roughly 180,000. The city lights beckoned the youngsters, while the hard-earned cash in their pockets empowered them to enjoy all it had to offer. Not everyone took the bait. "Some fellows would stay on the farm all summer long and never leave," one worker remembered, "because that was an expense." The purpose of the summer was to save money, not spend it. But ML did not have those concerns. The adventurous teen took every opportunity he could to journey to Hartford. "Yesterday we didn's [sic] work," he excitedly wrote to his mother during a rainy few days, "so we went to Hartford we really had a nice time there."[29]

Over the summer Tweed devoured city life. He visited department stores, enjoyed fine dining, dances, movie theaters, and cabarets. He was utterly amazed that he received equal service in Hartford's flagship stores. He visited the famed Metro-Goldwyn-Mayer (MGM) theater for movies and musicals—a particular novelty for all the tobacco boys from Atlanta. Atlanta's MGM and Fox theaters did not admit African Americans on an equal basis, and Dr. Mays discouraged Morehouse men from attending theaters that required Black patrons to sit in the balcony. It made the experience in Connecticut life-altering. Many Morehouse students inundated relatives and friends with letters attesting to having danced the latest dances in fine dance halls and seen the musical greats of the day performing alongside whites on a nonsegregated basis. Proctor recalled that they saw Lena Horne, Count Basie, and Charlie Barnett at the State Theatre in Hartford during the summer of 1944.[30]

But ML was not so much excited about the shows or celebrities themselves. Rather, being admitted to these establishments on an equal basis left the deepest impression. In Atlanta he avoided the movies and shows. He hated the way he had to demean himself by accepting Jim Crow just to enjoy a movie. Reflecting on his teenage years, he admitted that he had "the usual growing boy's pleasure in movies," but he only went to a movie theater once. "The experience of having to enter a rear door and sit in a filthy peanut gallery was so obnoxious that I could not enjoy the picture," he remembered.[31]

But all that changed in Hartford.

He sat wherever he wanted. He could even sit close to the celebrities if he wanted to do so. But ML did not bother mentioning the celebrities in his letters home. No celebrity sighting could match the thrill of walking into the theater without being challenged, degraded, or harassed. Here was the joy of choice. One of ML's coworkers felt the same excitement. "Down south you had to sit up in the balcony," he recalled thinking years later. "Around here, I could sit in front, and I said 'Jeez, this is great.'"[32]

These experiences had an incalculable influence upon ML. "Dear Mother Dear," he wrote, "I never thought that a person of my race could eat anywhere but we ate in one of the finest restaurants in Hartford. And we went to the largest shows there." He was garrulous in his excitement. It carried over in the barracks. Coworkers recalled he talked nonstop about the exhilaration and freedom he felt absent the humiliation of having to use "colored only" water fountains, bathrooms, waiting rooms, and railroad cars.[33]

Fifteen years later, still basking in the success of the Montgomery Bus Boycott, ML fondly reminisced about his trips to Hartford.

"I have very pleasant memories of this city," he told a University of Hartford audience. "Some fifteen years ago, I joined several of my fellow students in coming to Connecticut to work for the summer on one of the tobacco farms. . . . And all week long we would work very hard and the sun was very hot, and it was always a big relief for the weekend to come around when we could come to Hartford."[34]

The metropolis radically changed how ML viewed the possibilities of the commercial world.

Rural Simsbury, on the other hand, changed his interpersonal world. The small close-knit town gifted ML with opportunities to have kind, meaningful relationships with white people.

It began with the simple act of playing basketball. The Morehouse crew played hoops on the cinder court outside the bunkhouse. Often, they were joined by white immigrant workers from nearby farms. ML and Weasel teamed up, just as they did at the segregated Butler Street YMCA in Atlanta. But in Connecticut, the teams were racially integrated. ML, with his notorious "will-shoot" attitude, had not played basketball with whites since his childhood games in the backyard with his white neighbor, that is, until their friendship fell victim to what was "proper." Integrated basketball had yet to be achieved in college or the professional ranks. Daddy King thundered about it from the pulpit, calling segregated professional basketball a pure form of "injustice," practiced and defended by those who were not living "a Christlike life."[35]

But on the farm, the laborers gave little to no thought to race or color—just dribbling, passing, and shooting the ball. ML was able to recapture the carefree joy of his childhood games. He and his teammates did not have many examples on which to model themselves: most colleges refused to even allow Blacks and whites on the same court. But on the farm, the only thing that mattered was the score at the end of the game.[36]

That summer, ML also had transformative experiences with white women. Occasionally, white female migrant tobacco workers from the Midwest and South, including Florida, would join the Morehouse students during their one-hour lunch break. Other times the sun-kissed workers would meet up after work for cooling refreshments at Doyle's Drug Store, testing the store's advertised promise of being "20 Percent Cooler Than Outside!" There were Friday-night dances sponsored by the local YWCA. A restaurant—a cafeteria on Simsbury's Asylum Avenue established by local organizations and businesses for soldiers, workers, and students—had an interracial policy, allowing the Black male teens to socialize with the white female workers, while the Connecticut Council of Churches sponsored movie nights on various plantations. Eno Memorial Hall showed the latest Hollywood films on an integrated basis. "It was just an unfamiliar situation," one Morehouse worker remembered.[37]

It was unfamiliar because casual encounters between Black males and white females were one of the most heavily policed boundaries of Jim Crow. In 1944, interracial marriage was illegal in all the Southern states and all the Western states save Washington. African American men and even boys ML's age had been murdered for less. Just a few months before the Morehouse men and the white female workers from Florida left their respective homes for Connecticut, a fifteen-year-old Black boy named Willie James Howard was lynched by three white men in Suwannee County, Florida. His crime in this north Florida community was reportedly sending a flirtatious note to his white peer, Cynthia Goff.

On January 2, 1944, Alexander Phil Goff, the girl's father, and his two friends, Reginald H. Scott and Seldon B. McCullers, kidnapped Howard from his mother, Lulu, at gunpoint. They then picked up Howard's father, drove to a bridge, hog-tied the teen, and forced him into the Suwannee River below. He drowned. The father helplessly watched the men murder his only child. Local police and the sheriff apprehended Mr. Howard and forced him to sign an affidavit stating his son committed suicide. The case was closed. No charges were filed. The NAACP intervened, led by future Supreme Court Justice Thurgood Marshall. They pushed for an investigation; but on May 8,1944, a few weeks before the Black men and white women set off for Simsbury, an all-white grand jury refused to indict the men.[38]

Such events were seared into the collective memory and community ethos of Southern life, for both Black and white. For Black men and boys across the South, engaging in anything that could be construed as flirtation with a white woman was often akin to flirting with death.

In Simsbury, there were no such worries, no forbidden barriers. "They were workers just like we were," a Morehouse man remembered. "It was an unfamiliar situation that one could chat with a white person as a peer." Some of the white women felt similar. "We have two [social] passes a week," a Southern white girl working at a nearby tobacco farm told a local journalist during the summer of 1944, "to go to . . . Simsbury." They also enjoyed dancing. Their "Saturday night dances," another explained, were scheduled, casual affairs on the farm where they were joined by summer tobacco boys. "We have a jukebox and a piano. And we have boys from Tariffville and Simsbury."[39]

The interracial socializing was not universally harmonious. Some of the white Southern women felt obliged to maintain a commitment to Jim Crow in the light of day. Pickens recalled that the all-white attendees at a dance sponsored by the local fire department were not explicitly antagonistic. However, "getting one of the young ladies to dance with us was another question," he recalled. One woman dared to cross the color line, offering her hand to dance, but only, she patronizingly declared, with the man who had the lightest skin. "That fellow, of course, declined," Pickens remembered.[40]

Yet, the experience of socializing with white female peers—even from a distance—was still groundbreaking. Years later, Pickens put it simply. Growing up in Atlanta, he knew making a public romantic overture to a white women "would have led to a lynching." But in Connecticut, "We could talk with them . . . and not get taken to jail for it." It was a simple yet extraordinary experience for all the Southern tobacco boys.[41]

Especially ML. The last time ML had stood close to a white female stranger, she had slapped him. Now, in Connecticut, he was talking to white women, eating with them, enjoying milkshakes and candy bars with them at Doyles Drug Store, as well as the soda fountain at the canteen, laughing at movies, and enjoying their shared sense of the world as teenagers. They danced and commiserated over their labor—the persistent tinge of the tobacco stains on their clothes, the ever-present dirt under their fingernails, the seeming omnipresence of the foreman's shadow, and the unrelenting humidity. ML was able to get lost in the kaleidoscope of teenage social life, the awkward naivete of teenage flirtation and even the precocious discussions with white women about current events. Unlike Willie James Howard, fifteen-year-old ML did not have to worry about being lynched for simply speaking with a woman as a fellow human being.

ML also found that the white churches in Simsbury were open to him, even welcoming. White churches in the South generally did not receive African American parishioners. If the Black attendees could get beyond the front door, they were forced into segregated seating. Even the nationally known evangelists of the era, Billy Graham, dubbed America's Preacher, abided by Jim Crow regulations and maintained separate seating at his annual crusades and outdoor services, which attracted thousands of attendees.[42]

ML had every reason to expect this in Simsbury. The majority white hamlet did not have any Black churches, and so ML—presuming he had to travel to Hartford to worship at one of the city's two prominent Black Baptist churches, Shiloh Baptist or Union Baptist—made the trek during his first few weeks on the farm. Hartford was about fifteen miles away from the bunkhouse, a considerable distance to travel for one's humanity to be affirmed under God. However, work, weather, and precarious transportation often stood in the way. "I could not get to Hartford to church," ML confessed to his father, "but I am going next week."[43]

However, he soon learned that he could attend the white churches in Simsbury and not even have to sit in the back. "I went to church in Simsbury," he told his parents. "It was a white church . . . and we were the only negro's [sic] there," ML wrote in shock. "Negroes and whites go to the same church!" ML visited Simsbury's First Church of Christ. He and a few of the other Morehouse men were welcomed on an equal basis. It is not clear why they chose to attend the all-white Congregationalist church founded in the late seventeenth century. Perhaps it was simply because it was located near the main thoroughfare in town, on Hopmeadow Street, just a short walk from the dorm. Or perhaps it was the tradition of the Congregationalists—now known as the United Church of Christ (UCC)—for being abolitionists that drew the tobacco boys to the church. Or maybe some of the returning farmhands recommended the church. Or maybe they were invited by the pastor. Reverend E. Knox Mitchell Jr. was a Hartford Seminary–trained theologian who served as chairman of a religious outreach group known as the Committee of Character Building on Tobacco Farms.[44]

Whatever the reason, it was a fateful decision. ML and his fellow farmhands—sometimes upwards of sixty—would arrive to worship dressed in their Sunday best. Some walked while others elected to catch rides on the farm's old pickup trucks. They would hop off the makeshift benches mounted in the truck's bed, in exchange for the integrated church benches that welcomed them. During the summer, ML heard sermons that would have touched his aching but changing heart, including "Freedom's Holy Light," and a sermon series on "Foundations for a Peaceful World." The church became a home away from home for ML. He even sang in the choir, just as he occasionally did at Ebenezer. Bernice C. Martin, the wife of church choir director Garland Martin, recalled that a member of the congregation was struck when they heard ML singing in his pew during worship. ML's voice had deepened since he had stirred congregations to shouts and tears with his boyish rendition of "More Like Jesus." But his pitch and tonality remained. The parishioner brought ML to Garland, who then invited ML to join the choir. "When my husband asked Martin Luther King to join the choir," Mrs. Martin remembered, the shocked fifteen-year-old replied, "'You mean I can sing in a white man's choir?'" She recalled her husband offered a direct reply: "It isn't the color of your skin I am interested in, it's your voice." ML joined the choir and even sang a solo. "He had such a good voice," Mrs. Martin remembered. The Martins were impressed with more than just his voice. They developed a personal relationship with the teenager, even hosting him for dinner. They enjoyed his company, his inquisitive mind, and his love of history.[45]

Not every Morehouse student had this experience. A few were worshipping at the Methodist church in town, some of them even sang in the choir. That all ended abruptly when a group of white women and girls from Florida were imported to work in the tobacco fields. "They wouldn't come if the Morehouse College boys came," church member Irene Welden recalled. The church chose the white women over the Morehouse men.[46]

ML did not mention this in his letters home. Perhaps he did not know about the experience. Or perhaps he was not interested in chronicling what for him and his Southern coworkers was an ordinary life event. ML was focused on recounting what he considered extraordinary: integrated worship.

For the first time in his life, he attended an integrated worship service—sharing the same pews, holding the same hymnals, touching the same offering plates, taking communion, holding hands, singing and supplicating to the same God—with white people. It was ML's first experience with interracial Christian community, where the love of God triumphed over racism.

ML would seek to replicate this experience of beloved community for the rest of his life.

The Connecticut Valley helped ML see that racism was not inevitable. Jim Crow was not innate, as life in the South had tried to convince him. Rather, it was a social construction. In Connecticut, he discovered that racism was its own separate force—something that was cultivated, baked into laws and social customs, and then digested by hearts and minds. It caused white Americans to have a false sense of superiority and imposed on African Americans a false sense of inferiority. There was nothing natural about racism and inequality. Freedom was natural. Dignity and self-respect were God-given.

It was an equally revelatory experience for the all-white membership. "That was the only time we'd had any colored people in the church," Bernice Martin recalled. "I remember our minister saying that we should be cordial to them because there wasn't any reason not to be." Decades later, her fond memories remained. "They were very nice, agreeable students. We enjoyed having them." After hours around the dinner table, ML seemed to have left a particularly lasting impression upon the couple. "I will be interested in seeing what he is doing in times to come," Bernice recalled hearing her husband say the last time they saw ML. "That young man is capable of doing something special."[47]

. . .

ML (as well as many of his Southern colleagues who were interviewed years later) certainly had an idealized perception of Connecticut, and the Northern US more broadly. ML seemed not to notice or was simply not moved to chronicle or discuss the more subtle forms of racism he or his colleagues encountered during the summer. The Methodist church and the fire department dance did not appear to impact him. ML did not seem to notice or report on the gross employment discrimination he certainly encountered during his many commercial escapes. A 1943 statewide study found that there were no Black salesclerks employed in Hartford's major department stores. In fact, African Americans were almost universally excluded from white-collar occupations across the state. And some of the commercial spaces denied service to Blacks. George Hudson, a Jamaican migrant to the tobacco farms, was denied admittance to a movie theater in Hartford because of his race. Hudson, ten years older than ML, stated that bars were only slightly better. "When we went in to have a drink, the bartenders would break the glasses when we left." Connecticut, Pickens surmised years later, was "freer but still not quite free."[48]

But "freer" meant everything to teenage ML. "He talked about it," Pickens told a television reporter in 1998. "It was so different from our daily lives in the South under the situation of deep segregation, which we faced all of the time and everywhere." Enjoying free access to public accommodations—train cars, restaurants, theaters, as well as community organizations, churches, or the YWCA, opened a new, exhilarating form of existence for ML. As

Pickens surmised, he and ML recognized that they were experiencing "far more freedom than we were accustomed to. We really did not encounter [racism] to any extent similar to what we were encountering in our daily lives in the South." And that experience, Pickens noted, made the two teenagers feel "freer than we ever felt in our lives."[49]

ML was very conscious of the change, both in his circumstances and within himself. Years of battling Jim Crow had left him with deep scars of doubt and distrust of white Americans and society. He had started brandishing cynicism as his weapon and agnosticism as his shield. But in Connecticut, he was no longer at war. The freedom he experienced seemed like a dream, like something he had memorized from a Langston Hughes poem. ML and a few of his coworkers walked around white neighborhoods, almost pinching themselves, searching for the boundaries of their freedom. They waited to be harassed, arrested by police, or worse. But it never happened. Pickens recalled that they did walk into a barbershop, only to have the barber refuse to cut their hair. Yet that was the only restriction they encountered. Pickens, who later moved to Hartford as an adult, recalled that the two teenagers walked around freely, but somewhat in disbelief. At times, he admitted, they were "looking for signs that it was real."[50]

It was so real, it changed ML. It began the process of restoring his hope for white people. It resuscitated his optimism for America. The summer of 1944 unleashed a vision of how American society could be, and should be. There in the Connecticut Valley, ML had a mountaintop experience of freedom.

"And that feeling continued," Pickens noted. ML was so moved, his summer dormmate noted, that the teenager who had found refuge in agnosticism and anger began referring to the Connecticut Valley as "God's country."[51]

22
MALCOLM

You could not convince Malcolm Little Connecticut was God's country. He had seen too much to have faith in Christianity or white Northerners.

In the summer of 1944, the same summer ML was working under the tents, Malcolm, who would later be known as Malcolm X, was serving as a traveling salesman for a Boston tailor, selling suits to the battalion of Black farmhands in the tobacco fields of the Connecticut River Valley.[1]

The nineteen-year-old arrived in the valley having been fed a steady diet of Northern racism. Raised in Lansing, Michigan, his father, a Black nationalist Baptist preacher, was murdered by white supremacists. His mother, who imbued Malcolm and his siblings with racial pride, was deemed unfit by the state after a white insurance agent cheated her out of the life insurance money, leaving Malcolm a ward of the state. Living in a boys' home in rural Mason, Michigan, Malcolm attended Mason Junior High School, where he made the honor roll and was elected president of his all-white eighth-grade class. His success was blunted by daily taunts of "nigger" from classmates, teachers, and his court-appointed guardians. Yet Malcolm chose to believe they meant no harm.[2]

Like ML, his racial outlook changed when he was fifteen—except Malcolm's viewpoint became pessimistic. Malcolm had also decided he wanted to be a lawyer. Around 1940, he revealed his dream to his academic adviser and English teacher Richard Kaminska. Malcolm's white classmates remembered their white English teacher as towering and curt, but always supportive of their dreams, offering blunt but sound advice. Malcolm never forgot how his favorite teacher responded to his dreams. "You've got to be realistic about being a nigger," Kaminska lectured under his thick mustache. "A lawyer—that's no realistic goal for a nigger. You need to think about something you can be. . . . Why don't you plan on carpentry?"

Malcolm was devastated. "I was one of his top students, one of the school's top students," Malcolm reflected years later in his autobiography, "but all he could see for me was the kind of future 'in your place' that almost all white people see for black people."[3]

It was, Malcolm remembered, "the first major turning point of my life." Malcolm's outlook on faith, America, and its white citizens changed. "It was then that I began to change—inside," he remembered. He began his journey toward atheism and "drew away from white people."[4]

Malcolm left Michigan and moved to Boston's Black enclaves, spinning on a carousel of odd jobs—including the New Haven Railroad—and several illegal street hustles, outsmarting other con men and selling drugs and fantasies to white city slickers. In the summer of 1944, the tall, lanky teenager found himself selling suits as the only African American in the tailor's traveling convoy. When the tobacco boys prepared to venture from the farm, Malcolm did his best to convince them he could help them look their best. Often, he had barely unfolded his legs from the tailor's blue truck before he began his sales pitch for Stein's suits.

The brand possessed meaning for his Southern customers. Founded in the 1920s, Stein's was one of the largest menswear chains

in the country. In Atlanta, Stein's—"America's Greatest Clothier"—
opened "a modern and enlarged store" in 1936. The shop was only a
few blocks from ML's house, on the corner of Auburn and Peachtree.
Founder Joseph Stein, a native New Yorker, signaled his commitment to Southern mores and customs at the store opening. He told
the Atlanta press his suits came from Knoxville, Tennessee, and his
"experienced tailors work with the definite aim of supplying the best
of clothing for the southern man from a southern institution."[5] Jim
Crow was *the* Southern institution. The Morehouse farmhands in
Connecticut could not have walked into a Stein store in their native
Southland and received equal treatment. But on the farm, Malcolm
gave them top-notch service.

He had no trouble selling suits to the summer laborers of God's
country. While the Morehouse tobacco boys made only about five
dollars a day, the pricey thirty- to fifty-dollar suits sold well. It was
probably the easiest hustle of Malcolm's life. According to one tobacco boy, Charles Tisdale of Athens, Alabama, the Southern-born
farmhands were spellbound by Malcolm's charisma. His Northern
urban lingo sounded as fashionable as the suit covering his svelte
six-foot-four-inch frame. "He seemed to be so hip," Tisdale remembered thinking as an eighteen-year-old. "Guys from the South my
age were naturally drawn to that." Malcolm easily convinced them
that the fulfillment of all their dreams was just on the other side of
a new department-store suit lapel. "The only thing you need is a
brand-new suit," Tisdale recalled Malcolm saying in his sales pitch.[6]

It worked. Tisdale bought a forty-dollar Joseph Stein suit from
Malcolm. But he was not alone. "Several of us bought suits from
him," he fondly remembered. Indeed, according to the Morehouse
student newspaper, every summer the tobacco boys returned from
Connecticut armed with "new suits."[7] In the summer of 1944, these
youngsters likely had Malcolm to thank.

It is unclear if Malcolm and Martin met that summer. There is no evidence that the two teens laid eyes on one another or greeted one another.

Did talk of the tall hipster selling suits reach ML?

During that fateful summer, it is possible the towering Malcolm did not even bother to make his sales pitch to Martin, sizing up the younger, much shorter, eloquent tobacoo worker as an unlikely mark. If he did make his pitch to ML, young King likely rejected it. ML did not need the wares Malcolm was hustling; he had his own pricey collection of tailored tweed suits back at home.

Neither ever spoke of the chance encounter. As adults, the two men met only once, briefly, at the US Capitol in 1964; they barely had time to shake hands and pose for a photo. They were not able to meander down memory lane and discover that they both found themselves in a Connecticut tobacco field in the summer of 1944.

The two teens could not have known that their time in the valley was a historic moment, one that foreshadowed the eternal course of their public relationship. Like the summer of 1944, they always, somehow, managed to seem simultaneously so close, yet miles apart—freedom fighters with freedom dreams for their people, but with competing views of how to make those dreams a reality. Indeed, throughout their lives, Malcolm persistently and publicly dismissed the younger man, rejecting ML's dreams as nightmares.

ML's rejection of Malcolm also remained throughout adulthood. While he largely ignored Malcolm's overtures to publicly discuss and debate the issues facing Black Americans, ML admired Malcolm's intelligence and believed that Malcolm possessed important insights into the Black freedom struggle. But King abhorred Malcom's calls for violent self-defense.

But in the summer of 1944, the two teenagers were at a crossroads in their respective lives, just two young men trying to find their way. They likely departed the state as strangers, but with clearer paths for their respective futures. Malcolm's experience of racial discrimination in New England led him to further distrust and resent white people. For Malcolm it was not God's country. The region's de facto racism—residential and educational segregation, employment discrimination, the exclusion of Black workers from labor unions, and police brutality—made it the devil's lair. Perhaps the devil in New England was nicer than in the South, but a devil all the same.

A year and half later, Malcolm would be convicted of leading an interracial burglary ring in Boston. He was guilty, but according to the court, his major crime was being romantically involved with one of his white female co-conspirators. The district attorney told Malcolm, "If we had you Niggers down south, we would hang you." Instead, in a quintessential example of Northern racism: two of Malcolm's white female co-defendants received probation and were released, another, his lover Beatrice Caragulian Bazarian, served only seven months, but Malcolm received a minimum sentence of five and half years in Massachusetts' Charlestown State Prison. Malcolm Little, the street hustler, became inmate 22843. During his imprisonment, he joined the Nation of Islam. Shortly after his release, he became the group's national spokesman, declaring their Black nationalist gospel of salvation around the country. He would be known as Minister Malcolm X.[8]

New England had a different impact on ML. "As I got to see more of white people, my resentment was softened," he noted. In Connecticut, ML would rediscover his faith in America and God, and take his first step to becoming Minister ML King.

23
FIRST CONGREGATION

The farmworkers were ML's first congregation.

As the summer progressed, ML seemed obsessed with turning the world upside down—expanding God's country. He could not stop talking about changing society. Some on the farm dismissed the constant musings as juvenile chatter; they would have preferred more work and less talk from the youngster. Others saw ML's dreams as one of childhood's most precious but precarious luxuries: hope.

In Jim Crow America, such talk was as inspiring as it was dangerous. Young Black boys with big plans to change Jim Crow rarely made it to adulthood. Trying to bring their dreams to fruition often meant their lives would be cut short. Those who managed to reach adulthood usually followed one of two paths. As they witnessed their dreams being washed away in the flood of racism, they made bitterness, self-hatred, and rage their home. Others managed to harbor a modicum of self-love and humanity by making a tacit agreement with their segregated society: Grand childhood dreams were exchanged for localized, "practical" adult goals of improving one's station in life, without offending the steel sensibilities of Jim Crow.

On the farm, it was taken for granted that many college men had made such an agreement. They would aim to complete their education at the college and hash out a better life for themselves and their families. They would look no further than the bounds of their circumscribed existence in the South. However, in the summer of 1944, ML was too young to put his dreams to bed, and now too energized to stop imagining a better world.

And he could not stop talking about that world. ML, Pickens recalled, had "a great deal of energy." The energy was not sowed in the tobacco fields. Rather, he used it so sow dreams of a new Southland. Pickens noted that ML "would be one of the first out of the fields to get a drink of water and then prepare himself to go talk to the rest of us. . . . He wanted someone else around to talk to all the time . . . [and] he talked about segregation a lot . . . [and] imagining something that just didn't sound like it could work in a segregated society."

Even when the men held their "bull sessions" in the dorm, discussing Morehouse and teenage tales, ML would always, somehow, manage to steer the conversation toward his desire to make an impact in the South, to bring God's country to all. Coworker and Morehouse basketball star Silas "Smokey" Davis remembered ML always talking about doing "something different." Eighteen-years old at the time, the Alabama native recalled that the younger teenager was focused on his desire "to contribute to society in ways that no one else had ever done." That "something" was his intention to strike a death knell for Jim Crow. As one tobacco boy noted, despite the "very pleasant experiences" in Connecticut, ML made it clear that he "wanted to do something about racial segregation in the south." ML's body was present, sweating and toiling beneath the Connecticut sun, but his heart remained in the South.[1]

His inspiration proved contagious to others on the farm. His hope served as a reminder to his coworkers of childhood dreams long forgotten. He "was almost like a mascot," remembered one

Morehouse farmhand. As a representative of all that was good and hopeful, the men appointed ML their preacher.[2]

There were older Morehouse men on the farm who possessed the traditional markings of religious leadership. They had formal training, having completed semesters of Morehouse's required religious studies curriculum. On the farm, however, the once faithless teenager morphed into the leading evangelist for God's country. His hope was contagious. His carefully honed oratorical skills helped make his seemingly constant ruminations rousing. His musings were those of youthful hope, but expressed with adult clarity, and his lack of adult experience only reinforced the idea that he was naturally, perhaps divinely, gifted and called.[3]

ML was thrilled at his selection by the Morehouse men. The ink that relayed the news to his parents dripped with exaggeration born of excitement. He told his mother he was the "head of the religious Dept.," though it was less a department, more a voluntary association. For years, the Morehouse tobacco crew had organized a Sunday-morning worship service during breakfast in which the men shared speaking duties. But in the summer of 1944, the crew gave ML complete control. "I have to take charge of the Sunday service," he told his mother, "I have to speak on some text every Sunday to 107 boys."[4]

Despite his responsibilities, ML avoided calling himself the group's preacher. Maybe he was trying to avoid the title, a last-ditch effort to assert his autonomy over his father's smothering ways. Or maybe he liked the sound of "department head," which had a more professional ring to it than "preacher." However, no matter the title, ML's duties made his role clear: For the Morehouse men, he was their preacher, their chaplain, and their spiritual guide through the valley. Pickens summed up ML's role best: "We had religious ceremonies, and he was the preacher."[5]

It is difficult to overestimate the role of the Black preacher in the African American experience. The very status of "preacher," "minister," or "pastor" commands special esteem. White society enjoyed occupational differentiation; they had a plethora of elected officials, clergy, captains of industry, and civil servants to advance their political interests. The Black experience was hallmarked by the denial of the same. The Black preacher filled this void. This status led W. E. B. Du Bois, the first African American to receive a PhD at Harvard, to describe the Black preacher at the turn of the twentieth century as "a leader, a politician, an orator, a 'boss,' an intriguer, an idealist—all these he is, and ever, too, the center of a group of men."[6]

In the valley, fifteen-year-old ML began to embody the idea of the Black preacher. He was attuned to politics, constantly discussing statecraft while he traipsed across the farm. He loved big words and oratory, and had recently participated in that statewide competition. And he was an idealist, believing that the world could be changed and turned right side up. It all placed ML in the center of the group of Morehouse men.

Historically, the Black preacher also enjoyed influence and adulation based on the belief that Black clergy were endowed with supernatural gifts. Preachers received a "call" from God to be a divine representative and provide communities with biblical revelation as well as ethical and moral guidance. They were expected to see the invisible, to hear what others could not, and to speak what others could not or would not dare utter. This ability, it was believed, was divinely bestowed at birth. But it was the community—the congregation— that confirmed it so. In the Black Baptist tradition, a congregation or a group of followers had to authenticate their preacher's calling before a preacher was anointed as such. ML resisted the idea that he was called to the ministry and could not see himself in the pulpit. However, in the valley he encountered a group of peers and colleagues who felt differently. The community affirmed his calling long before ML accepted it himself.

ML's first congregation was stripped of the glitz and glamour that would come later when he was a renowned preacher. As an adult ML drew praise from listeners around the world for his preaching, including political and professional elites and celebrities. But young King began perfecting his preaching—not to an audience dressed in their Sunday best or perfumed to perfection—but to those drenched in sweat from the hot Connecticut sun, in denim overhauls and long-sleeve shirts stained with tobacco sap, with fingernails painted with dirt and soil. The preacher who loved big, academic words began his ministry preaching to laboring men.

ML would eventually preach in the world's most hallowed halls, but in 1944 he was far removed from the National Cathedral or auditoriums at Stanford University or the University of Oslo. The first worship services ML led were convened in the bare-bones recreation room of the tobacco farm. Only the ping-pong tables and a few scattered board games distinguished it from the beat-up sheds where the tobacco hung to cure. Occasionally the services were held in the mess hall, where ML's developing baritone voice competed with the clank of dishware, while his choreographed gestures cut through the haze of smoke that billowed from the wood-fired stoves.

And he seemed born to do it. When he ascended the makeshift pulpit in the recreation room of the dorm for the weekly 8:00 a.m. service, he had the bearing of an old pro. "You'd think he was already a trained minister," recalled Silas W. Davis. This is perhaps not surprising given that ML was no stranger to the ways of the preacher, having heard his dad preach since he was a child, watching him perform in the pulpit. His childhood was punctuated with visits by a plethora of Black Baptist preachers from across the country, preachers who fed ML's love of words.[7]

But ML's pulpit demeanor was far from mimicry. His was one of a professional, learned clergy. He had sworn off the ministry in part because of the emotional and expressive preaching style he witnessed on Auburn Avenue. His father's sermons were marked with Black vernacular and double descriptors (high-tall, low-down, kill-dead, more-better). The vernacular sermons were also chanted, beginning with conversational prose and then transitioning to a "metrical, tonal, and rhythmic chant," and interspersed with affirmations and shouts of "amen" and "preach it." If ML was not hearing such preaching from his father, he heard it blaring from the homes and shops along the Ave. Atlanta's Reverend James M. Gates became a celebrity preacher by selling his chanted sermons on Columbia Records and Paramount Records during the interwar period.[8] ML's maiden voyage in the pulpit was shaped less by the well-worn path of those he had been exposed to, and more by the path he believed was less traveled: the staid, lecture-style sermon.

On the farm, ML delivered his sermons with the meditative demeanor of a lawyer and the seriousness of a physician in surgery. The teenager, whose voice was emerging from puberty with depth, was very solemn—he was, Davis remembered, "always on a serious note." He delivered the homilies without the use of notes or a manuscript, relying instead on his profound memory and ability to recall long passages, as he had practiced for years bantering with Annie L. McPheeters at the Auburn Avenue Library. All of it—the demeanor, the baritone, the recitation of scholars—made it appear that he was a seasoned preacher speaking extemporaneously, not as himself but simply as a mouthpiece for the divine.[9]

ML's first efforts at sermonizing were a resounding success. "Sunday morning we had church in the boad [sic] house," ML hurriedly scribbled in a letter to his mother. By his own account, his preaching was good and inspiring, and the services were excellent overall. After a few weeks, he proudly told his parents, "we really have good meetings."[10]

The exact content of ML's first sermons have been lost to history, but their tenor lives on. Davis remarked that the young man's sermons were "always about helping people, always about elevating people." The topics likely spanned the range of his Sunday school lessons, the very lessons he had challenged: Jesus feeding the less fortunate, making the wounded whole, protecting the vulnerable, loving one's neighbor.[11]

He would tell his wife that it was on the farm where he "really began to feel the urge to preach."[12]

Indeed, these first sermons concerning helping and loving one's neighbor shaped ML's preaching for the remainder of his life, even in his final days. In his last sermon on April 3, 1968, the night before he was assassinated, he drew upon the parable of the Good Samaritan in the Gospel in Luke 10:25–37, which centers on a man from Judea who is robbed while traveling from Jerusalem to Jericho. The man is stripped of his clothes and his money, beaten, and left for dead. A passing temple priest refuses to assist the half-naked, dying man; an assistant to the temple priest does the same. However, a Samaritan—a man whose mixed-race heritage placed him on the margins of society—stops to assist the man, paying for his care. ML told the audience that he imagined the first two men asked themselves, "If I stop to help this man, what will happen to me?" However, he noted, "the Good Samaritan came by. And he reversed the question: 'If I do not stop to help this man, what will happen to him?'" This, ML preached on the night before his death, was what every Christian should ask themselves as they travel through life. He had long been taught that Christians should stop to help those who are hurting, injured, hungry, unsheltered, or left for dead. No matter the race, ethnicity, creed, or religion of a person in need, a Christian must stop to help, to elevate those who have fallen.

ML began preaching this theme of service almost twenty-five years before, as a fifteen-year-old preacher in the tobacco fields of Connecticut.

• • •

ML's imagination for service reached new heights on the farm.

In addition to feeding the souls of his fellow workers, ML also helped to feed their stomachs.

The teenager who did everything to avoid kitchen duty at home volunteered to work in the kitchen on the farm. "I have a job in the "Kicthin [sic]," he joyfully reported to his mother. "I get better food than any of the boys and more I get as much as I want!" he said in another attempt to calm her persistent worries.[13]

The dutiful son did not prepare food; that job was reserved for the seven cooks who knew how to utilize the kitchen's two wood-fired stoves. They gave the teenager the simple assignments: "I just do the extra work. I give out the lunches and serve whatever they have to drink," he explained to his mother. ML cleaned dishes and tables, and ladled out the milk and other beverages to his older co-workers as they filed through the cafeteria line. He also distributed sack lunches and, at the close of meals, collected and disposed of trash and leftovers.[14]

ML's kitchen duties had spiritual significance. Jesus served his disciples. He fed those who looked to him for spiritual guidance. ML, the budding preacher, decided to do likewise.

His service also had powerful social meaning. The young boy's social-class standing was obvious at first encounter; his superior "work" attire—especially the multiple pairs of shoes he requested his mother send him—his broad vocabulary, and callus-free hands spoke volumes. It was clear to everyone, one of ML's coworkers noted, that ML was "well placed socially." However, "that didn't mean much because he didn't make it mean much." ML's willingness to serve men who others might deem socially beneath him was a powerful message. ML did not view himself as superior, but as an equal.[15]

The men ML worked with in Connecticut had spent their lives serving the wealthier classes as porters, butlers, cooks, and drivers. However, on the farm, they were brought their food and drink by the scion of an upwardly mobile and well-educated Black family. Some had watched their mothers, wives, sisters, aunts, and grandmothers serve middle-class boys like ML, whose family had a Black female housekeeper. But on the farm, ML served them.

He was profoundly touched by this dynamic. One of his earliest memories stemmed from the overwhelming feelings of confusion and despair that came over him every time he saw the lingering effects of the Depression's economic collapse throughout the city of Atlanta. When he was just five years old, he asked his parents "about the numerous people standing in bread lines." Why were they there? Why is our family not there? What caused this? Can I help? He watched the women and men of Ebenezer Baptist Church organize to aid the needy, but given his age and his standing as the pastor's beloved son, he was often shielded from the hard work of service. The farm provided ML with the opportunity to engage in such Christian service on his own accord. He was not ordered to do so by his dad, or encouraged by his mother, nor assigned to as part of his Sunday school class. His instigating the good deeds made such selfless acts feel real, more authentic.[16]

ML had passionately voiced doubts about the Bible and the existence of God. Yet, on the farm he rediscovered Christ's charity.

His Sunday school lessons were replete with accounts of Christ's generosity—feeding the less fortunate, washing the feet of the weary, and welcoming outcasts. ML could recite them from memory, chapter and verse. The stories had marked his heart, no matter how much he rebelled.

The farm was a society within a society. And it slowly began to emerge as a model for how ML believed humanity could better meet the needs of the less fortunate. All the men, regardless of size or ability, received the same meal. This experience helped to shape ML's ideas about poverty and work. Throughout his adult ministry, including his acceptance speech for his Nobel Peace Prize, he stated that he had "the audacity to believe that peoples everywhere can have three meals a day for their bodies." Three meals a day, just like he helped to serve on the farm.

ML's preaching would forever be shaped by this experience. As an adult, he would utilize the metaphor of the mountaintop to symbolize the Christian pursuit of service, freedom, and hope. It was a message forged by his experience in the valley.

24
A BITTER FEELING

ML departed Simsbury on September 12, 1944, full of hope. He left with a pocketful of money, courtesy of his long hours, plus a twenty-five-dollar bonus for choosing to stay into September, and a free train ticket back home. The ability to frequent any restaurant, theater, or church left him optimistic about America. And in late August, his mother told him he had been admitted to Morehouse.[1] Finally, and perhaps most surprisingly, he discovered that he could serve his fellow man from the pulpit. Maybe, just maybe, the ministry was the platform from which he could turn the world upside down. Maybe he could diagnosis and remedy all of America's ailments from that platform.

Anything seemed possible.

He pondered all this as the bus pulled away from Simsbury toward the Hartford station. As one Morehouse man wrote of his departure from the tobacco fields:

There is a certain thrill, tempered, however, when the purple shadows of evening are falling upon you for the last time in Connecticut. The sun seems to set in its full glory and colorful array; the already beautiful scenery

takes on an extra ethereal halo. . . . When the bus taking [us] to the Hartford railroad station tops the highest
point surrounding the valley, [we] realize then that each
revolution of the wheels takes [us] farther from the place
where [we] have worked, played . . . [and we] look ever
homeward.[2]

ML looked homeward and saw his future. In Hartford, he
boarded the train bound for New York City. Once again, he stayed
in the city to explore. "I will leave here Sept 12," he wrote to his
mother on August 30, 1944, "and get home the 15th because I am
stoping [sic] in N. York for about a day." *The Maroon Tiger* noted
that during the return trip to Atlanta, several Morehouse tobacco
boys stopped in New York City to revel in the equal treatment they
received in the city's famed tourism sites, including "Radio City
[Music Hall], the subways, boat rides, [and] the Statute of Liberty."[3]
ML left New York City exhilarated by his experience of unprecedented freedom.

But the hope-filled journey changed once he reached the nation's
capital.

"It was a bitter feeling going back to segregation," ML remembered of the trip home. "It was hard to understand why I could ride
wherever I pleased on the train from New York to Washington, and
then had to change to a Jim Crow car at the nation's capital in order
to continue the trip to Atlanta."[4] He stepped off the Pennsylvania
Railroad and on to the Southern Railroad, and the Southern way
of life. It was hard for ML to comprehend how he could feel like a
dignified human being for months, and then, in what seemed like
a blink of an eye, be stripped of it. For months, social freedom had
become his new reality. But nothing, not even a temporary residence
in God's country, could change that he still resided under the regime

of Jim Crow America. And that reality dragged him from a feeling of goodwill to a profound sense of bitterness.

It was a shared feeling among all the tobacco boys. "The feeling . . . we all had was excruciatingly depressing," Pickens recalled. "It was very depressing on the return trip to once again get to Washington DC and have to go back into a segregated coach for the rest of the trip back south."[5]

ML and the tobacco boys had experienced a glimmer of freedom and equality, only to have it ripped from them, ironically, at the nation's capital, the seat of government for the home of the free.

• • •

ML was liberated from the Jim Crow car when the train arrived at Atlanta Terminal Station. He walked past the Jim Crow signs and hopped in the family car, bearing tales from the North. Words of hope and anger seemed to tumble out of his mouth, competing for center stage as the family made their way back to 193 Boulevard. "[He] came back buzzing with stories about the integrated life of the north, and how different for the negro such an existence was," Daddy King recounted. ML kept juxtaposing what it was like in the South compared to God's country, where there were no explicit laws meant to "turn people into things that were less than human," his father recalled.[6]

ML's summer vacation was bookended by two very traumatic incidents: He was humiliated and nearly attacked for protesting his treatment on a bus to Dublin, Georgia. And then at the end of the summer, he was forced to switch to the Jim Crow car in Washington to continue his trip to Atlanta. Sandwiched in the middle of these degrading experiences was the roughly four-month period that had brought him back to God, and to himself. The tough-guy image waned. The anger and grief receded. He became singularly focused on how he could bring God's country to all Black people. The boy who was obsessed with turning the world upside down returned, but with a renewed maturity and focus. His sister and closest confidante, Christine, noticed the change in her little brother. "When he got back home, there was something markedly different about him . . . he had undergone a sociological and philosophical metamorphosis." This was no exaggeration. ML took the experience very seriously. "We used to go to parties and everything," Christine remembered. "And then he decided, you know, that he's not going to parties. He'd be sitting there reading the Bible, and we'd go on out to parties. We couldn't get him to go." He even took a hiatus from social outings with girls. For a time, he completely turned inward. The fifteen-year-old left as a child, she noted, but seemed to return "a young man."[7]

The young man was clear he wanted to destroy segregation. But he was no longer sure which vocational path would best serve his purpose. Before going to Connecticut, he had sworn off the ministry, deciding law was the conduit to freedom. But after Connecticut he began to consider maybe the church house was his calling and the avenue to bring God's country to everyone.

The changed and charged young man looked to Morehouse College to provide the clarity he desperately desired and needed.

Part Four

FINDING A LIFE

MOREHOUSE COLLEGE

The Morehouse Alumnus, July 1948.

25

A MOREHOUSE MAN

Morehouse College was a guiding light. The hilltop campus rose above the city's industrial smoke clouds and the stereotypes of racism, challenging its students to do the same. Rising eleven hundred feet above sea level, the twelve-acre campus was built on the grounds of a Confederate Civil War outpost. What was once a space to protect Confederate soldiers and arm them for the cause of slavery was transformed into an educational fortress for the descendants of slaves.[1]

Morehouse had a tremendous impact upon ML, one that is too often ignored by biographers. ML, Coretta Scott King noted, "used to talk about Morehouse so much, it made a profound impression on him."[2] Indeed, the little college on the hill infused him with ministerial inspiration and imagination.

The fifteen-year-old freshmen did his best to look and act the part of a confident Morehouse man. He shed the goading adolescent nickname Tweed, introduced himself as ML. He quickly became known as the guy who was always groomed: shined shoes that glistened like glass, an assortment of suit jackets, and large-brimmed hats. But beneath the smooth threads was a tattered soul. After his time in Connecticut, he could not shake a nagging, terrifying sense that he was called into the ministry. The question stalked him. And as Morehouse provided ML with an image of what ministry could be, he could not stop talking about it. His friends grew weary of hearing about it. Despite their advice, he continued to deny the "inner urge" to pursue the ministry.

• • •

September 16, 1944.

ML King Jr. began his journey to becoming a Morehouse man.

As a commuter, his trek to school began by catching the West Fair Street trolley line to campus. On every trip, ML, his sister, and June Dobbs had to bypass the sign that sat above the conductor: "White People Shall Sit from the Front to the Back and Colored People Shall Sit from the Back to the Front." They were all careful not to accidently sit or stand in front or beside any white person for the roughly twenty-minute crosstown trip. For approximately one thousand two hundred seconds, they walked a tightrope, balancing obedience to the law while maintaining an inner sense of value as budding college students. The streetcar passed Terminal Station— the notorious and traumatizing bastion of antiblackness—bound for the Atlanta University Center, which was the home of Morehouse and Spelman, and Atlanta University, a citadel of Black affirmation.[3]

ML hopped off the street trolley at the corner of West Fair and Chestnut. He was set to join the largest freshman class in school history. Like ML, so many of the 191 promising Black men boasted famous names: Licinius Archias, John Wesley, Thomas Jefferson, and a few George Washingtons. Their monikers reflected the backlog of Black hope seeking fulfillment at the college.[4]

ML could feel the spirit in the air at freshman orientation. "There was a freer atmosphere at Morehouse," he recalled. It was not the kind of freedom that college students then and now relish. ML still lived in his childhood bedroom. There would be no wild parties nor independent living in a college dormitory. But Morehouse offered him an affirming liberty, one that was not encumbered by racial terror. The private-school professors were not caught in the clutches of state funds, they were free to teach what they wanted, say what they wanted, and to challenge their students to confront white supremacy. "For the first time in my life," ML reminisced, "I realized that nobody there was afraid."[5]

At Morehouse, ML could question the authority of the Western political tradition and not be attacked. He could commune with Plato, Socrates, and Aristotle on an equal basis. He could reach to touch the hand of God, and the divine would not withdraw. Morehouse satiated Black men who dared to cherish such freedom dreams.

• • •

Dr. Benjamin Elijah Mays and his wife, Sadie, never birthed their own children. But through Morehouse, they created many sons.

As president of Morehouse, Mays became a living legend at the school. It is difficult to overestimate his influence upon the school and its legacy. He completely transformed Morehouse from a school that had trailed other historically Black colleges in Atlanta—it was closer to a high school than a college—into a first-class liberal arts college for Black men.

When he returned to Morehouse in 1940, he was keenly aware of the massive task before him. Before becoming president, he endured a brief stint as acting dean at Morehouse. He braved ill-prepared students, poor facilities, and an even poorer salary. With no endowment, the college could not afford to pay him even the meager amount he was owed in salary. After completing his PhD at the

1944 Freshman Class photo:
ML, second row, seventh from right. At the time this was the largest freshman class in Morehouse history.

University of Chicago, he became the founding dean of the School of Religion at Howard University, only to return to the place where his teaching career began. He returned with an elite education and a master plan to match. He would lift morale and instill within Morehouse men "the idea that despite crippling circumscriptions, the sky was their limit."[6] He wanted Morehouse men to dream dreams. And thanks to his reforms the school enrolled one of the biggest dreamers the world has ever known.

Mays challenged his proverbial offspring to rise in the same manner he did: through a combination of brains and brawn, struggle and triumph. The svelte six-foot 180-pound former college football star looked as if he were built to shoulder responsibility. Both his upright posture and his standards were strict. He was a South Carolina–born bookworm, the offspring of enslaved parents who could not read. He picked cotton in the Old South, but was educated in the progressive North, receiving degrees from Bates College and the University of Chicago. He had a determination for freedom, born from his repulsion to Jim Crow's Southern dictates, and a persistent hope in the face of the broken promises of the North. Words were his weapon, sharpened as the debate-team captain at Bates and as an ordained Baptist minister. His iron-gray hair announced his mature wisdom, while his youthful, coal-black skin gave him the appearance of an energetic prodigy, ready to take on the monumental task of being a Black reformer in Jim Crow America. He would be the architect of the Morehouse man. His own life served as the blueprint, and young men like ML were the raw material awaiting construction.[7]

He envisioned that the Morehouse man would be part spiritual leader, part intellectual, part statesman, and always a gentleman in the service of the race. Mays called Morehouse men—whether in law, medicine, dentistry, engineering, ministry, teaching, business, or government service—to cast their lot with the forces of justice. He saddled them with the duty of lifting their voices against injustice wherever they found it, in the US or abroad. "If Germany through brutal means can build a kingdom of evil in one decade . . . we can democratize and Christianize America in one generation," he reasoned. Success was assured. The "moral order of the universe" supported justice. The planets, the sun, the moon, and the stars were on the side of justice. History was on the side of justice. And most important, God was on the side of justice.[8]

Mays commenced his educational vision for Morehouse with a series of reforms. As the first Morehouse president with an earned PhD, he demanded the faculty follow his intellectual accomplishments, replacing those who failed to do so. Salaries increased and the physical plant enjoyed investment. He challenged students to strive for excellence. He resisted recruiting for athletics. Accomplishments on the field of play came and went; distinction in a particular field of academics was an eternal mark. Their academic record, he liked to tell nervous freshmen, was "like death," it was a "permanent" fact one had to live with forever. "Make it respectable!" he demanded.

Mays also promoted an early admission program to beef up enrollment, which had been decimated by the outbreak of World War II and the military draft. The school was in danger of closing. The program helped open the school to talented high school students—students like ML.

He also breathed life into the school's finances. The students gave him the nickname "Buck Benny," because of his vigilant financial management of every "buck" that came into the college's coffers, and his ability to enlarge those coffers. During his presidency he racked up countless miles on the fundraising trail. He developed several crucial partnerships with corporate foundations. The Ford Foundation sponsored early admissions students like ML. The Field Foundation made major contributions to the endowment. William H. Danforth, CEO of Ralston Purina, appointed Mays to the Board of Trustees of the Danforth Foundation, while Danforth's daughter and grandson joined the Morehouse board. And Mays worked to appoint Charles E. Merrill Jr. as chairman of the Morehouse Board of Trustees. The son of the wealthy cofounder of Merrill Lynch held the post for more than a decade. He sponsored early admissions scholarships and made annual financial gifts to increase faculty salaries and support academic programs. These relationships with the scions of American enterprise helped Mays to transform the college from a financially struggling institution to one with a sprouting endowment. Mays not only saved the school from closing, he willed it to thrive.[9]

• • •

ML was a perfect fit for Mays's Morehouse. He was in a rush to become a Black man of distinction, and the school was beginning to
pride itself on making such men. He felt at home there. Many of his
high school friends were students, and the rules and expectations
were just like those in the King household. Students were inundated
with information on the "social maintenance" of the college. These
campus commandments were inscribed in *The Morehouse Companion*, a booklet given to every student. The first lesson was clear:
Morehouse was "emphatically a Christian school" created to educate Black men for leadership and service. "Morehouse is not a
winter resort," the booklet noted. "It is taken for granted that a
student elects Morehouse because he wants to further improve his
mind and . . . make a worth-while contribution to society." Students
chose Morehouse to learn the scholarly habits of work, study, and
intelligent expression. Their training in the liberal arts and sciences
would empower Morehouse men to be engaged citizens, to fully
understand humanity and to serve it.[10]

ML loved the school's sartorial expectations. The opening pages
of *The Morehouse Companion* directed students to list the essential
facts every Morehouse gentleman should know: hat size, shirt size,
make of his watch, height, and weight.[11] ML had begun keeping track
of such matters when he graduated from junior high and donned his
first of many tweed suits. Students were expected to sport collared
shirts, ties, coats, dress trousers, and sweaters. Peer pressure upped
the ante. *The Maroon Tiger* ran a regular column on attire. "Authentic Maroon Tiger Fashion" kept the students abreast of wardrobe
musts: a gray pin-striped or chalk-striped single-breasted or double-
breasted suit; a white broadcloth dress shirt; a patterned tie in blue,
red, or maroon; socks that matched the tie; a blue, gray, or black
herringbone tweed topcoat; a gray or blue snap-brim hat; and black
dress shoes. It was perfect for ML. Fellow freshman Charles V. Willie,

himself only sixteen, noted that ML quickly established his reputation as "a well-dressed and neat person who wore wide brimmed Big
Apple hats, fancy sport coats, and pegged-top pants."[12] Classmate
Robert Williams remembered being shocked when he discovered
that the debonair ML was not a distinguished twenty-five-year-old
man, but a fifteen-year-old teenager.[13]

He also earned the nickname Runt from his fellow freshmen.
It was tantamount to placing a target on his back. But ML refused
to relive the bullying he experienced as an undersize high schooler.
He wanted to alert his classmates that he was not an easy mark. He
chose fellow freshman Walter McCall as his proving ground. The
twenty-one-year-old World War II veteran had established himself as
the campus barber, offering ten-cent haircuts. Runt requested a cut.
After the trim, McCall remembered, ML casually told the Army vet
he would pay for the haircut later, claiming he was broke. How could
one of the best-dressed students not have a dime?[14]

"You and I both know you have a dime!" McCall recalled saying.
The teenager dismissively repeated that he would pay later, which
to McCall translated to never. "Man. I haven't got it now," ML repeated. "So there's nothing you can do about it, unless you want to
go to the grass."

McCall was bigger and six years older, but that did not matter to
ML. The teenager had learned a valuable lesson as the smallest guy
at Washington High. He could not become a target.

McCall tackled his customer and the two began wrestling. The
tussle spilled out onto the campus lawn, attracting onlookers, cheers,
and jeers. McCall claims the two wrestled to a draw.

ML had proven his point. Those who considered bullying the
class "Runt" now had reason to reconsider. In the end, ML not only
obtained a free haircut but also the respect of his peers, especially

McCall. As hypermasculine duels tend to resolve, their mutual respect gradually morphed into a lifelong friendship.[15]

Freshman squabbles aside, the rules at Morehouse were strict. The school prided itself on piety. "Morehouse College is essentially a small Christian college," noted the admissions policy, "and consequently selects its students on the basis of character, personality, and promise as constructive leaders, as well as on scholarship."[16] It did its best to give students a good education in literature and science, but "stress [was] placed upon moral training and the development of consecrated workers. Self-mastery, symmetrical character, high ideals and purposes are regarded as the chief end of education." Until students could obtain self-mastery, Morehouse tried to impose it. The body was the temple of the Holy Spirit, so alcohol consumption, on or off campus, was not allowed. Gambling, a favorite practice of sinners, was prohibited. Despite the prevalence of hunting in the South, guns were forbidden. The long list of rules probably reminded ML of Daddy King's parental lectures.[17]

Morehouse trusted its students, but it also verified. Curfew was enforced on underclassmen and expected of upperclassmen. The freshman curfew was 10:15 p.m. Sophomores received a forty-five-minute extension. Juniors and seniors were expected to "keep the hours of a gentleman," and no gentlemen would be caught out after midnight. Overnight guests—only male, of course—were prohibited without the permission and supervision of the dorm mother.[18] A Morehouse gentleman was expected to keep his room as tidy as his appearance. Passing the daily dorm inspections required fresh linens on the bed, clean clothes hung up in the closet, and dirty laundry hidden out of sight. Trash cans were to be used, but never full. Walls were to remain immaculate, free of writing, posters, or pictures.[19]

And every gentleman was expected to have table manners. More-house used the cafeteria to train men for fine dining. It was a foreign concept for some students, especially those from rural America. But it was routine for ML. Promptness was paramount. Like a reserva-tion, students had to arrive at the cafeteria at appointed times or risk not receiving service. Cafeteria doors opened for breakfast at 7:00 a.m. and closed at 7:25. The margin of error was even smaller for the remainder of the day: 12:45 p.m. to 12:48 for lunch, and 6:00 p.m. to 6:03 for dinner. "If you are late," *The Morehouse Companion* baldly in-structed, "be a good sport. Go away without complaint and resolve to be on time at the next meal."[20]

Morehouse rules of etiquette continued inside the cafeteria. Each student was assigned a seat at an eight-person table and instructed to remain standing until the blessing was sung. The Morehouse hymn was declared in part, "Holy Spirit, Holy Spirit, make us steadfast, honest, and true to Old Morehouse and her ideals and in all things that we do." This included eating in an orderly manner. Men were tutored on how to approach a dining chair, and the appropriate uten-sil to butter vegetables (always the fork). Waitstaff served the food. Students joked that the waiters wielded more power than the fac-ulty. Upperclassmen served as table hosts, positioned at the head, where they monitored the dissemination of food and the dedication to table manners. Students were forbidden to make any request to the waiter. All requests—a second portion, a refill, more napkins—went through the host.[21]

It was often a failed experiment. Cafeteria decorum was a perpetual battleground on campus. The student newspaper com-plained, "The conduct of some of the men in the dining hall is so boisterous and uncouth that it is deplorable." Men refused to stand in line and await their turn. Some even organized strikes of the dining hall, protesting the strict hours, upper-crust rules, and down-market fare. But ML was not among them. A Morehouse professor recalled that ML played the role of the etiquette watchman, embracing the orderly manner of dining and defending the administration. "I have heard students say that many times he would defend the administration or the dining room or some other [student] pet grief on the basis of moral rightness," the professor recalled in a 1963 interview. A few times, ML even attempted to play counselor to his peers. "Sometimes when the hot heads of the campus wanted to have a strike . . . he acted as a sobering influence of letting them think it through to see if they were really right or if the administration was right," the professor recalled. ML was always ready to remind his colleagues they were Morehouse men, with a moral charge to keep.[22]

And that charge followed them off campus as well. Students could not avoid the watchful eye of the faculty even if they did not dine in the cafeteria. Lerone Bennett, who arrived at Morehouse a year after ML, remembered, "If [the faculty] saw you at a restaurant . . . they taught then, and if you mispronounced a word, they would stop and, you know, and say, 'Young man, that—that's not the way that word . . .'"[23]

If a Morehouse man continually failed to keep the charge, on or off campus, Morehouse faculty reserved the right to expel him. No student was above the importance of maintaining the image.

The administration drilled key messages into the hearts and minds of first-year students through two campus requirements. The first was a weekly lecture course titled "Freshman Orientation and Hygiene." ML raised the course curve. Amid a roomful of freshmen attempting to dress to impress, ML stood out, gaining the admiration of his peers. Horace T. Ward, a native of rural Georgia, immediately noticed ML in class. ML, he remembered, was so "well dressed," "well groomed," and verbally polished.[24]

The Maroon Tiger, December 1946.

Daily chapel was the second requirement. "The Bible has a place in the regular course of study," Morehouse preached to its students. "In the life and discipline of the school, constant effort is made to inculcate Christian principles." This was routine for ML. The Kings held nightly family devotion in which the Bible was studied and verses committed to memory. The Morehouse instruction was no different for ML, especially since his dad was occasionally one of the chapel speakers. Leading local and national figures who addressed the student body during King's years included John Wesley Dobbs, cofounder of the Atlanta Negro Voters League; Walter White, head of the NAACP; Elmer W. Henderson, famous for his landmark law-suit against Southern Railway; and Henry A. Wallace, the US vice president from 1941 to 1945 and Progressive Party presidential nominee in 1948. These speakers fit with Morehouse's mission to feed the souls, hearts, and minds of its students. The Tuesday chapel program was reserved for President Mays. He would stroll into the seven-hundred-seat Sale Hall Chapel in his classic uniform of dark pin-striped suit, looking as if he had stepped out of the pages of *Gentleman's Quarterly*. When Mays walked into a room, students routinely muted themselves, unless they were complimenting his style or questioning their own sartorial choices.

The proper relationship between Christianity and democracy was Mays's favorite topic.[25] He believed the challenge of the twentieth century was to democratize and Christianize America. This was not Christian nationalism. It was an enduring Black liberal Protestantism, a social gospel that had faith in the ability and promise of Christianity and American democracy to achieve universal equality and freedom. "The Church," Mays often lamented in chapel, "is one of the most segregated institutions in the United States." It was wedded to the norms of society instead of transforming them. The Christian church had to break the shackles of segregation and become the one place were all human beings were treated equally. And the federal government had to become serious about fulfilling America's promises as articulated in its founding documents. The nation could form a more perfect union if there was a determined effort. A functioning democracy would rid itself of racialized violence and discrimination, as well as unemployment and poverty. Morehouse men would be a chorus of prophetic voices pushing "the Federal Government to be democratic and the church to be Christian."[26]

Mays challenged them to be morally courageous in pursuit of these ends. "A person is not entitled to live just because he happened to be born," Mays often reminded students. "The right to live must be earned by being great, by developing one's mind, and improving one's character."[27] This resonated with ML. He had long wanted to earn his right to live by doing something great for his people.

ML loved everything about Mays. He was constantly talking about the fifty-year-old man, styling and modeling himself after the president: the suits, the oratory, the phrases, the presence. Friends teased him, accusing him of "adoring" Mays. He had so much "reverence" for Mays, they taunted, he probably had an "idol" of the president. But ML's adoration of Buck Benny ran deeper than pinstripes. Mays spoke to ML's soul.[28]

Mays was a seer when it came to the religious needs of Black college students like ML. He published an article titled "The Religious Life and Needs of Negro Students" a month before taking the helm at Morehouse. He came to the job certain that most Black college students were "religiously confused" and were swearing off religion. Mays believed a weak background in religion was the cause. Most students had never had a scholarly course in religious studies. They arrived at college with a fundamentalist faith, a belief in biblical miracles—creation stories, seas that parted, animals that spoke, resurrections, and angels—all of which melted away under the microscope of modern science and history. With no faith, students were unable to establish a secure religious perspective. They developed critical eyes toward the faith. Instead of seeing the promise of Black faith, they saw peril. They pointed to the poor intellect of preachers and the irrelevancies of their sermons as proof of the impotence of faith, not the importance.[29]

This was ML.

After a few college classes, the teenager became notorious for ridiculing Black preachers and Black churches. He enjoyed mocking ministers who visited Ebenezer or those who turned up at the family dinner table. His stock skit was a joke about the typical sermon of a Black preacher. "God is love," ML would mockingly say, "but I'm not going to talk about God or love, but I am going to talk about is! like I is, like she is, like he is!" And then ML would start whooping. The whole bit was a mockery of ministers who had nothing intelligent or even religious to say. It was ML's way of ridiculing preachers who elevated wordplay and style above knowledge. He believed most Black preachers basked in anti-intellectualism. They were men who prioritized emotionalism as the chief sign of religious commitment.[30]

Yet Mays perceived that critical young minds like ML's had not completely given up on the faith of their fathers. They simply wanted to modernize it. "They have no sympathy for an otherworldly religion that promises reward in Heaven," Mays announced in an address on the religious needs of Black college students. "The function of religion, as they see it, is to give material security here and now." Students wanted a constructive religion, one that addressed their basic human needs. "If it does not strive to give that," Mays concluded, "it is no good."

Mays felt that students also wanted a religious life and social life that went hand in hand. In their view, there was nothing sinful about dancing, playing cards, or going to the theater. They had no patience for a faith that damned them to hell for "this or that." Black college students did not need another religious organization or social club. They needed professors who possessed academic respectability to present students with rigorous courses on the Bible and the history of Christianity. They also needed to see professors and administrators who were "actually stiving to live the religion of Jesus in an intelligent and sincere manner." Only this "intellectually commanding" and embodied faith could combat the antireligious attitude percolating among college students like ML.[31]

This was a faith that would reveal the significance and potential of Black churches as engines of educational, entrepreneurial, and social progress. Mays called it "a religious faith coupled with brain and intelligence" that directed students to fix their gaze not on heaven, but on human flourishing. This faith would challenge Black students to have some skin in the game, to engage in constructive criticism from inside the church, "rather than hurling epithets at it from the outside." This faith, Mays argued, would appeal to most Black students, it just needed to be proclaimed. Students would gladly and without compulsion listen to such a gospel. Students, Mays predicted, would pester the gospel teacher with questions "until the clock strikes midnight in quest of a . . . religion this pertinent to their lives."[32]

Young King fulfilled the prophecy. After chapel, ML routinely followed Mays to his office, peppering him with questions. He would pick the president's brain on subjects as varied as philosophy and haberdashery. Fellow freshmen Charles V. Willie watched in awe. Willie was a year older than ML but was inspired by the fifteen-year-old's boldness, particularly when ML raced after Mays to challenge the president's claims and propositions.[33]

Mays was pleasantly surprised by the teenage freshman. "I first became aware of the boy when he started questioning me closely after each of the Tuesday morning chapel sessions," Mays fondly remembered. Sometimes ML would wait just to tell the president that he agreed with the lecture. Other times, he would tell the president that he disagreed, or simply question the president's claims. "His questions were penetrating, and he often dropped by [my office] to discuss the subjects further. I perceived immediately that this boy was mature beyond his years; that he spoke as a man who should have had ten more years' experience than was possible." Mays could not know he was having a profound impact on the inquisitive, sometimes pestering youngster. But he clearly noticed one thing: ML was determined to fight the status quo one way or another. Whether it was racism, inequality, or military conflict, it was clear ML was going to "wage war against it."[34]

ML saw something in Mays, something he probably did not want to see, something he did not think was possible: a highly educated Black Baptist minister whose faith expression was staid, but whose labor was fervent. Mays was different from the Black Baptist ministers to which ML had grown accustomed. He was not a fundamentalist. He approached the Bible from a historical-critical method, interpreting Scripture in its historical context. This liberal theological perspective took the historical lessons and put them in conversation with modern knowledge.

This was the kind of faith for which ML thirsted. "My college training, especially the first two years, brought many doubts into my mind," ML noted. He began regretting that he was forced to go to church, finding himself at home in a "state of skepticism." But it was a welcome state of being. His Morehouse education challenged everything ML had known and seen of Black Protestant faith. "More and more could I see a gap between what I had learned in Sunday School and what I was learning in college." ML began to feel as if he were being set free religiously. Thanks in part to Mays's weekly lectures, ML wrote years later, "The shackles of fundamentalism were removed from my body."[35]

ML decided Mays would be the pastor he never had. Years later he declared that Mays was his "spiritual mentor" and "one of the greatest influences" of his life.[36] He loved that Mays practiced what he preached. One month into ML's freshman year, Mays was forcibly removed from a Southern Railway dining car enroute from Atlanta to New York and sent back to the Jim Crow car. Mays was incensed; he wanted to fight. Friends advised him to leave the matter alone. Bad publicity was kryptonite for his heroic fundraising efforts. He did not listen. He refused to accept the curtain, to be hidden away in the "Black car."

But he did not allow the treatment to fill his heart with the acid of hate. Mays did not just talk about the problem. He fought to de-mocratize the railroad. He teamed up with NAACP lawyer and fu-ture Supreme Court Justice Thurgood Marshall to fight it, taking Southern Railway before the ICC. "I had to try to do something about it," he reflected, "not for myself alone but for the cause of justice. . . . To refrain from this course because of fear would have been tantamount to accepting the path of expediency and inaction. This I could not do."[37]

ML was among many of the students who were simply amazed by Mays's action. His rival turned friend Walter McCall remembered how Mays's stance had "a terrific imprint upon us." The friends con-nected based on their mutual interest in law and its use as a tool to achieve racial equality. But Mays's action opened their eyes to another path. They discussed and dissected his ability to marshal the language of Christianity and democracy for the cause of jus-tice. They were inspired by his commitment to confront segregation wherever it reared its ugly head. The impact upon them, McCall re-membered, was "tremendous."[38]

Mays was, ML noted in a 1956 interview, "the ideal of what I wanted a minister to be." But as a freshman at Morehouse, ML would not dare to admit that Mays was also the kind of minister he could be.[39]

ML entered college dead set on a sociology major in prepara-tion for law school, but he felt he was being pushed into the minis-try. Not only had President Mays pierced his heart, the faculty also quickly recognized ML's lineage, expecting him to follow in his fa-ther's footsteps. And then there was the matter of Connecticut. The experience still simmered in his soul, as well as the souls of his fellow Morehouse farmworkers. Those who witnessed his first foray into preaching were all convinced the pulpit was his destiny.

After Connecticut, ML became completely preoccupied with his future. He was "consumed" by a war within, fellow tobacco boy William Pickens remembered. He was fighting "intellectually and psychologically, the array of forces that were . . . compelling him toward the ministry." Yet ML resisted, keeping his commitment to study law. He desperately sought support from his friends. He was selective with whom to discuss his future, choosing Morehouse men from Atlanta who knew him, the King family, and his father's social prominence. These friends, he thought, would be sympathetic to his point of view. They would cheer on his desire to break free from his father's shadow. Surely his dear friends would join him in his desire to pursue a career that was intellectually respectable and positioned to better the circumstances of their race.

ML always seemed to find a way to steer otherwise jovial and casual teenage conversation toward serious dialogue about his future. "ML presented his dilemma for review at every opportunity," Pickens noted. "When we would gather, invariably he would want to talk about his situation to us and he would want to air it and want us to respond to him." ML routinely told his crew of Morehouse friends that ministry was a small, provincial career. He wanted a vocation that would propel him to fundamentally change Black life. "I want to be a giant of a man," he started to tell his friends.[40]

"We guys would listen to him say that every now and then," Pickens said years later. "Nobody took him seriously, nobody . . . because [he] seemed [to] have been imagining something that just didn't sound [possible]." ML's desire to create an integrated and just society seemed implausible, the kind of wild dream that only a child could envision. So like the teenagers they were, the crew dismissed him. They ridiculed ML for his adult-size dreams with juvenile jeers and laughter. "Here was this very short fellow . . . talking about being a giant of a man," Pickens said. The crew retaliated with a steady stream of jokes aimed at ML's height.[41]

The jeers did not deter ML. The ridicule seemed to make him even more determined to resolve his inner struggle. "Some of the fellows sometimes would try to avoid him," Pickens confessed years later, "rather than hear ML, once again, rehash why he did not want to be a minister." However, Pickens and a few other Atlanta-born Morehouse students stuck it out with ML. They had the patience of Job, and listened to his standard complaints about the ministry and his desire to change society. They "tried to humor him," Pickens remembered, and they "tried to go along with him." But they were true companions, the kind of friends who refused to tell him what he wanted to hear. Instead, they told him what they felt he needed to hear. After witnessing his moving preaching and leadership in Connecticut, they felt the answer was clear: Ministry was destiny. "Our problem was that we could find no reason to join him in his belief that he had a choice," Pickens said. "I knew and the rest of the city guys knew that he had no choice; he was going to be a minister."[42]

ML would not hear it. He ignored Morehouse's pre-theological studies path and registered as a sociology major.

26
STRUGGLE FOR THE CROWN

Famed cleric and theologian Howard Thurman, a 1923 graduate of Morehouse, famously summed up the aspirational ethos of Morehouse: "Over the heads of her students, Morehouse holds a crown that she challenges them to grow tall enough to wear."[1]

Martin Luther King Jr. was not ready for his crown. "I shall never forget the hardships that I had upon entering college," ML remembered. "I was still reading at only an eighth-grade level."[2]

ML was not lazy in the classroom, nor dismissive of his college education, as some have argued. ML struggled in the classroom because he was ill-prepared. Racism, segregation, and a lack of resources had made his public-school education "inferior," he admitted. And years of skipping grades left him even more disadvantaged. His intellect and vocabulary were college-ready, but his writing skills and reading were not. He was so engrossed in discovering his future that he neglected to prepare for his present: being a fifteen-year-old college freshman. He had professional adult aspirations but mediocre teenage study skills and habits.

He sat toward the back of class in all his required first-year courses: Biology, Composition and Reading, Church History, Freshman Mathematics, History of Civilization. If he arrived early enough, he could secure his preferred seat in the last row. All his courses ran the duration of the year, allowing the youngster to establish a solid pattern.[3]

The dreaded class presentation—in his first-year History of Civilization with Professor Melvin Kennedy, chairman of the Department of History and Political Science, and a newly minted PhD from the University of Chicago—forced him to put on display his academic abilities.

There is so much at stake in a class presentation for a freshman. It is the opportunity to mark yourself either as a standout or a mediocre student. It provides the chance to confirm why you were admitted in the first place, to prove to your classmates, to the professor, and perhaps most importantly to yourself, that the admissions office did not make a mistake. This was especially true for ML. As an early admit, he was desperate to prove that he was a Morehouse man, not just in appearance, but also in intellect. And excellent oral presentations were important for his future plans. A good lawyer needed the ability to move a jury with words. It was not enough to detail facts; trial lawyers had to paint pictures. The cause of racial equality depended on it.

ML had every reason to be confident. He was steeped in the oratorical tools of Black preaching. He lived with a noted preacher, he heard famous preachers like William Holmes Borders over the radio, and Morehouse hosted some of the most noted speakers in the country. His life was a storehouse of moving rhetoricians. His second-place finish in the high school speech contest indicated that he was well on his way to joining the club of great speakers

Dr. Kennedy recalled that ML chose to present on Gandhi. It was a fitting topic. Gandhi, born to a privileged family in India, became a lawyer and a nonviolent activist against British colonialism. His efforts to throw off Western imperialism after World War I filled world news. The Black press called him "the Indian Messiah and Saint," and a model for the Black freedom struggle. Mays often reminded students that he had traveled to India in 1936 to meet Gandhi. ML had chosen the perfect topic. Gandhi seemed to be living the life ML dreamed for himself: a lawyer who was leading his people on a nonviolent crusade against colonial oppression.[4]

ML likely garnered much of his information on Gandhi from the Auburn Library. Annie McPheeters, ML's favorite librarian, recalled that he was fascinated by the library's books on Gandhi. "The thing that I am most conscious of Martin Luther was his interest in the books that we had in this collection that were on Gandhi and the Gandhi movement," she said in a 1992 interview. Once again, she told the youngster he could not check out books from the adult section. But she felt moved by ML's desire to read every one of the library's books on Gandhi. So they hatched a plan. "I told him to ask his father to come and get a library card, and I would check the books out to him on his father's card."[5]

ML's seemingly well-researched presentation was memorable, but not for its originality, but for its stunning mediocrity. There was no soaring rhetoric. No elaborate oratorical skills. No new or insightful information. Just a curious, shy, overwhelmed teenage freshman standing before his older, more mature, and better-prepared peers and the chairman of the history department. Professor Kennedy gave ML a passing grade, but noted the presentation was "not particularly impressive."[6]

ML was sorely disappointed, but he remained excited and dedicated to his education. Images of dazzling a courtroom—judges, all-white jurors, and Black clients—were still very much alive in his head.

· · ·

Luckily, ML was also taking a course in Composition and Reading that would help him with his public-speaking skills. Professor Gladstone Lewis Chandler designed the course to feed those, like ML, who hungered for big words. Chandler, who dubbed himself GLC, was a Caribbean-born wordsmith. He exuded charm and scholarly seriousness, transforming his classroom into a witty word banquet. He exhibited more than an affinity for literature and writing. His was a passionate love affair, an exciting excursion that students were invited to join. He paced around the room, placing himself at the center of great literary works. Othello, Shakespeare, and Homer became Black. His ability to recite works from memory made it difficult to know where the writer ended and the professor's lecture began. He almost seemed to speak in verse. His enamored students consistently rated him as one of the top professors at Morehouse during his thirty-four years on the faculty. He was known as "a teacher's teacher."[7]

"He impressed upon his students the importance of being scholarly, thorough, and progressive," one of ML's awed classmates wrote in his evaluation. "Literature became alive in his class."

"He was a fantastic, inspiring, and hard-working teacher, and he made me work hard," another student wrote.

Another remarked that Professor Chandler "enslaved metaphors and similes. . . . He prodded his pupils with a passion that made them conscientious converts."[8]

ML did not need to be converted. He was already a disciple of big words.

On the first day of class, the Harvard-educated professor addressed the freshmen in his customary formal manner:

Professor Gladstone Lewis Chandler, undated photo.

Gentlemen, some men are born great, others achieve greatness, and still others have greatness thrust upon them. None
of you were born great; none of you will have greatness
thrust upon you; therefore, you will have to achieve greatness. You will have to make the best of what you have.[9]

The professor spoke directly to ML's quest to achieve rhetorical
greatness.

He even provided a road map. "Gentlemen, we are going to establish a GLC Word Bank," he would announce between taking puffs
of his pipe. "You deposit some new words each class session, invest
them in congenial conversation, and withdraw with rich dividends."[10]

ML was a leading investor. He loved the course, mimicking and copying the man students referred to as "Channie." When GLC asked ML one day, "How are you doing?" ML could not simply respond "I'm fine." Instead, he went to the GLC Word Bank.

"Cogitating with the cosmic universe," ML delightfully remarked. "I surmise that my physical equilibrium is organically quiescent."[11]

ML would be forever indebted to GLC. As a lifelong member of the GLC Word Bank, he incorporated GLC's style into his own. A student who took the class with ML remembered the exhilaration the two felt after each class. After scribbling down every multisyllable word that sprang from Channie's lips, they would race to find a dictionary in order to learn and adopt the words. Anytime ML gave a speech, a homily, a sermon, an address, or a flirtatious line, it would be marked in part with a withdrawal slip from the GLC Word Bank. The civil rights movement and the soul of America reaped the dividends.[12]

Chandler designed the course to assist students in writing, reading, and rhetoric. He understood that many students like ML were orally and auditorily gifted, able to repeat things from memory, or sing or play instruments by ear. But GLC wanted their written communication to be equally advanced and clear. He believed writing and delivering compositions was the best way to help students master the English language.[13] The professor loved multisyllabic words, but he also loved succinctness. In a sexist, heteronormative manner, he constantly told his students, "Your written assignments should be like a lady's skirt: long enough to cover the subject, but short enough to be interesting."[14]

ML and his colleagues wrote their "skirt"-length essays and speeches and delivered them before their peers for the first three quarters of the course. "I am just as concerned with spelling and punctuation as performance of speech," he liked to say. Yet he did not want staid delivery. "I teach my students how to read a manuscript with all the spontaneity of an extemporaneous speech," he explained. And he was a notoriously tough grader. He expected students speeches to be well written and expertly delivered; students were to have eye contact with the audience 98 percent of the time, and 2 percent with their written manuscript. "For god's sake, don't have paper contact, but have audience contact!" he was fond of saying.[15]

Using this measure, he passed out failing grades accompanied by added unusual poetic flair. When a Spelman student who had decided to cross-register for his Morehouse course protested her failing grade, he reportedly told her, "Your eyes are like two pools of loveliness. Your lips are like twin blades of grass joined together by a pearly dew drop. . . . And if I were grading you on the basis of your pulchritude, I would give you an A, but, unfortunately, I'm grading you on the basis of your brains and I give you an F."[16]

GLC's penchant for being a tough grader was a bad sign for ML.

"He had the mind," Professor Chandler recalled in a 1963 interview, but ML also "had certain handicaps, coming up as he did through the public schools of Atlanta . . . he had certain deficiencies in fundamentals of English. . . . He had difficulty in spelling, punctuation, and the fundamentals of grammar," Chandler noted. "He had to work pretty hard to catch up."[17]

ML's baritone voice and passionate delivery could not save him from his poor preparation and the professor's stringent grading. "He did show promise as a speaker. . . . He had a good voice. . . . He had that organology of phonation, and a deep-seated voice that carries . . . but he had difficulties with pronunciation," Channie recalled. The professor commended the youngster for his honesty, conscientiousness, and hard work. ML was "always wanting to go beneath the surface to do some solid thinking. . . . He always had something to say, something meaty to say. . . . He worked hard at [written] expression. It gave him very great difficulty, but he worked hard on it . . . he always liked words, though he could not spell some of them," Channie frankly told an interviewer. "If I had been grading on effort, [he] certainly would have received an A." But Channie did not grade effort. He graded precision. ML's first-rate effort netted him second-rate results. "ML did not distinguish himself as a top-flight outstanding student. He was average or just a little above average but certainly at that time he did not show the sort of thing that he is now showing," Chandler noted in 1963. ML finished the yearlong course with a C. Chandler also gave him the same grade in sophomore English.[18]

ML put his lessons on display during his sophomore year at the college's inaugural John L. Webb Oratorical Contest. Directed by Professor Chandler, the contest was named in honor of the Black Baptist layman who was the director of the Universal Life Insurance Company of Memphis, Tennessee, and the Grand Master and Lecturer of the Masons in Mississippi. In 1945, he gave Morehouse College a contribution of $2,000 to endow the John L. Webb Oratorical Prize to promote excellence in public speaking. He was praised as the "first Negro to make such a substantial gift" to Morehouse.[19]

Students competed by choosing from five subjects from which they would speak without notes or manuscripts. Speeches could not be more than six minutes. Early rounds were judged by faculty. The finals were held in the chapel and judged by prominent members of the Atlanta community, including the NAACP attorney and former branch president A. T. Walden and noted journalist Ralph McGill. First place received twenty-five dollars, while second place received fifteen.[20]

ML's decision to participate shocked the campus "because [ML] did not speak in class," one classmate recalled of the shy sophomore. But at the contest, he "blew everybody away with his oratorical abilities!" Horace T. Ward, class of 1949, was amazed how such a slight body could produce such "forceful, eloquent, and thoughtful" speeches. The way ML commanded the room and persuaded the audience convinced Ward he was watching a lawyer in the making.[21]

ML reflected that the Webb contest, like the Elks Contest, helped him cultivate the ability to speak "without being tied down to a manuscript." Relying on his memory gave him freedom to look into the eyes and souls of his audience and move them with words and passion.[22] He did it as if he were born to it, because, in fact, he was born into it. "If I have any persuasion in speaking," ML recalled, "I don't think that I gained this from any book. I think that it's something that I have just grown up with."[23]

"He knew almost intuitively how to move an audience," Morehouse student Samuel DuBois Cook recalled. King marshaled the Black preaching tradition, presenting a six-minute monologue with cadence, voice modulation, haunting baritone, and beautiful, colorful phrases to implant a picture and pathos that the audience and judges would not soon forget. They were witnessing the maturation of a voice that would one day not just move a college campus, but a nation and the world. But all that would come later. ML, the sophomore, placed second in the contest, losing to Earl Edward Nance, a pre-theology student and future Baptist pastor.[24]

The confidence ML gained in the speech contest was tarnished by his experience that same semester in Math. He completed Freshman Mathematics with Professor Dansby, netting a B. But it all fell apart when he encountered Statistics. The course was important for a budding sociologist. But ML received an "incomplete." This was a first. ML always completed what he started. The "incomplete" jumped off his report card, making an indelible mark on his sense of shame. He talked about the "very difficult course" for years, especially in his sermons. His failure in math gave him an inferiority complex. ML used dogged strength to resist the inferior status Jim Crow thrust upon him. He did not have much strength in reserve to fight back against much else. He tried to find "the mead, mode, and medium, and standard deviation" in his problem sets, but ML only found that it subtracted from his self-worth.

The successes of one of ML's classmates in that course, Leif Cain, only accentuated ML's failure. The experience was so significant, ML mentioned it in a sermon more than a decade later.

Leif and ML arrived at Morehouse at the same time, but they were not in the same place academically. Leif breezed through math, especially statistics. ML watched with amazement as his classmate completed his assignments in what seemed like minutes. Leif was the picture not just of a budding mathematician, but a rising Morehouse man, and ML wanted to be him. "I knew I had the capacity of Leif Cain," ML reminisced in a 1957 sermon aptly titled "Overcoming an Inferiority Complex." "I [am] going to do this thing like Leif Cain," he told himself in several pep talks. Leif became ML's blueprint. ML tried to complete his problem sets and homework as fast as Leif. But what took Leif "one hour," required ML to spend "three hours." Getting the right answers would have provided some consolation, but even that escaped him. It was one of the most difficult experiences of his fledging academic career. Failure amid constant comparison robbed him of the little academic confidence he had. He wanted someone or something to blame. But the truth was a more stunning, difficult reality. "It was kind of difficult at first," ML admitted, "but I had to come to see that Leif Cain had a better mind than I had."

The hindsight of adulthood gave him perspective. "We should ask God to help us to accept ourselves and to use our tools no matter how dull they are. . . . I had to just come down to the point of accepting myself and my dull tools and doing it the best that I could, and this is the thing that every individual must do."[25] But self-acceptance is often a foreign land for souls navigating young adulthood. ML dropped the statistics class, forfeiting his GPA and self-esteem.

By the end of his sophomore year, ML had a C average.[26] Grading policy at Morehouse reserved C's for students who completed "average quality" work. ML arrived on campus bent on doing great things, grasping his crown. But there was no indication that the well-adorned prince of Ebenezer would be a leader on campus, let alone the city or the nation. According to his Morehouse report cards, Martin Luther King Jr. was just average.

Average was unacceptable in Daddy King's house. As ML wrestled with his future, difficulty maintaining C's, and an inferiority complex, he also had to manage his father's expectations. Morehouse kept close watch over students. Mid-semester and end-of-semester reports were sent to parents.[27] When report cards arrived at 193 Boulevard, Daddy King would throw a fit. He believed his oldest son was being lazy, cutting corners. Not even ML's sole B in Freshman Mathematics shielded him from his father's disgust. All he could see were the C's and the incomplete. Like a broken record, he would persistently fuss at ML. "If I could get through divinity school married with children and working full time, why can't you, single, being paid for, make A's!"[28]

It was tough growing up King. Daddy King's shadow loomed so large, he had difficulty seeing the world outside of it. Like many concerned and loving parents, he worked hard to spare his oldest son from the hardships he had experienced, but then harshly judged the child for lacking the experience of hardship.

But Daddy King's Morehouse was not ML's Morehouse. The school had changed a great deal since the 1920s and '30s. The faculty was more accomplished and brought with them higher academic standards.

Yet, Daddy King was blessed and cursed with certainty. His blind frustration got the best of him. He threatened ML that he would dispense the form of discipline he knew best: the leather strap. In a display of masculine dominance and foreboding embarrassment for his teenage son, Daddy King began visiting and calling ML's professors to check on ML's academic performance. He was, after all, an alum, a frequent chapel speaker, a city leader, and a paying parent. And as the president of Morehouse's Atlanta Alumni Association, he performed the concerned, invested alumnus and parent by showing his willingness to use physical force. Professor Chandler recalled the father's simple script. "Well, how is ML doing? He applying himself? Is he doing very much in your class?"

No matter the answers he received, he always closed with a parental boast and promise. "If at any time you find Martin not working up to his capacity you tell me. He's not too big for me to still strap him and whip him."[29]

ML surely found Daddy King's surveillance and threat of physical violence very difficult to handle, but it paled in comparison to peer embarrassment. The only thing worse than being one of the youngest and smallest Morehouse men was having your father boast on campus that he could and would bend you over his knee and spank you for lack of effort.

But effort was not the issue; and all of ML's first- and second-year professors knew it. Faculty conversations shared over coffee surmised that ML "showed great promise." He always wanted to delve deeper, go beneath surface arguments. Like Chandler, all agreed that the youngster deserved an "A for effort" in the classroom. But Morehouse men were not graded on potential and effort. They were assessed on performance, and in that area ML was far from an A. He displayed a love of words, but they were words he often did not know how to spell. He set the standard in clothing and decorum, but academically, he would not be "the student who set the curve," Professor Edward Jones noted. Jones, the chairman of the Modern Language Department and professor of French, saw through ML's C average in Elementary French and D average in Intermediate French. Professor Jones perceived that ML was "an unassuming, but serious student." He was quiet but earnest. He was rightfully admitted into college, but was simply overwhelmed.[30]

Professor Brailsford Brazeal, who served as Dean of Students and leader of the freshman lectures, also perceived ML was laboring to the best of his ability. Brazeal had an Ivy League PhD and was the foremost scholar of the Brotherhood of Sleeping Car Porters, the first African American labor union to receive a charter from the American Federation of Labor. He was the embodiment of a gentleman and a scholar. He walked ML and his colleagues through everything that pertained to college life, from bodily hygiene to study habits. He had a good feel for every first-year student. He perceived that ML was playing catch-up. "He had to work in order to build up his background to where it should be," Dean Brazeal remembered. ML was working overtime "to overcome a comparatively weak high school background."[31]

The quest for destiny and meaning, feelings of inferiority, and the humiliating threat of Dad's leather strap drove ML inward for his first two years of college. The social ML disappeared, giving way to a reclusive bookworm. Herman Bostick, a classmate in a few of ML's courses remembered, "ML was not one who stood on the corner to yack after class." If ML was standing on the corner, "he was waiting for the trolley to go home."[32]

ML's academic adviser, Dr. Melvin Kennedy, believed that was the problem. ML was spinning his wheels, spending too much time in the books and not enough in the schoolyard. This meant something coming from Kennedy. He was no stranger to hard work himself. He had received his PhD from the University of Chicago in 1944. When Kennedy received the routine call from Daddy King, he told the concerned, leather-strap-bearing father that ML was spending a "tremendous" amount of time studying, but not enough time exploring the social aspects of college. "I thought it might be worthwhile to explore the possibility of a more varied experience than he was having." ML was so focused on becoming a man of destiny that he was letting his adolescence pass him by. He was "tying himself down" to the problems and pressures of the world. That was too much for anyone to handle, let alone a child. ML needed to experience all that college had to offer. The adviser told Daddy King that he was encouraging the teenager to embrace his age, to "play more and roughhouse to relieve the pressure."[33] Remarkably, Daddy King found himself in agreement. He always wanted ML to be more of a fighter, to be a man's man.

But both men, Dr. Kennedy and Daddy King, were disappointed.

"There wasn't much we could do to get the boy to see it differently," Dr. Kennedy lamented. ML "seemed to be quite happy" just the way he was.[34] The youngster kept his head in the books.

Despite his tremendous efforts, ML only earned a 2.4 GPA in his first two years of college.[35]

But he remained committed to his dream of being a lawyer who would tear down white supremacy. Some friends believed it was his dreams that distracted him in the classroom. "I think he had a lot to hold on to," June Dodds reminisced, "a lot to dream about, a lot he wanted to do." He was so busy trying to figure out what he would do in the future that he struggled to thrive in the present.[36]

And yet Morehouse continued to hold out a crown, calling ML to be a man of merit and service, a man worthy to be a leader of his race.

A serious ML King Jr., circa 1947–1951.

27
DOWN TO BUSINESS

We aren't eager to marry white girls," ML scrawled across the page.

It was the summer of 1946, and ML was fed up. He had recently quit his summer job as a laborer at the Atlanta Railway Express Company after a white supervisor refused to call him by name, exclusively referring to him as "nigger." Soon after, on July 18, 1946, Black World War II veteran Maceo Snipes was shot by four white men, one of whom, Edward Williamson, was a white veteran. He died two days later, July 20, in a Butler, Georgia, hospital that had refused to give him a badly needed blood transfusion because they did not have any "colored blood." It was the first year the "whites only" Georgia Democratic Party gubernatorial primary was ruled unconstitutional. Snipes had been the only Black person to cast a ballot in Butler, Georgia, and it cost him his life. Snipes had served in the Pacific theater, avoiding the whizzing bullets and bombs of enemy combatants, only to return home to be shot in the back by his fellow countrymen for voting.[1]

Incensed, ML wrote an editorial and sent it to the editor of *The Atlanta Constitution*, the city's white daily newspaper. The words poured from his veins as he pondered the spilling of the innocent blood of Snipes and two Black couples—George and Mae Murray Dorsey, and Roger and Dorothy Malcolm—who were lynched five days later, on July 25, in Walton County, Georgia. Roger Malcolm had been accused of stabbing a white farmer during a fight. After posting bond with the help of the Dorseys, the two couples were surrounded by a mob of thirty unmasked white men. They tied the couples to a large oak tree and riddled their bodies with more than sixty bullets at close range. Mrs. Malcolm was seven months pregnant.[2]

Suspects in neither case—the Snipes murder nor the Walton County lynching—were ever convicted.

Using the tools he learned in his composition course, he penned "Kick Up Dust," decrying these crimes. It was published two weeks later. "I often find when decent treatment for the Negro is urged, a certain class of people hurry to raise the scarecrow of social mingling and intermarriage," ML wrote. Those opposed to Black equality often equated Black civil equality with miscegenation. But ML attacked this idea. Matters of the heart were not the heart of the matter. Fear of miscegenation was false, just an effort "to obscure the real question of rights and opportunities."[3] African Americans were American citizens. They deserved fair treatment and access to jobs for which they were qualified. Men like Maceo Snipes were entitled to the ballot as American citizens. And men like Robert Malcolm were entitled to equal treatment under the law. And Black children were entitled to safety and equal opportunities in education, health, recreation, and public accommodations. "We want and are entitled to the basic rights and opportunities of American citizens," ML declared.[4]

African Americans had been assaulted and killed for advocating equal rights, but ML showed no fear in speaking truth to the white newspaper. He did not hide behind a pen name or pseudonym. Nor did he hide his location. He proudly signed the editorial, "M.L. King, Jr. Morehouse College." He wanted everyone to know who he was, where he was, and for what he stood.

The Kings were pleasantly surprised. Daddy King loved the display of courage and academic accomplishment. Given ML's marks at Morehouse, his parents had conceded that young King would never have his own crown. They knew their son had ability, but it did not appear that he would be a man of independent distinction. If ML was going to enjoy any accomplishments, it seemed, they would largely be through familial connections. "Kick Up Dust" changed their minds. "[We] had no intimation of [ML's] developing greatness," Daddy King admitted years later, "until . . . he wrote a letter to the editor of a local paper which received widespread and favorable comment."[5]

ML was not surprised. He had doubts, but he never slept on his dream to change the world.

He approached his junior year in the fall of 1946 with the same hopes with which he started college. The lowly expectations of his professors did not lower the expectations he had for himself. The foreboding shadow of his dad did not block out the rays of his hope. He remained committed to changing the Black condition in America. Good marks were important, but commitment to others was paramount. He was a college student with average grades, "but," he recalled, "I never felt like a spectator in the race problem. I wanted to be involved in the very heart of it." The rousing reception for his editorial began to turn his dream into a living truth. "I could envision myself playing a part in breaking down the legal barriers to Negro rights."[6]

He confessed it all to Professor George Kelsey at the beginning of the school year. Professor Kelsey was a scholar's scholar. His wide-lapel suits, silk ties, clear-frame spectacles, and close-cropped hair with a perfect part down the middle seemed the perfect sartorial style for his academic stature. In his capacity as an ordained Baptist minister, Dr. Kelsey was accustomed to souls coming clean. But such confessions were unusual in the classroom, let alone on the first day of class. "At the outset, it was clear that he had come into the course with great seriousness and concern," Professor Kelsey recalled.[7]

ML wanted to impress the wunderkind. He embodied everything ML believed a Black minister should be: educated at the highest level, yet able to communicate with the common man, a professor with the emotionality of a traditional Black Baptist preacher. At just thirty-six years old, the bespectacled professor was young enough to challenge established traditions, but his newly minted PhD from Yale showed he understood the wisdom of the past.[8]

ML wanted to confess everything to Dr. Kelsey—the desire to be a better student, the nagging sense of academic inferiority, his disappointed dad, the inner turmoil concerning a career in the law or maybe ministry. And then there were the doubts he had about the respectability of the ministry.

"I still felt within that undying urge to serve God and humanity through the ministry," he confessed years later. Out of respect, admiration, and a tinge of guilt, ML unloaded all this on Dr. Kelsey. He admitted that his first two years of college had not gone very well. "But this year," ML told his professor "I have settled down to business!" He committed to working even harder on his studies.[9]

Dr. Kelsey likely welcomed the inquisitive, soul-searching young man. Kelsey believed the church needed youngsters like ML. In a report to the nation's three largest Baptist organizations concerning the education of Black ministers, Dr. Kelsey complained that all too often two kinds of Black males were encouraged to enter the ministry: (1) boys who lacked the critical reflection and analytic skills necessary to question the church's traditional ideals and practices, or (2) those that were just "dull, sedentary" boys. As a result, critical, bright young men "get the impression that religion is an affair of naive and stupid people." Kelsey believed Black America's best and brightest males might be willing to pursue the ministry if they were taught the difference "between essential religion and the crude manifestations of religion which [they have] seen."[10]

Kelsey's course, simply titled "The Bible," did this for ML. Like many college students then and now, this course would be the one ML would point to as the class that changed his life. Interestingly, it would be the only Morehouse course in which he obtained an A. And it would help him see what his life's business would be.[11]

Dr. George D. Kelsey, undated photo.

• • •

Dr. Kelsey was a serious scholar of the Bible and Christian Ethics. He merged conservative and liberal Protestant Christianity to reveal the faith's significance for individual and social reform. The major problem with conservative Christianity, Kelsey often told his students, was that it lead Christians to be primarily concerned with personal piety. The Bible did address the importance of soul salvation, but he cautioned his young pupils that a conservative focus on individual souls could easily lead to selfishness, making the Bible a pamphlet of personal moral instruction. But true faith had to move beyond prohibition of "drink[ing], sexual vice, theatergoing, card playing, and dancing." Christianity at its best should make Christians concerned with the matters about which Jesus was concerned. Yet he believed that liberal Protestant approaches to the Bible were also flawed. The historical-critical method helped to illuminate the Bible's relevance to modern culture and ways of improving collective social and political life. However, liberal Protestantism too often overlooked the importance of soul salvation, overestimating the human capacity for good. It also tended to identify the Kingdom of God with white bourgeois culture. What was needed was the best of both traditions—conservative and liberal approaches to Christianity.

True biblical Christianity would introduce souls to the radical, transformative love of God through the life of Jesus.[12] These baptized hearts would no longer govern their social and political relationships according to historical patterns, or racial, national, or class interests. To live and love according to racial segregation and discrimination was idolatry, "the worship of the creature instead of the creator." Jim Crow was not just a social arrangement; it was unbiblical. It was not simply a matter of personal preference. It was sinful. Christians understood that all human life was sacred because all humans were the children of a common Father. Racism splintered the human family. The love of God and the love of neighbor is one love.[13]

Dr. Kelsey's classroom lectures were a work of art. He used exegesis to squeeze every ounce of hidden, historical meaning from the Bible, and then challenged his students to find the modern-day application. Biblical miracles—animals that spoke, the appearance of angels, virgin births, and physical healings—were not dismissed as antimodern relics, but premodern stories full of modern truths that led to the creation of faithful Christians and the practice of true loving community. He loved to say, "The message of Jesus is not a message for the mere improvement of this life. It is a message concerning a completely new life. . . . It is revolutionary."[14]

Kelsey taught that Christian morality called for self-abandonment and self-denial. "We should turn ourselves over completely to God so that God may act through us. . . . The question is not what can man do? But what does God demand? and What is God doing?" His favorite Bible verses were Matthew 5:44–45, "Love your enemies, bless them that curse you, do good to them that hate you, and pray for them which despitefully use you, and persecute you; That ye may be the children of your Father which is in heaven." Christian love was the answer, he lectured. Every human being was made in the image of God, therefore, every Christian was called to love, even one's enemies. "We are not commanded to love our enemies in order to bring our enemies around to loving us," Kelsey lectured. It was a desirable end, but not the ultimate end. Following God was the goal of Christian ethics. "We are commanded . . . to love our enemies," Dr. Kelsey told his students, "because God does!"[15]

This was not a weak, passive love. Christianity demanded an active resistance to evil. When confronted—cursed, despitefully used, or persecuted—Christian love demanded moral protest. One should never inflict violence upon one's enemy. The best expression of Christian love was working nonviolently to defeat evil systems, not people.

"I had believed that Jesus' 'turn the other cheek' philosophy and the 'love your enemies' philosophy could only be useful when individuals were in conflict with other individuals," ML reflected. It seemed when racial groups and nations were in conflict, "a more realistic approach seemed necessary." But Professor Kelsey helped ML see the error of his way. The way of Jesus revolutionized all relationships, including communal and national life. The goal of a Christian protest was to bring communal life in harmony with the Gospel. The aim was always justice and democracy, "not the substitution of one tyranny for another." As Professor Kelsey told his students, Christian protest always sought "the good of all."[16]

Kelsey introduced students to Henry David Thoreau as one example. It was a transformative meeting for ML. Students read Thoreau's 1849 essay, "Civil Disobedience." Originally published as "Resistance to Civil Government," the essay argued that citizens had a moral obligation to nonviolently disobey unjust laws. "This," ML wrote, "was my first intellectual contact with the theory of nonviolent resistance." ML was inspired by Thoreau's choice to go to jail rather than pay taxes that supported the Mexican-American War and the spread of slavery. "[I was] fascinated by the idea of refusing to cooperate with an evil system," ML noted. "I was so deeply moved that I re-read the work several times. I became convinced then that non-cooperation with evil is as much a moral obligation as is cooperation with good."[17] ML had this impulse in his heart when he refused to give up his seat on the bus when he was fifteen. But Thoreau provided him with the intellectual reasoning behind the impulse.

The course had ML enraptured. He never experienced someone break down Scripture like Dr. Kelsey. Mays's presidential lectures outlined how the Black church could perfect American democracy, but Professor Kelsey's lectures illustrated the biblical support. The course made young King grow in the faith. He heard the sayings of Jesus and the prophets all his life, but Professor Kelsey made him hear the call of Jesus anew.[18]

"Martin stood out in class," Dr. Kelsey noted years later. It was not simply because ML was an A student. It was the way ML personalized the lessons. "He absorbed Jesus' teachings with his whole being." Kelsey remembered that when he lectured on the biblical Jesus and the calling of the disciples, he witnessed the calling of another disciple. ML's eyes would light up. His face would be transfigured with his characteristic wide, cheeky smile. ML's reactions touched the professor. Decades later, Kelsey noted, "The sight of a young man just seventeen years old responding to the 'hard sayings' of Jesus in rapturous delight had its effect upon me."[19]

ML cherished his class assignments. Through "critical reflection," Professor Kelsey noted years later, ML met Christ, again. Indeed, ML's view of the Bible was completely revolutionized in Dr. Kelsey's class. "I came to see," ML joyously admitted years later, "that behind the legends and myths of the Book were many profound truths which one could not escape." The papers and exams are among the few undergraduate assignments ML kept. He journeyed through the Bible using a historical-critical approach. He studied ancient Near Eastern culture and how it differed from modern American culture. "We no longer see the naive anthropomorphic God," he wrote for one of his exams. There was no longer a need to attribute human form or characteristics to God. God was a "holy and spiritual" entity. ML examined pseudonymous authorship. He wrote about literary

criticism of biblical texts. And he surveyed the role of human beings and traditions in the formation of the Bible itself. "Books were
chosen in the Old Testament on the basis of there [*sic*] moral and
spiritual fulfillment," he noted in a test right before Christmas 1946.
In one of his last tests in the yearlong course, he concluded the Bible
was not a staid text, but a book of "progressive revelation."[20]

ML was especially attracted to the truths spoken by the prophets of the Old Testament. "It is obvious," he noted with newfound
confidence in another blue-book exam "that prophets address
themselves to the conditions existing in their time. Prophecy is a
moral, not a magical thing." Prophets are not so much concerned
with supernaturally predicating the future as they are with fixing
the moral and political realities of the present. Later, in a foreboding essay for another class, he would write about how societies
tend to handle religious leaders who seriously challenge the moral
and political status quo: "What is societies [*sic*] reaction to such
men? It has reacted, and always will re-act, in the only way open to
it. It destroys such men."[21]

Indeed, one truth he came to embrace in the course and for the
rest of his life was the fact that even the righteous, those who oppose
evildoers, will experience pain and suffering. In an essay question on
"the problem of the book of Job," ML found meaning in the pain
and suffering experienced by the righteous Job. "Job ended up seeing
God," he wrote. "The righteous shall see God."[22]

ML was also mesmerized with the prophet Amos. The eponymous book of the Bible presents Amos as an average citizen who
answered a divine call to be a prophet. Amos addressed the corrupt
governing structure and empty worship of a nation, calling the nation to dedicate itself to justice. ML's favorite verse was from chapter 5, in which Amos speaks for God, declaring, "Take away from

me the noise of your songs, but let justice roll down like water, and righteousness like a mighty stream." God was not interested in the conspicuous praise and worship of governing leaders while they committed and allowed injustice. ML would famously adopt this line in his own preaching.

Teacher and pupil developed a lasting relationship. After class ML followed Kelsey to his office for further conversation. He scheduled visits at the professor's home and, as Kelsey comedically remembered, any number of other locations where ML could manage to bend his ear. "I liked to get in over my head," ML recalled in a 1957 interview with *Time* magazine and then bombard professors like Kelsey "with questions." ML was seeking more than just a closer relationship with his professor; he was seeking a closer, renewed relationship with the Jesus of whom Dr. Kelsey spoke.[23]

ML's renewed relationship to the faith was not just one of intellect, but also emotion. He had long believed that the emotionalism of Black Protestantism hindered the church from being a vehicle of modernity. He despised the shouting and foot stomping. "I revolted," ML admitted. "I didn't understand it, and it embarrassed me." He doubted Black religion "could be intellectually respectable as well as emotionally satisfying."[24] His embarrassment and doubts were put to rest during Professor Kelsey's course. ML learned there was nothing wrong with expressive worship. In fact, it was part of the Black religious experience stemming from West Africa. Emotions in worship did not need to be eliminated, they just needed to be channeled in the right direction. Religious fervor did not begin and end in the sanctuary, it had to flow out into the world. Every passionate "Amen" uttered during worship had to be matched with passionate action in the world. The same hands that fervently clapped and the same feet that tapped during worship needed to be just as committed to work and to stride toward freedom.

Professor Kelsey was right: ML met Christ anew during his class. He saw ML experience the fascination and majesty of the life and teachings of Christ. ML also came to realize that human beings perpetually fall short of the exulted Christ. "Accordingly, humility is engendered and the sense of the constant need of divine grace enriches the human spirit," Professor Kelsey observed in his student. "It was this kind of religious experience which was the power and source of Martin's life of non-violence."[25] ML carried this duality of grace and guilt with him for the rest of his life.

ML forever pinpointed the course as a transformative moment. He told parishioners, journalists, and anyone who would listen that Dr. Kelsey, along with the steady influence of Dr. Mays, forced him to change his mind about the intellectual respectability of the ministry and emotional worship. As he told an interviewer in 1967, "Those two men changed my life and affected me very profoundly." "Both were ministers, both deeply religious," he often repeated, "and yet both were learned men, aware of modern thinking."[26] In addition to Mays's weekly lectures, Kelsey's course helped him resolve the conflict between the faith of his father—the faith he learned at Ebenezer—and the faith he was learning at Morehouse. ML had entered the course very cynical of biblical Christianity. "My studies," he acknowledged—from biology to the History of Western Civilization—"had made me skeptical, and I couldn't see how many of the facts of science could be squared with religion." Dr. Kelsey changed all that. The professor introduced ML to a Bible that was not preoccupied with magic, but morality, justice, and human flourishing. "[It] convinced me that religion could be intellectually respectable as well as spiritually satisfying."[27]

This was the Christianity that ML had desperately sought. As an adult, he came to believe that his experience of being agnostic as a preteen and becoming a true believer during his late teens actually strengthened his faith. "The fact that I had challenged the church and then come back and was able to live with it," he said, actually "deepened my faith."[28] Indeed, in Kelsey's class ML discovered a faith he could proclaim in good conscience. It was a faith that could save souls and save the soul of America, pushing the nation to be true to its founding documents. It was a faith he could live with and die for.

The course pushed ML to raise the white flag of surrender. No more inner turmoil about the ministry. No more doubts about his experience in Connecticut. No more late-night monologues with his friends, begging for affirmation and confirmation of his disgruntlements with the church and the ministry. He was no longer seeking excuses for his future. That was ML the shy freshman, the struggling sophomore. "During my junior year," ML joyfully reminisced, "I changed my mind." Years later, he would tell *Harper's Magazine*, "that inner urge grasped me and I couldn't stay away." He was not quite ready to tell his parents. But he wanted all his friends to know he had been captured, especially all those who had listened to his doubts and fears. William G. Pickens, his friend and fellow tobacco boy, was one of the first he told. As their junior year ended, ML spotted him at the campus snack bar. "Garfield, I want you to be the first to know," Pickens remembered ML saying, gushing with pride and glee. "I have figured out how I will be able to be a minister and still have social purpose." Pickens was thrilled for his friend. He knew the inner "turmoil" ML had been experiencing. But he was not surprised. "ML, that's great news," Pickens recalled telling ML. "I told you you would be a preacher."

All Robert Williams could do was laugh when he heard. Finally, he thought, ML had come to his senses.[29]

• • •

If ML was going to represent a God of love and grace, he knew he needed to overcome his hate toward white Americans. ML's resentment had persisted through his first two years of college. Every news story of racial discrimination and violence was fuel for the flames. It was the propellent for "Kick Up Dust," while the mundane—such as the everyday indignity of inferior bathrooms, services, and facilities, and racial epithets—fanned the flames. White America had hated, used, cursed, and persecuted him his entire life, now he had to learn to love and bless them that persecuted him.

His parents constantly pointed him to Christ's prescriptions for his pain and anger: The Sermon on the Mount. When he wept in his mother's lap on account of losing his first friends because they were white and he was a "nigger," his parents reminded him that the faith called him to "love your enemies." When the bus driver cursed at him for refusing to give up his seat he was reminded that the Bible advised him to "bless them that curse you." Every time a white parent chastised their child for playing hide-and-seek with ML in the grocery store, he was summoned to "do good to them that hate you." When he was refused equal service on the train because he was Black, he was reminded to "pray for those that despitefully use you." And when a white woman slapped ML in the face because she wrongly believed he had stepped on her foot, Jesus beckoned him to "love those that persecute you."

But now those very same words had new meaning. They were not the empty platitudes of his parents, nor premodern biblical superstitions. These were the tough sayings of Jesus, and thanks to Dr. Kelsey, ML went beyond "the legends and myths of the Book," as he described them, to discover "the many profound truths which one could not escape."

ML challenged his hate, face-to-face. He joined the Intercollegiate Council and Forum, an interracial group comprised of Black students from Morehouse, Spelman, Morris Brown, and Atlanta University, along with white students from Emory and Georgia Tech. For weeks at home, ML raved about the group. Dad took little notice of his son's rays of joy; that is, until he realized the group was integrated. Daddy King was a captive of history, a past that taught him not to trust white leaders. Even the best well-intentioned white clergy often could not escape the clutches of white supremacy. He burned with anger. "I don't like it, ML!" he remembered shouting at his son. He demanded his son quit the council. "You don't need to risk any betrayals from them," he berated his junior, "and that's mainly what you'll get."[30]

ML understood. The weight of resentment was still anchored in his own heart. But, he told his father, he had to take the risk. Hate was too easy. "Dad," the son calmly lectured, "I know I could resent every person in the white race, and it would be easy. That's the point. It would be too easy, and I know the answer to so much of this is more complicated." He forced hope upon himself; hope that he could forgive white Americans, and hope that white Americans could rediscover their humanity and come to grips with the evils of white supremacy. To do otherwise—to make hatred a home— would make him and his father the very kind of people they claimed to be fighting. If he had learned anything at Morehouse, he told his dad, he learned that a moral fight had to be fueled with morality. No matter the enemy, they had to act morally. "There is time," he counseled his dad. "I know we have time if we build from among all the groups we can depend on and trust. And I know they're out there!"[31]

The inner wounds of white supremacy—wounds Daddy King

allowed to fester—made distrust seep from his veins. He did not want his son to experience an ounce of the disappointment he had. ML, as was his habit, listened politely to his father's ranting, robotically saying, "Yes. Uh huh. I see." His father knew his son well enough to recognize when he was fighting a losing battle. ML was not going to quit, but maybe he would pull back. "We've got to work with them, God knows this," his dad pivoted. "But be careful about these meetings, this willingness to trust those who can be friends or enemies from one day to the next." But it was to no avail. "Even in my desire to make him a little more cautious," Daddy King admitted, "I'd run out of arguments." ML continued going to the meetings with a heart that was as scared as it was open.[32]

The group met monthly in the belly of the beast: the all-white male Emory University. ML forced himself to confront his feelings even as the superiority of Emory's facilities confronted him at every meeting. ML, as a newly committed minister, opened his heart and allowed the Emory students to work on it.

For Emory, hosting Black students at the white Methodist university was forward thinking at the time. Georgia state law denied tax exempt status to private schools that practiced racial integration in admissions. The meetings were the closest the students could get to learning together without breaking the law. The interracial group gathered to listen to faculty and guest speakers address poverty, prison reform, and the ill effects of segregation upon whites and Blacks. But more importantly, they listened to one another. They shared their experiences as fellow residents of Atlanta. Although they lived and went to school only a few miles from one another, they existed in two totally different worlds.

The exchanges were charged. ML and the Morehouse students

came face-to-face with men who resembled and even sounded like the segregationists and Klansmen who oppressed them. They bared their souls to the grandsons of Confederate soldiers. They shared their bone-trembling tales of discrimination with the children of men who shepherded segregated churches and operated segregated businesses. They shared their experiences of segregated movie houses, the indignity of paying the same fare as white passengers but being pushed to the back of every train and bus. Stories of being prohibited from Atlanta's city parks and public swimming pools or dilapidated recreational facilities abounded. The white Emory students heard, perhaps for the first time, that what they took for granted in their daily lives was a privilege, one that Black students could not enjoy nor fathom.

These white-male college students were told by their fathers, mothers, and forebearers that it was their God-given duty to perpetuate the America the Morehouse men struggled to transform.

But in their own way, the white students refused to hold up their end of the bargain with their parents or ancestors. They joined the interracial student group to try, in some manner, to make a change. Joining the group was a small, radical step. The aim of racial segregation was not just physical separation, but dehumanization; to prevent the recognition of Black humanity and to perpetuate white innocence at all cost. Every interracial gathering was a challenge. It physically brought Black and white together in equality and presented Black and white flesh as equal flesh.

The white students listened, with shock, to their Morehouse interlocutors. They affirmed the extraordinary and quotidian travails of their crosstown colleagues—the challenges of travel, the difficulty of learning in overcrowded schools, the toil of securing paid labor, the indignity of Jim Crow signs, and the loss of loved ones—mothers, fathers, uncles, aunts, cousins, neighborhoods—who dared to challenge these strictures. The racial revelations planted the seeds of guilt and accountability, seeds that bore the fruit of commitment. The white students pledged to change the world they had inherited.

But the white students were not the only ones changed. Years later, ML would write that his resentment dissipated as a result of the meetings. "I did not conquer this anti White feeling," ML confessed, "until . . . I came in contact with white students through working in the interracial organization."[33] Standing face-to-face with these white men changed him. Hearing their desire to end segregation inspired him. Their voices, with their white Southern drawls, sounded like the barks and curses he heard as he traveled throughout life. Yet their confessions that they often lacked the courage to stand up against white supremacy moved him. It helped him to see the humanity of white people, something ML rarely witnessed in Southern whites. He recognized that racism had not just distorted white people, it had also distorted his own heart. "As I got to see more of white people," he confessed, "my resentment was softened, and a spirit of cooperation took its place."[34]

The interracial group opened the door for ML to share his self, his gifts, his talent, and his time. He began to display a remarkable comfort with the group helping others to also feel at ease while engaging in charged exchanges. He passionately conveyed his desire to topple Jim Crow. He helped everyone to see that racism was not inevitable. Integration and equal opportunity were necessary if America was going to be true to its founding documents. The Christian church had to lead the way if America was ever going to reach such a promised land. He fervently argued for these ideas, while managing to comfort and win over his white colleagues. He displayed a level of single-minded commitment and grace that even impressed his professor. "He was so convincing!" Professor Brazeal noted. ML was "able to cause people to develop confidence in his ability." ML's leadership skills were bubbling to the surface. "We didn't know that he would blossom into the leader that he became," Professor Brazeal admitted, but ML's leadership in the group was undeniable.[35]

It was a sign of things to come. ML would reflect that "the wholesome relations we had in the Intercollegiate Council convinced me that we had many white persons as allies, particularly among the younger generation." From that day forward, ML pledged to work with any white person who was interested in putting an end to white supremacy, both in their individual soul and the soul of the nation. ML would spend the rest of his life working with white people, helping them to see Black humanity and to rediscover their own.[36]

• • •

ML had surrendered his will to the ministry. He surrendered his resentment of white people. Now he had to surrender to the Morehouse Minister's Union. The group was comprised of students in the Morehouse School of Religion, pre-theology students and students who were preparing for the ministry. The objective of the club was to provide support and dialogue concerning the promises and challenges of the ministry.[37]

It made logical sense for ML to join. Membership was a rite of passage for all Morehouse men going into the ministry. However, the reputation of the Minister's Union made joining difficult. It embodied everything ML had previously believed about the ministry. At Morehouse, theology students were thought to lack intellectual creditability. It was considered the easiest course of study, a degree for those who could not manage a "real" major. The debates spilled over into the campus newspaper. *The Maroon Tiger* monitored the "hot" dispute around campus concerning "the ignorance that exists among the pre-theological students." It had become widely accepted on campus that too many students majored in religion "because they don't have enough mentality to prepare themselves for other fields."[38]

ML was allergic to such slurs. He was trying to carve out his own space in the ministry as a preacher who was emotive but was also intellectual. He had announced it from the rooftops across campus. He was going to be a learned preacher. How could he now join an organization whose motto, the campus organ teased, was "The spirit over the intellect"?[39]

Nevertheless, ML joined the group and started to identify as a "pre-theology student." He heard all the jokes, the whispers, and the ridicule. But he wanted everyone to know that he was different. While the perception of the Minister's Union was that its members believed "the only requisite for entering the ministry is to accept religion as it is, to 'put a little gravy in it,' and throw it to their parishioners." ML had other ideas. He set his sights on breaking the mold, becoming an enlightened minister. He would usher in a new reputation for the Minister's Union, fulfilling the call of *The Maroon Tiger* for a preacher who "makes use of other fields of inquiry," a minister who "emphasized 'tuition over intuition.'"[40]

ML, who had sprouted to his adult height of five seven by his junior year, made known his plans not to conform. In the group's annual photo, all the distinguished older gentlemen donned suits with ties, befitting a traditional minister. ML refused. The young man known for his fancy ties sported a sports coat with no tie. ML was going to be a minister, but not the traditional minister many had in mind.

Picture of Morehouse Minister's Union, 1946–1947.
ML is in the second row, second from right.

• • •

With direction came purpose. ML's fullhearted decision to make ministry his destiny gave him a newfound confidence. He no longer sat quietly in the back of the classroom. He felt awake to his education. And he believed he could help his classmates feel the same. The fledging minister began urging his peers to rediscover the exhilaration of education. As his junior year drew to a close, ML used the bullhorn of the student newspaper to shout his convictions. He drafted "The Purpose of Education," a homily that drew from President Mays's Tuesday lectures, but was remixed for his own generation.

"As I engage in the so-called 'bull sessions' around and about the school," ML lectured, "I too often find that most college men have a misconception of the purpose of education." Too many students believed the point of education was to equip them with the skills to exploit the masses or gain wealth. Both views were wrong, ML thought. The purpose of education was twofold: "Intelligence plus character." The former taught one how to think critically, how to filter truth from the chaff of lies and bias that flowed freely from the pulpit and the press. But critical thinking was not enough. One needed a commitment to morality. "The most dangerous criminal may be the man gifted with reason, but with no morals," ML wrote.[41]

Education without character was a great menace to society, he explained. ML used Georgia Governor Eugene Talmadge as exhibit A. Talmadge was a graduate of the University of Georgia, had an honorary degree from Oglethorpe University, and was a member of Phi Beta Kappa, one of the most prestigious academic honor societies recognizing elite achievement in the liberal arts and sciences. He was also an honorary member of the Ku Klux Klan. He ordered the firing of University of Georgia faculty and staff who championed integrated classrooms, including the dean of the School of Education. And in the 1946 Georgia gubernatorial election, Talmadge ran for a fourth term using a race-baiting campaign slogan: "The only issue in this race is White Supremacy." Voters agreed. He won a fourth term. "Mr. Talmadge could think critically and intensively," ML declared, "yet he contends that I am an inferior being. Are those the types of men we call educated?"[42]

ML closed with a warning for Black and white, as well as for students and teachers. "The complete education gives one not only power of concentration, but worthy objectives upon which to concentrate. . . . If we are not careful, our colleges will produce a group of close-minded, unscientific, illogical propagandists, consumed with immoral acts. Be careful, 'brethren!' Be careful, teachers!"[43]

• • •

ML got down to business during his junior year. Within the pages of the Bible he discovered a map for truth, love, and community. He found a way to merge his love of learning and his love of neighbor into a meaningful career—a quest for knowledge and respectability combined with his desire to serve. And he proclaimed it to all who would listen. The shy, quiet student morphed into a loudmouth for justice and equality. In doing so, he discovered a profession worthy of his time, talents, and treasure. He found his life by deciding he would lose it for the cause of Christ.

As the school year came to a close, he still did not tell his parents about his decision to preach. As a teenager attempting to test his independence, he preferred to leave some things left untold. Besides, he did not want the coronation his father would surely orchestrate. He told a friend that he was not prepared for the attention and notoriety that came with being a minister, especially one who would have such a momentous stage as Ebenezer. He simply did not want to be wrecked by "the potholes" of fame.[44] He did not feel ready. He was just learning to be at peace with his newfound self and his newfound destiny. ML was ready to preach a gospel of freedom and equality. He was ready to be Minister Martin Luther King Jr.

He was just not ready to tell his parents.

Instead, ML decided to return to the place where it all began: Connecticut. He told his parents he was headed back to earn money. Tuition and fees at Morehouse had almost doubled since he was admitted. At the price of $90 per semester, plus an annual fee of $28, the cost of attendance had soared to more than $200 a year. The teenager yearning to be independent could earn that in the tobacco fields. There were plenty of summer jobs in Atlanta where he could engage in less strenuous labor and still make that kind of money.

His dad had plenty of connections to such jobs. But the trip back to Connecticut was about more than just money.

The steamy tobacco fields were the perfect place to live out the call he had just accepted, away from the spotlight and lofty pulpit of Ebenezer. Just a few barns and a few young men: his very first captive audience.

In the midst of exercising his calling in God's country, he would painfully discover that even God's country was not cleansed from the sins of racial violence and discrimination.

28
THE POLICE

I t started with a party, as most tales of teenage revelry gone wrong
seem to.

• • •

ML was busy preaching that summer—crafting his own voice with
a deliberateness derived from his decision to enter the ministry. His
first summer in Connecticut he preached as a novice. The second
summer he preached like a preacher. Dr. Mays had given his brain a
revised image of what a preacher could be. Dr. Kelsey had given him
new eyes to see the Bible. Channie had revived his love for literature
and the sound of poetic flourishes rolling off his tongue.

ML preached about loving one's enemies and waging peace. Now
that he knew his life's destiny, he preached with revived purpose.

"He would preach about Christian subjects that were normally
heard in a Christian church," Pickens remembered of the 1947 summer. But unlike the summer of 1944, ML was not just trying his
hand at preaching, he was preaching like a man who was preparing
for the rest of his life. "It seemed to me that he was not only whet-

ting his appetite but developing his skills as a minister." Pickens recalled.[1]

The days had a monotonous routine. Early mornings, breakfast
was served by ML. Then he worked in the sweltering tobacco fields.
Lunch. More baking fields. Dinner. And on Sunday, a passionate sermon by ML.

The men then enjoyed their time of recreation.

Lights out.

Repeat.

The Morehouse men did occasionally interrupt their summer
ritual with a party. ML joined in. He was no longer the perpetually pensive college student. The burden of finding a path to an
exceptional future had been lifted, freeing him to be an ordinary
teen.

After one of these parties, ML was stopped by the police. Larry
Williams, ML's childhood friend and a member of Ebenezer, heard
about it back on campus. Rumors spread, claiming there was beer
and teenage horseplay involved. But other than that one secondhand
account, no concrete details have emerged. There was no arrest. No
jail time. And no citation.[2]

Biographers have paid little attention to the incident, trivializing
it as a harmless encounter. But for ML, or for any Black person, there
was no such thing as a minor police stop in the 1940s. It was an era
when police stops involving Black Americans often ended tragically,
with no evidence of prior wrongdoing. No citations. No tickets.
Only the crime of being Black.

For most Black Americans, being accosted by police was the formal ritual marking one's entry into adulthood. ML was eighteen
years old in the summer of 1947. It was his turn to become a Black
adult male.

• • •

Given the lack of detail in that secondhand account, one can only speculate on the location of the festivities and the resulting police encounter. A party at the Bond Hotel in Hartford that summer is a likely candidate. It was planned to be the party of all parties. The men were excited. Working long hours in the hot tobacco fields gave them plenty of time, too much time, to plan their outfits, the party, and how to exploit the freedom of God's country.

Their excitement was matched by a group of coeds from Spelman College. Those young women were in Hartford along with twenty-five other women from fourteen different colleges for the Students in Industry Project. For two months, the students stayed on the campus of Hartford Seminary and were tasked with finding employment in an industry of their choice. They were to work their jobs and study the endemic problems of labor and management within the industry. Twice a week the Industry Project hosted industry business executives and pelted them with polite but stern questions regarding labor conditions. The students did all the cooking and cleaning at the Seminary, and even attended vesper services every evening. Weekends were reserved for much-needed free time and opportunities to explore the leisure activities of Hartford. The Morehouse men, especially returning tobacco boys like ML, were all too willing to show them the way.[3]

The "dancing party" was special. The Spelmanites wrote glowingly about the affair for the student newspaper, and the national Black press covered the party as well. The fifty Morehouse men were the perfect hosts and guides. They traded in their dungarees and workshirts for their Sunday best. Some wore their finest suit, while others purchased brand-new suits from that summer's Malcolm Little, the traveling salesman outfitting the tobacco boys. Nothing was too good for the party of the summer.[4]

Their attire matched the party décor. The Bond Hotel was the newest and largest hotel in Hartford. Only the vaulted ceilings of the exquisite ballroom could cap the high hopes the coeds had for the party. They had food, and they had drinks. The Morehouse men returning from World War II were old enough to purchase and consume alcohol. ML was underage, but that did not stop him. He was not a heavy drinker, but like teenagers before and after him, he sampled. A little dabble here, a quick sip there. And they had music and dancing. For ML, drinking was like dancing. It was an activity that he believed was harmless—a point of departure from the traditional Baptist faith of his childhood.[5]

The dancing was intense. The students stayed on the floor all night, pausing only to sing their respective school songs, putting their Morehouse-Spelman mark on the festivities.[6]

Then it was back to dancing, sweating out all their cares and labors. The joy saturated them. They were free from Jim Crow laws and free from the eyes of their foremen, supervisors, and chaperones.[7]

ML knew this feeling so well. The young king of the dance floor displayed his lindy-hopping, jitterbugging, gyrating, laughing, joking, swooning, and flirting like an eighteen-year-old does when they have not a care in the world.

After the party, old friends said goodbye, with pledges to see one another back on campus. New friends exchanged contact information on scraps of paper, made sacred by the promise of young love. ML walked out into the night, floating on the high of the dance. He had money in his pocket. He once again secured his throne as king of the dance floor. His future life as a minister awaited. Life was good.

Until it wasn't.

It is very possible that ML had his encounter with the police following the party. By the summer of 1947, Hartford, and the entire
urban region, was on red alert concerning the dangers of young
Black Southern migrants. "We found prejudice when we were off
the farm," Alfred Chambers noted. The Jamaican-born tobacco boy
recalled that anytime they ventured into the city and the surrounding areas, police officers "would stop us and question where we were
going." Fitzroy Parkinson added, "They would want to arrest us for
the slightest thing."[8]

The top law enforcement agency in the country sounded the
alarm. J. Edgar Hoover, the director of the FBI, was busy warning
the nation of a rise in juvenile crime following World War II, especially caused by eighteen-year-old men like ML. The nation's top
cop told the nation's policemen to be on the lookout for "a growing infection in our society": an era of juvenile lawlessness. Hoover
placed the blame on the lack of individual morality. His "FBI Law
Enforcement Bulletin," a monthly "confidential" mailing that was
"restricted" to state and local law enforcement officials, warned that
eighteen-year-old men were leading the nation in arrests, according
to FBI data—data that was not verified by any other party. It warned
"irresponsible youth are a constant danger to law enforcement officers and law-abiding citizens." The FBI Law Enforcement Bulletin also supplied local newspapers with unverified tales of drunken
youths committing murder, vandalism, and assault. Hoover directed
the nation's law enforcement officers to be on the lookout for juve-
niles who seemed destined to be "tomorrow's gangsters." In one way
or another, ML would remain a high priority for J. Edgar Hoover's
FBI for his entire adult life.

Locals decided Black migrants fit the description. Southern

Black migrants had begun pouring into the state, especially Hartford. During the decade, more than twenty thousand Black migrants
made their way to the state, many deciding to make Hartford their
home, unleashing a 200 percent increase in the city's Black population. They were disproportionately young, under the age of twenty-
five, and male, just like ML. The demographic shift unleashed a
torrent of xenophobia. Newspapers across the Northeast and Connecticut ran stories warning of a crime wave caused by "itinerant
southern negroes."[9]

But crime statistics did not support these fears. Crime did not
proportionately rise with the growth of Black urban populations.
The Connecticut Interracial Commission, founded in 1944 to handle the state's changing racial demographics, found that migrants
were often the victims, not the perpetrators, of crime. A 1946 report
noted that Black migrants experienced illegal discrimination in the
areas of employment, housing, education, and public accommodations. In fact, in 1947, the commission found that when racial discrimination was reported, too often policemen "threatened to arrest
the complainant for breach of the peace" instead of investigating
the complaint. The commission recommended special police training to acquaint officers with the rights of African Americans to public accommodations, and to teach them to abide by civil rights laws
during "interracial" police encounters.[10]

But facts, figures, and commission reports rarely deter those invested in narratives of racial "crime waves" and "invasions." Journalists and residents advocated for the police to accost Southern Black
migrants, discouraging them from settling in Connecticut.[11]

In 1947, *The Hartford Chronicle*, the city's Black newspaper,
warned that police were bent on "promoting a little private crime
wave of their own."[12] Front-page headlines of white publications

seemed to confirm it: "Police Determined to Shoot to Kill to End Itinerant Crime Wave"; while another said point-blank: "Police Patience Exhausted as They Crack Down on Southern Muggers with Bullets to Check Crime Wave; Will Shoot to Kill." Incidents of Black men being shot by white policemen while "in the act of committing a crime" began to increase as if it were a sport. There was no stated police policy to shoot Black migrants. However, according to one newsmagazine, "there was a general understanding" emerging among policeman of the urban North: Run Black Southern migrants out of town or "use them as first-class targets for pistol shooting." An unnamed Northern policeman confirmed this modus operandi to the media:

> I think the best method is to place a bullet in his head. That will do more to check the mugging and law-breaking going on in the city by that bunch of men and women more than anything else.[13]

ML and his crew may have been swept up in this hysteria.

The discriminatory practices of society guaranteed he would always fit the description. He was young. He was Black. He was male. He was Southern. He was a migrant worker. He was a top threat.

That was the political atmosphere ML walked into as he departed the party.

And whether it was that night or at some other point during that summer, he was stopped by the police.[14]

Being held by law enforcement as an African American male, especially in the 1940s, was never a minor incident. There was no such thing as a routine stop. Violent and degrading police stops were all too common for Black Americans. It was an ever-present nightmare. After the Civil War, law enforcement evolved into a system of maintaining a racial hierarchy. With a few exceptions, local, state, and federal police departments were restricted to white officers. These officers regularly inflicted indiscriminate violence against Black citizens with impunity thanks to a complicit legal system.

ML knew the reality of police brutality. He had been warned about it his entire life. Instructions on how to handle a policeman had been drilled into his being. His earliest memories were stained with blood spilled in Atlanta: police beatings at the Atlanta train station, Klansmen, and police, sometimes one and the same, assaulting and killing African Americans under the banner of law and order.

Indeed, ML's teenage years, like many Black teens then and now, were filled with such police violence. Black newspapers read like a roll call memorial of Black Americans who became targets of police violence while they were simply trying to go about their everyday affairs.

On March 26, 1944, when ML was fifteen, a white mob with the help of Mississippi police took the life of Reverend Isaac Simmons by shooting him three times and cutting out his tongue because they wanted his prosperous farmland. Police arrested his family, who witnessed the crime, and threatened them against testifying.

Three months later, on June 16, 1944, fourteen-year-old George Stinney became the youngest American to be executed. The state of South Carolina sentenced him to death by the electric chair for the rape and murder of two white girls. There was no incriminating evidence.

On June 12, 1945, when ML was sixteen, Niecey Brown, a seventy-four-year-old Black woman, died from a fractured skull after George Booker, an off-duty Alabama police officer, forcibly entered her house with no warrant and beat her with a bottle. Her crime: She denied him entry into her home. During Brown's September 1945 trial, his lawyer cautioned the all-white jury, "[I]f we convict this brave man who is upholding the banner of white supremacy by his actions, then we may as well give all our guns to the niggers and let them run the Black Belt." Booker was acquitted of all charges.

On February 12, 1946, when ML was seventeen, World War II veteran Sergeant Isaac Woodard was beaten unconscious by South Carolina Police Chief Lynwood Shull. His crime: asking a Greyhound bus driver to stop for a restroom break. The beating left the uniformed Woodard permanently blind.

And at the start of ML's junior year of college, the lynching of Maceo Brown, as well as the Moore's Ford Bridge lynching in Georgia in July 1946 pushed ML to his boiling point, compelling him to write his first letter to the editor.[15]

Now at eighteen, he was face-to-face with the threat of the same nightmare. Surely, the flashing police lights must have set off memories of all the names and unnamed souls who met their end on account of a police stop.

As the officer approached ML, the officer likely could not discern that this was the face of a studious college student; nor could he have known that it was the face of a young man who had recently dedicated his life to the ministry of the gospel of the meek and lowly Jesus Christ; that it was the face of a young man who would change America. All he saw was the face of someone who was labeled the face of crime.

One moment ML was having the time of his life with his friends; the next he faced the possibility of losing his life.

ML was indeed one of the lucky ones. He was just questioned and accosted but not shot or murdered. Things could have turned out differently. This particular cop let him go.

His first police encounter disabused him of the teenage myth of immortality. It was so significant, he told at least one friend about it when he returned to campus in the fall. But he did not tell his parents.

He decided it was time to tell them something else: his future plans. He had reached the point of no return. There was no turning back.

29
MINISTER ML KING

When the phone rang at 193 Boulevard, it seemed like an ordinary phone call, like the ones that had taken place countless times before. When ML was away on the farm, Daddy King recalled, he routinely called his mother in search of the warmth that only her doting voice could provide.

Yet this phone call, in the summer of 1947, was not routine. It changed the course of history.

Daddy King and Alberta recounted the story in an unpublished autobiography of Daddy King.

"Hello?" Alberta said softly when she picked up the phone.

"I am going to preach, Mother Dear," ML hurriedly said. In his excitement and certainty, ML did not notice the silence on the other end. He was happy to fill the void, rattling the receiver with his baritone voice. "Daddy is not going to believe it," he said. ML knew his father too well. Daddy King had given up on the idea of the boy following in his footsteps and accepted what seemed inevitable. He had even begun to steer ML toward the law and away from the ministry, and started falling in love with the idea of his son becoming a successful lawyer endowed with the wealth that accompanied such a career.

"You're going to have to talk to him about it," ML pleaded with his mother. "But my mind is made up," he said, recovering his confidence, and independence. "I'm going to be a preacher!"

Mother Dear kept her quintessential cool. Showing too much excitement would have smothered the eighteen-year-old's sense of autonomy. "You don't know what your daddy will say," she remembered calmly replying. Ever supportive, she told ML, "You know he will be proud if he knows you're going to be a preacher."

"Well, anyway," she remembered ML saying somewhat dismissively, "you talk to him and ask him what I have to do: Whether I have to talk to the deacons to get a hearing to do a trial sermon? Whom do I talk to? Or just what?"

"You don't have to talk to anybody but your daddy," she assured him. Daddy King was the pastor and he called the shots.

"Well," ML compromised, "you talk to him first."

It had all come down to this. Warring with Jim Crow, dreaming of law school, picking tobacco, freely socializing and serving in God's country, and preaching countless sermons in the fields of Connecticut had produced one outcome: ML would be a preacher.

When he returned from his second trip to God's country about a month later, at the tail end of the summer of 1947, ML was immediately greeted by his father at the notorious Terminal Station.

By his own account, Daddy King's greeting felt more like an ambush than a welcome-home reception.

"ML, your mother says you want to preach. Is that true?"

ML answered in the affirmative. "Yes, sir. That is what I'm *going* to do," he said, removing the aspirational desirous "want" from the equation.

"Are you sure of it?" his father asked.

ML just nodded.

"That is not a lucrative field. You won't make much money,"

Daddy King warned. The father had once turned the same pros-ecutorial line of questioning on himself; when he was attending Morehouse in the late 1920s, he had faced his own doubts about continuing his career in the ministry. He had strongly considered leaving the ministry for a more lucrative profession. Now he threw down the same gauntlet at his son's feet.

"You would make a lot more in law or some other calling," Daddy King admonished. "So you should be sure, absolutely sure, that that's what you want to do," he recalled saying.

"I know that," ML reportedly replied confidently. "I'm not look-ing for money. I'm looking forward to serving my fellow man."

A satisfied Daddy King did not waste another second. "When do you want to preach your trial sermon?" he quickly asked.

"As soon as I can," ML replied, equally in a hurry.

Daddy King, attempting to hide his excitement, calmly replied, "Well, we'll arrange it."[1]

• • •

"Can't hold 'em!" Daddy King proudly announced from the front row on a fall afternoon in 1947. The makeshift chapel in the church basement was swelling beyond capacity. Daddy King always sched-uled trial sermons in this multiple-purpose room. The lower ceilings, the smaller seating capacity, and the old wooden lectern were per-fect for neophytes and probationary sermons. The sanctuary was reserved for prime time, for those who had proven themselves wor-thy, those who were licensed and ordained. But the crowd kept filing in to witness the prince of Ebenezer take his step toward destiny. Larry Williams remembers seeing Alberta's face shine with pride as ML's majestic baritone began his sermon, and feet scurried across the 3,200-square-foot fellowship hall looking in vain for a seat. "Can't hold 'em!" Daddy King shouted again, stopping his eighteen-year-old son mid-sentence. "We're going upstairs," the proud pastor declared.

"Wait a minute, brother Pastor," Larry overhead Deacon Edwards say, "it's tradition to hold trial sermons in the basement."

According to Larry, Daddy King quickly dismissed his head deacon. "Yeah, but it's too crowded."

As the congregation made its way upstairs, Larry saw the preacher of the hour give his mother a furtive glance before putting his hand on her shoulder. Larry believed ML was embarrassed by his father's extraordinary measures.[2]

But soon even the pews in the red-carpeted sanctuary were filled. "That was a new experience for us," Daddy King admitted years later. The church was rarely filled to capacity when he preached on Sundays. But ML's first sermon at Ebenezer drew a crowd. "Never before had we seen so many people in that auditorium," Daddy King admitted. "My son was a drawing card."[3]

Friends, family, and parishioners all came out to see the pastor's son. All of them likely had multiple, overlapping motivations for crowding into the sanctuary to hear ML. He had developed a small reputation as a compelling communicator. He won the local Elks contest a few years prior, and he had written a popular, brave letter to the editor a few months before. Others had more sentimental reasons. They had watched ML grow up. He was a son of the church, making him a surrogate son to countless church members. The little boy who had sung about being more like Jesus was now a man committing his life to preaching about Jesus. Georgia Lewis, the family housekeeper, was beaming with joy. The child she had fed and helped to raise was about to preach. Others, perhaps, came out of pure curiosity. Would this be their first chance to catch a glimpse of the young man who would likely be their next pastor? Other souls were probably compelled by disbelief. The rebellious child—the one who was at times unruly while his father preached, the child that had questioned the Bible, the youngster who had doubted the very existence of God, and had run from the pulpit—was now walking into the pulpit.

He did not disappoint. As he ascended the prime-time platform, Georgia Lewis shouted her nervous affirmation. Everybody was nervous: Dad, Mom, and even a few Morehouse friends who came to see the fulfillment of something they had long believed would happen.[4] ML opened his mouth to finish what he started in the church basement, a task that had its true origins in Connecticut.

His sermon title was "Life Is What You Make It." Years later, Larry Williams claimed ML's sermon was a riff on the sermons of others, borrowing and integrating words and phrases from other musicians, authors, and popular preachers. Williams's memory is, perhaps, influenced by the fact that he and ML used to sneak out of Ebenezer while Daddy King was preaching to go listen to other Black ministers in Atlanta. When the two boys made their respective decisions to pursue the ministry, they made a point to learn and glean from the styles and phrasing they heard in the city's pulpits. But borrowing is a part of the Black preaching tradition. Sermons were not scholarly works to be published, they were to be performed. And like a jazz musician, ML riffed and improvised his sermons, creating new sermonic songs. Songs he would sing until his dying day. A song that still reverberates to this day.[5]

His exact words are lost to history—dust swept off the pews of the old Ebenezer church—but the spirit of what he said and how he said it are not forgotten. Content and delivery are inseparable in Black preaching. It is not just what ML said that day, but also the way he proclaimed it that matters. Like an improvised song, the methods and style of his sermon can be recalled, even if the exact words and notes cannot.[6]

According to Williams and June Dobbs, the sermon was a lecture-style message of encouragement and empowerment to Black Christians. White supremacy was real. It encompassed everything: legislation, education, employment, commerce, even the built environment. Black folk could still shape their own lives according to Christ. Rather than malice or misfortune, Christians should always respond with grace and kindness. They should strive for excellence in everything. They should labor, study, and live as if they were doing it unto Christ. And all should work, in some way, big and small, to make the world a better place, until all of God's children could taste the sweetness of freedom. Christianity was meaningless if it could not make us kinder, freer, and more human. This was the core message of Christianity.[7] It was virtually the same message he had been preaching in Connecticut.

June Dobbs was pleased that her friend did not try to mimic his father. Instead, he combined the styles of the men he admired. He adopted Mays's stance, standing erect, never moving beyond the pulpit. He did not stroll through the aisles and jump on pews like his dad. But he did not completely neglect the emotion of Black preaching, Professor Kelsey helped him overcome his resentment of the pathos of Black religion. He imitated Dr. Kelsey's extensive vocabulary, while displaying controlled but sincere emotion. His sermon built momentum at just the right pace. It started off slow, building to a faster, forceful crescendo. That booming, melodic voice. The pitch-perfect timing. He used his hands to emphasize points. He embodied the Black folk sermon, using repetition to stress his points. He modulated his melodic voice to stress certain words. He hit his first syllables hard and then stretched his vowels, Christianity became: "CHRIS-ti-ANNNN-NI-TEEE. Freedom became, "FREEEEE-dom." It was an amalgamated style that was all his own "He had touch," June recalled, "a way of putting it that went straight to your heart. . . . And he was sincere. He never changed from that."[8]

The church bore witness. At the conclusion of his sermon, the congregation rose to their feet and shouted in affirmation. "His sermon was hailed enthusiastically as a homiletic masterpiece," Reverend King said years later, still beaming with pride and astonishment. His firstborn son owned the moment. ML's rare combination of voice, delivery, intelligence, and sermon structure, his incredulous dad said, "Set [ML] apart from anyone I'd ever heard in my life." This was not the opinion of a dad blinded by parental love. This was the seasoned opinion of Reverend Martin Luther King Sr. ML did not preach like a nervous man on probation. No. ML, he recalled, "preached like a veteran, like a man with years of experience behind him."[9]

ML was a veteran of sorts. Without the help of a microphone, or the elevated platform of a pulpit, he had amplified his booming voice across wood planks and cots in Connecticut for two summers. He learned to preach on the same level as his audience. Not in lofty, cushy sanctuaries, but in ramshackle buildings. He preached not to the upper classes, but to working, dirty, farming boys and men. Soul to soul.

He walked into the church basement as ML.

He departed the main sanctuary with a new name: Minister ML King Jr., assistant pastor of Ebenezar Baptist Church.

30
AN AMERICAN TEENAGE BOY

M L was officially ordained, but he was also every bit a postwar teenager. The eighteen-year-old college senior was not prepared to inherit all that came with the throne of Ebenezer. He was still young. And the same ministry that called him to humility, fidelity, and service also brought extreme adulation and temptation.

Being the prince of Ebenezer brought new clarity, but also the murky lure of seduction. He confided to June Dobbs that mothers of the church, church visitors, and even society women, began throwing themselves, their daughters, and their nieces at him. For some, ML's newfound power was an aphrodisiac, while for others, he represented the assurance of economic security. This was no longer high school puppy love. ML was a man with a future, leading some women to extreme measures to chase him and his promised future. According to June Dobbs, ML told her that women began to approach under the pretext of spiritual fulfillment, seeking prayer, counsel, or comfort, but all too often, he told June, it turned out to be for physical fulfillment. He was shocked how quickly things turned from the spiritual to the flesh. Some propositioned him for marriage, others tried to kiss him, a few, he confided, got him alone, presumably for prayer, and simply began undressing.[1]

He told June he tried to discourage it. There were so many expectations to live up to: those of his father, those of his God, and
those he had for himself. But there were also the dangerous expectations of Black Christian masculinity. Too much Christian piety,
the Morehouse student newspaper argued, was easily equated with
"effeminate prudence." Muscular Christianity called for displays of
"physical prowess" and virile heterosexuality.[2] ML felt this pressure
acutely, making the teenager—like many teenagers—extremely sensitive to how others evaluated him.

Years later, an adult ML purportedly confessed to fellow civil
rights activist Dorothy Cotton that during his later years at Morehouse he suffered from a nagging feeling of insecurity concerning his looks, height, and perceived masculinity. As a minister, as a
leader, and as a Morehouse man, he was expected to stand tall in all
areas of life: a difficult task when one is weighed down by invisible,
yet ever-present insecurities. His dad labeled him "too sensitive." He
did not like to fight. He was shorter than most. He was younger too.
Classmates teased him for it, taunting him as the "Runt." Handsome
suits, ties, and shoes could not atone. Sports were a potential venue
to lay claim to physical prowess, but his stature placed a ceiling on
that.[3]

So, he confided to Dorothy, he tried to escape the shadow of his
stalking insecurities, in part by wooing the girlfriend of the tallest,
"handsomest guy" on campus.[4]

It made his father proud. "He's gone out with some of the finest
girls, beautiful girls," his dad liked to apologetically brag, "and then
he just seems to lose interest."[5]

The reality was a little different. Sometimes ML did lose interest; but at other times, he failed to gain the interest of women, or
they simply lost interest in him. Many biographers have assumed

that ML's dating life was always successful. They have also misunderstood the nature of "dating" in 1940s America. Teenagers were rarely allowed to socialize with the opposite sex without supervision. Dating in this sense meant a man calling upon a girl at her house while being supervised by parents or attending a movie with a third-party chaperone. Yet even in this context, the teenager at times fell into the all-too-common heterosexual male trap of measuring his masculinity by the number of women who were romantically interested in him. It was, Dorothy believed, the start of a lifelong habit, the ailment of a lingering sense of insecurity.[6]

And it all started at Morehouse.

• • •

With his future decided, ML began to embrace more of campus life, starting with intramural basketball.

The basketball court became a space for him to display his masculinity and show that even though he was going to be a minister, he was still able to enjoy life.

He teamed up with his old friends from the neighborhood to form the City Slicks, an intramural squad. The team's name was deliberate. "City slickers" was a popular phrase of the day. The *Atlanta Daily World* referred to the city's pickpockets and thieves as "city slickers." ML and crew—Proctor, Cash, and another Atlanta native, Jefferson C. Nash—adopted the name to let everyone know they were smooth, urbane, popular guys, prepared to steal the ball and wins.[7]

The intramural team put it all on display in Morehouse's seven-hundred-seat gymnasium. The games tipped before varsity games, often drawing enthusiastic crowds that rivaled the varsity game. The intramural games "appealed to everyone" on campus, *The Maroon Tiger* noted. Shockingly, even the notoriously stiff Minister's Union came to the game. No doubt to check out their newest member.[8]

The Minister's Union and fans were introduced to ML's basketball alter ego: "Will Shoot." The City Slickers played against the Be-Bops, the Rattlers, the Hustlers, the Hornets, as well as the team of Florida boys, the boys from Birmingham, Black fraternities, and even faculty. No matter the opponent, they all received the same treatment from ML: bombs away.[9]

The team made it all the way to the championship game during one intramural session. They handled the Crabs, eliminating the freshman squad in the first round of the playoffs. Next, the Slicks stomped the Kappas, 35–14. In the semifinals, ML and crew calmed the "scrappy" Omegas, defeating the eventual third-place finishers by 8 points.[10]

In the championship, they clashed with a team of war veterans who called themselves "Shell Shocked." The teams faced off before a crowd described by the local news as a "loud," "rabid" "colorful fracas."

The war veterans were riddled with injuries during the final game, forcing them to play the second half with only four players. But the war vets were no strangers to long odds, scoring most of their points while shorthanded. Henry "Coot" Warner led the four-man squad. He was seemingly the perfect counterpart to ML—a "husky, ambidextrous" guard just like ML, but he was six feet, 185 pounds. He was a former Benedict College basketball star, turned World War II soldier, who had returned home and become a star Morehouse varsity basketball and football player.

There were no rules against varsity athletes playing intramurals.

Perhaps there should have been. ML was no match for the older, bigger, and stronger man with the "famed set shot." Warner schooled the undersize teenager—and any other Slick that tried to pick his pockets on the court—for an intramural record 32 points (without the help of a three-point line). The shorthanded Shell Shocked shocked the City Slicks, beating them 56–47 to win the championship. Point guard Nash led the City Slicks with 13 points. Will Shoot netted 8 points in the losing effort.[11]

Will Shoot transformed back into ML after the game. Win or lose, he cleansed himself of the stench of selfish play, exchanged shorts, T-shirts, and tank tops for his debonair uniform of collared shirts, dress slacks, sport coats, and fancy shoes. Studying could wait. The newly destined minister stayed around to cheer on the varsity basketball players.

He had the same team spirit during football season, posting up in the stands with the City Slicks to cheer on the fighting Maroon Tigers. He was determined to show that he was going to be a minister who still enjoyed all that life had to offer.

After the varsity games, everybody headed to "the Block." Yates and Milton Drug Store No. 2 sat right outside the campus gates, at the intersection of West Fair and Chestnut Streets, affectionately dubbed "the Block." It was *the* Morehouse hangout. It was close enough to campus that students could walk to it, but far enough to be considered off campus. It was an institution, synonymous with Morehouse social life. "It is almost impossible to conceive of 'Morehouse,'" *The Maroon Tiger* noted in 1947, "unless somewhere in the mind is an image of Yates & Milton No. 2." The Block had all the necessities for postwar college social life—food, a soda fountain, milkshakes, and a jukebox.

And perhaps most importantly, "the Block" was also outside the

"After game bull session is in process at 'The Block.'"
The Maroon Tiger, Senior Edition, 1947.

ML's lifelong muse, noted poet and writer Langston Hughes, at "the Block"
with unidentified students from A.U., Morehouse, and Spelman in 1947 during
a visiting professorship at Atlanta University. Hughes's class does not appear on
ML's college transcript, but it is possible ML attended lectures or socialized
with Hughes at "the Block."

purview of the college administration.[12] On campus, Morehouse kept a watchful eye, policing all social events. *The Morehouse Companion* stipulated the date, time, and place had to be planned in conjunction with the Faculty Social Committee, and then cleared by the Dean's office. Each party, afternoon tea, or dance was required to have at least two faculty members present. And it was the responsibility of the students to plead, beg, and secure "the professors or teachers to chaperone their parties." Faculty chaperones then had to be registered in the Dean's office.[13] However, at "the Block," students only needed to register their food and beverage order and which song they wanted to play on the jukebox.

The soundtrack of "the Block" was a blend of Black popular music like Joel Lutcher's "Hot the Block," mixed with the rhythm of the constant grind of the milkshake machine, impatient shouts for food, postgame quarterbacking, juvenile chatter, voyeurism, and laughter.

ML and crew—including Proctor and McCall—were established contributors to the soundtrack. They planted themselves at the Block. Like the jazz blaring from the jukebox, the discussions were improvisational, unfolding according to the whimsical and impulsive dictates of youth. Proctor recalled discussing everything under the sun. Commentary on Morehouse football and basketball games—"The 'House really shot 'em out of the gym tonight"—to baseball, such as Jackie Robinson's 1947 breakthrough as the first African American player in America's pastime with the Brooklyn Dodgers. It made ML a Dodgers fan. "I was deeply moved by the fact that Branch Rickey (president, general manager, and partial owner of the Dodgers) was willing to be this courageous," he reflected years later. Such conversations were followed by questions about homework assignments. The grapevine was tapped for the latest social gossip—who was going to be homecoming queen, affectionately and reverently known as Miss Maroon and White; who was the newest couple going steady—followed by wisecracks, and extended debates of politics, theology, and tradition. Nothing escaped scrutiny. Proctor and even Morehouse faculty recalled that ML and McCall seemed to always be in a rhetorical tussle regarding everything from military service to the most expedient pathways to racial equality. Verbal jousting seemed to be their love language. In a 1970 interview, he recalled nudging ML about church tradition. "Tweedy," he asked, "would it be alright if I came to your church without a tie? Is it mandatory to wear a tie in Sunday School?" Or "Would you preach in your church without a tie and a black suit?" ML had purposely posed for his Minister's Union photo in a light-colored jacket without a tie. The answer was obvious.[14]

Occasionally, the bull sessions were so deep, the strapping college students would continue long after "the Block," closed, moving to the dormitories, burning the midnight oil. ML would crash on the floor, exchanging bull until the wee hours of the morning.[15]

ML was always ready with a smooth answer, regardless of the topic. The older McCall remembered that if the conversation turned to a matter that exceeded ML's teenage experience, he turned to the wellspring of teenage wisdom: popular culture. He loved to make remarks and offer commentary that were peppered with lyrics from popular songs. It was a fruit born of his love of words and his desire to show others that while he was a minister, he was still hip. If the conversation turned pessimistic, ML quoted Johnny Mercer's 1940's Grammy nominated "Ac-Cent-Tchu-Ate the Positive." The song was a riff on the teachings of an interracial religious movement led by Father Divine, known as the International Peace Mission Movement. ML would encourage his friends to hold tight to positivity and hope.[16]

When the conversation turned to romance and sex, as it inevi-

tably did for college students, ML authored a glossary of pop culture euphemisms. Just call us "the Wreckers," ML and Larry started
telling classmates. They took the moniker from Robinson and Stevens Wreckers, a local wrecking company, because, ML would say
through his big grin, "We wreck girls."[17] Even by the standards of
the 1940s, ML's audacious comments and jokes reeked of an insecure teenager attempting to project confidence and swagger to his
older, all-male classmates.

In addition to the Wreckers, ML authored a lexicon of teenage euphemisms that were reflective of America's patriarchal culture, teenage imagination, and Black church references. He labeled
women he believed to be potential excellent sexual partners, but
not wives, as "one-time wreckers." He referred to potential female
sexual partners as "doctor," someone who could meet his physical
needs, helping to heal all his ailments. "Don't let the doctor catch
you with your shoes off" was a running joke for the young minister
and his crew of Black church aficionados. Feet serve as a common

A cartoon in the Morehouse student newspaper depicted students obsessed with
the opposite sex, while the world around them was ablaze.
The Maroon Tiger, December 1946.

euphemism for male genitals in the Old Testament, as in the story of Ruth and Boaz in the book of Ruth. Shoes became a euphemism for condoms, which exploded in availability and use during and after the war. It was advisable, ML and friends joked, to keep one's "feet" covered with "shoes" when visiting the "doctor."[18]

Female students considered to be the most attractive were discussed as having the "highest constitution." Shapely and full-figured women were labeled "highly endowed" and "well established."[19] ML nudged his friends anytime and every time a "doctor" floated by. He stared far too long when he saw a woman who was "highly endowed" with "the highest constitution."[20] It is unclear if he became sexually active as a teenager, but American pop culture steadily fed his already active imagination, creating a world of wonder, consumption, euphemisms, and exaggerations.

• • •

The dance floor was the venue where ML's colorful glossary and lyrics collided with the real world. He had the moves; but he also had a dad who opposed dancing. Daddy King believed dancing was a sin, the sway of the devil. Dances with Morehouse faculty chaperones did not mean a thing to the elder King. Sin was sin.

ML tried to maneuver around the old man. Begging his mother was the path of least resistance. His mother listened to reason, especially when it was ML offering the reason. Mama routinely gave her permission for him to attend, but always with the caveat, "Be sure to ask your dad too." ML always gave up. "Well, we just won't go," his mother recalled her son saying, hoisting the white flag. "I just as well go before the Supreme Court before I go before him." Like the Supreme Court, ML hoped the judgment would go in his favor, but experience taught him otherwise. Living at home as a college student saved money, but it came with other costs.

A few times, ML, accompanied by Walter McCall or Larry Williams, stealthily attended the dances anyway. The former wrestling rivals jostled on the dance floor for romantic affection.[21]

When Daddy King discovered that his son and Larry Williams had gone to a YWCA dance, he let out his wrath in curses on the two young ministers. He threatened to put them out of the church. Baptists do not dance! As a warning, he made ML and Larry stand before the entire church and confess their sins. They were forced to plead for their mercy, apologize, and pledge to sin no more.[22] That meant no going to public parties.

The experience taught father and son valuable lessons. Daddy King learned that parenting that made attending public dances impossible made unsupervised house parties virtually inevitable. And ML learned if he could not go to the party, he would bring the party to him.

After his confession, ML hosted house parties. Being a city student, commuting back and forth to campus, was a detriment to his social life. But ML turned it into an advantage, hosting coed dance parties, when his parents were away ministering.[23]

Christine helped invite the girls from Spelman. Her invitations provided her Spelman sisters temporary parole from Spelman's velvet cage of Victorian Christian womanhood. Spelman College was "emphatically Christian." The school motto and crest boasted "Our Whole School for Christ." The school aimed to develop Christian virtues in its female students. Chapel attendance was required every weekday at 8:00 a.m., as well as a midweek prayer meeting, and Sunday worship at 3:00 p.m. Morehouse men were allowed daily social visits to the campus for one hour, from 4:30 p.m. to 5:30. The

Spelman administration had oversight of any social event attended by Spelman students regardless of location. And Spelmanites, as they were called, were discouraged from venturing off campus and were permitted only with parental permission. Beyond the campus borders, students were required to wear gloves and a hat. The rest of their bodies also had to be modestly covered. "Elaborate or extensive wardrobes" were prohibited. Conspicuous consumption and adornment did not cohere "with the standards and ideals of Spelman College." The Spelman student newspaper reminded students, "As soon as we step out of our room, our behavior and our appearance become a matter of observation to others. Above all things one should never be conspicuous in clothes, make-up, conversation, or conduct." Instead, each student was required to have at least one "simply made" plain white washable dress, a uniform symbol of purity. And "at least two dark aprons or smocks" for domestic work. They were instructed never to chew gum, to avoid public displays of affection, and never to apply makeup in public. Morehouse men found it absurd. The piety and "lack of freedom" at Spelman, *The Maroon Tiger* claimed, was unrivaled in the modern world, having been "last experienced by the Puritans in 'Old Boston.'"[24]

But when Christine invited them, the invitation was viewed as having come from the preacher's daughter, providing Spelman sisters the necessary alibi they needed for their off-campus adventure. Awaiting them was reprieve, however fleeting, on ML's makeshift dance floor.

At 193 Boulevard, they played all the hits from "the Block," including the leading Juke Box Race Records of the day, such as Louis Jordan's hits "Boogie Woogie Blue Plate" and "Let the Good Times Roll."[25]

That was until Daddy King rained on their hit parade. Eventually, Reverend King became aware of the social gatherings. Surprisingly, the preacher extended grace. He allowed them to continue. He preferred the prince and princess of Ebenezer to socialize with the opposite sex in the sanctuary of their home as long as it was innocent fun. However, like the FBI would years later, he surveilled his son.[26] One night he came home while the house party had a particularly "good time going," McCall joyously remembered. King Sr. witnessed ML and a crew of Morehouse and Spelman students jitterbugging and lindy-hopping to their hearts' content. They "were just swinging away on into the night." But the whole scene apparently went too far for Daddy King. Having social visits was permissible. Dancing was not. He burst in and began to fuss, lecture, and scream. "We were so embarrassed," McCall remembered.[27]

Yet his father's strictness did not put a dent into ML's romantic escapades.[28] According to Larry Williams, ML was attracted to "fair-skinned" African American girls with Eurocentric facial features. Long straight hair and slender noses always caught his attention. Equally important was her standing among Morehouse men. The more prominent she was on campus and the more desired by his classmates, the more teenage ML desired her.[29]

His track record was long, and he seemed to pursue whomever was most popular at the time. He was rumored to have called upon light-skinned coeds like Madeline Knight and Gloria Royster. Others were the cherished scions of Black Atlanta's elite. Mattawilda Dobbs was homecoming queen, and the daughter of the local Masonic Worshipful Master. She went on to become an internationally known operatic soprano. Rose Martin was the daughter of the vice president of Atlanta Life Insurance Company; and Betty Milton was the daughter of the president of Citizens Trust Bank.[30]

ML attempted to charm the belles with his clothes, smooth baritone, and developing intellect. Morehouse and Spelman newspapers complained that Morehouse men were "slipping too far away from the good" and were forgetting "their basic home discipline" when engaging Spelman women, especially in their speech patterns. Morehouse men were challenged to speak to women as if they were hosting them for tea. ML led the way. According to these women, he was a perfect gentleman. He put Professor Chandler's yearlong course in General Literature to full use. Female recipients of his visits and phone calls were treated to tales of the Rubicons he would cross for them; and the Troys whose destruction their beauty caused. Edgar Allan Poe's "To Helen" was a favorite, always on the tip of his tongue. With ML's near-perfect memory, the poem was transformed, as ML easily substituted the name "Helen" with the object of his affection. "Helen, thy beauty is to me" was remixed into Mattawilda, or Rose, or . . .[31]

And of course, ML had access to the love songs of America's burgeoning race record industry. Billy Eckstine's "Prisoner of Love" was a constant at the Block, ranking at the top of Billboard's most played Race Records in America's jukeboxes from 1946 to 1947. It had perfect longing lyrics of unrequited love featuring a man who longed for a woman who already had a lover.[32]

For very special occasions, there was Nat King Cole's 1948 hit "Nature Boy." McCall recalled that ML loved to repeat the lyrics, citing that loving someone and having that love requited was the greatest thing in life.[33]

But beyond the boisterous, teenage flirting, ML also listened. He asked questions about their studies, their dreams, and their politics. He told them about his aspirations, how he was going to smother Jim Crow and push America to be true to its founding documents.[34]

In all of this, there was one popular woman who became more

than just a souvenir along ML's ego trip. King biographies have mentioned her in passing, but her place in ML's life was far from fleeting. His parents wanted him to marry her. They believed she was the perfect first lady for the budding minister. ML agreed. He had every intention of making her his first lady, his very own Mrs. Martin Luther King Jr.

Juanita Garnetta Sellers: "Popular, comely and possessing the charm to make and keep any friendship warm."
Voted "Best Dressed."
Campus Mirror, May 1948.

31
JUANITA

Her name was Juanita Garnetta Sellers. She was the "it" girl. She was the daughter of one of the most prosperous morticians in Atlanta. Next to Black churches, Black funeral homes were one of the most prominent independent anchor institutions in Black communities, serving not only as spaces for the dead, but also doubling as lodging facilities for Black travelers who were racially prohibited from hotels. And Sellers Brothers Funeral Home embodied this reality. With locations in Carrollton and Fairburn, Georgia, as well as Atlanta, the Sellers possessed significant financial and social capital in Black Atlanta.

Juanita enjoyed the status. She was popular, voted Spelman's best dressed and Morehouse's homecoming queen. Every Spelman sister wanted to be her, and every Morehouse man wanted to date her. It made her the perfect prize for ML.

Juanita embodied what her classmates called "that Spelman Look." Her flawless dark caramel complexion complemented her radiant white smile. She stood upright, her posture straight, as was her permed hair. Her demeanor was graceful and poised. She walked like she had a book affixed to the top of her head.[1]

She wore smart vertical-striped long wool skirts that "elimi-nate[d] the negative and accentuate[d] the positive," according to the Spelman *Campus Mirror*. She chose colorful blouses, with boat and square necklines; solid-colored suits; and accessorized with colorful but tasteful necklaces, pearls, earrings, and bracelets.[2]

The sloped campus terrain did not stop her from wearing styl-ish heels every day. Juanita preferred peep-toed heels, showing just enough skin to be interesting, but still sufficiently respectable.[3]

Her intellect matched her closet. Just six months older than ML, she also passed the early entrance exam and enrolled at Spelman at the age of sixteen. She majored in English, with a minor in music. While most of her Spelman sisters and Morehouse brothers, includ-ing ML, used the summer to work, make money, or travel, Juanita took more classes at Atlanta University. Friends teased her that she spent all her time studying in the library or fussing about the 99 per-cent she received on an exam, as opposed to a perfect 100.[4]

Beyond her studies, she was a member of the glee club and the chorus, the advertising manager of the *Campus Mirror*, and a noted "sports enthusiast" who studied the *Atlanta Daily World* sports pages like it was her homework. Yet she still managed to have time to attend the latest soirees and parties. Given her style, exacting bril-liance, popularity, and well-rounded nature, her classmates predicted she would be a "favorite daughter of Wall Street," employed by Du-Pont or some other leading corporation of the day. She was "every woman," the total package.[5]

The men at Morehouse agreed, selecting her Miss Maroon and White. It was the ultimate seal of approval. The homecoming queen was chosen as the embodiment of "beauty, personality, and those characteristics that make for fine womanhood," including "charac-ter, personality, intelligence." Only a fool, the Morehouse student newspaper noted, would "try and step out on Juanita Sellers."[6]

Morehouse Homecoming Queen "Miss Maroon and White"
and her attendants. From left to right: Mary Bowman; newly
crowned Miss Maroon & White Juanita Sellers; and Eloise Dunn.
Campus Mirror, November 1947.

It is difficult to overstate the social significance of the annual weekend affair of homecoming and the crown that came with it. The front page of the *Atlanta Daily World* announced, "Juanita Sellers to Reign Over Maroon and White Classic," while the *Chicago Defender* featured a full-length body shot of the newly minted maiden. On the first day of homecoming festivities, "the attractive" coed was the featured guest at the Morehouse morning chapel service, followed by a pep rally. On Friday evening, she hosted the Miss Maroon and White reception. On Saturday morning, she was treated to "all of the pomp and trapping[s] of royalty" as she waved at well-wishers during the "colorful parade" of floats. She formally received her crown on Saturday afternoon, November 8, 1947, during half-time of the 47th annual homecoming game against rival South Carolina State College. The captain of the football team always crowned Her Highness. The honor in 1947 belonged to the strapping World War II veteran and starting quarterback Edwin "Pony-Express" Smith. The football and basketball star strolled his five eleven, 160-pound svelte frame across the field to present Queen Juanita with the game ball and her well-deserved crown.[7]

The crowning achievement put her in ML's crosshairs. She would be the spoils of his inner war to secure a measure of masculine assurance.

She knew ML's reputation. It preceded him like an emergency siren, with all its warnings and enticements. But she also knew him—they were both students at the Atlanta Laboratory School as kids and tested into college early—and she knew his family were good stock that formed his bedrock.[8]

She was treated to ML's whirlwind Channie-like verses and lyrics, discussions of their respective futures, the war on Jim Crow, and how he intended to enlist her services. Yet, she also loved that he was well-rounded. He knew how to have fun. And he was a genius when it came to knowing how to make her laugh. "He had a wonderful sense of humor," Juanita reminisced on the sixtieth anniversary of their college graduation. "He knew when to be conservative, but he was also fun-loving."[9]

It all swept her off her feet.

Their romance unfurled at ML's house, a scandal in the making. Social norms called for ML, as the male, to visit her, to "call" on her at her house under the supervision of her parents. However, ML's appeal and social status led Juanita to violate everything she was taught to hold sacred, while her parents turned a blind eye. Class etiquette, Christian piety, and her Spelman image went out the window when it came to ML. It was a small gesture with massive significance. ML, the short, not-so-handsome guy, had Miss Maroon and White willing to sacrifice her reputation, while his was bolstered.[10]

ML policed Juanita's physical appearance. She was known for always being put together, the embodiment of "that Spelman Look." When they ventured out together, she recalled years later, he would advise her to "go put on some fresh lipstick and freshen up."[11]

Juanita knew ML enjoyed showing her off. One day he told her he wanted her to meet somebody important. She agreed. When she stood to leave to go to the meeting, he said, "No, no . . ." They could not leave until she performed what would become their ritual prior to any outing: a fresh coat of lipstick, a touch-up of her makeup, and a mist of perfume. He took her to meet Reverend Dudley of Liberty Baptist Church. Reverend Dudley was special to ML. He was one of the first Baptist ministers outside the King family who opened his pulpit to the young preacher. ML, Juanita, and Reverend Dudley had a lovely visit; good casual conversation, interspersed by refreshing sips of Southern sweet tea.[12]

But Juanita was initially unsure about the status of her relationship with ML. What did this mean? Was ML just showing her off? Was he looking for approval from someone he admired? Was it a meeting to determine if Juanita was first lady material? What other women had met Reverend Dudley? In a world without social media and the internet, the grapevine was the best source of information; but it often lied. She attempted to draft Christine into her investigation. If anybody would know about ML's love life, it would be his sister.

Juanita made a habit of calling Christine. They sat on the phone in what would become a game of cat and mouse. After small talk about the goings-on at Spelman, Juanita would drop hints, asking questions—What's ML up to these days? What are his plans for the weekend?—hoping Christine would take the bait. But Christine was faithful to her baby brother. No friendship, no Spelman sisterhood, and no budding feminism could break the bond she had with him. "I always had to fight to pull any information out of Christine," Juanita complained to her own mother.[13]

Juanita's prying was not completely in vain. Christine did give her a morsel of data. After ML took Juanita to see Reverend Dudley, Christine explained the visit to Juanita. Reverend Dudley was the pastor of Jean, a woman ML had been dating. The Reverend Dudley excursion, Christine relayed to Juanita, was "a ceremony" of sorts, a public announcement. It was ML's "politic way" of informing Reverend Dudley that he was no longer seeing Jean, that Juanita was his new girl. Juanita welcomed the news.[14]

ML began to dream about Juanita as Mrs. Martin Luther King Jr. As graduation drew closer, he started to see things more clearly. He knew a wife could help make or break his ministerial career. And ML was in a hurry to secure his career. Once he knew his life's destination, he grew impatient, desiring to get there as fast as he could. He wanted to secure his wife and move on to the next thing.

"I will be a pastor of a large Negro church in the South," ML declared in a bull session and to anybody who would listen. "That's where I plan to live and work. I want the kind of wife who will fit into that kind of situation." Juanita was a Southern belle, nursed, fed, and fashioned in the Black church. She was long a member of West Hunter Street Baptist Church. Just like ML she had been baptized as a young child. She sang in the church youth choir. As a first soprano she was a coveted soloist, and even took piano lessons for a time. The Black Baptist church was her cultural oxygen and soundscape.[15] He would lead a church that would serve hearts and minds and save souls. She would be his first lady, and by loving and serving him, she would serve the people, and perhaps even save him from his worst, most destructive, insecure impulses.

But the attraction was more than just cold pragmatism. The love was also sincere. She was everything ML loved about Mama and Mother Dear, the two women he idolized and adored most. She was fashionable. Refined. Smart. And she was gifted musically. She was dedicated to the race, steeped in church and civic activities. He was convinced, he told his friends, "I must have a wife who will be as dedicated as I am." But Juanita was also everything he wished Mother Dear was. She was outspoken. Assertive. Expressive. He worried that he could too easily become "disenchanted" in marriage. He needed someone special to maintain the intellectual spark. "I don't want a wife I can't communicate with," June Dobbs recalled ML telling her. He loved that Juanita was more than just a pretty face. She was, he admitted, "a fine girl," but also a fine mind. He wanted a woman who was going to be his equal in the marriage; a woman who possessed her own thoughts about the world. I need someone I can respect, he persisted, not someone who was willing to be "a doormat."[16] Juanita Sellers was far from a doormat. She had her own light to shine.

And she was a family favorite. She and Christine worked side by side at the *Campus Mirror*, exchanging journalistic tidbits between juicy college gossip. Later, Juanita would be Christine's maid of honor. Mom and Dad King loved her too. Her pedigree was superb and her social résumé was second to none. Her family were already at the top, and their daughter was the perfect complement to their son. She was eyeing an Ivy League graduate degree. "We love that girl," Daddy King was fond of saying.[17]

Many people spend their entire lives searching for the perfect match. Juanita and ML seemed to have found it while still teenagers.

ML, third from left, attending the Morehouse Annual Institute on Marriage and Family, attentively seated in the front row, circa 1946–1948.

• • •

As graduation approached, ML began to take marriage very seriously.

Morehouse championed marriage. If the race was going to progress, the educated few had to lead the way. Marriage was the primary institution by which progress could be made. In the spring of 1946, the college launched periodic gatherings on marriage. "The Institute on Building for Successful Marriage and Family Living" was led by the department of sociology, ML's major department. With his heart and future on the line, he began attending the lectures, taking his seat in the front row.[18]

ML was treated to a series of groundbreaking conversations, panels, and workshops on all things related to sex, dating, and marriage. Leading ministers, scholars, social workers, and physicians led panel discussions and even hosted personal consultations on the importance of choosing the right mate, and the step-by-step process to get there.

President Mays offered what he called "The Ten Commandments of a Successful Marriage," including spiritual compatibility, physical compatibility, and shared responsibility.

Juanita checked all the boxes.

Reverend Maynard Jackson guided ML on "features that make for incompatibility—namely, attitudes, feelings, psychosomatic relations and interpersonal actions." Reverend Jackson spoke from experience. When the New Orleans native was a Morehouse student in the 1930s, he met and married Irene Dobbs. She was the Spelman valedictorian and daughter of John Wesley Dobbs, the "mayor" of Auburn Avenue. Reverend Jackson and Irene were a dynamic duo. He went on to lead Friendship Baptist Church, one of the most prominent African American churches in Atlanta. She became a professor of French at Spelman. They were civil rights activists, leading the effort to integrate Atlanta's public libraries. Reverend Jackson's life was a testimony: A man who desired prominence and leadership for the cause of Black civil rights, especially a man of the cloth, had to have a prominent woman as his partner.

Reverend Homer C. McEwen, pastor of the First Congregational Church, Atlanta, and Mrs. Marie S. Key, a consultant for the Planned Parenthood Federation, gave their views on "What Constitutes a Smooth Date," reminding the men of their gentlemanly duties, such as opening doors, walking on the curb side, and teaching them how to properly "call" upon a woman. Juanita, and perhaps a list of belles, were the beneficiaries of this consultation.

Fortunate men took the date to the next level. Miss Faith Jones, dean of Women at Hampton Institute, followed with a lecture on proper "Courtship and Engagement," giving the men a cheat sheet on the appropriate ways to court a woman and how to win her hand in marriage. It was a conversation that made ML, who usually sat in the back in class, sit front and center.

Dean Jones also warned against "petting problems," her chaste way of referring to the dangers and problems of premarital sex. It was a necessary but awkward lecture in a room full of teen-age boys and war veterans. There was no mention of "one-time wreckers," or "doctors," or "well-established" women. Just facts and warnings.

William M. Cooper, director of Extension at Hampton Institute, pointed to the necessity of budgeting to ensure the economic structure of family life. This was an important matter for ML. He was starting to see economics as a significant force in personal and social conflicts. He even published an essay in the inaugural volume of the Morehouse *Annual Sociology Seminar Digest* titled "Economic Basis of Cultural Conflict." He was questioning capitalism and the economic life he wanted to lead. His views were likely influenced by Walter Chivers, a Morehouse sociology professor and local labor union president. While ML never spoke of Chivers's influence, he did take several courses with the labor leader, who worked tirelessly to unionize public workers. ML was from the professional class, but witnessing inequality and exposure to new economic ideas made him uncertain if he wanted to live like it. Juanita was also from the professional class, but she was sure she wanted to keep it that way.[19]

Dr. Raymond H. Carter, a local physician, gave advice on how to be prepared for marital sex. His "Sexual Adjustment in Marriage" pointed to the importance of patience and communication for sexual fulfillment in marriage. There was no room for quips about "shoes" and "feet," only honest and intimate conversation.[20]

The institute shaped ML's view of marriage as a loving yet practical arrangement. During the sessions, he jotted down several proverbs in his notebook: "We must satisfy our emotional needs." "Only the person you love can hurt you emotionally." "You can't cling to your mother & father and give yourself completely to marriage." "Marriage is more that [sic] a physical union between two people, it is an emotional union between two people."[21]

These pragmatic, functional ideas guided his approach to marriage for the remainer of his life and ministry. "Marriage is at bottom a state of adjustment between two individuals who are seeking to be one," he wrote to a soul seeking his counsel on marriage in 1957. Love was key, he admitted, "but love must always be tempered with reason. Love devoid of rational and practical considerations can become a wild and fanatical emotion that can only lead to psychological disintegration."[22]

ML and Juanita began to have their own frank, rational, and practical conversations about marriage with their respective families. Daddy King was keen on it. Like the overbearing parent he could be, he confused his own desires with those of ML. "There were so many girls who liked him," Daddy King reasoned. "They were pushing him. I was afraid he would get tied up with one we did not like." They liked Juanita. She was from a prominent local family, and Daddy King wanted ML to marry an Atlanta girl so his son would be close to home and become his full-time assistant pastor and eventual successor.[23]

The Sellerses approved the match as well. ML became the cherished son they never had. Mr. Sellers and ML greeted one another with big smiles, warm hugs, and familial backslaps, while Mrs. Sellers was showered with sweet compliments and cheek kisses from ML. They called ML "son," and ML returned the favor, referring to them as "Dad and Mom Sellers."[24]

Marriage was discussed, not in terms of "if," but "when." When would the proposal take place? When would the wedding be held?

ML and Juanita, as well as their respective families, agreed to the
plan. The two would wed. Word began to spread throughout Black
Atlanta society that they were officially betrothed.[25]

• • •

For the next four and a half years, it appears ML and Juanita carried
the burden and safety of young, betrothed love. The weight of expectation was heavy; but the security offered levity to outside dalliances and flighty flirtations. It was a push and pull that they both
enjoyed. Their relationship had the predictable unpredictability of
young love. It whiplashed between being everything and nothing.
It ebbed and flowed, at times a tidal wave of passion, at other times
barely a trickle of a mention. It was as serious and silly as any first
love. They would achieve the kind of equilibrium and normalcy that
young love too often dismisses as boredom. They would dip into the
valleys of jealousy and insecurity, and doubt brought on by Juanita's independence and ML's tendency to make a sport of women's
hearts. Rivers of doubts flowed as both questioned the other's commitment. ML grew concerned that Juanita's conspicuous consumption and embrace of capitalism blinded her to the plight of the Black
masses, the very people he planned to work with and for. Juanita
came to believe that ML would be too controlling, foreclosing her
career opportunities. Then they would perpetually return to the
comforting familiarity of reconciliation and safety, catapulting them
back to the mountaintop highs of passion. Wash. Rinse. Repeat.[26]

But all these inconvenient truths and concerning patterns on the
horizon were blurred by the euphoria of young love and the security
of betrothal.

ML had his entire life planned with all the clarity that accom-
panies ambition and teenage ignorance. He would go to seminary,

become an intellectually respectable and credentialed minister. He would then marry Juanita. Mrs. Juanita Sellers King: his love and perfect partner for the war he waged within and the war he planned to rage against Jim Crow. Together they would live out their days serving God and humanity.

It had all the makings of a perfect Black fairy tale.

32

REVEREND ML KING JR.

"Now Daddy, I want to go to seminary," Daddy King recalled his son telling him in the fall of 1947.[1]

ML had rallied the troops before he told Daddy King about his seminary dreams. He told Mother Dear. She gave her blessing. Christine was next. She was proud of her little brother, while AD continued to stand in awe of his big brother. After ML received everyone's approval, he finally confronted the lone resister: Dad.[2]

The elder King had his own vision for his son's future. He wanted ML to be co-pastor of Ebenezer.

It was the perfect plan. ML had a great voice. He preached like a seasoned man. He was mature. He was dedicated, and he was gaining experience by the day, preaching and teaching. But perhaps most importantly in the eyes of Daddy King, he was the pastor's son. It was the perfect pairing. Two kings on the throne of Ebenezer—the elder, the king, and the younger, the prince. ML pledged to his father that he would help his dad spread the gospel of equality. Daddy King believed it was time for ML to fulfill his promise.

In an unpublished autobiography, Daddy King vividly recounted their conversation. "Now, Daddy, I want to go to a white seminary," ML blurted out before his dad could protest. "And I have certain thoughts about it." It was an audacious proposition. ML would need financial assistance, and his grades did not scream graduate school. He was carrying a C average and graduation was near. But long odds had never stopped him before.

All the men he admired—Mays, Channie, Kelsey—had attended graduate school, particularly predominantly white schools in the North. ML had made up his mind that he would do the same. Seminary would offer him the intellectual respectability he craved for his ministry.

He did not tell his dad he wanted to go to a white school because he wanted to be like his professors. Rather, he pointed to race leadership, a claim he knew his dad would understand.

"I am convinced that white folk need to be informed that all blacks are not dumb, as so many seem to believe," he told his dad. "So I would like to attend one of their schools of religion for my post-graduate work." Daddy King loved his son's desire to shine, but he did not share his son's idea that singular Black excellence could change the hearts and minds of white Americans. Nevertheless, a defeated Daddy King reluctantly agreed.[3]

King told his dad he was considering three seminaries, all in the North: Union Theological Seminary in New York City; Andover-Newton Theological Seminary in Newton, Massachusetts; and Crozer Theological Seminary in Upland, Pennsylvania, just outside of Chester.[4]

ML decided on Crozer Theological Seminary, against his father's wishes. "You are mighty young to go to Crozer," his father recalled telling his eighteen-year-old son, a response he would likely have given for any of the seminaries. Dad probably believed that his son was too young to be that far from home. But ML had his mind made up. Dr. Edwin E. Aubrey, the president of Crozer, had taught Benjamin Mays at the University of Chicago. ML wanted to study with the man who taught the man he admired so much. And faculty, such as Dr. Aubrey, lived on campus, offering opportunities for personal engagement outside the classroom, just like at Morehouse. Students were also permitted to take courses at the University of Pennsylvania, an Ivy League school. It was the perfect place for ML to credential himself and authenticate his ministry.[5]

On October 27, 1947, Minister ML King Jr. wrote to Crozer Theological Seminary for an application. He bypassed the office of admissions and the dean, writing straight to President Aubrey, expressing how "intensely interested" he was in Crozer. He requested that the application and course catalogue be sent to him "as soon as possible."[6]

• • •

The pressure was on.

Daddy King refused to give up. He vowed to himself that he would always love his children, he would love them, as he put it to his wife, "too much to deny them anything, especially themselves."[7] But that did not mean he would stop trying to make his dream ML's dream also. He told ML that he had arranged for him to sit before an ordination committee on February 18, 1948. A group of ministers would question ML on his fitness for ordained ministry. Ordination would elevate him from Minister ML King Jr. to Reverend ML King Jr., giving him the authority to perform solemn ceremonies—marriages, funerals, and baptisms. And perhaps most important for his dad, it would authorize him to function as a pastor, specifically co-pastor of Ebenezer. Daddy King hoped ordination—the enticement of the title, the newfound authority, and the new responsibilities—would change his son's mind about going off to seminary. [8]

He was wrong.

ML completed his application to Crozer just a week or so before the ordination council.

As the now nineteen-year-old sat down to answer the application query, "Give your personal reasons for the decision to study for the Gospel Ministry," he was forced to consider everything that had happened, all the events that had brought him to this point.

He had known, it seemed, forever that his life's blueprint was to make a difference in the struggle for Black humanity. Now he had all the raw material he needed to build that very life.

He had the resolute foundation of his personhood, hewed out of the mountain of racism. He lost his earliest friends simply because he was Black and they were white. He was brutally slapped in the face simply because he was Black. He could not buy new shoes simply because of the color of his skin. He was cursed and threatened, forced to stand up on the bus because he was born of African descent. He was refused equal service in the dining car on the train, put behind a curtain as if to shield others from his grotesque skin. He watched human limbs be battered and bruised because they were Black limbs. He read about bodies being raped and murdered because they were Black bodies. And he experienced the stalking fear of police because he was Black. Yet, with the help of his parents and the rock of Ebenezer, he had managed to create the groundwork of somebody-ness.

He had grown skeptical of the Bible and blasphemed the fundamentalist theology he was taught. He struggled in school, barely surviving his sociology major. He walked around at war with himself, desperately searching for a destiny and respectable profession. But he never lost hope that somehow his singular life could, no matter his grades or his grammar, make a difference.

He concretized his plans with the hope of the Gospel. His

conversations and debates with Mays rewired his ideas of what a minister could be and should be. Professor Kelsey electrified his understanding of the Bible, putting the text in motion. Professor Channie flipped the switch, empowering ML to use his love of words for the sake of the Gospel.

And then there were the log-cabin dormitories of Connecticut, the acres of country dirt, God's country dirt, where it all had come together.

"My call to the ministry was quite different from most explanations Ive [*sic*] heard . . ." he wrote pensively.

"This dicision [*sic*] came about in the summer of 1944 when I felt an inescapable urge to serve society. In short, I felt a sense of responsibility which I could not escape."[9]

Shortly after he mailed off his application, his dad bestowed upon him his new title: Reverend ML King Jr., Associate Pastor of Ebenezer Baptist Church, Atlanta, Georgia.[10]

But ML had accepted so much more than just a title and a profession. He had, finally, accepted himself and made peace with his life's blueprint.

33
COMMENCEMENT

Commencement: A time when all focus is on endings. The end of the school year. The end of a degree program.

But the word denotes the start of something new; the beginning of a new stage, a new plan, a new world.

As ML approached the beginning of the rest of his life, he had changed so much. Physically he looked much the same in his cap and gown as he did during freshman orientation, jostling to stand next to someone shorter than him while donning a grin that radiated confidence. Intellectually he seemed the same as well, graduating with a 2.48 GPA.[1]

But so much had changed. He had stopped fighting with himself concerning his calling to the ministry. He stopped wrestling with God. He began crafting an image of a minister, one that borrowed from the men in his life—Mays, Kelsey, and Channie—to create something that was altogether different.

The "inner urge" had taken over. It became a groundswell, shaping how ML viewed everything.

He would write, "There have been times that I have been carried out of myself by something greater than myself and to that something I gave myself."[2]

Class of 1948 Graduation Photo: At the time, it was "the largest graduation in the history of Morehouse College."
ML is in the front row, second from left. His City Slick teammate Jefferson C. Nash is next to him, third from left. Friend William Pickens is in the second row, sixth from left. Walter McCall is in the fourth row, seventh from left.

His beloved professor Dr. George D. Kelsey noticed ML's surrender. He told a colleague that ML had become "quite serious about the ministry." He felt that ML seemed to have "a call rather than a professional urge."[3] ML was not pursuing the ministry as just another job. He was on a divine errand to give himself to something greater.

Dr. Kelsey was not the only faculty member to see this. The faculty that witnessed his mediocre classroom performance and subpar academic work began to believe ML was going to be a great minister. Morehouse Dean of Men Dr. Brailsford Brazeal wrote in his recommendation letter to Crozer that ML's grades were average, but the youngster had "developed considerably." Given the opportunity, Brazeal predicted, ML would blossom at Crozer.

Morehouse religion professor Lucius Tobin, who also served on ML's ordination committee, acknowledged ML's grades were just "a little above average." Yet, he wrote, "I do not hesitate in saying that he should do well in the ministry, once he has had the type of training given at Crozer."

Mays sensed the same. Never one to pull his punches, he wrote for ML and McCall, "You will see from their records that they are not brilliant students," he said baldly, "but they do have good minds." He continued, "I am of the opinion that they both can do substantial B work and with good competition, they may do even better."[4]

All his professors saw his potential.

And ML would make these men prophets.

In recognition of his growth and potential, the Morehouse faculty chose ML to be the first speaker for the senior week chapel services in Sale Hall Chapel. The shy, quiet freshman who refused to talk in class was now a recognized orator, a proclaimer of the Gospel. The remaining speakers of the week were all paired in duos. ML was the only one chosen to speak solo. His singular reputation preceded him.[5]

He ascended the sacred desk on Sunday, May 23, at 9:00 a.m. and proceeded to bring down the house. The scene was "forever etched" in the memory of classmate Samuel DuBois Cook. "I remember it as though it were yesterday," Cook said decades later. "I can still see him now in the Chapel in Sale Hall delivering that speech. He electrified us." He was dressed "sharp as a tack." ML expounded upon the theme for the week: "The Social Responsibilities of the College Man."[6] In "great oratorical flourish," Cook recalled, ML stated a principle, an ideal he would go on to repeat throughout his life. "There are moral laws of the universe that we cannot violate with impunity," he harmonized to his classmates, "anymore than we can violate the physical laws of the universe with impunity." ML then addressed the importance of means being commensurate with ends, another message he would preach all his life. If the college man recognized these facts, ML concluded, he would be a social leader who fulfilled his cosmic obligations. "The brother soared," Cook said, "I mean, he was just, he just took off. So we knew he was going to be a great preacher, a great, great speaker, a great orator and so forth."[7]

Despite Cook's praise, ML's oratorical mastery was still a few years away. During senior week, President Mays awarded ML second prize in the John L. Webb oratorical contest. King was outdone by another future minister, freshman James N. Mitchell. The overachieving first-year student took first prize in 1948 and for the next two years. He went on to Oberlin to study theology and pursued a career in Chaplaincy.

ML garnered the fifteen-dollar second-place prize with a speech that portended his focus on legal equality. He titled his address "Should the Fair Employment Practice Committee (FEPC) Become a Federal Law." The FEPC was created in 1941 by President Roosevelt to ensure "the full and equitable participation of all workers in defense industries, without discrimination because of race, creed, color, or national origin." As ML crossed the stage, President Truman was trying to push Congress to make the FEPC federal law. The president failed. Fifteen years later, ML would give another rousing speech to persuade his audience of the necessity of a federal law barring employment discrimination. Using the oratory he used for the Webb contest and the poetry of Langston Hughes he learned in seventh grade, he couched his speech in a dream. It became known as "I Have a Dream." The speech moved the audience and the soul of the nation, pushing Congress to pass the 1964 Civil Rights Bill, outlawing discrimination in public accommodations, education, and hiring. Students would recite the speech for years to come, just like ML recited Hughes. And the speech, which began as a second-prize speech at Morehouse, eventually helped him to garner a new prize: the Nobel Peace Prize.[8]

• • •

The Kings' graduation celebration was a familial and community affair, like most graduations in the Black experience. In 1948, only about 2 percent of Black men and women graduated from college. The King family was about to contribute not one but two members to that elite group, making their familial accomplishment worthy of communal merriment.

But even by those standards, the King graduation affair was extravagant. The children's attire set the tone: ML and AD sported matching white double-breasted tuxedo jackets, black pants, and bow ties. Christine wore a matching black-and-white formal dress and floral corsage.

The Kings hosted the party at their two-story "palatial" yellow

The family gathers to celebrate the college graduates with a photo of Mama on the mantel, June 1948.
Starting at left: Alfred, Christine, ML, Mother Dear, and Daddy King.

brick house at 193 Boulevard. ML's makeshift dance floor was transformed into a white tie banquet hall. The children and their parents
formed a receiving line, greeting guests—community leaders, society women, church members, and newspaper men—as they arrived.
A vibrant "galaxy of gladioli and lilies" formed a second receiving
line. The flowers' symbolic meaning of character, faithfulness, and
integrity made it a purposeful choice, physically welcoming visitors
into their home and metaphorically into the new worlds in which
the college graduates were about to embark. The sword lilies stood
at attention, forming a military-like salute to the accomplishments
of the King children and the parents who raised them.[9]

The parents, as is the privilege of proud parentage, took a moment to congratulate themselves by announcing the accomplishments of their children. AD was headed to the tobacco farm in
Connecticut, following in the footsteps of his older brother, and
then to Morehouse. Christine would finally best her competitive
bother, officially graduating twenty-four hours before him. She was
Ivy League bound, enrolling in graduate school at Columbia University on a "segregation scholarship." Prior to the 1954 Brown v. Board
of Education decision ruling school segregation unconstitutional, it
was illegal to admit Black students into graduate and professional
programs at the historically white "public" universities across the
South. In an odd twist on the doctrine of "separate but equal,"
Southern states like Georgia paid for Black students like Christine
to attend graduate and professional school in the North rather than
admit them or pay tuition dollars to the few historical Black colleges
that had graduate and professional schools. Christine noted, "The
state of Georgia paid my tuition, my room and board, everything
because I couldn't go to the University [of Georgia]."[10] She set her
heart on majoring in Economics. But that would not last long. She
was the only woman and the only African American in the econom-

ics course of study. Her white male economics professor ignored her raised hand and questions. She would switch to Education after the first semester.[11]

ML, to his father's visible delight, was all set to serve as assistant pastor for the summer, running the church while his dad took a much needed summer break. Leading such a prominent congregation while being only nineteen years old was an impressive feat. But it was not enough to make ML want to stay. Against his father's wishes, he was set to attend divinity school at Crozer in the fall. Yet nothing could put a damper on the moment. AD was growing. Christine was solidly Christine, fulfilling the "most distinctive" superlative her classmates bestowed upon her. And young King finally seemed fit for his crown. His mother would tell him, "Remember ML, we're expecting great things from you." And ML seemed fit to exceed those expectations.[12]

The family celebrated the graduations in formal style. No detail was overlooked. Musicians from Ebenezer, all nurtured by Mrs. King, provided live classical music and church hymns. Miss Emma Lyons, a classically trained pianist and singer, and Miss Frankie Lowe, a soloist in the girls' chorus, provided the vocals. C. Reese Lyons, an organist, and Clarence Render, a classically trained violinist, provided accompaniment.[13]

A boogie-woogie celebration would have to wait.

But ML's main dance partner was present. Juanita Sellers was there in her full Spelman look. All the other young woman were put to work. June Dobbs presided at the punch bowl and assisted in the dining room. Several young women from the church maintained the guest book. Even AD's longtime girlfriend, Naomi Barber, whom he would wed two years later, served as one of the many "floating hostesses." But not Juanita. ML's sweetheart had one assignment: Be ML's sweetheart. The *Atlanta Daily World* noted her presence, receiving and greeting guests alongside the graduate like she was a member of the King family. She did not have to say who she was or why she, a recent Spelman graduate also on her way to Columbia on a segregation scholarship, was there. Everybody knew she was there as the future Mrs. Martin Luther King Jr.[14]

• • •

On Tuesday, June 8, 1948, 10:30 a.m., ML's quest for his Morehouse crown ended where it all began: Sale Hall Chapel. The chapel was bursting at the seams. The old building seemed to sweat and swell as the temperature was already a muggy eighty-two degrees, well on its way to the day's high of ninety-two degrees. An overflow crowd gladly spilled on to the campus yard, exchanging the tight humid quarters for the shade of the trees and the clear blue sky. There they listened to the services via speakers that were set up outside for the largest graduation in Morehouse history. ML and 112 men laid hold of their degrees. Clad in black robes that gripped soggy skin, and with mortarboard tassels stuck to the right side of sweaty beards and stubble, they crossed the threshold to become college graduates, a minority within a minority.[15]

It was a combination of high church worship and tent revival. ML's glee club bellowed Handel's "Hallelujah." The packed audience joined in when the Morehouse Quartet thundered "Rise Up, O Men of God" and the college hymn, "Dear Old Morehouse." Dignified attire stood next to overhauls. Head nods and applause were dwarfed by passionate, perspiring shouts of religious joy as names symbolizing distinction and Black hope— Benjamin Franklin Jenkins, John Wesley Adams, Frederick Douglass Jackson Jr., and Martin Luther King Jr.—were called across the stage to receive their Morehouse degrees and crowns.[16]

The graduation speaker was Dr. Kenneth Irving Brown, president of Denison University. The leader of the Baptist-affiliated college challenged the graduates. "If you can do one single thing towards a just, durable, and creative peace you will have fulfilled your major obligation to the world." The charge stuck to ML. Dr. Brown told them not to bother preaching against the major isms of the day, but to simply focus on waging peace. "Your job for the next fifty years," the aging sage told the youthful graduates, "and mine for the next twenty will be to work toward world peace, which is your dream and mine."[17]

Nobody would have guessed on that glorious sunny day in 1948 that nineteen-year-old ML, not the elder Dr. Brown, was the one who only had twenty years from that day to fulfill his major obligation to the world. And no one, not even ML, could have predicted that in those twenty years his dream—one that was cultivated on a tobacco farm in Connecticut—would be the dream that so many would come to embrace and share.

Part Five

FINDING A WIFE

34
CROZER

T oo long has the Baptist church preached against dancing . . ." a
seminary-bound ML declared before a statewide Georgia Baptist
Convention, held on June 15–16, 1948. He only had his college degree for a week, but he was already publicly challenging his dad and
what seemed like an eternity of Baptist practice.[1]

Less than 10 percent of Black Baptist ministers were seminary
trained. ML was a minority in the Black Baptist church regarding
education and his beliefs. He told the convention that Black Baptists
had spent too long thinking of the physical act of dancing as sinful.
They were stuck in tradition, not adjusting to the modern world.
Dancing itself was not sinful. Rather, what determined the ethics of
dancing, he countered, was one's "state of mind while dancing."[2] He
did not change the state of mind of the majority of Black Baptists.
The National Baptist Convention maintained its official prohibition
against dancing. And he certainly did not change his father's mind.

It was clear, ML was ready for seminary. He was ready to examine
long-held beliefs and practices under the microscope of modern science. As he wrote a few months later in his Crozer Theological Seminary orientation notebook, "the minister or religious leader must be
like a scientist. He must reject all hypothesis [sic] that reject the facts."[3]

• • •

Life and Morehouse prepared ML for the theological challenge of Crozer. As an adult, ML would say that Mays and Kelsey were the ones who enlightened him; while his graduate studies armed him with the lexicon of the Western philosophical and theological canon.[4] These tools would not alter a great deal of what he learned at Morehouse. Rather, Crozer would help ML communicate these ideas to a broader, largely white scholarly audience.

Like Professors Mays and Kelsey, the Crozer faculty challenged fundamentalist readings of the Bible. In fact, the school had developed a reputation for going even further, engaging in a historical criticism that seemingly ripped the Bible apart. One faculty member joked, "We used to say that we would get rid of Moses in the first semester, and dispose of Jesus in the second."[5]

ML was academically prepared, but he was not ready for the all-white setting. Returning to an all-white environment triggered a social anxiety experienced by some African Americans in the past and even today. Right or wrong, ML keenly felt the microscope of the white normative gaze. He felt the respectability of his entire race rested on his shoulders. "I was aware of the typical white stereotype of the Negro," he recalled of his nineteen-year-old self. "He is always late, that he's loud and always laughing, that he's dirty and messy." ML went to extremes to deflate these myths, leading him to wrestle with the peculiar sense of "double consciousness." He admitted, "For a while I was terribly conscious of trying to avoid identification with [these stereotypes]. If I were a minute late to class, I was almost morbidly conscious of it and sure that everyone else noticed." He even hid his naturally playful side. "Rather than be thought of as always laughing, I'm afraid I was grimly serious for a time," leading some faculty and students to describe him as shy or snobbish. It did not help that ML felt compelled to jazz up an already dapper wardrobe. While the rest of the students looked like students, King admitted, "I had a tendency to overdress, to keep my room spotless, my shoes perfectly shined, and my clothes immaculately pressed." One professor attested, "I never saw Martin in class without a suit, white shirt and tie with his shoes polished." ML was even conscious of the food he consumed. "I remember once at an outing how worried I was when I found they were serving watermelon. I didn't want to be seen eating it because of the association in many peoples' minds between Negroes and watermelon." He even attempted to police the behavior of the few other Black students. He chastised one Black student for having beer in his room. He lectured him that they needed to be beyond reproach because "the burdens of the Negro race" were on their shoulders. The older student replied, "So what?" The beer stayed.[6]

Eventually, ML resolved these issues. As students teased him for being neat, overly clean, and well dressed, he began to relax. He expelled the hyperconsciousness, recognizing it as the baggage of racism. "It was silly, I know," a more mature ML reflected, "but it shows how white prejudice can affect a Negro."[7]

ML adjusted. During his second semester, he turned twenty and began to display maturity and clarity of purpose that helped him show up as his full, fun-loving self. He grew comfortable in his new surroundings, adjusting to the integrated environment. White maids cleaned his dorm room. White chefs prepared his meals. At times, he expressed guilt. Similar to his time in Connecticut, he wondered why all African Americans could not live in such a world. He emerged as a top-notch student at Crozer. After carrying a C average his first term, he maintained at least a B average for the remainder of his degree program. But, according to June Dobbs, Daddy King still found fault. "You ought to be making all As," she remembered hearing the patriarch fuss. "I pay all your bills!" which included a five-dollar weekly allowance in his student post office box.[8]

ML met the challenge, staying up all night if necessary to perfect his studies, building on the theological base he obtained at Morehouse. He became class president and the eventual class valedictorian. "He played," his father remembered, "but always when [it was] time to study, he'd go in." His father proudly recalled hearing his son say, "I'm not going to be a dishwasher, I'm going to be a scholar."[9]

The Dean of Crozer sent word to Morehouse, attesting to the success of their alum. "King is one of our most outstanding students," Charles E. Batten wrote. He noted that ML was "held universally in high regard by faculty, staff, and students and is undoubtedly one of the best men in our entire student body." Indeed, ML was even hired to babysit for one of his white professors. The Old Testament professor paid his student thirty-five cents an hour.[10]

The admiration was based on more than just ML's classroom performance. ML gained the respect of the Crozer community by calmly staring down the barrel of a gun that was wielded by an enraged racist. Dormitory hijinks precipitated the near-death experience. Lucius Z. Hall, a veteran from South Carolina, lived a few doors down from ML. He was known to refer to Black students as "darkies" and to venerate the Confederate flag. He was also a notorious prankster: water buckets above dormitory doors that soaked unwitting targets with ice-cold water when they entered; rearranging or hiding a target's dormitory furniture was another favorite. Others joined in the fun, making it an ongoing dormitory joke. When ML walked into his dorm, room 52, and discovered his mattress was missing, he immediately assumed it was Hall. He found his bedding in the dormitory basement. As he carried his mattress up three flights of stairs, he plotted his revenge. ML and a few other recipients of Hall's mischief struck back. They removed all of Hall's dormitory furniture—mattress, bed, table, chairs, and desk—and placed it on the front lawn of the dorm, careful to arrange it in the same configuration as his dorm room. Classmates recalled that Hall returned and was furious. He spotted ML watching from his dormitory window, and immediately set out to kill "the darkie." He grabbed his pistol and busted into room 52.

"Martin, I'm going to kill you!"

ML, pretending to read a book, remained calm. He held on to the book without flinching. It was not the first time he had faced an assault or near death at the hands of an enraged racist. And it would not be his last.

Classmates intervened. "Hall, don't do that," Marcus Garvey Wood recalled saying as he stood in ML's dorm room. "It's all fun. . . . You don't even know [if ML] did it!" It did not matter. Hall had decided ML's skin made him guilty. Words were exchanged by both parties. Somehow the situation was deescalated. The exact words have been lost to time, but Wood remembered it took about an hour of tense conversation to convince Hall to take the sights of his pistol off ML. The next day, Dean Batten met with the men. He banned the practice of "room raids." ML's calm, fearless reaction, and his seeming indifference toward death, became legendary on campus.[11]

ML had another face-off with a gun in nearby New Jersey. In the wee hours of Monday, June 12, 1950, ML and Walter McCall, accompanied by McCall's girlfriend, Pearl E. Smith, and her roommate, Doris Wilson, were returning from an evening church service. Around 12:45 a.m., the group, all still dressed in their Sunday best, stopped at Mary's Cafe in Maple Shade, New Jersey, for a drink. According to Pearl, she, Doris, and ML found a table in the taproom, while McCall went to the bar to place their order: two beers and four glasses. Bartender Ernest Nichols refused to

serve them. The German immigrant cited the illegality of selling package goods on Sunday. McCall, confused, consorted with
his friends. They wondered, according to their filed complaint, if
Nichols "was refusing to serve us because it was Sunday and a
bottled beer was considered package goods." Cunningly, they sent
McCall back to the bar to ask for four glasses of beer instead. The
fifty-four-year-old barkeep refused. According to his lawyer, Nichols shouted at McCall, "No beer, Mr.! Today is Sunday!"[12]

McCall, sensing something afoot, then asked for four ginger ales.
Nichols became incensed. In a whirlwind, he went to his apartment,
retrieved his .45, and returned to the tavern. He then flung the door
open and fired a shot in the air. Pearl told the authorities Nichols then
came back in the tavern and began waving the gun around while he
rained down curses on the group. It was just like when fifteen-year-
old ML was cursed and threatened by the bus driver. Frightened for
their lives, the four fled out the door. Nichols reportedly yelled at
them, "I'll kill for less!" They peeled off in McCall's car and sped
to the local police station. They filed a complaint against Nichols,
stating he had violated the state's 1945 antidiscrimination law, one
of the first in the country. The official complaint states that Nichols
"willfully refused to serve beverages of any kind, used profane and
obscene language, and intimidation by weapon . . . such refusal being
by reason of complainants' color." Three of the four signed the complaint accordingly: Pearl E. Smith, W. R. McCall, and ML King Jr.[13]

The group of four, accompanied by police, returned to the
tavern. Police confiscated Nichols's gun. Nichols maintained his
innocence, claiming his treatment of ML and crew had nothing to
do with race. Rather, he refused to serve them because he believed
they were trying to trap him into violating the state's prohibition
of alcohol sales on Sunday or after 10:00 p.m. He said nothing
about the ginger ale. His lawyer also claimed that the gunshot was

nothing but a misunderstanding. "Mr. Nichols claims that this act was not intended as a threat to his colored patrons. The colored patrons, on the other hand, while they admit that the gun was not pointed at them seemed to think that it was a threat. Mr. Nichols on the other hand states that he has been held up before and he wanted to alert his watchdog who was somewhere outside on the tavern grounds." ML testified at the hearing for the weapons charge. "He was a very good witness," the Maple Shade prosecutor remembered. "He was direct and positive with his answers. You had the feeling he was telling the truth." Nichols was found guilty on weapons charges and fined fifty dollars.[14]

However, the hearing for the discrimination charges was another matter. The Camden, New Jersey, branch of the NAACP took up the case. Three white male students from the University of Pennsylvania Law School were sent to Mary's Cafe to test Nichols's commitment to state law. They had no problem getting beer. They pledged to testify before the grand jury. However, they backed out. The law students feared their testimonies would brand them race traitors and harm their career prospects. News of the betrayal wounded ML. When he and Pearl were summoned back to New Jersey to testify, they did not even bother to show up. According to McCall, they all felt the case was hopeless without any corroborating evidence from white citizens. "We just dropped the thing," he noted years later. The judge dismissed the case.[15]

Once again, ML was confronted by the limits of Northern integration and equality.

• • •

High classroom marks, heroics, and civil rights protest aside, Daddy King was concerned what the seminary was doing to his son. ML seemed to become more liberal. "He often seemed to be drifting away from the basics . . . that I felt very strongly about," the father noted in his autobiography. This included personal morality. When Daddy visited his junior, ML casually ushered him into the school's poolroom while smoking a cigarette. The smoke-filled poolroom was located under the seminary's chapel, a sign of the school's liberal orientation. Daddy King detested his son's smoking and the poolroom. That place, as evidenced by the cigarette smoke, was for sinners, not young ministers. ML teased his father for being too old-fashioned, putting personal piety over the importance of interpersonal relations. ML enthusiastically showed off the behind-the-back trick shot he had developed at Crozer as if it was a new biblical revelation. Between shots, he reminded his dad the smoke-filled poolroom was like dancing: The act of shooting pool was not sinful. It was the mindset and the plans that too often accompanied the pool hall that were sinful. The two battled to a stalemate: Daddy King protested with his hands restlessly sequestered in his pockets, while ML aimed for the corner pocket.[16]

But Daddy King did not suffer silently through all of ML's evolving liberalism and its baggage. The father handled it the best way he knew how. He scolded the child as he had done when ML was a self-professed agnostic thirteen-year-old. "There were some sharp exchanges," Daddy King admitted. "I may even have raised my voice a few times." But ML's emerging skill in the pulpit provided the father with the balm of fatherly pride. ML joined his Morehouse and seminary education with the oratory of the Black preaching tradition. And with his memory, he could cite long literary passages and quotes without the aid of any notes, further mesmerizing listeners. "Students would always look forward to King's sermons," Crozer classmate George Lawrence remembered. "The way he preached.

The content. He was a born orator . . . he put his whole heart and soul into it."

Daddy King also became an admirer, watching with pride as his son filled the Ebenezer pulpit during the summer, delivering crafty sermons that merged the ancient words of the Bible with contemporary knowledge, applying it all to present-day problems. Daddy King marveled at how his namesake "combined so many of the Bible's truths with wisdom of the modern world . . . interwoven into a most compelling, stirring oratory."[17] It was a distinctive voice and style he had begun rehearsing in the tobacco barns of Connecticut.

Daddy King had no choice but to agree with Dean Batten's progress report on the budding preacher. "[ML] King seems to know where he wants to go and how to get there," the dean concluded, and "he is making remarkable progress in arriving."[18]

35

WILL YOU MARRY ME?

Getting Juanita to the altar remained a desired destination for ML. She was just 120 miles away at Columbia University with his sister, Christine.

Christine recalled when she and Juanita took the train to enroll at Columbia, their trek north was just as degrading as ML's initial journey north had been. They deferred the packed lunches their parents gave them, electing to eat in the dining car. Christine ruefully remembered the experience. "We were separated from the white passengers by two curtains."[1]

ML made occasional visits to see Jaunita and his sister in New York. The girls were forbidden by their parents to explore New York beyond the places they needed to go for their immediate needs. But when ML visited, they could venture further, seeing the parts of New York City they had only heard about. He even brought Walter McCall for one trip. "Juanita and I waited like giddy schoolgirls for their arrival," Christine remembered. The foursome explored the metropolis's neighborhoods, chewing up as much of the Big Apple as they could.

Juanita and Christine also visited ML at Crozer, staying with a friend of the King family. The group even arranged a New York City reunion with ML's beloved Professor George Kelsey in January 1949. They swapped stories and fondly sang the songs of their beloved Morehouse and Spelman.[2]

These visits also served as check-ins for ML and Juanita, touch points in their betrothed relationship as both continued to pursue their careers and entertain romantic suitors. ML did not hide the fact that he dated. Perhaps he concealed it from Christine and Juanita, but not his mother. He kept her abreast of his dating life. "Do you know the girl I used to date at Spelman, Gloria Royster?" he said, half expecting his mother to remember his rotation of dates. "She is in school at Temple, and I have been to see her twice." He relayed his interactions with new infatuations as well. "Also, I met a fine chick in Phila [Philadelphia] who has gone wild over the old boy," he joked.

Reverend J. Pius Barbour, Chester, Pennsylvania, pastor and family friend, unwittingly played wingman for ML. "Since Barbor [sic] told the members of his church that my family was rich, the girls are running me down," he joked to his mother. "Of course," he quickly pivoted, "I don't ever think about them. I am too busy studying."

Alberta and Daddy King did not seem to worry much about their son's dating. In fact, the father took a measure of pride in it. It was a display of masculinity. But they still held on to the hope that when he was ready, he would settle down and marry Juanita. Preferably sooner than later.[3]

But they were unaware that ML dated his first and only white woman at Crozer. In Connecticut, fifteen-year-old ML had enjoyed talking with white women. At Crozer, he took things even further with Amelia Elizabeth Moitz. The daughter of the school's campus dietician and cook, Betty, as he called her, lived on campus. The forbidden couple attended the movies together, and even kissed and held hands in public. Betty said she loved him. She was completely impressed by his gifts, sense of humor, and sincerity.

"One thing ML knew at age nineteen," she noted in a 2016 interview, "was that he could change the world." And ML loved her. He had pursued her, winning her affections away from one of his professors. Dr. Kenneth Smith, Crozer's twenty-five-year-old professor of applied Christianity, was dating Betty while ML was his student. In a 1983 interview, the white Virginian remembered ML as "driven" in the classroom, obtaining an A in Smith's Christian Social Philosophy course and an A-minus in Christianity and Society. He, understandably, offered less information about the love triangle. "Martin and I dated the same girl once," he told the interviewer, "and that's all I'm going to say about that one."

ML seriously considered disappointing his parents by ending his arranged relationship with Juanita so he could marry Betty. He thought an interracial marriage, more than marriage to a Black professional like Juanita, could make great strides toward interracial harmony. But older classmates convinced him otherwise. Marcus Wood, nine years older than ML, recalled, "The more we warned ML that marriage was out of the question—especially if he hoped to become a pastor in the South—the more he refused to break off the potentially controversial relationship." Reverend Horace Edward Whitaker, known affectionately as Whit, was a war veteran and eleven years older than ML. He told ML that perhaps in another time and another day ML and Betty could marry, but 1950s America was not that time. ML knew Wood and Whit were right. At the time, every single Southern state—sixteen in all—had an anti-miscegenation law prohibiting interracial marriage (the US Supreme Court ruled such laws unconstitutional in 1967). In 1958, Gallup launched its first public opinion poll on interracial marriage:

94 percent of white Americans disapproved. It would take until the year 2021 for 94 percent of whites to approve, representing one of the largest transformations of public opinion in Gallup's history. ML imagined that world, but knew he did not yet live in it. He eventually accepted the wise counsel of his seminary elders, finally admitting that a white wife and pastoring in the South did not mix. "She liked me, and I found myself liking her," he purportedly told a friend years later. "But finally, I had to tell her resolutely that my plans for the future did not include marriage to a white woman." Years later, Betty would claim she was the one who put an end to the talk of marriage, leaving ML angry that societal norms would not allow their fledging love to grow. "Our romance," Betty reminisced in 2016, "was short and sweet."[4]

After graduation, ML, along with the eleven other Black students, set his heart on changing the world. Crozer had been like "a miniature kingdom of God where there was no discrimination," Marcus Wood recounted. "We had a white cook, we had white maids to clean up our rooms, and most of the faculty was [sic] white." Wood remembered ML and other Black students joking about white maids cleaning the rooms of Black students: "Oh, we've reached the Kingdom of God!" they joked. Jesting aside, Wood said that the experience at Crozer made all the Black students "concerned that as we moved up in life that we would make all of society a free society, a society where one would not be known by his race, creed or color." ML had carried that burden since his time in Connecticut. He often told Wood that he felt so much guilt enjoying the "heaven" of Crozer, while so many Blacks in the American South were living through hell.[5]

ML believed he needed a wife, a partner, to assist him in delivering his people. He told family and friends he would graduate in the spring of 1951, tie the knot that summer, obtain his PhD, and then pastor in the South. "His goal was to finish his degrees . . . and marry someone whom he really loved and go wherever the first church called him," one friend recalled. ML naturally assumed his promised bride would say yes, but she was busy building a life of her own. She graduated from Columbia in 1949 and began teaching at Savannah State University in Savannah, Georgia. She was well on her way to becoming an award-winning teacher and sought-after speaker, while also fielding romantic interests from a rotating crew of Atlanta's most eligible Black society bachelors.[6]

When the summer of 1951 did not produce a Mrs. ML King Jr., friends like Whit assumed ML was still too busy playing the field. "Apparently," he wrote to ML, "you are still meeting these girls who are one-time wreckers." Whit reminded ML of his own advice: "Watch the doctor! Don't let one catch [you] with your shoes off."[7]

Whether he was playing Casanova or not, ML was not married because Juanita had broken his heart. According to June Dobbs, ML did propose marriage to Juanita in the summer of 1951. The proposal occurred amid a heated summer of disagreement. He was upset Juanita had signed a contract to teach over the summer at Savannah State instead of coming home to Atlanta where he was filling the pulpit at Ebenezer. She had returned to Atlanta the previous summer. ML thought she would do the same in 1951.

After cold months apart, the summer was the time for their love to blossom again. "He was very upset," Juanita recalled. She said ML's reaction made it plain to her: "Women don't sign contracts." ML had loved that Juanita was not a "doormat." She was assertive and independent, it was one of the things that attracted him most. But according to Juanita, ML also saw that virtue as her greatest vice. ML believed, "[No] woman would let a contract stand ahead of her man," she mockingly remembered.[8]

The matter brought the love affair to a boil. Both issued ultimatums. ML proposed marriage and proposed that Juanita begin adjusting herself to being a pastor's wife, a spouse who would submit herself to being the primary caregiver and the queen of the domestic sphere. ML's attitude regarding the roles of women reflected not only his environment, but American culture. He believed women were as capable as men. There should be no glass ceilings in the professional world. But there would be one in his personal world. Being married to a career woman was perhaps fine for somebody else. But not for him. He wanted his wife to have the mind of a professional, someone he could intellectually engage, but have the primary existence of a "homemaker" and a mother.

Indeed, ML told friends and dates that he expected to come home to a clean house, a warm meal, and a brilliant beautiful wife patiently waiting for him. "You know I need a wife who is going to be home," one date recalled ML telling her. "Some men can do it, but I have to have a wife who will be home most of the time, and when I come home I want my wife to be there." He felt the same way about his wife working. "I'm supposed to take care of my wife, I'm supposed to earn enough money for me to take care of my family. You take care of me and you take care of the children." This was the life that was still very common in midcentury middle-class America. And it was the life he had seen his father live.[9]

But Juanita was determined to have her own life and her own career. According to June, Juanita told ML she needed some assurances before she would give her hand in marriage. She asked ML to promise they would settle in Atlanta. She knew the city. It offered plenty of teaching jobs for a Black woman, including her alma mater. And if all else failed, she could work at her family's business there.[10]

ML would not and could not guarantee that. God had spoken

to him, he told Juanita. He was supposed to obtain the PhD and then go wherever God directed him. His mission was to help God's children combat white supremacy, even if that was in the small, fictitious Southern town of "Chitlin Switch, Georgia," he was prone to say.[11]

Juanita was not moved. "My best friend was engaged to him," June Dobbs Butts recalled in an 2006 interview, "and she said 'I can't do that.'" June recalled Juanita's retelling of the story. "I'll go crazy," Juanita told ML. "I can't live in any little hick town." In the South, small towns not only lacked urban amenities, they were usually overrun with white supremacist violence under the cover of law and order.

"Well, I've got to do this," Juanita recalled ML saying, " 'cause God wants me to do this."[12]

Juanita remained resolute. She was willing to compromise many things—her propriety by visiting his house and his dorm while he was in seminary, and even rumors of his dalliances. But she was not willing to give up the plans she had for her life just so ML could fulfill his. Many women went to pieces for ML, but not Juanita. She had, June Dobbs remembered, what the French dubbed "sangfroid." She was self-possessed and cool, even when under pressure. She was "cold-blooded!" Dobbs said of Juanita's dealings with ML. She was on her way to building a life according to her own desires. Not even smooth-talking ML could talk her out of her destiny.[13]

Both decided a marriage was not worth their respective futures. The engagement was off. Juanita believed the events of the summer of 1951 marked "the beginning of the end" of their marriage contract.[14]

"Juanita could have lived the life that ML wanted her to," June Dobbs Butts told one interviewer, "but she didn't want to be exposed to white racism and that kind of thing. . . . She didn't want to devote her whole life. She wanted more of a calm life."[15]

Juanita preferred to put it more bluntly. "I was too independent . . . too liberated for him."[16]

Indeed, Juanita continued to teach, and in 1952, according to the *Atlanta Daily World*, she was "rapidly becoming known for her challenging and inspiring addresses to church and school groups" throughout the state. She also continued to court. The society page of the paper kept readers updated on her dates and escorts. Juanita was living her life.[17]

Over the next year, ML followed the spirit and moved to Boston to complete his PhD in theology. He was drawn to Boston University Graduate School for its emphasis on personalism, a school of thought that emphasized a personal and knowable God; the immortal spiritual nature of humanity; God's interests in each human soul; and the life of Jesus as God's blueprint for every human being. It was a philosophical rendering of the Black Baptist faith he imbibed as a child. As ML would later write, personalism offered a "metaphysical and philosophical grounding for the idea of a personal God, and it gave me a metaphysical basis for the dignity and worth of all human personality."

In Boston he found himself, once again, confronted with the limits of Northern freedom. He had difficulty finding an apartment in Boston. "I went into place after place where there were signs that rooms were for rent," he recalled in a 1965 *Boston Globe* article. "They were for rent until they found out I was a Negro and suddenly they had just been rented."[18]

He finally landed at 170 Saint Botolph Street. Once settled, his calls and poetic overtures to Juanita continued, but they slowed to a trickle. The few letters he sent were missives of doubt. He pointed out their gendered differences in expectations and her conspicuous class status. It all seemed increasingly insurmountable. He was riddled with skepticism regarding the possibility of their shared future.[19]

Doubting his future with Juanita, ML hit the streets of Boston looking for a wife. He was, a friend joked with him, "galivanting around Boston, [like] the most eligible and popular bachelor in town."[20]

36
JEWELLE

"Y ou look like a princess," she remembered ML saying to her through that broad smile that seemed to occupy his entire head. It was the fall of 1951, and it was the first time he was meeting the princess.[1]

Her name was Jewelle Taylor. She was an eighteen-year-old freshman at Radcliffe College in Cambridge, Massachusetts. ML's parents helped to make the connection. They became aware of the Connecticut-born Jewelle while attending the National Baptist Convention. They overheard her father, a prominent Black Baptist preacher, boasting about his daughter's educational accomplishments. Both were young, intelligent children of the Baptist cloth, removed from their families. ML's parents secured her phone number so the two could meet. The connection was supposed to be a supportive, platonic relationship.

But ML was not interested in being friends. He was looking for a wife. He started asking Jewelle out on dates. She kept declining, telling him she was too busy with her studies for dates. But that was not the whole truth. She and her circle of Radcliffe coeds were indeed looking for husbands. "It was the early 1950s," she reflected. "Many of us were obsessed with maximizing our strategies to find a suitable husband, preferably before we graduated. Feminist mantras about careers and independence had not yet entered our consciousness or our vocabularies." She acknowledged ML had many admirable qualities. She enjoyed their robust conversations about justice and the evils of racial segregation. However, she admittedly became "defensive" when ML turned his critique on the North. He knew her native land of Connecticut too well to indulge her explanations and excuses. Yet, she relished their debates on the best strategic solutions to racism. She deeply respected his commitment to the ministry and his desire to return South and declare war on Jim Crow. But she drew the line at being a pastor's wife. She watched her mother live under the burdens and responsibilities of being a first lady. Jewelle decided the burden was too heavy a load for her. Besides, she thought, "I ha[ve] neither the temperament nor the fortitude to live in the segregated south."[2]

Jewelle tried to be diplomatic when she rebuffed his romantic interest. She did not want to cause "friction" between their families. She told him she was busy for the next several weekends. Instead, she offered to meet him for coffee after class. It would be a study date. "This was a strategy I had learned from my popular dorm-mates to save the weekend for the big dates and let the less desirable guys take you out for coffee on a study date during the week," she admitted years later. She was hoping to hear from "a cute guy," a "female deprived black male at [all-male] Harvard." The dating numbers were in Jewelle's favor, and she planned to enjoy it.

But ML, according to Jewelle, was persistent and principled. He was not interested in a coffee date, nor study date. He wanted a church date. He wanted Jewelle to hear him preach. Unaware of her pledge to never marry a preacher, the church date was ML's way to observe her fitness to be a first lady. And perhaps, in the process use the charisma of the pulpit to dismantle Jewelle's wall of romantic rejection, brick by brick.

"After several lengthy phone conversations," she recalled, "I finally capitulated."

When he picked her up for church, he looked her over and immediately commented on her red suit and promise as a first lady. He called her a princess, and then through his spacious smile, declared, "You'll be a big hit with the church ladies."

Initially, ML's plan seemed to be working. Jewelle remembered being very impressed with him. "I was surprised at how confident and smooth he was in the pulpit," she admitted. She admired how well organized his sermons were, how he passionately sprinkled them with lengthy quotes from learned men. And, she confessed, "I was . . . pleased when I caught him smiling down at me with a twinkle in his eye at the end of the sermon." Afterward, church members invited the young couple to a traditional fried chicken dinner. The meal was, Jewelle fondly recalled, "a welcome change from the bland Yankee food" at Radcliffe.

They repeated their Sunday "date" routine two more times—complete with ML's earnest preaching, stealthily twinkled glances, and soul food dinners. Things seemed to be going according to ML's plan.

That was a problem for Jewelle. ML, she recalled, "definitely seemed to be seeking an eligible wife and helpmate." But Jewelle remained serious about her pledge not to marry a minister. "I knew that it was time to take our relationship from this serious heavenly plane to a more casual level, where I would feel more comfortable and less concerned about any commitment." She recalled breaking the news to him as they drove from their last church service back to Radcliffe. She loved his sermons and the soul food dinners, she told him, but going to church was not her idea of "a fun date." She was the daughter of a pastor. She had to go to church every Sunday and live her social life under the microscope of the impossible expectation to be what she called an "earth-bound angel." She wanted to be free—liberated from church expectations and serious commitments—and just have fun. "If you want to see me again," she plainly told him, "please invite me to a movie or a party."

ML, according to Jewelle, was crushed. He wanted a wife and a first lady, a woman who loved church as much as he did. He clearly began to think Jewelle was the one. She seemed to enjoy going to church with him, being on his arm, and being the recipient of his adoring glances from the pulpit. And then, seemingly out of the blue, she told him otherwise. All of this came on the heels of Juanita's rejection, likely sharpening the sting of Jewelle's unrequited interest. The look on his face was imprinted on her memory. He was speechless, she remembered, looking embarrassed, "as if he had been scolded by a favorite teacher."

She immediately felt bad. She did not want to hurt his feelings. She impulsively hugged him and gently kissed him on the cheek. Their first time sharing physical affection was a sympathy hug and a consolation kiss. But that did not seem to matter to ML. Jewelle recalled that ML smiled as he turned to leave, bounding down the steps of her dorm as if he had just hit the winning shot in a basketball game. "[Now] I had to worry whether I had conveyed exactly the wrong message by my spontaneous show of affection," she thought.[3]

ML got the message. He did not contact Jewelle for several weeks.

And then her phone rang in the spring of 1952. She was pleasantly surprised to hear ML's slow, deep-baritone voice on the other end. He invited her to a party at his apartment. She happily accepted. She missed their playful banter and debates. But just in case ML had plans to resurrect his romantic feelings for her, she took along a friend from Radcliffe.

ML played host at the party. He was the perfect gentleman. He greeted Jewelle and her friend as he did everyone when they entered the small apartment. It was a friendly, intimate affair, attended by Boston's Black undergraduates, graduate students, as well as sororities and fraternities from across the Boston area. They found strength and joy in their small, scattered numbers. By the spring of every academic year, everybody in this budding circle of Black Boston's talented tenth knew everybody. With all the close relations, ML spent the party doing more talking than showing off his storied dance moves.

Jewelle immediately recognized the usual suspects. But then, scanning the room, she recalled her shock when she laid eyes on an unfamiliar face. "A very attractive young black woman with long dark wavy hair," she vividly remembered, "and skin the color of caramel taffy, sitting in a corner with her eyes riveted on Martin." Jewelle could not resist staring. Who was this stranger? During the party, the woman barely spoke to anyone. She was kind when spoken to, but still very reserved. "There was an air of mystery about her, as if there were depths of emotion hidden beneath her placid exterior," Jewelle remembered thinking. ML occasionally checked on her during the party, but the woman just sat in the corner in what Jewelle described as a "Sphinx-like pose, radiat[ing] a sense of quiet dignity and inner strength."[4]

Who was this mystery woman?

Jewelle just had to know. "Within minutes, unable to contain my curiosity, I introduced myself to the newcomer."

The newcomer quietly stated that her name was Coretta Scott.

Coretta Scott.

37
CORETTA

ML and Coretta Scott met in Boston in February 1952. The two were introduced by Mary Powell, a King family friend from Atlanta studying at the New England Conservatory of Music. ML told Mary he was growing "cynical" about love—no doubt a result of a series of rejections. There was Juanita Sellers, Jewelle Taylor, and then there was a woman from the New England Conservatory. He met LaVerne Weston at Sharaf's Cafeteria. He approached the aspiring opera singer while she was eating alone. She remembered his sharp wardrobe and charisma. She enjoyed their conversation. He talked a lot, but he also asked good questions. He even bragged a bit. "I'm going to kill Jim Crow," she recalled him saying. She did not say anything. But she did remember thinking, "I wonder, how is he going to do that as a preacher?" She was intrigued enough to go out on two dates with him. He quickly brought up marriage, telling her he was looking for a wife who would take care of him like his mother. That was not the "happily ever after" for which LaVerne was looking. Besides, she thought to herself, he was just too short.[1]

These disappointing rejections were creeping into cynicism, so he asked Mary if she knew any single women.

Mary told the pessimistic twenty-three-year-old bachelor about two fellow students also attending the conservatory. The first was LaVerne. "Oh, I've met her," Mary recalled ML casually saying, before trailing off. The second was Coretta Scott. Mary told ML that Coretta was a small-town Southern girl from Heiberger, Alabama, an unincorporated community about ten miles outside of Marion. The population was less than three thousand. The soon to be twenty-five-year-old soprano was a voice and music education major, in her second semester just like ML. Her fair skin set against her long, coal-black hair made her face shine like the sun breaking through at midnight, while her soft smile seemed to whisper poise. She had that Spelman look. But she was educated at Antioch College in Yellow Springs, Ohio, where she majored in elementary education and music. Mary warned ML that Coretta was not a religious fundamentalist. Rather, she was a woman with a critical intelligence, a mind of her own, and a disposition that had been cultivated by parents who taught her she was a child of God despite the racist social mores of her native rural Alabama.[2]

Mary failed to mention that Coretta also considered herself allergic to preachers. She was religious, raised in church. But she had come to be dismissive of most Black ministers as fundamentalist, unintelligent, and lacking commitment. Years later, Coretta remembered dismissing ML as soon as Mary brought him up. "I thought this Martin Luther King was probably some older man, pious, narrow-minded and not too well trained, like most of the preachers I had known."[3]

ML, on the other hand, was intrigued. "I want to meet her," he told Mary. Coretta told Mary to forget the setup. Mary ignored her. She gave ML Coretta's number.

ML called her immediately, commencing a courtship of romance, intellectual exchange, and gamesmanship that only young love could create and enjoy.

• • •

ML rushed in during their first phone call, bombarding Coretta with his tried-and-tested lyrics. He channeled Professor Channie's poetics through the phone. King would later tell audiences that courting Coretta compelled him to add Shakespeare's poetic take on loving desire to his repertoire:

> Love is not love which alters when it alteration finds,
> Or bends with the remover to remove.
> O no, it is an ever-fixèd mark
> That looks on tempests and is never shaken;
> It is the star to every wand'ring bark . . .[4]

"It was intellectual jive," Coretta recalled. "Of course, I kind of enjoyed it," she admitted years later. But in the moment she refused to let on.

"That's absurd," she recalled saying through the telephone receiver. "You don't even know me."[5] That was about to change.

ML asked her to meet him for lunch the next day. Coretta remembered being tentative. She had a full schedule of classes. Finding time for an impromptu date was not a priority. King pleaded, asking if he could see her as soon as possible. "You know every Napoleon has his Waterloo," he told her. "I'm like Napoleon. I'm at my Waterloo, and I'm on my knees." She conceded to lunch later that week.[6]

ML had a green 1950 Chevy, a gift from Daddy King following his top-notch graduation from Crozer. "[It] usually takes ten minutes to make the trip from B.U.," he flirtatiously told her, "but tomorrow I'll do it in seven."[7]

Coretta waited in the drizzling rain outside the conservatory on

Huntington Street for her lunch date in the green Chevy. She was dressed in a tightly buttoned coat and a light-blue suit. It was the perfect canvas to highlight her long, loose hair and bangs. The driver wasted no time flirting with her. "He looked at me all the way from my feet to my head." Coretta remembered. "He looked me over so intently that I felt self-conscious." He canvassed her again when she took off her coat. "When I took off my coat," Coretta told an audience of college students in 1965, "typical of any male, I suppose, he got a good look and of course I was very, I tried to appear very unmoved." ML liked what he saw. Later, he would tell Mary through a slick grin, "I owe you a thousand dollars for introducing me to this girl," and gushed to his old friend Larry Williams about "the fine chick" named Coretta he had just met. Eventually, he would tell Coretta that he looked at her and thought, "She could be very attractive, she could be one of the most beautiful women in America, but she needs some help on dress and style." But in the moment he simply complimented her hair.[8]

Coretta could not say the same. She was not impressed. When he pulled up in his green Chevy, Coretta was concerned about "the little man" who seemed to fit all too well in the small car. "My first thought was, 'How short he seems,'" she confessed years later. It was bad enough that he was almost two years younger than she was. Being only two inches taller made it worse. "I'd always liked tall men," she told her five-foot-seven husband years later. "You looked so short sitting there in your little Chevy that I wasn't even sure I was going into the restaurant with you." She looked him over as they zoomed to Sharaf's Cafeteria on Massachusetts Avenue. He looks "unimpressive," she told herself. He had a wide nose, small ears, and a large forehead that seemed to be forcing his hairline into retreat. "He doesn't look like much," she remembered thinking as she shuffled out of the small car.[9]

Short. Not handsome. It was as if she were reading his diary of insecurities.

During that first date, he radiated charm. He showered her with poetic compliments. He listened. He asked her questions about her studies. He discussed serving others, economic inequality, racism, and his plans to put Jim Crow on its deathbed. Coretta recalled that at some point during the conversation, she said something which prompted ML to say, "Oh, I see you know about some other things besides music?" ML had no idea. At the time, Coretta was more of an activist than he was. She had come under the sway of nonviolent activist Bayard Rustin while still a high school student. As the first Black student to major in elementary education at Antioch College, she joined the Young Progressive League, attended the Progressive Party's national convention as a student delegate, and was a member of the campus branch of the NAACP. She protested when a local barbershop refused to cut Black hair, and she attempted to organize a protest when the all-white local schools would not accept her as a student teacher on account of her race. Coretta was well on her way to being a nonviolent soldier. "When I met her, she was very concerned about all of the things we are trying to do now," ML noted in a 1965 interview with Arnold Michaelis. "I never will forget the first discussion we had when we met was the whole question of racial injustice and economic injustice and the question of peace. And in her college days, she had been actively engaged in movements dealing with these problems." It has been the standard narrative to assume, as did Michaelis, that ML taught Coretta how to put her faith in nonviolent action. But this was not so. "It may have been the other way . . . ," ML told Michaelis. "I wish I could say to satisfy my masculine ego that I led her down this path, but I must say we went down together." And, he added, "at many points she educated me."[10]

During their first date, Coretta sensed that ML was sincere in his desire to shape a new world. It made her see the short minister in a new light. "In those few minutes I had forgotten about Martin being short," she later confessed. "And I completely revised my first impression. . . . This young man became increasingly better-looking as he talked." And she remembered saying to herself, "He doesn't seem like a minister. He's so different . . . he is so different from the ministers that I have known." Suddenly, the unhandsome runt morphed into a "very masculine" suitor. Her presumption of an unlearned, self-righteous minister dissipated, revealing an intelligent man of flesh and blood. This was not a selfish person of narrow concerns, she thought, but a broad-minded, self-possessed man who knew "exactly where he was going and how he was going to get there."[11]

ML wanted to get to the altar. According to his pattern, he was content to cram their entire courtship into their first date. He decided that Coretta was everything he wanted and needed—beautiful, smart, pious, and committed—a true partner in love and ministry. When their date ended, he turned to her and softly said, "You have everything I have ever wanted in a wife." Coretta, content to exit his Chevy and the date, was speechless. ML continued, guided by his mantra of love, tempered by reason. "The four things that I look for in a wife are: character, intelligence, personality, and beauty. And you have them all. I want to see you again. When can I?"[12]

"I was not so young that I, you know, was swept off my feet by this comment," she said years later, "but I did think about it." So she elected to play it cool. "I'll have to check my schedule," she demurely responded. "But you may call me . . ."[13]

Their dance played out accordingly: ML chased after Coretta's heart, while Coretta half-heartedly fled. "Martin pursued me," Coretta noted, "not that I ran very hard."[14]

While she did her best to remain uninterested, she began to recognize that she and ML actually "had a great deal in common," she said years later, "even though we had different backgrounds."[15]

They did grow up very differently. ML was a member of the urban Black middle class and Coretta hailed from the agrarian world of Heiberger, Alabama. And they had very different class backgrounds. "He came from a middle-class background," Coretta noted, "and I came from a poor underprivileged background where I had struggled most of my life, and he had never known these kinds of struggles."[16] As students, ML had the financial support of his family, a car, a checkbook, and income from preaching; while Coretta was largely on her own, earning money doing odd jobs, including being a maid. At times her pockets were stretched so thin, she ate fruit, graham crackers, and peanut butter for dinner. Admittedly, his urbane background made the farm girl skeptical of his interest. "I wondered whether his expressions were genuine because he had come from a middle class background and had not known conditions as I had."[17] Yet they were both Southerners who had, as Coretta would put it, to fight to overcome the "feeling of inadequacy" that Jim Crow imposed on all Black flesh. They both found themselves focused on changing the world, a desire both fully developed while living in the North.[18] Coretta called her time attending Antioch College as "one of the most important phases of my life." Like ML, she found destiny in the North. "I grew up," she told an interviewer of her time at Antioch, "I discovered myself."[19] Coretta's perception of white people was also transformed in the North. In Ohio, she was able, for the first time, to work with white people who were not completely blinded by Jim Crow. "For a southerner, particularly a southern Negro," she wrote in 1948, "it seems to me important to find out that there really are some white people working for racial equality and to be able to work with them." She acknowledged the South had its share of white people fighting for racial justice, but Southern mores made it difficult to partner across racial lines. But in Ohio, she even babysat for a white family, caring for a young John Lithgow, the future Emmy- and Tony-winning and Oscar-nominated actor.[20] And she also had an interracial romance, dating a white man for two years while attending Antioch.[21] Both ML and Coretta grew up in the South, but they came of age in the North.[22]

ML wasted no time communicating his urgent desires and expectations. "Martin showed every sign of someone falling in love at first sight," Coretta fondly remembered. "He impressed me as a man on a mission, on an urgent assignment who knew exactly what he wanted and wanted to rush on." He told her he "believed that women are just as intelligent and capable as men and that they should hold positions of authority and influence, but when it came to his own situation, he thought in terms of his wife being a home-maker and a mother for his children. He was very definite that he would expect whoever he married to be home waiting for him."[23]

It was all too much for Coretta. She was flattered, but she viewed his proposition as a hindrance to her career. While many women of the 1950s yearned to be married by their early to mid-twenties, Coretta was not most women. She wanted to travel the world as a concert singer, not be a first lady of a church or a stay-at-home wife. "The more I saw of Martin, the more I liked him," she admitted years later, "but I was resisting falling in love because I was determined that nothing would stop me from doing what I wanted to do and reaching my goals." Privately, Coretta was also nursing her own broken heart, a festering wound inflicting by a previous lover. She told herself she could not afford to make the same mistake twice. It was much safer to focus on her career than on love. "With Martin I had all my defenses up, Coretta admitted, "but in my heart I knew they were not too strong."[24]

As they continued to casually court she found she loved their conversations: Kant, Hegel, and Nietzsche; classical music, the social gospel, and of course, the role of Black faith in the struggle for racial equality. She was pleasantly surprised by his insistence to follow Christ's command to "love your enemies." When discussing Christian theology and eternal reward, she distinctly remembered ML telling her, "I'm not concerned with the temperature of hell or the furnishings of heaven, but with the things men do here on earth." And she loved his questioning of extravagant wealth and his concern for poverty. "I think a society based on making all the money you can and ignoring people's needs is wrong," he told her during one of their countless intellectual exchanges. He even issued a stern warning to his future wife. "I don't want to own a lot of things."[25]

Coretta could tell he was sincere, and it was music to her ears. A few months prior to meeting him she had written in a class assignment that America suffered from "an overdevelopment of the material and the underdevelopment of the spiritual aspects of living." But staring into each other's eyes, neither could fathom just how far King would go in his aversion to wealth. In the future he would refuse to own a new vehicle, accept the royalties from his books, or even the money from the Noble Peace Prize. "It almost became a fetish," Reverend Wyatt T. Walker noted of ML's perspective on money during an interview in 1963. Walker was a close associate and friend of ML beginning in the late 1950s and served as executive director of King's Southern Christian Leadership Conference from 1960 to 1964. He believed that once ML committed himself to the ministry, he began a slow process of "rebelling" against middle-class accoutrements. Wyatt confided that ML's home was very modest. "It's a slum, to tell you the truth." ML even opposed carpeting fearing it appeared materialistic. He conceded to Coretta's wishes, but only in their bedroom, where no one would see it. Even the preacher's dandy appearance shifted. When Wyatt first met ML, he

remembered ML being "as neat as a pin." But as his involvement in
the civil rights struggle progressed, ML began to dress less flashy
even looking "scrubby" at times. His suit pants would be "wearing
out in the pockets and his shoes run over."[26]

But those days were off in the future. When they were dating
ML maintained his dandy appearance. He even gave Coretta gentle
grooming suggestions. They might have annoyed another woman,
but not Coretta. Prior to meeting ML, she admittedly did not give
her appearance much thought. "I might comb my hair in the morning and I wouldn't think about it anymore during the rest of the day,"
she confessed. "I would put on makeup in the morning when I left
for school and that was it." But she enjoyed that ML cared so much
about her appearance. "Perhaps you'd like to go to the ladies' room
and comb your hair?" he would gently say to her. Or, "You look so
pretty with lipstick on. Why don't you put on some makeup?" He
even commented on her clothes: "Why don't you buy that pretty red
coat we saw in Filene's window?" Coretta received these comments
as a form of loving care, signs that ML paid close attention to every
detail that concerned her. "Having a man around to tell you that
you looked nice when you went out, you know you look forward to
that," she said. "He made me feel like a real woman."[27]

Coretta also loved that he was adept in the lighter side of life,
especially his sense of humor. "He was a great tease," she remembered. And he was a master on the dance floor. "He was . . . a good
dancer," she joyously boasted. "He could do everything from the
jitterbug to the waltz."[28]

But Coretta was still apprehensive about marrying ML. The conversation was great. The mutual respect was ideal. The growing attraction was a green light brighter than his Chevy. But Coretta did
not want to trade in her dream of traveling the world as a concert
singer to be caged in the life of being a preacher's wife.[29]

But ML was convinced that Coretta was the one. He was just waiting for her to realize it.

Coretta did her best to be nonchalant. She continually pushed back against his desire for marriage, a proposition that seemed to be discussed at the end of every date. "I'm not ready to get married," she would tell him. Sometimes she would just ignore him. He would ask her if she could be a good preacher's wife. "I didn't answer," she recalled. "He could decide that for himself," she reasoned.[30] At one point, she even told ML (while simultaneously trying to convince herself) that she would not be bothered if they stopped dating. "It wouldn't matter," she told him. ML, Coretta recalled, did his best to resist the bait. "Oh, it wouldn't?" he casually responded, attempting to keep the shock out of his voice. Coretta confidently shot back, "No. It wouldn't."[31]

He tried to make her jealous, hoping the attention of other women would open her closed heart. For one of their early dates, they attended a party in Waterbury, Connecticut, about 130 miles from Boston. ML was the center of attention. His reputation as a promising preacher made many of the women crown him a prize bachelor. He relished the experience. Coretta recalled watching just about every woman at the soiree fight a losing battle for his attention. "For someone only five foot seven and twenty-three years old, his personality was such that all the girls seem to look up to him," Coretta noted. "You know women are hero-worshippers," Coretta recalled ML explaining. It was ML's blatant attempt to get the hesitant Coretta to see what the other women at the party saw. "He was just so pleased because he wanted to impress me," she figured.[32]

And it worked. Coretta admitted all the attention "certainly heightened" her "interest" in ML. "Virtually every woman in the place would have traded places with me gladly," she remembered. "It always helps to know that a man you might be interested in is in demand." Yet she did her best to conceal her feelings, electing to remain outwardly unbothered. "I was very cool," she noted.[33]

But ML saw cracks in Coretta's façade. It even became a running joke for the couple. "Why don't you simply tell her that I swept you off your feet," ML teased Coretta, interrupting her during a 1956 interview on their courtship. Laughing, ML added, "And don't forget to mention that when you saw all those girls talking to me at that party in Waterbury, you started looking at me in a new light." All Coretta could do was laugh, the journalist noted, and "admit it was true."[34]

After a semester of courting, ML increased the pressure. After completing his first year of PhD studies, he invited Coretta to visit him in Atlanta during the summer of 1952. He would be filling the pulpit for his dad the entire summer. His aim was to win her heart and the approval of his parents in one triumphant swoop. But Coretta initially rejected his flattering invitation, in part, because of Juanita. She knew about Juanita all along. "I was told by Mary Powell that he was engaged to a girl in Atlanta," she admitted years later. "But he immediately started pursuing me and he kept talking about marriage." She remembered thinking, "Now how do you explain this?" Coretta reasoned that if ML was serious about Juanita he would not be pursuing her. "Before I became emotionally involved, it didn't bother me," she told an interviewer in 1968. She told herself that she was focused on her career anyway. But everything changed as her love for ML grew. "I was getting emotionally involved and there was nothing I could do about it," she confessed. So she waited to see if ML would tell her about Juanita. Eventually he did. "What impressed me most about Martin was his integrity and how he himself told me about 'the other woman.'"[35]

ML downplayed his feelings for Juanita, blaming his dad. He admitted Juanita was "a fine girl," and that they had dated "rather seriously," but the engagement, he truthfully admitted, "was more an assumption" between the two of them and their respective families, an informal rather than "a formal arrangement." This was true. But ML failed to mention that it was Juanita who put a pause on making it formal. He told Coretta that it was Daddy King who really wanted him to marry Juanita, that any feelings he had for Juanita he did more as a surrogate. "My father is very keen on it," he told Coretta. "But I am going to make my own decisions. . . ." Back in college, he had written in his old marriage institute notebook that a man could not cling to his parents but must give himself completely to marriage. Now he was going to have to put those words into action. "I know the kind of wife I need. . . . I will choose my wife," he told Coretta, "and I choose you."[36]

Despite ML's assurances, Coretta feared going to Atlanta. She did not want to be embarrassed or become another woman fawning after the promising minister.[37] Coretta believed ML, but feared "he was not strong enough" to stand up to the wishes of his dad. Mary Powell, who knew the family well, wholeheartedly agreed. Coretta recalled Mary's warning: "He's not strong enough. He will probably marry Juanita. I think he will be forced to do that."

Yet Coretta decided to go to Atlanta for a short summer visit to see for herself. "For the first time I felt that here is a man I really could fall in love with, if I could just let myself," she recalled thinking. But she still wanted to test ML, she reasoned, "to see if he really wanted me or not." So she told him she was not coming to visit. She explained she was too busy to meet his family. Besides, she knew he was still dating women in Atlanta. She encouraged him to focus on the other matters in Atlanta that required his attention. The test worked. ML was so upset, he issued an ultimatum, threatening to end their relationship. "If you don't want to come, just forget everything!" he snapped. "Forget it. Forget the whole thing!"[38] Coretta

saw the emotional outburst as a good sign. "Hmmm, I thought . . .
He really wants me to meet his parents. He really cares."[39]

ML departed for Atlanta, his emotions continuing to boil. "Dear
Miss Scott," he scribbled in a letter dated July 14, 1952. The salu-
tation was a drastic departure from his usual romantic greeting.
"I must regretfully confess I am in no mood for writing you. . . . I
see you mean to insult me on every hand." He apologized for his
tone, but he was angry that Coretta refused to visit him. He enclosed five dollars so Coretta could buy herself "something nice."
He closed the letter by chastising her for her decision: "P.S. Either
you are under the influence of some frustrated women and men
or you just don't give a damn."[40]

Coretta's exact response is not known. Her letters to ML have
not been made public. But whatever she wrote back to ML clearly
softened his heart. "Dearest Coco," he wrote on July 18, "your letter
was sweet and refreshing to my heart, which had well-nigh grown
cold toward you." He told her he was convinced he was in love with
her. Waxing poetic, he scribbled, "Darling I miss you so much. In
fact, much to [sic] much for my own good. . . . My life without you
is like a year without a spring time." He described himself as a king
in desperate need of a queen. "Can you imagine the frustration that
a King without a throne would face?" he asked her. "Such would
be my frustration if I in my little kinghood could not reign at the
throne of Coretta." He issued a halfhearted apology for his fanciful
flight. "But how else can we express the deep emotions of life other
than in poetry?" he asked rhetorically. "Isn't love too ineffable to be
grasped by the cold calculating heads of intellect?"[41]

He went on to discuss the book Coretta gave him, Edward Bel-
lamy's 1888 novel, *Looking Backward: 2000–1887*. The book envisions
Boston in the year 2000. The nation has experienced an awakening.
Capitalism has been replaced by a more just means of wealth dis-

tribution. Society has become classless, racially integrated, and the concept of war is foreign. Yet women remain stuck in time as second-class citizens. Perhaps Coretta gave him the book to see if he would comment on the evolution of ideas of class, while gender inequality remained. But ML failed to do so in his love letter. Instead, he praised the warless, economic, and humanitarian vision of the book, while never mentioning the gender component. "Much of its content is in line with my basic ideas," he told Coretta. Yet he criticized Bellamy for being too optimistic about the capacity of humanity to progress without submitting to God. "Ultimately our problem is [a] theological one," he surmised. "Let us continue to hope, work, and pray that in the future we will live to see a warless world, a better distribution of wealth, and a brotherhood that transcends race or color. This is the gospel that I will preach to the world," he promised her. "Thank you a million times for introducing me to such a stimulating book; you are sweet and thoughtful indeed."[42]

He quickly turned to the visit. "As to your visit to Atlanta. . . . It hurt me very much to know that you believe that I would invite you to Atlanta and then mistreat you." He asked one last time if she would visit. He promised it would be the last time he would ask. His dying heart needed to be put out of its misery, and his practical side needed to know so he could "make the arrangements."

But, he told her, if she did not come, it could mean the end. "Of course if you don't come I will know that you have no confidence in me and I will proceed to think out our courtship in those lines. I hope we won't have to break up about this trip."

He closed with, "Be sweet and remember that daddy still loves you."[43]

Coretta finally told ML she would come visit him. She loved him, and she reasoned that she owed it to herself and to the relationship to meet the Kings to see if she should surrender the throne of her heart to ML King Jr.[44]

"I am overjoyed to know that you are coming to Atlanta," ML wrote to her on July 29. "I'm sure that you will not regret a minute of the visit."[45]

Coretta did regret the visit. Her fear of being mistreated came to fruition.

The visit, which began in early August, started off as well as could be expected. Coretta, admittedly "on guard," enjoyed polite but awkward conversations with mom and dad King. The Kings were polite, but not warm; welcoming, but not open. "When I came home I met her," Daddy King remembered years later. "I didn't pay much attention to Coretta. . . . I wanted him to marry Juanita."[46]

Coretta boarded at Mary Powell's house, but attended church with Christine under the guise of being Christine's friend, not ML's love interest. Neither Daddy King nor the congregation was ready to hear that the prince of Ebenezer was considering marrying someone other than Juanita, let alone a musical performer. ML preached a sermon titled "Communism's Challenge to Christianity." ML acknowledged that communism and Christianity were incompatible, but he summoned his home church to learn from communism. "It should challenge us first to be more concerned about social justice," he told them.[47]

After a few days, Coretta went to Alabama to visit her parents. She wanted ML to come with her, but he was too busy with preaching engagements and running Ebenezer. The couple agreed Coretta would come back to Atlanta and drive back to Boston with ML. But Coretta's mother saw ML's failure to visit as a bad sign. She told her daughter to skip the return trip to Atlanta. She would be better off just going back to Boston by herself.[48]

But the two hearts missed one another. A flurry of love letters flooded their respective mailboxes in Atlanta and Heiberger. While Coretta's are not public, ML's letters reveal a couple falling in love.

"Dearest Coco," ML wrote on August 13, while confined to bed with an illness, "I could hardly adjust myself to your leaving, but somehow these things must be faced." He assured her that his family loved her. "My parents were very impressed with you, and ever since your leaving I have heard nothing but Coco." This was certainly an exaggeration born of blind love. A week later he thanked Coretta for her "sweet letter," noting, "Darling you are so inspirational. A word from you comes as spiritual food to a soul that is well-nigh starved." The couple exchanged photos. "I spend all day looking at the large on [sic] that you gave me." ML raved, "Everyone comments on how beautiful it is." He signed the letter, "Your Lover, M.L."[49]

Against her mother's wishes, Coretta returned to Atlanta in early September. The couple planned to depart for Boston on Tuesday morning, September 9. On Sunday, September 7, ML preached on "Mental and Spiritual Slavery." That evening, he told Coretta he needed to go visit a few sick parishioners and say goodbye to others, those older members who had watched him transform from a religious skeptic to a sincere preacher. He told Coretta to wait at his parent's house because he would return shortly. As night fell, ML did not return. "I waited and waited and waited," Coretta remembered. The later it got, the angrier she got. Her efforts to hide her anger and frustration boiled over. She knew he was not coming home. And she knew exactly where he was: with Juanita.[50]

"They were over there, uhh . . ." Coretta remembered years later. "Well I guess I shouldn't tell what they were doing . . . but anyway . . ."[51]

Mother Dear and Christine knew it too. To help their son and brother, as they always did, they intervened. They fixed up a spare room for Coretta and politely told her to go to bed. Coretta, ever the gentle soul, remained courteous and begrudgingly did as she was told.

With Coretta tucked away, Alberta immediately called Juanita.

ML came to the phone. The mother told her son he was messing up. Coretta had been visibly angry. If he was serious about her, Alberta told her son, he needed to return home at once.

ML did his best to stay calm and not alert Juanita and her family about the situation. "Yes, Mother Dear," he said trying to rush her off the phone. "Yes, you want me to bring you some barbecue on my way home. Uhhhh huh. Is that right? Okay. I'll bring you some barbecue. Uhh huh, okay bye." He did not take his mother's advice. He spent the night at Juanita's house.[52]

"The next morning when I woke up, I was just so unhappy," Coretta remembered. She came downstairs to breakfast and ML was there, smiling as if nothing had happened. He told Coretta he had grown weary from all the parishioner visits and simply fell asleep at a member's house. Coretta could barely look at him. "I was about to burst. . . . I felt like crying. I knew I had been mistreated." Years later, Coretta admitted that she was not so much angry that ML was still seeing other women. She knew about that. She felt he had the right to date because she had not given him an exclusive commitment. After having his own heart broken, ML was, she noted, simply "playing it very safe." But she was angry that he did so in such a dismissive and embarrassing manner.[53] Monday was a blur. On Tuesday, the two packed up the car and quietly drove back to Boston. The silence in the car was so loud, it made an already long drive feel like an eternity.

Eventually ML confessed. These confessions became a pattern of their courtship. "If he ever did something a little wrong, or committed a selfish act, his conscience fairly devoured him," Coretta told an interviewer in 1968. "The one thing that I realized even in courtship was . . . he would have to tell me. . . . For example," she continued, "he might go out with a girl or he might almost get caught up in a situation . . . well he would always tell me eventually . . . he may not tell me right then, but he had to tell me the truth and one thing that I noticed was that he had a very strong moral conscience and he could not do wrong and not feel guilty. He would feel guilt that would just about eat him up. The guilt was so strong that he would have to say something. He'd have to . . . And this was one thing that I always noticed in courtship."

Coretta came to trust ML, not despite the episode with Juanita, but in part because he told her about it, and any other "situation." "I came to see . . . the one thing that would keep Martin straight was . . . his conscience. . . . He was always looking for a sin to clean up, starting with sins in himself."[54]

According to Coretta, ML began the cleanup soon after they arrived back in Boston. He confessed that he had been with Juanita. He told her about Alberta's phone call, the Sellers' efforts to maintain the relationship, everything. But he insisted his visit was only to inform Juanita and her parents that the long, betrothal was finally and officially over. Despite the Sellers' disappointment and attempts to convince him otherwise, ML stood firm: He told them another lover possessed his heart.[55]

ML may have deliberately orchestrated the whole ordeal to test Coretta, to see if she would truly be unbothered if their courtship ended; to see if her noncommittal words were betraying a committed heart. Coretta admitted that he teased her about the ordeal a few months later. "When I go home this girl's got to be there and every time that I start to break up with her, you know, she is so charming that it is just so hard for me to do it because she is such a fine girl." ML continued to pour it on, "She's not just a girl that you could put aside. She's really a fine girl. And it's so hard. When I go home, you won't be there and she'll be there and so I just think . . . I just about decided that I'll go ahead and marry her."[56]

Coretta was furious. "Go. Go away from me!" she remembered

telling him. "Just don't say anything else to me!" She refused to speak to him.

"Wait a minute," she remembered ML saying. "I want to tell you something."

"I don't want to hear anything that you've got to say. This is just it!" she said as she began to cry.

Coretta remembered ML laughing. "Now, wait a minute now. I just want to say one thing." This went on for what felt like forever to Coretta.

"I was just teasing you," he told her, with his characteristic smile transfiguring his face. "You said that you did not care if I broke up with you." Clearly that was not true. "The truth of the matter is," he told Coretta, "I don't plan to marry her." The plan all along, he told Coretta, was to marry her.

Throughout the fall of 1952, ML and Coretta continued to date, splitting their time between classes—in addition to his classes at Boston University, ML also enrolled in a Philosophy of Plato course at Harvard—and seeing one another almost every day. Perhaps they were spending too much time together, as ML failed his required exam in German.

But he was succeeding in winning more and more of Coretta's love. In keeping with the gender norms of the time, she felt she needed to marry "a strong man" like ML, a man who was willing to occupy his "natural place as the head of the household." She loved the fact that ML was, as she put it, "too sure of his manhood." If ML was not, she feared she would "wear the pants" in the relationship. Coretta wanted a man, a partner she "could look up to and respect." She decided ML was that man. He was not going to be an ordinary minister. "His life is going to be different . . . than the stereotypical minister," she remembered thinking. ML was a man with a divine plan, on a mission to fight for and with all of God's children who were oppressed.[57]

And Coretta came to believe that it was God's plan for her to help him do so. She had long believed in fate. During her undergraduate studies at Antioch College she wrote at length about it. In a 1951 term paper she stated she had only "one basic assumption" in life: "Life is purposeful." She admitted she could not prove this proposition by reason alone. Rather, she was "forced to rely on the evidence perceived through my senses which I describe as bits of understanding, of love, and beauty."[58] Her senses led her to believe her meeting and connection with ML was purposeful, filled with love and beauty. They were destined for marriage. "I was meant to be Martin Luther King's wife," she told an interviewer in 1963.[59]

"Of course I prayed about this," she wrote years later, "it was not an easy decision . . . [but it] was the most important decision that I would ever make in my life." She prayed and pondered over the course of several months while continuing to date ML. She thought, "If I am serious about a commitment to service, how better could I serve than as a minister's wife?"[60]

And there was love. She asked herself, "Do I love him enough to make any sacrifices? Or can I give him up and not miss him?" She decided, "I couldn't give him up and that was that." She switched her major from performing arts to musical education. "Regardless of what happens after I marry Martin," she pledged, "I will adjust myself to these conditions, whatever they may be." Like Ruth in the Bible, she vowed fidelity, "Wherever Martin lives, I will live there too. Whatever he does, I will be involved in it."

ML finally gained Coretta's commitment, but his parents' approval still evaded him, largely because Juanita's shadow was still present. Tellingly, later that fall, a friend from Boston asked ML if he was married yet, and if so, "Which one was it?"[61]

The question came to a head that November when his parents

came to visit ML in Boston. During the visit Daddy King began bragging about his twenty-three-year-old son's dating prowess in Atlanta, telling Coretta his son had courted "the daughters of some fine, solid Atlanta families." He even mentioned ML's proposal to Juanita. He told Coretta that Juanita and her urbane family, as opposed to Coretta's rural one, had "much to offer."

Coretta sternly shot back, "I have something to offer too, Reverend King!"

Reverend King ignored her, continuing his praise of Juanita. "A fine family," Daddy King boasted, sounding like a car salesman. "[She is] very talented . . . wonderful . . . radiant personality. Beautiful girl. We love that girl. . . . I don't know what he [ML] is going to decide."[62]

ML did not say a word during his father's sales pitch. "He just sat there grinning like an embarrassed schoolboy," Coretta remembered. She was perturbed. Why was ML not challenging his father?[63]

ML used his tried-and-true method of handling the patriarch: He put on a veneer of acquiescence but then proceeded to make his own decision. "He was always so respectful of his father," Coretta remembered, "and yet he was completely his own man. . . . He made his decision, and whenever he didn't want to tell his father something he would just go out and make it." Indeed, ML arose from his seat, walked into the kitchen, and whispered to his mother: "You know, Coretta is going to be my wife." Alberta gave her son her blessing, as she always did for her middle child. A few days later, she told her husband about the private conversation. He refused to hear it.

Even though Juanita was Christine's friend, she'd given up on his marrying Juanita. She knew when her baby brother was in love, and she knew when ML had made up his mind. "She's a fine girl," she told her stubborn dad. "You must accept it, for Martin is going to marry her."

Dad refused to accept anything other than Juanita. Besides, ML

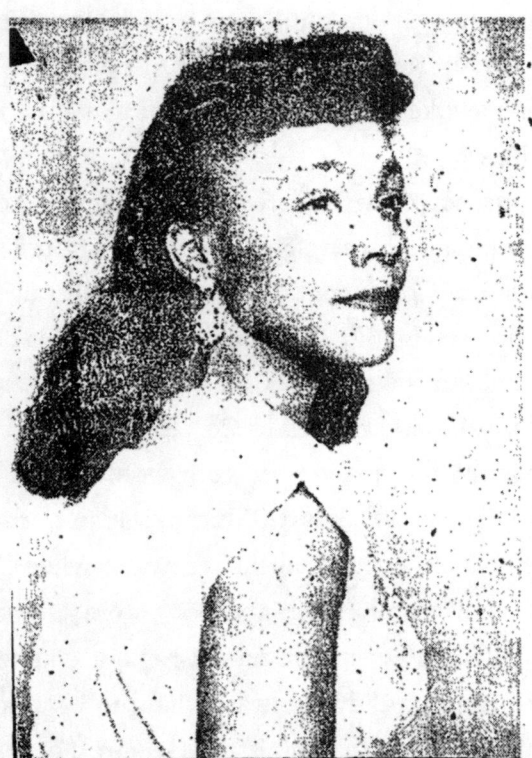

ENGAGEMENT ANNOUNCED — Mr. and Mrs. Obie Scott of Heiberger, Alabama announce the engagement of their daughter, Coretta to Rev. Martin Luther King, Jr., son of Rev. and Mrs. Martin Luther King, Sr. of Atlanta, Georgia.

The bride-elect is a graduate of Antioch College and presently studying at the New England Conservatory of Music.

Rev. King is a graduate of Morehouse College, Crozer Theological Seminary and at present is a candidate for the Ph. D. Degree at Boston University and special student in Philosophy at Harvard University.

ML and Coretta's engagement announcement in the *Atlanta Daily World*, April 5, 1953.

was going to be a minister, he told the family. He could not marry a concert singer.[64]

Coretta wondered if ML could stand up to his father. She knew ML loved her, but she also knew how much his dad's approval meant to him. Her restlessness was put to rest by a dream: She and Juanita stood before Daddy King. Daddy King turned to her, not Juanita, and smiled. She awoke convinced the dream was a miraculous foretelling of his blessing.[65]

And so it was. ML drove the green Chevy back to Atlanta during the Christmas holiday season to get the go-ahead from his father. ML was his own man, as Coretta put it, but the son still craved his father's approval and, if need be, financial support. He sat his dad down for a conversation about the merits of marrying Coretta as opposed to Juanita. "Coco," ML later relayed to Coretta, "I put you both on the scale." He weighed the qualities of both women for his dad. Both were beautiful. Attractive. Smart. Educated. Juanita came from an upwardly mobile family with financial resources, while Coretta's parents owned a small, rural "mom and pop" store. But only Coretta was willing to change her major, and the major course of her life, to be Mrs. ML King Jr. Only she was willing to be a partner in his ministry, no matter where that ministry led them. Those were life decisions Juanita refused to make. The conversation worked. "I can see that that is your choice," Daddy King gruffly said to his son. "I agree to it because I respect your choice and opinion." ML relayed the news to Coretta like she had just won the lottery. "Coco, you won!"[66]

The couple waited until Easter to officially announce their engagement in the *Atlanta Daily World*.

Coretta's vision became reality. Daddy King did choose her. Almost sixteen months to the day of the couple's first encounter, Daddy King officiated their wedding on the lawn of Coretta's parents' home outside Marion, Alabama, on June 18, 1953. ML wore a white tuxedo jacket and black pants. It was probably the same one he donned when he graduated from college five years early. He had not changed much since then. His June 2, 1953, health examination revealed that he measured five feet, six and a half inches and weighed 166 pounds. Coretta, in keeping with her sense of independence, rejected wearing a white dress, electing to wear a pale-blue short-sleeve dress, with a lace jacket, netted gloves, and shoes dyed to match. She wore a single string of pearls, a gift from the groom. She had the traditional language of "obey" removed from her vows. Coretta feared it would anger her husband-to-be, or that perhaps he would feel embarrassed or emasculated by such a revolutionary act in 1950s America. But to her surprise, "Martin didn't object," Coretta wrote years later, "because his view of women was more progressive than that of most men of his generation."[67]

There were no nearby hotels that would accept Black patrons, so the newlyweds spent their wedding night in the home of a friend, a prominent undertaker, just like the Sellers family. Throughout their marriage ML would tease that they spent their lively honeymoon in a funeral parlor.[68]

● ● ●

Juanita was surprised to learn of Coretta's version of events when they were published in Coretta's 1969 book. Juanita never publicly stated exactly what happened during ML's overnight stay, but in a 1984 interview, she stated she did not need a rendezvous to confirm the "engagement" was over. Yet she proudly reiterated to the interviewer, "I'm the one ML was supposed to have married, but I was too liberated."[69]

Juanita got married a year and a half after ML, to another accomplished man with a PhD. On December 26, 1954, she wed

Dr. Vernon Wayland Stone, a man thirteen years her senior and her colleague at Savannah State University. Christine King celebrated her friend by hosting a bridal shower and luncheon. The bride was married in a waltz-length ivory gown; the tall, handsome groom wore a dignified tuxedo. The couple wed in her parents' home on Hunter Street in Atlanta. After their nuptials, Dr. and Mrs. Stone moved to Tallahassee, Florida, where they both taught at Florida A&M University, and later at the University of Maryland Eastern Shore. The Stones moved to Atlanta in 1968 when Dr. Stone was named the first African American full professor at Georgia State. They had two children—Joy and Keith—and were married for forty-nine years. In 1999, the society page of the *Atlanta Daily World* included the couple in its list of "Atlanta's Twenty Most Romantic Couples," based on their commitment to being friends, communicating, and "respect[ing] each other's rights." Dr. Stone died on October 7, 2004, at the age of eighty-nine, just two months shy of the couple's golden anniversary.[70]

During the marriage and as a widow, Juanita lived the professional life she had always planned for herself. She was president of Sellers Brothers Funeral Home for more than thirty years. Her work was validated with the Woman of the Year Award from the National Funeral Directors and Morticians Association. She was also given the Pioneer Award from the Atlanta Business League, and the Businesswoman of the Year Award from Iota Phi Lambda Sorority, the first African American Greek-lettered business sorority. She was crowned with the Spelman College Enterprise Award, and served on the board of directors of Citizens Trust Bank, a rare achievement for a woman. The local news named her among the "Fifty Outstanding Mothers Who Maintain Fantastic Careers." She was recognized as a religious leader and a businesswoman whose vocation and community involvement had not hampered her commitment to motherhood.

Ironically, her life and accomplishments kept her connected to the former lover who wanted her to put a cap on her professional life. She served as a trustee and president of the missionary society at West Hunter Street Baptist Church, where ML's close friend and civil rights movement lieutenant Reverend Ralph David Abernathy served as senior pastor. She donned a turquoise ballerina-length silk organza gown that matched Coretta Scott King's when they both walked down the aisle of Ebenezer Baptist Church as bridesmaids in Christine King's wedding. The city of Atlanta recognized her life's work, featuring her on a Black History Month calendar of famous Atlantans, and Mayor William Campbell declared March 18, 2000, "Juanita Sellers Stone Day," accompanied by a commendation from Georgia Governor Roy Barnes. It was a small but significant holiday, especially for a Black woman in the South. But it was dwarfed by the national holiday recognizing her former lover. She died on May 30, 2018, at the age of eighty-nine. She lived out most of her adult years working at the family business and serving the community from her base on Hunter Street, which in 1976 was renamed Martin Luther King Jr. Drive.[71]

38
MONTGOMERY

In the fall of 1953, ML and Coco began their life together in a rented apartment in an old house at 396 Northampton Street in Boston. Apartment 5 had four rooms: a kitchen, bedroom, den, and a living room. They paid thirty-five dollars a month. For a time, Minister Malcolm X lived about two miles away at 5 Wellington Street. He held court every Sunday in his living room, giving lectures and sermons on the teachings of the Honorable Elijah Muhammed and the Nation of Islam. There is no record of a meeting or a chance encounter. If they passed one another on the street, they both would have been too busy to notice. Paroled the previous year, 1953 found Malcolm X rapidly establishing the Nation of Islam's Temple No. 11, about two miles south of the newlyweds. ML and his bride were preoccupied establishing a marriage while also attempting to finish their degree programs. They divided up the scholastic boundaries of the house. ML studied in the den, while Coretta took the bedroom. Coretta rushed to finish her degree so she could settle in to being "a new bride." She took thirteen courses that year and was a student teacher in an all-white school, an opportunity Antioch had denied her.[1]

ML adjusted his masculine notions during the first, and all too often rough, year of their marriage. Although their relationship hewed to certain gender conventions of the time, particularly King's belief that Coretta be the primary caregiver and the homemaker, at times it did challenge other dominant social mores. While ML never enjoyed housework, he dutifully pitched in while his beloved stretched herself to finish her degree. He did all the heavy cleaning, including scrubbing and washing the clothes. Coretta appreciated the effort, but not the results. When ML hung up the clean clothes on their makeshift clothesline, which dangled across the kitchen, they often looked worse instead of better. "I never told him," Coretta confessed, but without fail the clothes "looked like the 'before' on TV commercials, she remembered." He was better in the kitchen. Thursday was his night to cook since Coretta had a late class. He recreated the meals and smells he had as a youngster, drenching the small apartment in the savory, heavy aromas of smothered cabbage, pork chops, fried chicken, and turnip greens. The one exception was the cornbread. He could not do that from scratch; he relied on a premade mix.[2]

The newlyweds continued to enjoy a shared intellectual life. Together, the dynamic couple hosted a philosophy club, which ML dubbed the Dialectical Society. The group was organized by ML and other Black theology students in Boston. They met monthly on Friday night. ML served as president of the budding group of intellectuals—described by one member as "the gang in the room solving the problems of the world, politically, socially, and in the theological realm." The group would discuss and debate one another's arguments concerning how to best address American inequality. Eventually, the group became integrated with the participation of a few whites.[3]

ML maintained his playful side. He and Coretta went to amusement parks. They danced. And they roller-skated like their lives depended on it. ML and friends laughed, roughhoused, and showed off their fancy turns, gyrations, and dance moves while on the move. Coretta's mother was amazed that the son-in-law whose preaching she came to admire also had a lighthearted inner child. "You know," Coretta's mother said to him during one visit, "you act like you are about four years old."[4]

In the spring of 1954, ML completed his PhD residency requirements. Coretta was set to receive her degree. It was time for ML to look for a job. He had an offer to be Dean of the School of Religion at Shaw University and an offer to join the faculty of Morehouse. The young couple was attracted to the idea of living out their lives in an academic environment. ML had always wanted to be a recognized, educated minister. But something did not feel right. Just ten years prior, in Connecticut, he had received the calling to serve his people. And the masses of African Americans were not found on the grassy knolls of Black college campuses. ML was also offered positions in Northern churches—one in New York and another in Massachusetts—where his reputation as a remarkable young preacher was established. He also was invited to lead two churches in the South: First Baptist Church in Chattanooga, Tennessee, and Dexter Avenue Baptist Church in Montgomery, Alabama.[5]

Coretta wanted to stay in the North. Maybe someday they would return South, but not yet. "I [want] to breathe the freer air and the richer cultural life of the north a while longer," twenty-seven-year-old Coretta told her twenty-five-year-old husband, "and enjoy the greater opportunities a northern city . . . [offers] for furthering my musical career." ML understood. He questioned himself. "Can I return to a society that condones a system I have abhorred since childhood?" They prayed. After several days of prayer, contemplation, and mulling it over with their friends, ML decided.

"I am going back South," he told his wife, "I am going to live in the South because that is where I am needed." ML acknowledged all the disadvantages but, he reasoned with Coretta, "Our greatest service could be rendered in our native south. . . . We [have] something of a moral obligation to return . . . to do something about the problems that we had felt so keenly as youngsters." Those problems: The oppressive Jim Crow signs and waiting rooms. The refusal of service based on race. The police brutality. The discriminatory hiring and pay. The segregated schools, starved of resources. The bigoted bus rides. The embarrassing, dehumanizing curtains on the train. The lurking sense of nobody-ness. It all came rushing back to him. Yet, it was one of those times when he felt he was being carried out of himself by something greater, and he decided he was going to give himself to it. Coretta conceded. She could see it in his eyes, she remembered. He was in such a hurry "to get on with his destiny."[6]

Dexter Avenue Baptist Church in Montgomery was the next stop on destiny's road. Coretta maintained her hesitancy. Montgomery was the first capital of the Confederacy, where Jefferson Davis was sworn in as the first president of the Confederacy. It was rabidly racist and offered few opportunities for her. And it did not help that the church was across the street from the state capitol building, where state politicians made a sport of proposing, passing, and defending white-supremacist legislation. The thought of having to rock her future children to sleep in the cradle of the Confederacy unnerved her.

But ML saw so much potential in the church. It was small, comprised of the educated Black middle class, most affiliated with the Alabama State College for Negroes (now Alabama State University). It was a staid church, lacking emotionalism. ML loved that. The church had parted ways with its previous pastor for trying to unsettle the congregation from their middle-class comfort. That was scary. It hit close to home. But he still wanted the job. An anxious

ML gave himself a pep talk before he preached his candidacy sermon. He had preached so many times before; but now he was "on
trial" for the position. "Keep Martin Luther King in the background
and God in the foreground and everything will be all right," he whispered to himself. "Remember you're a channel of the gospel, not
the source."[7]

On Sunday morning, January 24, 1954, ML channeled the Gospel
for his trial sermon: "Three Dimensions of a Complete Life." He
had preached the sermon before and he would continue to preach
it for the remaining fourteen years of his life. Like so many of his
sermons, he committed it to his extensive memory. Life is measured
by the length, breadth, and height, ML told the congregation. The
length of life was the concern for one's own ambition and welfare.
But a life that was only concerned with self and not the welfare of
others was "meaningless and godless." We all need to expand our
breadth of life, "the outward concern for the welfare of others."
Remembering all the stories and confessions he heard during the
interracial forum, he boldly told the congregation that too many
white Southerners defended segregation because they were entirely
concerned with the length of life—the welfare of their so-called way
of life—rather than the breadth of life, the regard for the welfare
of others. Finally, he told the enraptured congregation, there is the
height of life, "the upward reach for God." God is the source of everything.

Pulling from his philosophy classes, he preached, "Everything
that we see in life is something of a shadow cast by that which we do
not see." Plato was right: "The visible is a shadow cast by the invisible." We are spiritual beings, thirsty until we find God. "St. Augustine
was right: we were made for God; we will be restless until we find
rest in him." ML had lived this reality. Material possessions—cars,
homes, televisions, money, can never fulfill the God-shaped hole in

our lives. "So let us go out with a cultivation of the third dimension, for it can give life new meaning," he told an excited church. "When we add height to length and breadth we have the complete life."[8] The silk-stocking church responded with dignified head nods and staid amens. The search for a new pastor was over.

ML officially accepted the position of pastor of Dexter Avenue on April 14, 1954, wrestling the pulpit away from another finalist, his old nemesis turned friend, Walter McCall. ML was thrilled, his head full of dreams for what the congregation could become. Coretta had a third sense about it as well. "Being in Montgomery was like a drama that was unfolding," she remembered. "Martin and I and the people . . . were like actors in a play, the end of which we had not yet read. Yet we felt a sense of destiny, of being propelled in a certain positive direction."[9]

It was a drama for which ML was prepared; he had been in preparation since the summer of 1944. He just needed to get his congregation on the same page.

His first sermon as pastor of Dexter Avenue would have pleased his old Bible professor Dr. George Kelsey. It was simply titled: "Love Your Enemies."[10]

He followed up the sermon with a vision statement for the church. He wrote it out and submitted it to his new congregation. He told them the church was in dire need of establishing a scholarship committee for talented high-school students to attend college, a cultural committee to enrich the life of the congregation, and a social service committee to aid those in need. He pushed the church to start a "strong and dynamic" Women's Council, to organize and bend the church's ear and pocketbook toward the needs of women. And he demanded that "every member of Dexter must be a registered voter." This was an onerous, urgent demand. White violence and trickery had limited Black access to the ballot. While African Americans comprised about 35 percent of the population, they accounted for less than 4 percent of Montgomery's voters at the time.[11]

Finally, he established a social and political action committee. The committee was charged with keeping the church abreast of the social, political, and economic conditions of Black Americans. Desegregation was the main concern. The ink was barely dry on the US Supreme Court decision outlawing racial segregation in public schools in the *Brown v. Board of Education* case. There was a great deal of hope in Black America, but also fear and uncertainty concerning how the nation would right its wrongs and how and where the backlash would occur. "The gospel of Jesus is a social gospel as well as a personal gospel," ML reminded his new church, "seeking to save the whole man." The committee would seek to save humanity from its social sins, so that individual souls would have a chance. The committee would prove crucial in starting and sustaining the Montgomery Bus Boycott the following year.[12]

The new pastor acknowledged that his vision was expansive, especially for a small church of just 365 members who were known for their middle-class complacency. But he promised his tireless dedication and requested the same from them. He invited the congregation to dream with him—a dream he had been crafting since he was a fifteen-year-old staring up at the Connecticut sky. If they kept their mutual promises, he predicted:

"Dexter will rise to such heights as will stagger the imagination of generations yet unborn, and which even God himself will smile upon."[13]

And it was so . . .

Acknowledgments

I am indebted to so many. First, I want to thank Coretta Scott King. In her wisdom and foresight, she created the Martin Luther King, Jr. Papers Project, an endeavor that continues to this day thanks to the King family and Stanford University. This book would be impossible without the papers. I would also like to thank the past souls who have labored in that vineyard, and the current staff who continue to build upon that foundation—Regina Covington, Jackie Santiago, David Lai, Rabiah Choksi, Hazel Lowy, Jorden Mikel Sharick, Tenisha Armstong, Meghan Cook Weaver, Brynn Raymond, and Ryan Butler. In addition to the hundreds of past and present Stanford students who worked on the papers project, I also benefited from the research and insights from Stanford students Warda Ali, Cahron Cross, and Rabiah Kabir. And the project was made better by the kindness of Issac Newton Farris and Joy Bennett.

I am so grateful for the scholarship and generosity of Lerone Bennett (my namesake), Jonathan Eig, Jeanne Theoharis, Patrick Parr, Jason Miller, David Levering Lewis, David Garrow, and Taylor Branch. And thanks be to God for David Kuhn and Biz Mitchell for believing in me, and in this book. I also want to express my gratitude to several dexterous archivists across the country: Jena Jones at the Atlanta History Center, Kris Ford at the Atlanta University Center Robert W. Woodruff Library, Jasmine Gurley of Morehouse

College, Bella Jankowski at Clarivate, Mary Huelsbeck and the State Historical Society of Wisconsin, Holly A. Smith of the Women's Research & Resource Center of Spelman College, and Scott Sanders of Antioch College. A special thank you to Pam McDonald, retired Librarian at Westminster School, Simsbury, Connecticut. Your research and generosity were transformative.

Finally, to my family—by choice and by blood. To my ever-expanding California family by choice—the Browns, the Butlers, the Camarillos, the Days, the Pearmans, the Smiths, the Winns, and Nya and Ashley—you all have sustained me along the way with love, laughter, encouragement, and babysitting (smile).

And to my family by blood: Mom and Dad, thank you, as always, for loving me and for all the lessons. My siblings: Nicole, Tony, Danielle, and Libra, thank you for loving and supporting me. Mom and Dad Reese, thank you for supporting me and the family along the way. We could not do this without you.

To my children: Bishop, Benjamin, and Livingston, thank you for inspiring me—each in your own special way—to write this book. And to my personal superwoman and beautiful wife, Richelle. There aren't enough words, baby, so I will just say this: Thank you for everything and for all that you are to me, and to us. I love you.

A Partial Reconstruction of Martin Luther King Jr.'s Early Reading List

Edward Bellamy, *Looking Backward: 2000–1887*, 1888

William Holmes Borders, *Seven Minutes at the 'Mike' in the Deep South*, 1949 (a compilation of sermons broadcast over the Atlanta airwaves in the 1940s)

Donald C. Bryant and Karl R. Wallace, *Fundamentals of Public Speaking*, 1947

Henry Sloane Coffin, *What to Preach*, 1926

Mohandas Gandhi, *The Story of My Experiments with Truth*, First US Edition, 1948

Langston Hughes, *The Dream Keeper and Other Poems*, 1932

George Kelsey, "The Nature of the Christian Ethic," *Journal of Religious Thought*, 1945

Benjamin Mays, *Disturbed About Man*, 1969 (a collection of his sermons throughout the years, published shortly after King's death in honor of King)

The Morehouse Companion, 1944–1945, https://radar.auctr.edu/companion-1944-1945

Reinhold Niebuhr, *Moral Man and Immoral Society: A Study of Ethics and Politics*, 1932

Edgar Allen Poe, *The Raven and Other Poems*, 1845

Walter Rauschenbusch, *Christianity and the Social Crisis*, 1907

Corwin Roach, *Preaching Values in the Bible*, 1946

Friedrich Schleiermacher, *The Christian Faith*, 1830

Alfred Lord Tennyson, *Locksley Hall*, 1842

Henry David Thoreau "Civil Disobedience," 1849

Howard Thurman, *Jesus and the Disinherited*, 1949

Notes

Introduction

1. Martin Luther King Jr., *The Papers of Martin Luther King, Jr., Volume I*, ed. Clayborne Carson, Ralph E. Luker, Penny Russell (Berkeley, Calif: University of California Press, 1992).
2. Martin Luther King Jr., *The Papers of Martin Luther King, Jr., Volume I*.
3. Anna Malaika Tubbs, *The Three Mothers: How the Mothers of Martin Luther King, Jr., Malcolm X, and James Baldwin Shaped a Nation* (New York: Flatiron Books, 2021), 133.
4. *Hartford Courant*, January 18, 2011, A1.
5. See, for example, Phillip Atiba Goff et al., "The essence of innocence: consequences of dehumanizing Black children," *Journal of Personality and Social Psychology* 106, no.4 (2014): 526–45.

1. Little Mike

1. See birth accounts in Reverend Martin Luther King Sr. with Clayton Riley, *Daddy King: An Autobiography* (Boston: Beacon Press, 1980), 73–79; "The Autobiography of Daddy King as Told to Edward A. Jones" (August 1973), 100–101, unpublished; Christine King Farris, "The Young Martin," *Ebony*, January 1986; see also, Dharathula H. Millender, *Martin Luther King, Jr.: Boy with a Dream* (Indianapolis: Bobbs-Merrill, 1969).

    On flu pandemic, see, *Atlanta Constitution*, January 4, 1929, 5; January 13, 1929, 13; *Washington Post*, January 13, 1929.

    On angina, see "Transcript of Interview with Coretta Scott King," Hatch Papers, box 22, 6, tape 14.

    On infant and maternal mortality, see US Department of Commerce, "Twenty-Ninth Annual Report: Mortality Statistics 1928" (Washington, DC: US Government Printing Office, 1930); see also, Katherine Eriksson, Gregory T. Niemesh, and Melissa Thomasson, "Revising Infant Mortality Rates for the Early Twentieth Century United States," *Demography* 55, no. 6 (December 2018): 2001–24; Jeffrey P. Brosco, "The Early History of the Infant Mortality Rate in America: A Reflection Upon the Past and a Prophecy of the Future," *Pediatrics* 103, no. 2 (February 1999); Tamara Savage, "Maternal Mortality and the Progressive Era: A Critical Examination of the Past to Inform the Present, *Open Journal of Social Sciences* 8 (2020); Gopal

K. Singh and Stella M. Yu, "Infant Mortality in the United States, 1915–2017: Large Social Inequalities Have Persisted for Over a Century," *International Journal of Maternal and Child Health and AIDS* 8, no. 1 (2019): 19–31; Jamil Drake, "'Fit to Be a Midwife': Protestantism, Moral Character, and the State Supervision of Black Lay Midwives, 1931–1946," *Religion and American Culture: A Journal of Interpretation* 33, no.1 (Winter 2023): 75–114.

2. King Sr., *Daddy King*, 73–79; "The Autobiography of Daddy King as Told to Edward A. Jones," 100–101; Millender, *Martin Luther King, Jr.*; *Atlanta Constitution*, January 4, 1929, 5; January 13, 1929, 13; *Washington Post*, January 13, 1929.

3. See birth accounts in King Sr., *Daddy King*; "The Autobiography of Daddy King," 100–101; Millender, *Martin Luther King, Jr.*; Anna Malaika Tubbs, *The Three Mothers: How the Mothers of Martin Luther King, Jr., Malcolm X, and James Baldwin Shaped a Nation* (New York: Flatiron Books, 2021), 133.

4. Interview with Martin Luther King Sr. in "My Life with Martin Luther King," stenographer notebook, box 23, folder 3, Alden and Allene G. Hatch Papers, MS Group 077, Special and Area Studies Collections, George A. Smathers Libraries, University of Florida; L. D. Reddick, *Crusader Without Violence: The Biography of Martin Luther King, Jr.* (Montgomery, AL: New South Books, 2018), 60.

5. See birth accounts in King Sr., *Daddy King*; "The Autobiography of Daddy King," 100–101; Millender, *Martin Luther King, Jr.*; Tubbs, *The Three Mothers*.

2. 501 Auburn Avenue

1. Martin Luther King, "An Autobiography of Religious Development," Crozer Theological Seminary, 1950, Martin Luther King, Jr. Research and Education Institute, Stanford University, https://kinginstitute.stanford.edu/king-papers/documents/autobiography-religious-development#fn10; Gary M. Pomerantz, *Where Peachtree Meets Sweet Auburn: The Saga of Two Families and the Making of Atlanta* (New York: Scribner, 1996), 121–25; Lerone A. Martin, *Preaching on Wax: The Phonograph and the Shaping of Modern African American Religion* (New York and London: New York University Press, 2014); Scott Henry, "Timeline: The Long, Risqué History of Atlanta's Nightlife," *Atlanta Magazine*, September 19, 2019; King Williams, "The Royal Peacock Is One of Atlanta's Last Remaining Third Places," *Atlanta Magazine*, May 17, 2024; Willard Lewis, "Citizens Trust Bank," *New Georgia Encyclopedia*; Edward Hatfield, "Auburn Avenue," *New Georgia Encyclopedia*; Alexa Henderson, "Atlanta Life Insurance Company," *New Georgia Encyclopedia*; Christine King Farris, *Through It All: Reflections on My Life, My Family, and My Faith* (New York: Atria, 2010), 25–27; "Notes from interviews with MLK April 15–May 18, 1967" by David Halberstam, David Halberstam Collection, box 11, folder 5, Howard Gotlieb Archival Research Center, Boston University.

2. King, "Autobiography of Religious Development"; Pomerantz, *Where Peachtree Meets Sweet Auburn*, 121–25.

3. King, "Autobiography of Religious Development." See also, "Notes from interviews with MLK"; Christine King Farris, The HistoryMakers A2010.074, interviewed by Julieanna L. Richardson, July 11, 2010, session 1, tape 6, story 1, The HistoryMakers Digital Archive; Farris, *Through It All*.

4. On grandma and her influence, see King, "Autobiography of Religious Development"; *Time*, "The South: An Attack on the Conscience," February 18, 1957; Christine King Farris, "Young Martin," *Ebony*, January 1986; *Atlanta Daily World*, May 22, 1941, 1; Farris, *Through It All*; L. D. Reddick, *Crusader Without Violence: The Biography of Martin Luther King, Jr.* (Montgomery, AL: New South Books, 2018), 62.
   On the ideology and activism of Black Baptist women and the National Association of Colored Women's Clubs, see Evelyn Brooks Higginbotham, *Righteous Discontent: The Women's Movement in the Black Baptist Church, 1880–1920* (Cambridge, MA: Harvard University Press, 1993); Deborah G. White, *Too Heavy a Load: Black Women in Defense of Themselves, 1894–1994*, 1st ed. (New York: W. W. Norton, 1999). See also Martin Luther King, Jr. Research and Education Institute, Stanford University, "Family History of Martin Luther King, Jr.," https://kinginstitute.stanford.edu/family-history-martin -luther-king-jr.

5. On grandma and her influence, see King, "Autobiography of Religious Development"; *Time*, "The South: An Attack on the Conscience"; Farris, "Young Martin"; Farris, The HistoryMakers A2010.074, July 11, 2010, session 1, tape 1, story 2; Farris, *Through It All*; Reddick, *Crusader Without Violence*, 62.
   On the ideology and activism of Black Baptist women and the National Association of Colored Women's Clubs, see Higginbotham, *Righteous Discontent*; White, *Too Heavy a Load*. See also Martin Luther King, Jr. Research and Education Institute, Stanford University, "Family History of Martin Luther King, Jr."

6. King, "Autobiography of Religious Development"; King family and friends interview in Farris, "Young Martin"; *Afro-American*, June 8, 1957, A1; *Face to Face*, interview with Martin Luther King Jr. (London: BBC, 1961). See also Tubbs, *The Three Mothers*, 67–73.

7. King Sr., "*Daddy King*," 109–13; *Face to Face*; Farris, The HistoryMakers A2010.074, session 1, tape 1, story 3; Farris, *Through It All*; Lerone Bennett Jr., *What Manner of Man: A Biography of Martin Luther King, Jr.* (Chicago: Johnson Publishing Co., 1964); Reddick, *Crusader Without Violence*; Tubbs, *The Three Mothers*; Harvard Sitkoff, *King: Pilgrimage to the Mountaintop* (New York: Hill and Wang, 2009); Jonathan Eig, *King: A Life* (New York: Farrar, Straus and Giroux, 2023).

8. MLK Letters to Daddy King in MLK Papers, vol. 1.

9. King Sr., *Daddy King*; Farris, *Through It All*; Bennett Jr., *What Manner of Man*; Reddick, *Crusader Without Violence*; Tubbs, *The Three Mothers*; Sitkoff, *King*; Eig, *King: A Life*.

10. King Sr., *Daddy King*, 85, 113.

11. Farris, The HistoryMakers A2010.074, session 1, tape 2, story 1; Farris, *Through It All*, 16–18. Italics in original.

12. Farris, "Young Martin"; Farris, *Through It All*; Farris, *My Brother Martin* (New York & London: Aladdin Paperbacks, 2003); *Time*, "The South: An Attack on the Conscience," 17–20; Reddick, *Crusader Without Violence*; Bennett Jr., *What Manner of Man*.

13. Farris, The HistoryMakers A2010.074, session 1, tape 2, story 1; Farris, *Through It All*, 16–18.

14. Farris, The HistoryMakers A2010.074, session 1, tape 2, story 1; Farris, *Through It All*, 16–18.

15. On grandma and her influence, see King, "Autobiography of Religious Development";

Time, "The South: An Attack on the Conscience"; Farris, "Young Martin"; Farris, The HistoryMakers A2010.074, July 11, 2010, session 1, tape 1, story 2; Farris, *Through It All*; Reddick, *Crusader Without Violence,* 62.

On the ideology and activism of Black Baptist women and the National Association of Colored Women's Clubs, see Higginbotham, *Righteous Discontent*; White, *Too Heavy a Load.* See also Martin Luther King, Jr. Research and Education Institute, Stanford University, "Family History of Martin Luther King, Jr."

16. King, "An Autobiography of Religious Development."

3. Church

1. Tommy H. Jones, *Ebenezer Baptist Church Historic Structure Report* (Atlanta: Cultural Resources, Southeast Region, National Park Service, 2001); Martin Luther King, Jr. Research and Education Institute, Stanford University, "Ebenezer Baptist Church," https://kinginstitute.stanford.edu/ebenezer-baptist-church-atlanta-georgia; relative cost of a project is measured as a multiple of the resources used in its production. This would include the labor, capital, and materials used to produce the project. This measure uses GDP per capita; see "Purchasing Power Today of a US Dollar Transaction in the Past," MeasuringWorth, 2024, www.measuringworth.com/ppowerus/.

2. Martin Luther King, "An Autobiography of Religious Development," Crozer Theological Seminary, 1950, Martin Luther King, Jr. Research and Education Institute, Stanford University, https://kinginstitute.stanford.edu/king-papers/documents/autobiography-religious-development#fn10; Christine King Farris, The HistoryMakers A2010.074, interviewed by Julieanna L. Richardson, July 11, 2010, session 1, tape 1, story 7, and tape 3, story 4; tape 5, story 5, The HistoryMakers Digital Archive; Jones, *Ebenezer Baptist Church Historic Structure Report*; King Institute, "Ebenezer Baptist Church."

3. King, "An Autobiography of Religious Development."

4. King, "An Autobiography of Religious Development."

5. Interview with Martin Luther King Sr. in "My Life with Martin Luther King," stenographer notebook, box 23, folder 3. Alden and Allene G. Hatch Papers, MS Group 077, Special and Area Studies Collections, George A. Smathers Libraries, University of Florida; Ted Poston, "Martin Luther King," Parts 1–6, *Afro-American,* June 8, June 15, June 22, June 29, July 6, July 13, 1957; Farris, The HistoryMakers A2010.074, session 1, tape 1, story 7–8, The HistoryMakers Digital Archive; Christine King Farris, *Through It All: Reflections on My Life, My Family, and My Faith* (New York: Atria, 2010), 26–27; Lerone Bennett Jr., *What Manner of Man: A Biography of Martin Luther King, Jr.* (Chicago: Johnson Publishing Co., Inc., 1964), 17; L. D. Reddick, *Crusader Without Violence: The Biography of Martin Luther King, Jr.* (Montgomery, AL: New South Books, 2018), 65–69; David Levering Lewis, *King: A Biography* (Chicago: University of Illinois Press, 2013), 13; "More Like Jesus," composed by J. M. Stillman, *Good Will* (Chicago: Fleming H. Revell, 1878), number 39; *Journal of the General Missionary Baptist Convention of Georgia,*1934, reprinted in Clarence M. Wagner, *Profiles of Black Georgia Baptists* (Atlanta: Bennett Brothers Printing Company, 1980), 94.

4. Play

1. *Sixteen '74,* "Remembering Mrs. Alberta King," video interview, Walter J. Brown Media Archives and Peabody Awards Collection, University of Georgia, http://dlg.galileo.usg .edu/peabody/id:1974_74055_pst_1.

2. Christine King Farris, The HistoryMakers A2010.074, interviewed by Julieanna L. Richardson, July 11, 2010, Session 1, tape 6, story 1, The HistoryMakers Digital Archive; Christine King Farris, *My Brother Martin* (New York & London: Aladdin Paperbacks, 2003). See also, "The Autobiography of Daddy King as Told to Edward A. Jones" (August 1973), 166, unpublished; L. D. Reddick, *Crusader Without Violence: The Biography of Martin Luther King, Jr.* (Montgomery, AL: New South Books, 1959), 62.

3. Farris, The HistoryMakers A2010.074, session 1, tape 6, story 1.

4. On the childhood pranks, see Christine King Farris, "The Young Martin," *Ebony*, January 1986; Farris, *My Brother Martin*; Christine King Farris, *Through It All: Reflections on My Life, My Family, and My Faith* (New York: Atria, 2010), 20–31.

5. Farris, *Through It All*, 20–31.

6. Ted Poston, "Martin Luther King," Parts 1–6, *Afro-American*, June 8, June 15, June 22, June 29, July 6, July 13, 1957; William Peters, "Our Weapon Is Love," *Redbook*, August 1956.

5. Big Words

1. Interview with Martin Luther King Sr. in "My Life with Martin Luther King," stenographer notebook, box 23, folder 3. Alden and Allene G. Hatch Papers, MS Group 077, Special and Area Studies Collections, George A. Smathers Libraries, University of Florida.

2. Interview with Martin Luther King Sr. in "My Life with Martin Luther King"; Ted Poston, "Martin Luther King"; Parts 1–6, Afro-American, June 8, June 15, June 22, June 29, July 6, July 13, 1957; Christine King Farris, *Through It All: Reflections on My Life, My Family, and My Faith* (New York: Atria, 2010), 26–27; Lerone Bennett Jr., *What Manner of Man: A Biography of Martin Luther King, Jr.* (Chicago: Johnson Publishing Co., Inc., 1964), 17; L. D. Reddick, *Crusader Without Violence: The Biography of Martin Luther King, Jr.* (Montgomery, AL: New South Books, 2018), 65–69; David Levering Lewis, *King: A Biography* (Urbana and Chicago: University of Illinois Press, 2013), 13.

3. *Atlanta Constitution*, April 4, 1970, 1B; Christine King Farris, *Through It All*, 20–23.

4. Interview with Martin Luther King Sr. in "My Life with Martin Luther King"; Farris, "The Young Martin"; Poston, "Martin Luther King"; Farris, *Through It All*, 26–27; Bennett Jr., *What Manner of Man*, 17; L. D. Reddick, *Crusader Without Violence*, 65–69; Lewis, *King: A Biography*, 13; "More Like Jesus," composed by J. M. Stillman, *Good Will* (Chicago, Illinois: Fleming H. Revell, 1878), number 39.

5. Detailed in Reverend Martin Luther King Sr. with Clayton Riley, *Daddy King: An Autobiography* (Boston: Beacon Press, 1980), 78–88. See also Christine King Farris, The HistoryMakers A2010.074, interviewed by Julieanna L. Richardson, July 11, 2010, session 1, tape 5, story 2, The HistoryMakers Digital Archive.

6. Taylor Branch interview with Mr. Leathers on April 1, 1970 in Taylor Branch Papers Folder 701, Southern Historical Collection, Wilson Library, University on North Carolina

at Chapel Hill; interview with Martin Luther King Sr. in "My Life with Martin Luther King."

7. Annie L. McPheeters, interviewed by Kathryn L. Nasstrom, June 8, 1992, P1992-09, Series J: Black and White Women in Atlanta Public Life, Georgia Government Documentation Project, Special Collections and Archives, Georgia State University Library, Atlanta, GA.

8. McPheeters, interviewed by Nasstrom.

9. McPheeters, interviewed by Nasstrom.

10. McPheeters, interviewed by Nasstrom.

6. Saved

1. Martin Luther King, "An Autobiography of Religious Development."

2. King, "An Autobiography of Religious Development"; see also King Chronology, Martin Luther King, Jr. Research and Education Institute, Stanford University, https://kinginstitute .stanford.edu/king-resources/king-encyclopedia/chronology; Christine King Farris, The HistoryMakers A2010.074, interviewed by Julieanna L. Richardson, July 11, 2010, session 1, tape 1, story 7, The HistoryMakers Digital Archive.

3. King, "An Autobiography of Religious Development."

7. The Talk

1. King told this story in several places throughout his life to varying degrees of detail, see, for example, Martin Luther King, "An Autobiography of Religious Development"; Ted Poston, "Martin Luther King," Part 1, Afro-American, June 8, 1957, A1; Martin Luther King Jr., Stride Toward Freedom: The Montgomery Story (New York & London: Harper & Row, 1958), 18–19; see also King's retelling to Lerone Bennett in Lerone Bennett Jr., What Manner of Man: A Biography of Martin Luther King, Jr. (Chicago: Johnson Publishing Co., Inc., 1964), 18–20. Family members also recalled the incident, see Christine King Farris, The HistoryMakers A2010.074, interviewed by Julieanna L. Richardson, July 11, 2010, session 1, tape 3, story 2, The HistoryMakers Digital Archive; Christine King Farris, Through It All: Reflections on My Life, My Family, and My Faith (New York: Atria, 2010), 24–25; Christine King Farris, My Brother Martin (New York & London: Aladdin Paperbacks, 2003); Reverend Martin Luther King Sr. with Clayton Riley, Daddy King: An Autobiography (Boston: Beacon Press, 1980), 113.

2. Martin Luther King, "An Autobiography of Religious Development"; Poston, "Martin Luther King," Part 1; Martin Luther King Jr., Stride Toward Freedom, 18–19; Bennett Jr., What Manner of Man, 18–20; Farris, My Brother Martin; Farris, The HistoryMakers A2010.074, interviewed by Julieanna L. Richardson, July 11, 2010, session 1, tape 3, story 2; Farris, Through It All, 24–25.

3. Martin Luther King, "An Autobiography of Religious Development"; Poston, "Martin Luther King," Part 1; Martin Luther King Jr., Stride Toward Freedom, 18–19; Bennett Jr., What Manner of Man, 18–20; Farris, My Brother Martin; Farris, The HistoryMakers A2010.074, interviewed by Julieanna L. Richardson, July 11, 2010, session 1, tape 3, story 2; Farris, Through It All, 24–25.

4. Martin Luther King, "An Autobiography of Religious Development"; Poston, "Martin Luther King," Part 1; Martin Luther King Jr., *Stride Toward Freedom*, 18–19; Bennett Jr., *What Manner of Man*, 18–20; Farris, *My Brother Martin*; Farris, The HistoryMakers A2010.074, interviewed by Julieanna L. Richardson, July 11, 2010, session 1, tape 3, story 2; Farris, *Through It All*, 24–25.

5. Martin Luther King, "An Autobiography of Religious Development"; Poston, "Martin Luther King," Part 1; Martin Luther King Jr., *Stride Toward Freedom*, 18–19; Bennett Jr., *What Manner of Man*, 18–20; Farris, *My Brother Martin*; Farris, The HistoryMakers A2010.074, interviewed by Julieanna L. Richardson, July 11, 2010, session 1, tape 3, story 2; Farris, *Through It All*, 24–25.

   On Alberta and the marriage bar, see Christine Farris King, "The Young Martin," *Ebony*, January 1986; see also Anna Malaika Tubbs, *The Three Mothers: How the Mothers of Martin Luther King, Jr., Malcolm X, and James Baldwin Shaped a Nation* (New York: Flatiron Books, 2021), 70.

6. Poston, "Martin Luther King"; Martin Luther King Jr., *Stride Toward Freedom*, 18–19.

7. Martin Luther King, "An Autobiography of Religious Development"; *Face to Face*, "Interview with Martin Luther King, Jr." (London: BBC, 1961); Farris, *My Brother Martin*, 26.

8. Poston, "Martin Luther King," Part 1, *Afro-American*, June 8, 1957, A1.

9. *Face to Face*; Poston, "Martin Luther King," Part 2, *Afro-American*, June 15, 1957, A3; L. D. Reddick, *Crusader Without Violence: The Biography of Martin Luther King, Jr.* (Montgomery, AL: New South Books, 1959), 72.

10. *Atlanta Daily World*, November 11, 1937, 1; Reddick, *Crusader Without Violence*, 68–69.

11. Martin Luther King Jr., *Stride Toward Freedom*, 19–20; *Face to Face*; Poston, "Martin Luther King," Part 1; King Sr. with Clayton Riley, *Daddy King*, 98–99; "The Autobiography of Daddy King as Told to Edward A. Jones" (August 1973), 35–36.

12. Martin Luther King Jr., *Stride Toward Freedom*, 19–20; *Face to Face*; Poston, "Martin Luther King," Part 1; King Sr. with Clayton Riley, *Daddy King*, 98–99; "The Autobiography of Daddy King as Told to Edward A. Jones" (August 1973), 35–36..

13. Martin Luther King Jr., Stride Toward Freedom, 19–20; *Face to Face*; Poston, "Martin Luther King," Part 1; King Sr. with Clayton Riley, *Daddy King*, 98–99; "The Autobiography of Daddy King as Told to Edward A. Jones" (August 1973), 35–36.

14. King Sr. with Clayton Riley, *Daddy King*, 98–99.

15. Reddick, *Crusader Without Violence*, 68–69.

16. Martin Luther King Jr., "Growing Up in Atlanta," April 1965, Lawrence D. Reddick papers, Sc MG 974, Box 14, Folder 1, Schomburg Center for Research in Black Culture, Manuscripts, Archives and Rare Books Division, The New York Public Library. While the transcript does not have an exact date, the speech was probably given around April 6, 1965; see *Baltimore Afro-American*, April 10, 1965, 1.

17. W. E. B. Du Bois, *The Souls of Black Folk* (Chicago: A. C. McClurg and Co., 1903).

18. Martin Luther King Jr., "My Pilgrimage to Nonviolence," *Fellowship*, September 1958, Martin Luther King, Jr. Research and Education Institute, Stanford University, https://kinginstitute.stanford.edu/king-papers/documents/my-pilgrimage-nonviolence#ftnref7;

Martin Luther King interview with Mike Wallace, WNTA-TV, transcript reprinted in *New York Post Magazine*, "Self-Portrait of a Symbol: Martin Luther King," February 15, 1961, 6.

19. *Face to Face*.

20. "Notes from interviews with MLK April 15–May 18, 1967," by David Halberstam, David Halberstam Collection, box 11, folder 5, Howard Gotlieb Archival Research Center, Boston University.

21. On studies by Kenneth and Mamie Clark, see, for example, "Segregation as a Factor in the Racial Identification of Negro Preschool Children: A Preliminary Report," *Journal Experimental Education* 11 (1939): 161–63; "The Development of Consciousness of Self and the Emergence of Racial Identification in Negro Preschool Children," *Journal Social Psychology* 10 (1939): 591–99; "Skin Color as a Factor in Racial Identification of Negro Preschool Children," *Journal Social Psychology* 11 (1940): 159–69; "Emotional Factors in Racial Identification and Preference in Negro Children," *Journal of Negro Education* 19, no. 3 (1950): 341–50.

22. M. S. Bynum et al., "Racism Experiences and Psychological Functioning in African American College Freshmen: Is Racial Socialization a Buffer?" *Cultural Diversity and Ethnic Minority Psychology* 13, no. 1 (200): 64–71; E. W. Neblett et al., "Patterns of Racial Socialization and Psychological Adjustment: Can Parental Communications About Race Reduce the Impact of Racial Discrimination?" *Journal of Research on Adolescence* 18 (2008): 477–515; M. T. Wang et al., "Parental Racial Socialization as a Moderator of the Effects of Racial Discrimination on Educational Success Among African American Adolescents," *Child Development* 83 (2012): 1716–31; V. C. McLoyd, "Spotlighting Black Adolescent Development in the Shadow of Racism: A Commentary," *Journal of Research on Adolescence: The Official Journal of the Society for Research on Adolescence* 32, no. 1 (2022): 295–301.

23. James Baldwin, "The Dangerous Road Before Martin Luther King, Jr.," *Harper's Magazine*, February 1961.

24. "Notes from interviews with MLK."

8. Fight

1. Ted Poston, "Martin Luther King," Part 2, *Afro-American*, June15, 1957, A3. On AD's tendency to fight see "The Autobiography of Daddy King as Told to Edward A. Jones" (August 1973), unpublished; Reverend Martin Luther King Sr. with Clayton Riley, *Daddy King: An Autobiography* (Boston: Beacon Press, 1980); Christine King Farris, *Through It All: Reflections on My Life, My Family, and My Faith* (New York: Atria, 2010); L. D. Reddick, *Crusader Without Violence: The Biography of Martin Luther King, Jr.* (Montgomery, AL: New South Books, 1959); Lerone Bennett Jr., *What Manner of Man: A Biography of Martin Luther King, Jr.* (Chicago: Johnson Publishing Co., Inc., 1964).

2. Poston, "Martin Luther King, Part 2; Christine King Farris, The HistoryMakers A2010.074, interviewed by Julieanna L. Richardson, July 11, 2010, session 1, tape 1, story 6, The HistoryMakers Digital Archive.

3. Poston, "Martin Luther King," Parts 1–6, *Afro-American* June 8, June 15, June 22, June 29, July 6, July 13, 1957; William Peters, "Our Weapon Is Love," *Redbook* August 1, 1956.

4. See King's memory of the event in Poston, *Afro-American*, "Martin Luther King, Part 2; family members recalled the incident as well, see, L. D. Reddick, *Crusader Without Violence*, 72; Dharathula H. Millender, *Martin Luther King, Jr.: Boy with a Dream* (Indianapolis, IN: Bobbs-Merrill, 1969).

5. *Afro-American*, June15, 1957, A3; Christine King Farris, The HistoryMakers A2010.074, interviewed by Julieanna L. Richardson, July 11, 2010, session 1, tape 1, story 6, The HistoryMakers Digital Archive.

6. Christine King Farris, "The Young Martin," *Ebony*, January 1986; Poston, "Martin Luther King," Parts 1–6; King Sr., *Daddy King*, 109; Bennett Jr., *What Manner of Man*, 24; Reddick, *Crusader Without Violence*, 62, 72–77.

7. King Sr., *Daddy King*, 113; Reddick, *Crusader Without Violence*, 72.

8. King Sr., *Daddy King*, 113; *Face to Face*, interview with Martin Luther King Jr. (London: BBC, 1961); Andrew Young interview with Tom Dent, February 1, 1984, Amistad Research Center, Tom Dent papers, item 4; Bennett Jr., *What Manner of Man*, 24.

9. King Sr., *Daddy King*, 113; Reddick, Crusader Without Violence, 72.

9. A Dreamer

1. *Atlanta Daily World*, March 6, 1938; March 13, 1938; September 13, 1939; September 11, 1940; September 19, 1943; *Atlanta University Bulletin*, no. 32, December 1940; no. 38, April 1942; Carolyn Kindred, "Elizabeth Elaine Lemon: Trailblazing Woman," in *Trailblazing African American Women of Coastal Georgia*, a program presented by the Ashantilly Center at St. Cyprian's Episcopal Church and Parish Hall, February 29, 2020; Dharathula H. Millender, *Martin Luther King, Jr.: Boy with a Dream* (Indianapolis: Bobbs-Merrill, 1969). See also familial reflections, L. D. Reddick, *Crusader Without Violence: The Biography of Martin Luther King, Jr.* (Montgomery, AL: New South Books, 1959); Lerone Bennett Jr., *What Manner of Man: A Biography of Martin Luther King, Jr.* (Chicago: Johnson Publishing Co., Inc., 1964); "The Autobiography of Daddy King as Told to Edward A. Jones" (August 1973), unpublished; Reverend Martin Luther King Sr. with Clayton Riley, *Daddy King: An Autobiography* (Boston: Beacon Press, 1980); Christine King Farris, *Through It All: Reflections on My Life, My Family, and My Faith* (New York: Atria, 2010).
On Black income, see US Bureau of Labor Statistics, "The Economic Situation of Negroes in the United States," US Government Printing Office, 1962.
On family expenditures, see US Bureau of Labor Statistics, *Monthly Labor Review*, October 1940; as late as 1949, the median income of Black families in Atlanta had risen to $1,343; see US Department of Commerce, Bureau of the Census, "1950 Census Population Preliminary Reports: Characteristics of the Population of the Atlanta, GA Standard Metropolitan Area: April 1, 1950," May 27, 1951.

2. *The Herald: The Official Organ of the Georgia Teachers and Education Association* 3, no. 2 (1936), University of Georgia Libraries, Black Teacher Archive; Aaron Brown "An Evaluation of the Accredited Secondary Schools for Negroes in the South," *Journal of Negro Education* 13, no. 4 (Autumn 1944): 488–98; Educational Policies Commission, *Learning the Ways of Democracy: A Case Book of Civic Education* (Washington, DC: Educational Policies

Commission, National Education Association of the United States and the American Association of School Administrators, 1940), 186–87.

3. MLK letter to Alberta King in MLK Papers, vol. 1.

4. *Atlanta Daily World*, March 6, 1938; March 13, 1938; September 13, 1939; September 11, 1940; September 19, 1943; *Atlanta University Bulletin*, no. 38, April 1942; Kindred, "Elizabeth Elaine Lemon"; Millender, *Martin Luther King, Jr.* See also familial reflections, Reddick, *Crusader Without Violence*; Bennett Jr., *What Manner of Man*; "The Autobiography of Daddy"; King Sr., *Daddy King*; Farris, *Through It All*.

5. Kindred, "Elizabeth Elaine Lemon"; Millender, *Martin Luther King, Jr.*

6. Kindred, "Elizabeth Elaine Lemon"; Millender, *Martin Luther King, Jr.*

7. Kindred, "Elizabeth Elaine Lemon"; Millender, *Martin Luther King, Jr.*

8. Kindred, "Elizabeth Elaine Lemon"; Millender, *Martin Luther King, Jr.*

9. Dewey M. Clayton and Maya Todd, "Voter Suppression Laws and the Racial Turnout Gap in America," *Journal of Black Studies*, July 12, 2025, https://doi.org/10.1177/00219347251346186; see also Constitutional Rights Foundation, "Race and Voting in the Segregated South," https://teachdemocracy.org/bill-of-rights-in-action/bria-12-2-b-race-and-voting-in-the-segregated-south, accessed August 12, 2025; Kindred, "Elizabeth Elaine Lemon"; Millender, *Martin Luther King, Jr.*

10. Kindred, "Elizabeth Elaine Lemon"; Millender, *Martin Luther King, Jr.*

11. Millender, *Martin Luther King, Jr.*

12. *Atlanta Daily World*, March 6, 1938; March 13, 1938; September 13, 1939; September 11, 1940; September 19, 1943; Miss Lemon's recollections recorded in Kindred, "Elizabeth Elaine Lemon: Trailblazing Woman"; Millender, *Martin Luther King, Jr.*

13. *Atlanta Daily World*, March 6, 1938; March 13, 1938; September 13, 1939; September 11, 1940; September 19, 1943; Kindred, "Elizabeth Elaine Lemon: Trailblazing Woman"; Millender, *Martin Luther King, Jr.*

14. *Atlanta Daily World*, March 6, 1938; March 13, 1938; September 13, 1939; September 11, 1940; September 19, 1943; Miss Lemon's recollections recorded in Carolyn Kindred, "Elizabeth Elaine Lemon: Trailblazing Woman"; Millender, *Martin Luther King, Jr.*

15. Kindred, "Elizabeth Elaine Lemon"; Millender, *Martin Luther King, Jr.*

16. See Wallace D. Best, *Langston's Salvation* (New York: New York University Press, 2017); W. Jason Miller, *Langston Hughes* (Chicago: University of Chicago Press, 2020). A special thanks to W. Jason Miller for helping me with this connection, personal email to author, April 26, 2024.

17. W. Jason Miller, *Origins of the Dream: Hughes's Poetry and King's Rhetoric* (Gainesville: University of Florida Press, 2015), 1.

10. Mama

1. Martin Luther King, "An Autobiography of Religious Development."

2. Family members recalled the incident in Christine King Farris, "The Young Martin," *Ebony*, January 1986; Christine King Farris, *Through It All: Reflections on My Life, My Family, and My Faith* (New York: Atria, 2010), 11–12; Martin Luther King, Jr. Research and Educa-

tion Institute, Stanford University, "Family History of Martin Luther King, Jr.," https://kinginstitute.stanford.edu/family-history-martin-luther-king-jr; Reverend Martin Luther King Sr. with Clayton Riley, *Daddy King: An Autobiography* (Boston: Beacon Press, 1980), 99–100; L. D. Reddick, *Crusader Without Violence: The Biography of Martin Luther King, Jr.* (Montgomery, AL: New South Books, 1959), 73; Lerone Bennett Jr., *What Manner of Man: A Biography of Martin Luther King, Jr.* (Chicago: Johnson Publishing Company, Inc., 1964). See also, *Time*, "America's Gandhi: Rev. Martin Luther King Jr.," January 3, 1964.

3. Farris, "The Young Martin"; Farris, *Through It All*, 11–12; King Sr., *Daddy King*, 99–100; Reddick, *Crusader Without Violence*, 73; Bennett Jr., *What Manner of Man*; *Time*, "America's Gandhi."

4. See, for example, D. R. Cohen et al., "Applying an Ecosocial Framework to Address Racial Disparities in Suicide Risk Among Black Youth," *Psychology in Schools* 591 no. 12 (2021); F. T. Saleem et al., "Addressing the Myth of Racial Trauma: Developmental and Ecological Considerations for Youth of Color," *Journal of Clinical Child and Family Psychology Review* 23 (2020): 1–14.

5. Family members recalled the incident in Farris, "The Young Martin"; Farris, *Through It All*, 11–12; King Sr., *Daddy King*, 99–100; *Time*, "America's Gandhi."

6. Family members recalled the incident in Farris, "The Young Martin"; Farris, *Through It All*, 11–12; King Sr., *Daddy King*, 99–100; *Time*, "America's Gandhi: Rev. Martin Luther King Jr.," January 3, 1964.

7. Family members recalled the incident in Farris, "The Young Martin"; Farris, *Through It All*, 11–12; King Sr., *Daddy King*, 99–100; *Time*, "America's Gandhi: Rev. Martin Luther King Jr.," January 3, 1964.

8. *Atlanta Daily World*, May 22, 1941, September 24, 1941; Farris, *Through It All*, 11–12.

9. King, "An Autobiography of Religious Development"; *Time*, "The South: An Attack on the Conscience," February 18, 1957; Farris, "The Young Martin"; Gary M. Pomerantz, *Where Peachtree Meets Sweet Auburn: The Saga of Two Families and the Making of Atlanta* (New York: Scribner, 1996), 158–59; Farris, *Through It All*, 12; King Sr., *Daddy King*, 99–100.

10. King, "An Autobiography of Religious Development"; Farris, *Through It All*, 12; King Sr., *Daddy King*, 99–100. See also, King Chronology, Martin Luther King, Jr. Research and Education Institute, Stanford University, https://kinginstitute.stanford.edu/king-resources/king-encyclopedia/chronology; and Jonathan Eig, *King: A Life* (New York: Farrar, Straus and Giroux, 2023), 47.

11. Clarence Jones, "My Life in the Aftermath of Martin Luther King Jr.'s Assassination," *New Yorker*, July 18, 2023.
    On King sermons describing his death, see, for example, his sermon on January 27, 1957, at Dexter Avenue Baptist, in which King preached, "If I had to die tomorrow morning I would die happy, because I've been to the mountaintop and I've seen the promised land and it's going to be here in Montgomery," MLK Papers, vol. 4; see also King's sermon "The Perfect Faith," delivered at Ebenezer Baptist Church on October 7, 1962, in which King notes that God is his "bodyguard," MLK Papers, vol. 8, forthcoming. For more examples of King's acceptance of his death, see, Coretta Scott King, transcript, Hatch Papers, box 22, folder 6, tape 14; David Halberstam, "Notes from the Bottom of the

Mountain," *Harper's*, June 1, 1968; June Dobbs Butts interview, *Voices of the Civil Rights Movement*, Comcast NBC Universal, no date; June Dobbs Butts, interviewed by Franklin Abbott, January 29, 2016, Activist Women Oral History Project, Archives for Research on Women and Gender, Special Collections and Archives, Georgia State University; Eig, *King: A Life*.

12. King, "An Autobiography of Religious Development."

11. Agnostic

1. Martin Luther King, "An Autobiography of Religious Development"; David Halberstam, "The Second Coming of Martin Luther King, Jr.," *Harper's*, August 1, 1967; "Notes from interviews with MLK April 15–May 18, 1967" by David Halberstam, David Halberstam Collection, box 11, folder 5, Howard Gotlieb Archival Research Center, Boston University.
2. "Notes from interviews with MLK."
3. Christine King Farris, The HistoryMakers A2010.074, interviewed by Julieanna L. Richardson, July 11, 2010, session 1, tape 1, story 7, The HistoryMakers Digital Archive.
4. "Notes from interviews with MLK."
5. Christine King Farris, *Through It All: Reflections on My Life, My Family, and My Faith* (New York: Atria, 2010), 12.
6. *Time*, "The South: An Attack on the Conscience," February 18, 1957; King Jr., *The Autobiography of Martin Luther King*, Chapter 2: Morehouse College, Martin Luther King, Jr. Research and Education Institute, Stanford University, https://kinginstitute.stanford.edu/publications/autobiography-martin-luther-king-jr/chapter-2-morehouse-college.
7. *Time*, "The South: An Attack on the Conscience"; "America's Gandhi: Rev. Martin Luther King Jr.," January 3, 1964.
8. W. E. B. Du Bois, *Souls of Black Folk* (Chicago: A. C. McClurg and Co., 1903).
9. *Time*, "The South: An Attack on the Conscience"; see also Lerone Bennett Jr., *What Manner of Man: A Biography of Martin Luther King, Jr.* (Chicago: Johnson Publishing Co., Inc., 1964), 20–26.

12. A Tough Guy

1. "Notes from interviews with MLK April 15–May 18, 1967" by David Halberstam, David Halberstam Collection, box 11, folder 5, Howard Gotlieb Archival Research Center, Boston University; King Sr., Comments at Coppin State University, no date, Lawrence D. Reddick papers, Sc MG 974, Box 14, Folder 1, Schomburg Center for Research in Black Culture, Manuscripts, Archives and Rare Books Division, The New York Public Library.
2. Report Card in P.E. Atlanta University Laboratory High School, January 23, 1942, copy at MLK Institute Stanford University.
3. *Atlanta University Bulletin*, no. 38, April 1942,
4. King, "Statement on Meredith March," Grenada, Mississippi, June 16, 1966, MLK Papers, vol. 11, forthcoming.

5. *Atlanta University Bulletin,* no. 32, December 1940, no. 38, April 1942; Sarah Grace Bradley, *Atlanta Daily World,* September 20, 1942, 3.

6. Naomi King, The HistoryMakers A2010.071, interviewed by Denise Gines, July 14, 2010, session 1, tape 2, story 2; June Dobbs Butts, The HistoryMakers A2006.076, interviewed by Shawn Wilson, April 13, 2006, session 1, tape 1, story 10, The HistoryMakers Digital Archive.

7. Christine King Farris, "The Young Martin," *Ebony,* January 1986; Christine King Farris, *Through It All: Reflections on My Life, My Family, and My Faith* (New York: Atria, 2010), 27; L. D. Reddick, *Crusader Without Violence: The Biography of Martin Luther King, Jr.* (Montgomery, AL: New South Books, 1959), 65–68.

8. Ted Poston, "Martin Luther King," Parts 1–6, *Afro-American,* June 8, June 15, June 22, June 29, July 6, July 13, 1957.

9. Mattiwilda Dobbs Janzon, The HistoryMakers A2005.056, interviewed by Racine Tucker Hamilton, March 1, 2005, session 1, tape 2, story 9, The HistoryMakers Digital Archive.

10. Poston, "Martin Luther King."

11. June Dobbs Butts, "Good Memories of a Great Man's Childhood," *The Tennessean,* January 18, 1993, 11A; June Dobbs Butts, The HistoryMakers A2006.076, interviewed by Shawn Wilson, April 13, 2006, session 1, tape 2, story 7, The HistoryMakers Digital Archive; June Dobbs Butts, interviewed by Franklin Abbott, January 29, 2016, Activist Women Oral History Project, Archives for Research on Women and Gender. Special Collections and Archives, Georgia State University.

12. Poston, "Martin Luther King," Parts 1–6; see also, William Peters, "Our Weapon Is Love," *Redbook,* August 1956.

13. Basketball

1. Ted Poston, "Martin Luther King," Parts 1–6, *Afro-American,* June 8, June 15, June 22, June 29, July 6, July 13, 1957.

2. Poston, "Martin Luther King."

3. *Atlanta Journal Constitution,* January 15, 2018, A11.

4. Coretta Scott King interview, Hatch Papers, tape 3; Reverend Peter Johnson interview with author, January 13, 2023.

5. *Atlanta Daily World,* January 12, 1940, 5; January 20, 1942, 5; January 30, 1942, 5; March 19, 1942, 5; April 2, 1942, 5; April 6, 1942, 5.

6. *Atlanta Daily World,* January 12, 1940, 5; January 20, 1942, 5; January 30, 1942, 5; March 19, 1942, 5; April 2, 1942, 5; April 6, 1942, 5.

7. *Atlanta Journal Constitution;* Poston, "Martin Luther King," June 15, 1957, A3.

8. Poston, "Martin Luther King," June 15, 1957, A3.

14. Dating

1. Ted Poston, "Martin Luther King," Parts 1–6, *Afro-American,* June 8, June 15, June 22, June 29, July 6, July 13, 1957; interview with Martin Luther King Sr., no date, stenographer notes, Alden and Allene G. Hatch Papers, box 22, folder 2 and folder 3; L. D. Reddick,

Crusader Without Violence: The Biography of Martin Luther King, Jr. (Montgomery, AL: New South Books, 1959), 67.

2. Reddick, *Crusader Without Violence*, 67.

3. Christine King Farris, "The Young Martin," *Ebony*, January 1986; Poston, "Martin Luther King," Parts 1–6.

15. School Shooting

1. *Atlanta Daily World*, June 4, 1943, 5; October 28, 1943, 6; November 3, 1943, 1; November 5, 1943, 1; February 17, 1944, 1; December 1, 1944, 3. As a result of his academic record and character witnesses, Livingston was not charged with a felony. Instead, he was charged with several misdemeanors, fined, and given a probationary sentence of four years. He graduated with his class in 1944 and joined his three brothers in the Army to join the war effort.

2. *Atlanta Daily World*, June 4, 1943, 5; October 28, 1943, 6; November 3, 1943, 1; November 5, 1943, 1; February 17, 1944, 1; December 1, 1944, 3.

16. The Bus

1. MLK's grades for the entire academic year are listed on his Booker T. Washington High School Report Card, dated January 28, 1944. MLK Papers, vol. 1.

2. Jonathan Eig, *King: A Life* (New York: Farrar, Straus and Giroux, 2023), 65–67.

3. *Norfolk Journal and Guide*, November 27, 1926, 11; *Atlanta Daily World*, July 25, 1943, 2; August 22, 1943, 2; August 31, 1943, 1; April 16, 1944, 2; September 7, 1944, 1; April 22, 1947, 1.

   On Bradley and her influence upon King, see King interview with Donald Smith, November 29, 1963, in MLK Papers, vol. 8, forthcoming. See Bradley's obituary, *Atlanta Daily World*, October 9, 1953, 1; Michelle O'Donnell, "Black Elks Honor Rituals as Membership Dwindles," *New York Times*, September 20, 2004.

4. *Atlanta Daily World*, April 16, 1944, 2.

5. *Atlanta Daily World*, July 25, 1943, 2; July 30, 1943, 1.

6. *Atlanta Daily World*, April 22, 1944, 3; Eig, *King: A Life*, 51.

7. *Atlanta Daily World*, April 22, 1944, 3; September 2, 1945, 1; October 9, 1953, 1; *The Savannah Tribune*, September 13, 1945, 1; September 5, 1959, 5; November 16, 1957, 1.

8. *Atlanta Daily World*, April 22, 1944, 3; September 2, 1945, 1; October 9, 1953, 1; Eig, *King: A Life*, 51.

9. ML recounted this incident throughout his life, see Ted Poston, "Martin Luther King," Parts 1–6, *Afro-American*, June 8, June 15, June 22, June 29, July 6, July 13, 1957; *Time*, "America's Gandhi: Rev. Martin Luther King Jr.," January 3, 1964; Martin Luther King Jr., interview with Alex Haley, unedited transcript of *Playboy* interview, Rubenstein Library, Duke University, October 23, 1964. Special thanks to Jonathan Eig for sending this my way. See published version in *Playboy*, January 1965.

   On Bradley and her influence upon King, see King interview with Donald Smith, November 29, 1963, in MLK Papers, vol. 8, forthcoming. See Bradley's obituary, *Atlanta Daily World*, October 9, 1953, 1.

10. King, "Statement on Meredith March," Grenada, Mississippi, June 16, 1966, Martin Luther King, Jr. Research and Education Institute, Stanford University.

11. Poston, "Martin Luther King"; *Time*, January 3, 1964; Martin Luther King Jr., interview with Alex Haley, unedited transcript of *Playboy* interview, Rubenstein Library, Duke University, October 23, 1964; see also *Playboy*, January 1965.

12. See for example, *Baltimore Afro American*, March 25, 1944, 1, May 20, 1944, 9; *New York Amsterdam News*, April 1, 1944, 1A; *Philadelphia Tribune*, March 25, 1944, 2; *The Cleveland Call and Post*, March 25, 1944, 1B; *Michigan Chronicle*, April 15, 1944, 6, May 20, 1994, 1; *Atlanta Daily World*, May 16, 1944, 1

13. Martin Luther King Jr., interview with Alex Haley.

14. Poston, "Martin Luther King"; *Time*, "America's Gandhi: Rev. Martin Luther King Jr."; Martin Luther King Jr., interview with Alex Haley.

15. *Atlanta Daily World*, September 2, 1944, 1; September 7, 1944, 1; Bruce Beezer, "Black Teachers' Salaries and the Federal Courts Before Brown v. Board of Education: One Beginning for Equity," *Journal of Negro Education*, vol. 55, no. 2 (Spring 1986).

16. Christine King Farris, The HistoryMakers A2010.074, interviewed by Julieanna L. Richardson, July 11, 2010, session 1, tape 3, story 4, The HistoryMakers Digital Archive; June Dobbs Butts, interviewed by Franklin Abbott, January 29, 2016, Activist Women Oral History Project, Archives for Research on Women and Gender. Special Collections and Archives, Georgia State University; June Dobbs Butts, The HistoryMakers A2006.076, interviewed by Shawn Wilson, April 13, 2006, session 1, tape 1, story 10, The HistoryMakers Digital Archive; Lakshmi Pandey David L. Sjoquist, "An Exploration of Racial Residential Segregation Trends in Atlanta: 1970–2020," Working Paper 22-01, Center for State and Local Finance, Andrew Young School, Georgia State University, April 18, 2022; David Halberstam, "The Second Coming of Martin Luther King, Jr." *Harper's*, August 1, 1967; "Notes from interviews with MLK, April 15–May 18, 1967" by David Halberstam, David Halberstam Collection, box 11, folder 5, Howard Gotlieb Archival Research Center, Boston University.

17. See brief background on program in *Atlanta Daily World*, September 4, 1941, 1.

18. *Morehouse College Bulletin*, May 1944, May 1945.

19. In the 1940 government census, King reported his annual salary as $2,500. This income is the approximate equivalent to $300,000 in 2023.

20. Reverend Martin Luther King Sr. with Clayton Riley, *Daddy King: An Autobiography* (Boston: Beacon Press, 1980), 122; interview with Martin Luther King Sr. in "My Life with Martin Luther King," stenographer notebook, box 23, folder 3, Alden and Allene G. Hatch Papers, MS Group 077, Special and Area Studies Collections, George A. Smathers Libraries, University of Florida.

21. Martin Luther King Jr., "My Pilgrimage to Nonviolence," *Fellowship*, September 1958, Martin Luther King, Jr. Research and Education Institute, Stanford University, https://kinginstitute.stanford.edu/king-papers/documents/my-pilgrimage-nonviolence#ftnref7; *Atlanta Daily World*, July 2, 1941, 1.

22. Interview with Emmett Proctor, April 15, 1970, transcript notes in Taylor Branch Papers, folder 701, Southern Historical Collection, Wilson Library, University on North Carolina at Chapel Hill; Emmett Proctor telephone interview with Pam McDonald, August 16, 2000, Pam McDonald Collection, Simsbury Historical Society; *Atlanta Daily World*, September 4, 1941, 1; King, Letter to Alberta, August 30, 1944, MLK Papers, vol. 1, 117; "Tribute to Claude B. Dansby," *Morehouse College Bulletin*, Summer 1973; Alex Wood, "Blacks Recall Connecticut Tobacco Farms," *Journal Inquirer*, July 17, 1989, 21–22.

23. Interview with Emmett Proctor, April 15, 1970; interview transcript, William G. Pickens, *Connecticut Journal*, episode 126, aired on Connecticut Public Television (CPTV), May 8, 1998, transcribed by Pam McDonald, circa 2000, in Pam McDonald Collection; Wood, "Blacks Recall Connecticut Tobacco Farms."

24. Benjamin E. Mays, *Born to Rebel: An Autobiography* (Athens & London: University of Georgia Press, 1971), 76–77.

17. Terminal Station

1. *Atlanta Daily World*, February 10, 1944, 6; John Michael Giggie, *After Redemption: Jim Crow and the Transformation of African American Religion in the Delta, 1875–1915* (New York: Oxford University Press, 2008), 23–28.
   On Reverend Gates, see Lerone A. Martin, *Preaching on Wax: The Phonograph and the Shaping of Modern African American Religion* (New York and London: New York University Press, 2014).

2. *Maroon Tiger*, November 1944.

3. *Atlanta Daily World*, January 1, 1944, 1; January 9, 1944, 4; January 28, 1944, 1; *Pittsburgh Courier*, February 12, 1944, 2.

4. *Atlanta Daily World*, December 31, 1943; January 1, 1944, 1; January 9, 1944, 4; January 28, 1944, 1; *Pittsburgh Courier*, February 12, 1944, 2; "Purchasing Power Today of a US Dollar Transaction in the Past," Measuring Worth, 2023, www.measuringworth.com/ppowerus.

5. *Atlanta Daily World*, November 30, 1942, 1; July 17, 1943; July 20, 1943, 6; September 13, 1944, 1.

6. Interview transcript, William G. Pickens, *Connecticut Journal*, episode 126, aired on Connecticut Public Television (CPTV), May 8, 1998, transcribed by Pam McDonald, circa 2000, in Pam McDonald Collection.

7. *Maroon Tiger*, November 1944; *Atlanta Constitution*, March 5, D2; May 14, 1905, E1; "Atlanta Terminal of the Southern of the Southern Railway," *International Railway Journal* 13, no. 5 (August 1905); "Finding Aid," and "In House Correspondence," (n.d.), Atlanta Terminal Station Records, 1940–1952, Atlanta History Center James G. Kenan Research Center Manuscript Collections MSS 733, box 1.

8. *Atlanta Constitution*, March 5, D2; May 14, 1905, E1; "Atlanta Terminal of the Southern of the Southern Railway," *International Railway Journal*.

9. *Atlanta Daily World*, November 27, 1935, 6; May 8, 1940, 1; Mays, *Born to Rebel*, 75–79; *New York Times*, November 8, 1967, 40; Jackson McQuigg, "Southern Railway Serves the

South," Atlanta History Center, January 6, 2022, https://www.atlantahistorycenter.com
/blog/tsouthern-railway-serves-the-south/; Ray Stannard Baker, *Following the Color Line:
An Account of Negro Citizenship in the American Democracy* (New York: Doubleday, Page &
Company,1908), 34.

10. Mays, *Born to Rebel*, 75–79.

11. "Atlanta Terminal of the Southern of the Southern Railway," *International Railway Journal*;
Atlanta Daily World, March 16, 1941, 4; Mays, *Born to Rebel*, 75–79.

12. *Atlanta Constitution*, March 5, D2; May 14, 1905, E1; Mays, *Born to Rebel*, 75–79; "Atlanta
Terminal of the Southern of the Southern Railway," *International Railway Journal*.

13. *Atlanta Constitution*, March 5, D2; May 14, 1905, E1.

14. "Atlanta Terminal of the Southern of the Southern Railway," *International Railway Journal*;
W. E. B. Du Bois, "On Being Black," *New Republic*, February 18, 1920; Mays, *Born to Rebel*,
75–79.

15. Mays, *Born to Rebel*, 75–79.

16. *Atlanta Daily World*, March 30, 1941, 4.

17. *Atlanta Constitution*, March 5, D2; May 14, 1905, E1; Baker, *Following the Color Line*, 34.

18. Martin Luther King Jr., *Stride Toward Freedom: The Montgomery Story* (New York & London: Harper & Row, 1958), 20–21.

18. The Price of the Ticket

1. W. E. B. Du Bois, "On Being Black," *New Republic*, February 18, 1920.

2. Du Bois, "On Being Black"; Benjamin E. Mays, *Born to Rebel: An Autobiography* (Athens &
London: University of Georgia Press, 1971), 75–79.

3. British royalty and celebrities continue to sport expensive horsehair bedding. See Sarah
Cummings, "The History of the Bed: From Horse Hair to Now," *Victorian Era*, October
27, 2017; Julie Sagoskin, "Dream On: Mattress Brand Beloved by Royals & Stars Like
Drake Can Cost Over $650K—A Luxe Detail Was Taken from Swedish Noblemen," *The
Sun*, August 23, 2024; *Mitchell v. United States*, 313 U.S. 80 (1941); Arthur D. Durbin, *Some
Classic Trains* (Milwaukee, WI: Kalmbach Publishing, 1964), 108–123; Mia Bay, *Traveling
Black* (Cambridge, MA: Harvard University Press, 2021), 88–97.

4. Georgia General Assembly, Acts and Resolutions of the General Assembly of the State of
Georgia 1899, Volume 1, 67, https://hdl.handle.net/2027/nyp.33433009067129.

5. Thomas Montgomery Gregory, "The Jim Crow Car: An NAACP Investigation," Part 3,
The Crisis, February 1916, 195–98; Mays, *Born to Rebel*, 196–97.

6. Georgia General Assembly, Acts and Resolutions of the General Assembly of the State
of Georgia 1899; Mays, *Born to Rebel*, 75–79, 196–97. For more on *Mitchell v. United States*
see Bay, 233-240.

7. Mays, *Born to Rebel*, 96–97.

8. Bay, *Traveling Black*, 88–97; Pullman Company, Pullman Advertising Folder, Chicago, IL,
circa 1920, in Durbin, *Some Classic Trains*. On Bessie Smith, see Jackie Kay, *Bessie Smith*
(New York: Absolute, 1997); Chris Albertson, *Bessie* (New Haven & London: Yale University Press, 2003).

19. The Jim Crow Car

1. "Looking Through the Window of a Jim Crow Train," *New York Amsterdam News*, November 13, 1943, B; Arthur D. Durbin, "Crescent Limited," in *Trains: The Magazine of Railroading* 24, no. 9 (July 1964): 20–35; Burke Davis, *The Southern Railway* (Chapel Hill and London: University of North Carolina Press, 1985).

2. Stannard Baker, *Following the Color Line: An Account of Negro Citizenship in the American Democracy* (New York: Doubleday, Page & Company, 1908), 31; Gunnar Myrdal, *An American Dilemma: The Negro Problem and Modern Democracy* (New York & London: Harper & Row Publishers, 1944, 1962), 635.

3. "In House Correspondence," Atlanta Terminal Station Records, 1940–1952, Atlanta History Center, James G. Kenan Research Center Manuscript Collections MSS 733, box 1, folder 3; Arthur D. Durbin, "Crescent Limited"; Southern Railway, "The Southern Crescent—A History of Good Service," Southern Railway's Public Relations and Advertising Department, circa 1972.

4. "In House Correspondence," Atlanta Terminal Station Records, 1940–1952; Durbin, "Crescent Limited"; Southern Railway, "The Southern Crescent—A History of Good Service." For a general executive history of Southern Railway, see Davis, *The Southern Railway*.

5. W. E. B. Du Bois, "On Being Black," *New Republic*, February 18, 1920.

6. Bay, *Traveling Black*, 64–75.

7. James E. McCulloch, ed., *The Human Way: Addresses on Race Problems at the Southern Sociological Congress, Atlanta, 1913* (Nashville: Southern Sociological Congress, 1913), 70–77.

8. Bay, *Traveling Black*, 64–75; Mays, *Born to Rebel*, 77–79; Du Bois, "On Being Black"; Thomas Montgomery Gregory, "The Jim Crow Car: An NAACP Investigation," Part 1, *The Crisis*, December 1915, 87–90, Part 2, January 1916, 137–38.

9. Bay, *Traveling Black*, 64–75; Mays, *Born to Rebel*, 77–79; Du Bois, "On Being Black"; Gregory, "The Jim Crow Car: An NAACP Investigation," Part 1, Part 2.

10. "Looking Through the Window of a Jim Crow Train," *New York Amsterdam News*, November 13, 1943, B; *The Chicago Defender*, August 26, 1922, 2; Gregory, "The Jim Crow Car: An NAACP Investigation," Part 2.

11. Bay, *Traveling Black: A Story of Race and Resistance*, 64–75; Mays, *Born to Rebel*, 77–79; Du Bois, "On Being Black."

12. Bay, *Traveling Black*, 64–75; Mays, *Born to Rebel*, 77–79; Du Bois, "On Being Black"; Gregory, "The Jim Crow Car: An NAACP Investigation," Part 2.

13. Bay, *Traveling Black*, 64–75; Mays, *Born to Rebel*, 77–79; Du Bois, "On Being Black"; *Chicago Defender*, August 26, 1922, 2.

14. Interview transcript, William G. Pickens, *Connecticut Journal*, episode 126, aired on Connecticut Public Television (CPTV), May 8, 1998, transcribed by Pam McDonald, circa 2000, in Pam McDonald Collection.

15. Bay, *Traveling Black*, 64–75; Mays, *Born to Rebel*, 77–79; Du Bois, "On Being Black."

16. Mays, *Born to Rebel*, 76–77.

17. *Pittsburgh Courier*, September 5, 1942, 1; Mays, *Born to Rebel*, 77–79.

18. Bay, *Traveling Black*, 64–75; Mays, *Born to Rebel*, 77–79; Du Bois, "On Being Black"; Gregory, "The Jim Crow Car: An NAACP Investigation," Part 1.

19. Quoted in Bay, *Traveling Black*, 69–70.

20. Martin Luther King Jr., *Stride Toward Freedom: The Montgomery Story* (New York & London: Harper & Row, 1958), 20.

21. Arthur D. Durbin, "Crescent Limited"; Durbin, *Some Classic Trains*, Southern Railway, "The Southern Crescent—A History of Good Service."

22. King, "Statement on Meredith March," Grenada, Mississippi, June 16, 1966, MLK Papers Project, vol. 11, forthcoming.

20. The Curtain

1. Mike Schafer, *More Classic American Railroads* (Osceola, WI: MBI Publishing Company, 2000), 127; Arthur D. Durbin, "Crescent Limited," in *Trains: The Magazine of Railroading* 24, no. 9 (July 1964): 20–35.

2. Thomas Montgomery Gregory, "The Jim Crow Car: An NAACP Investigation," Part 3, *The Crisis*, February 1916, 195–98; William Pickens, "Jim-Crowed," *Socialist Review* 9, no. 2 (July 1920), 75–76; W. E. B. Du Bois, "On Being Black," *New Republic*, February 18, 1920.

3. *Pittsburgh Courier*, August 7, 1943, 15; *Henderson v. United States*, 339 U.S. 816, 820 n.2 (1950).

4. *Chicago Defender*, August 26, 1922.

5. "Looking Through the Window of a Jim Crow Train," *New York Amsterdam News*, November 13, 1943, B.

6. Reverend King T. Hayes, telephone interview with Pam McDonald, August 4, 2000.

7. *Henderson v. United States*; Benjamin E. Mays, *Born to Rebel: An Autobiography* (Athens & London: University of Georgia Press, 1971),197; Burke Davis, *The Southern Railway* (Chapel Hill and London: University of North Carolina Press, 1985), 75.

8. Mays, *Born to Rebel*, 198; Stetson Kennedy, *Jim Crow Guide to the USA: The Laws, Customs and Etiquette Governing the Conduct of Nonwhites and Other Minorities as Second-Class Citizens* (Tuscaloosa, AL: University of Alabama Press, 1959), 187.

9. *Henderson v. United States*, 63 F. Supp. 906, 910 (D. Md. 1945); *Henderson v. United States*, 339 U.S. 816, 820 n.2 (1950).

10. *Henderson v. United States*, 63 F. Supp. 906, 910; (D. Md. 1945); *Henderson v. United States*, 339 U.S. 816, 820 n.2 (1950).

11. Elmer Henderson Obituary, *The Guardian*, July 22, 2001; *Pittsburgh Courier*, October 9, 1948, 1; *Henderson v. United States*, 63 F. Supp. 906, 910 (D. Md. 1945); *Henderson v. United States*, 339 U.S. 816, 820 n.2 (1950). Henderson's case was appealed to the US Supreme Court, which ruled in Henderson's favor 8–0 in 1950. It did not rule on the doctrine of "separate but equal," but rather ruled that segregation in the form of reserved tables and curtains in interstate railroad dining cars was unconstitutional under the Interstate Commerce Act. Southern Railway still tried to maintain segregation. Following the ruling, the railroad instructed its dining-car stewards to seat white passengers "from the buffet or kitchen end of the dining car, and colored persons from the opposite end." See Kennedy, *Jim Crow Guide to the USA*, 187.

12. Martin Luther King Jr., *Stride Toward Freedom: The Montgomery Story* (New York & London: Harper & Row, 1958), 20.

13. Letters in MLK Papers, vol. 1.

14. Interview transcript, William G. Pickens, *Connecticut Journal*, episode 126, aired on Connecticut Public Television (CPTV), May 8, 1998, transcribed by Pam McDonald, circa 2000, in Pam McDonald Collection.

15. *Maroon Tiger*, November 1944; interview transcript, William G. Pickens, *Connecticut Journal*.

16. *Maroon Tiger*, November 1944.

21. Simsbury

1. Interview transcript, William G. Pickens, *Connecticut Journal*, episode 126, aired on Connecticut Public Television (CPTV), May 8, 1998, transcribed by Pam McDonald, circa 2000, in Pam McDonald Collection.

2. *Maroon Tiger*, November 1944.

3. *Maroon Tiger*, November 1944; letters in MLK Papers, vol. 1.

4. Letters in MLK Papers, vol. 1.

5. Interview transcript, William G. Pickens, *Connecticut Journal*; Mike Swift, "King's Summers in State Fostered Famous Dream of Freedom," *Hartford Courant*, January 21, 1991, A1G.

6. "Attack on the Conscience," *Time* 69 (7). 1957, 17–20.

7. Interview transcript, William G. Pickens, *Connecticut Journal*; Swift, "King's Summers in State Fostered Famous Dream of Freedom," *Hartford Courant*, January 21, 1991, A1G; Reverdy C. Ransom, III, "Jamaican Workers in the State of Connecticut," *Journal of Negro Education* 15, no. 4 (Autumn, 1946), 717–21; Ralph L. Guyette, "Growing a Crop Under Tents," *Popular Mechanics*, July 1947, 132–34, 220, 224.

8. Interview transcript, William G. Pickens, *Connecticut Journal*; Swift, "King's Summers in State Fostered Famous Dream of Freedom"; Ransom, III, "Jamaican Workers in the State of Connecticut," 717–21; Guyette, "Growing a Crop Under Tents," 132–34, 220, 224.

9. *Maroon Tiger*, October 1938; Alex Wood, "Blacks Recall Connecticut Tobacco Farms," *Journal Inquirer*, July 17, 1989, 21–22.

10. *Maroon Tiger*, November 1944; *Atlanta Daily World*, October 8, 1944, 3.

11. *Maroon Tiger*, November 1944.

12. *Maroon Tiger*, October 1938.

13. Emmett Proctor telephone interview with Pam McDonald, August 16, 2000, Pam McDonald Collection, Simsbury Historical Society; interview transcript, William G. Pickens, *Connecticut Journal*; Alex Wood, "Blacks Recall Connecticut Tobacco Farms," *Journal Inquirer*, July 17, 1989, 21–22; *Maroon Tiger*, November 1944.

14. Letters in MLK Papers, vol. 1.

15. Arthur L. Johnson, *Race and Remembrance: A Memoir* (Detroit, MI: Wayne State University Press, 2008), 27–31; "Written and Photographic Documentation of Cullman Brothers, Inc. Tobacco Barns," Prepared for Fuss & O'Neill, Inc. Manchester, Connecticut, by Bruce Clouette, Archaeological and Historical Services, Inc., Storrs, Connecticut, June 2009.

16. *Maroon Tiger*, October 1938 and November 1945; Guyette, "Growing a Crop Under Tents"; Wood, "Blacks Recall Connecticut Tobacco Farms"; Swift, "King's Summers In State Fostered Famous Dream of Freedom"; interview transcript, William G. Pickens,

Connecticut Journal. See also, Patrick Parr, *The Seminarian* (Chicago: Lawrence Hill Books, 2018), 7–9.

17. *Maroon Tiger*, October 1938 and November 1945; Guyette, "Growing a Crop Under Tents"; interview transcript, William G. Pickens, *Connecticut Journal*.

18. *Maroon Tiger*, October 1938 and November 1945; Guyette, "Growing a Crop Under Tents"; interview transcript, William G. Pickens, *Connecticut Journal*. The pay is equivalent to about eighty-five dollars for an eight-hour work day in 2024 or roughly $10 an hour. See Samuel H. Williamson, "Seven Ways to Compute the Relative Value of a U.S. Dollar Amount, 1790 to present," MeasuringWorth, 2024.

19. MLK Letter to his parents in MLK Papers, vol. 1, strike-through in original.

20. Wood, "Blacks Recall Connecticut Tobacco Farms."

21. Proctor telephone interview with Pam McDonald; Wood, "Blacks Recall Connecticut Tobacco Farms"; Swift, "King's Summers in State Fostered Famous Dream of Freedom."

22. Proctor telephone interview with Pam McDonald; Wood, "Blacks Recall Connecticut Tobacco Farms"; Swift, "King's Summers in State Fostered Famous Dream of Freedom"; interview transcript, William G. Pickens, *Connecticut Journal*.

23. Wood, "Blacks Recall Connecticut Tobacco Farms."

24. Wood, "Blacks Recall Connecticut Tobacco Farms."

25. Proctor telephone interview with Pam McDonald; Wood, "Blacks Recall Connecticut Tobacco Farms."

26. Interview with Emmett Proctor, April 15, 1970, transcript notes in Taylor Branch Papers, folder 701, Southern Historical Collection, Wilson Library, University on North Carolina at Chapel Hill; Wood, "Blacks Recall Connecticut Tobacco Farms"; Swift, "King's Summers in State Fostered Famous Dream of Freedom."

27. MLK Papers, vol. 1, italics mine.

28. Interview transcript, William G. Pickens, *Connecticut Journal*.

29. MLK Papers, vol. 1; Wood, "Blacks Recall Connecticut Tobacco Farms"; Swift, "King's Summers in State Fostered Famous Dream of Freedom."

30. MLK Papers, vol. 1; Wood, "Blacks Recall Connecticut Tobacco Farms"; Swift, "King's Summers in State Fostered Famous Dream of Freedom"; Proctor telephone interview with Pam McDonald.

31. Martin Luther King Jr., *Stride Toward Freedom: The Montgomery Story* (New York & London: Harper & Row, 1958), 20–21.

32. MLK Papers, vol. 1.

33. MLK Papers, vol. 1; Swift, "King's Summers in State Fostered Famous Dream of Freedom."

34. Transcript of "The Future of Integration" by Martin Luther King Jr., May 7, 1959, University of Hartford, Keller Lectures Collection (ARCH075), University of Hartford Archives & Special Collections. Transcribed by Sean Parke, University Archivist, March 2020.

35. Proctor telephone interview with Pam McDonald; *Atlanta Daily World*, August 3, 1943, 3.

36. Wood, "Blacks Recall Connecticut Tobacco Farms."

37. Wood, "Blacks Recall Connecticut Tobacco Farms"; Reverend King T. Hayes, telephone interview with Pam McDonald, August 4, 2000. See also, *Hartford Times*, July 22, 1943; *Farmington Valley Herald*, July 24, 1947, 3, Pam McDonald Collection.

38. For more on this case, see Julie Buckner Armstrong, "How My Heart Grows Weary: Willie James Howard and the Suwanee River," *Journal of Florida Studies* 1, no. 9; Equal Justice Initiative calendar, https://calendar.eji.org/racial-injustice/jan/2.

39. *Hartford Courant,* July 27, 1944; Reverend King T. Hayes, telephone interview with Pam McDonald; Wood, "Blacks Recall Connecticut Tobacco Farms"; Swift, "King's Summers in State Fostered Famous Dream of Freedom."

40. Reverend King T. Hayes, telephone interview with Pam McDonald; Wood, "Blacks Recall Connecticut Tobacco Farms"; Swift, "King's Summers in State Fostered Famous Dream of Freedom."

41. Wood, "Blacks Recall Connecticut Tobacco Farms"; Swift, "King's Summers in State Fostered Famous Dream of Freedom"; interview transcript, William G. Pickens, *Connecticut Journal.*

42. Graham began the stepwise process of stopping segregated seating in 1953. See Michael E. Long, *Billy Graham and the Beloved Community: America's Evangelist and the Dream of Martin Luther King, Jr.* (New York: Palgrave Macmillan, 2006); Steven P. Miller, *Billy Graham and the Rise of the Republican South* (Philadelphia: University of Pennsylvania Press, 2009).

43. MLK Papers, vol. 1.

44. MLK Papers, vol. 1; see stories on Mitchell in *Hartford Times,* April 10, 11, 12, 1946; Swift, "King's Summers in State Fostered Famous Dream of Freedom."

45. Bernice Martin interviewed in "Simsbury's Connection with Martin Luther King," McLean Retirement Community Newsletter, July 2005; Bernice Martin interviewed on *Connecticut Journal,* episode 126, aired on Connecticut Public Television (CPTV), May 8, 1998. On attendance and sermon titles, see *Farmington Valley Herald,* June 29, 1944; July 6, 1944; July 13, 1944, in Pam McDonald Collection; Wood, "Blacks Recall Connecticut Tobacco Farms"; Swift, "King's Summers in State Fostered Famous Dream of Freedom."

46. Wood, "Blacks Recall Connecticut Tobacco Farms."

47. Wood, "Blacks Recall Connecticut Tobacco Farms"; Swift, "King's Summers in State Fostered Famous Dream of Freedom"; Martin interviewed on *Connecticut Journal.*

48. Jeremy Brecher, Connecticut Humanities Council Researcher, interviewed on *Connecticut Journal,* episode 126, aired on Connecticut Public Television (CPTV), May 8, 1998; Swift, "King's Summers in State Fostered Famous Dream of Freedom"; Wood, "Blacks Recall Connecticut Tobacco Farms"; Fay Clarke Johnson, *Soldiers of the Soil* (New York: Vantage Press, 1995), 63–64.

49. Swift, "King's Summers in State Fostered Famous Dream of Freedom"; Wood, "Blacks Recall Connecticut Tobacco Farms"; interview transcript, William G. Pickens, *Connecticut Journal.*

50. Interview transcript, William G. Pickens, *Connecticut Journal;* Swift, "King's Summers in State Fostered Famous Dream of Freedom."

51. Interview transcript, William G. Pickens, *Connecticut Journal;* Swift, "King's Summers in State Fostered Famous Dream of Freedom."

22. Malcolm

1. Malcolm's experience in the Connecticut Tobacco fields is chronicled in Les Payne and Tamara Payne, *The Dead Are Arising: The Life of Malcolm X* (New York: Liveright Publishing Corp., 2020), 202–205.

2. Malcolm X with Alex Haley, *The Autobiography of Malcolm X* (New York: Random House, 1964), 43–46.

3. In Malcolm's autobiography he uses the pseudonym Mr. Ostrowski for his teacher. See, Malcolm X, *The Autobiography of Malcolm X*; Payne and Payne, *The Dead Are Arising*, 138–39.

4. Malcolm X, *The Autobiography of Malcolm X*, 43–46.

5. *Atlanta Daily World*, October 17, 1936, 5; *Atlanta Constitution*, October 16, 1936, 24.

6. Payne and Payne, *The Dead Are Arising*, 138–39; Patrick Parr, *Malcolm Before X* (Amherst & Boston: University of Massachusetts Press, 2024), 88–91.

7. *Maroon Tiger*, November 1945.

8. Malcolm X, *The Autobiography of Malcolm X*; Payne and Payne, *The Dead Are Arising*; Parr, *Malcolm Before X*, 19–20.

23. First Congregation

1. Alex Wood, "Blacks Recall Connecticut Tobacco Farms," *Journal Inquirer,* July 17, 1989; Mike Swift, "King's Summers in State Fostered Famous Dream of Freedom," *Hartford Courant,* January 21, 1991, A1G; William G. Pickens, *Connecticut Journal,* episode 126, aired on Connecticut Public Television (CPTV), May 8, 1998, transcribed by Pam McDonald, circa 2000, in Pam McDonald Collection.

2. Wood, "Blacks Recall Connecticut Tobacco Farms"; Swift, "King's Summers in State Fostered Famous Dream of Freedom."

3. Wood, "Blacks Recall Connecticut Tobacco Farms"; Swift, "King's Summers in State Fostered Famous Dream of Freedom"; MLK letter home, MLK Papers, vol. 1.

4. MLK letter home, MLK Papers, vol. 1.

5. Wood, "Blacks Recall Connecticut Tobacco Farms"; Swift, "King's Summers in State Fostered Famous Dream of Freedom."

6. W. E. B. Du Bois, *The Souls of Black Folk* (Chicago: A. C. McClurg and Co., 1903).

7. Swift, "King's Summers in State Fostered Famous Dream of Freedom."

8. On Black vernacular and Black chanted sermons, see, Lerone A. Martin, *Preaching on Wax: The Phonograph and the Shaping of Modern African American Religion* (New York and London: New York University Press, 2014).

9. Swift, "King's Summers in State Fostered Famous Dream of Freedom."

10. MLK Papers, vol. 1.

11. Wood, "Blacks Recall Connecticut Tobacco Farms"; Swift, "King's Summers in State Fostered Famous Dream of Freedom."

12. Coretta Scott King interview, Hatch Papers, Tape 3.

13. MLK letters home in MLK Papers, vol. 1.

14. MLK letters home in MLK Papers, vol. 1; Wood, "Blacks Recall Connecticut Tobacco Farms."

15. MLK letters in MLK Papers, vol. 1; Wood, "Blacks Recall Connecticut Tobacco Farms"; Swift, "King's Summers in State Fostered Famous Dream of Freedom."

16. Martin Luther King, "An Autobiography of Religious Development."

24. A Bitter Feeling

1. MLK Papers, vol. 1.
2. *Maroon Tiger,* November 1945.
3. MLK Papers, vol. 1; *Maroon Tiger,* November 1944.
4. *Baltimore Afro-American,* June 22, 1957, A3.
5. Interview transcript, William G. Pickens, *Connecticut Journal,* episode 126, aired on Connecticut Public Television (CPTV), May 8, 1998, transcribed by Pam McDonald, circa 2000, in Pam McDonald Collection.
6. Reverend Martin Luther King Sr. with Clayton Riley, *Daddy King: An Autobiography* (Boston: Beacon Press, 1980), 128.
7. Christine King Farris, The HistoryMakers A2010.074, interviewed by Julieanna L. Richardson, July 11, 2010, session 1, tape 3, story 4, The HistoryMakers Digital Archive; Coretta Scott King interview, Hatch Papers, Tape 3; Christine King Farris, *Through It All: Reflections on My Life, My Family, and My Faith* (New York: Atria, 2010), 38.

25. A Morehouse Man

1. *Morehouse College Bulletin,* May 1944; interview with Herman Bostick, April 6, 1970, transcript in Taylor Branch Papers, folder 701, Southern Historical Collection, Wilson Library, University on North Carolina at Chapel Hill; *Morehouse College Bulletin,* May 1945; Edward A. Jones, *A Candle in the Dark: A History of Morehouse College* (Valley Forge, PA: Judson Press, 1967), 50.
2. Coretta Scott King interview Hatch Papers, Tape 3.
3. June Dobbs Butts, interviewed by Franklin Abbott, January 29, 2016, Activist Women Oral History Project, Archives for Research on Women and Gender. Special Collections and Archives, Georgia State University.
4. *Morehouse College Bulletin,* May 1944.
5. W. E. B. Du Bois, *The Souls of Black Folk* (Chicago: A. C. McClurg and Co., 1903), 81; *Afro-American,* June 22, 1957, A3; Jones, *A Candle in the Dark.*
6. Benjamin E. Mays, *Born to Rebel: An Autobiography* (Athens & London: University of Georgia Press, 1971),172.
7. On Mays see, Mays, *Born to Rebel,* 170–92; Benjamin E. Mays, "The Religious Life and Needs of Negro Students," *Journal of Negro Education* 9, no. 3 (July 1940); see also Randal Maurice Jelks, *Benjamin Elijah Mays: Schoolmaster of the Movement* (Chapel Hill: University of North Carolina Press, 2014).
8. Benjamin E. Mays, "Democratizing and Christianizing America in this Generation," *Journal of Negro Education* 14, no. 4 (1945); Barbara Dianne Savage, *Your Spirits Walk Beside Us: The Politics of Black Religion* (Cambridge, MA: Belknap Press of Harvard University Press, 2008), 205–237.
9. See, Mays, *Born to Rebel,* 170–92; Mays, "The Religious Life and Needs of Negro Students"; Mays, "Freshmen," *Pittsburgh Courier,* September 20, 1947; see also, Randal Maurice Jelks, *Benjamin Elijah Mays.*
10. *The Morehouse Companion,* 1944–1945; *Morehouse College Bulletin,* May 1944.

11. *The Morehouse Companion*, 1944–1945.

12. *Maroon Tiger*, November 1945 and December 1946; "Remembering the Young King," *Ebony*, January 1988.

13. Interview with Robert Williams, April 3, 1984, notes in Taylor Branch Papers, folder 701.

14. Interview, Patrick Parr with Reverend Samuel McKinney," in Patrick Parr, "Reverend Samuel McKinney Remembers His Friend Dr. King," *Seattle Magazine*, January 15, 2015, https://seattlemag.com/reverend-samuel-mckinney-remembers-his-friend-dr-king/; Parr, *The Seminarian*, 45–47; Jonathan Eig, *King: A Life* (New York: Farrar, Straus and Giroux, 2023), 58.

15. Eig, *King: A Life*, 58.

16. *Morehouse College Bulletin*, May 1944.

17. *The Morehouse Companion*, 1944–1945.

18. *The Morehouse Companion*, 1944–1945.

19. *The Morehouse Companion*, 1944–1945.

20. *The Morehouse Companion*, 1944–1945; Donald H. Smith interview of Gladstone Louis Chandler, November 29, 1963, or December 4, 1963, Donald H. Smith Tape Recordings, State Historical Society of Wisconsin, Madison, Wis. UC344A.

21. Words of *Morehouse Hymn* adapted by J. O. B. Moseley, class of 1929. *The Morehouse Companion*, 1944–1945, 1945–1946; *Maroon Tiger*, November 1945; *Maroon Tiger*, Senior Edition, 1947; interview with Robert Williams, April 3, 1984, Taylor Branch Papers, folder 701, Southern Historical Collection, Wilson Library, University of North Carolina at Chapel Hill; interview, Dr. Herman Bostick by Herbert Holmes, April 6, 1970, MLK Memorial Center Oral History Project.

22. *Maroon Tiger*, November 1945, Senior Edition, 1947, January 1948; interview with Robert Williams, April 3, 1984; Smith interview of Gladstone Louis Chandler, November 29, 1963 or December 4, 1963, Donald H. Smith Tape Recordings, State Historical Society of Wisconsin, Madison, Wis. UC344A, tape 9, side 1, parts 1 & 2; tape 10, side 1, part 1, copy located at King Institute ML's classmate and later executive editor of *Ebony* magazine Robert E. Johnson claims King participated in the cafeteria strike/protest. See Eric Stirgus, "King's Classmates Recall Young Leader," *Atlanta Journal Constitution*, January 15, 2018, A1.

23. Lerone Bennett, The HistoryMakers A2002.167, interviewed by Julieanna L. Richardson, August 29, 2002, session 1, tape 3, story 1, The HistoryMakers Digital Archive.

24. "Remembering the Young King."

25. Jelks, *Benjamin Elijah Mays*, 161–64.

26. Mays, "Democratizing and Christianizing America in this Generation"; Savage, *Your Spirits Walk Beside Us*, 205–237; Mays, *Born to Rebel*, 170–92; Mays, "The Religious Life and Needs of Negro Students"; Mays, "Freshmen," *Pittsburgh Courier*, September 20, 1947; see also Jelks, *Benjamin Elijah Mays*.

27. *Atlanta Daily World*, September 13, 1944, 1; September 19, 1944, 3; October 8, 1944, 3; for Mays's style and impact on Morehouse, see Jelks, *Benjamin Elijah Mays*.

28. *Atlanta Daily World*, September 13, 1944, 1; September 19, 1944, 3; October 8, 1944, 3; Mays, "Democratizing and Christianizing America in this Generation"; interview, Oliver

"Sack" Jones with Herbert Holmes, April 8, 1970, Martin Luther King, Jr. Memorial Center Oral History Project; interview with Juanita Sellers Stone, notes in Taylor Branch Papers, folder 701; "Remembering the Young King."

29. Mays, "The Religious Life and Needs of Negro Students."
30. Interview with Edward Whitaker, July 31, 1984, notes in in Taylor Branch Papers, folder 703; "Remembering the Young King."
31. Mays, "The Religious Life and Needs of Negro Students."
32. Mays, "The Religious Life and Needs of Negro Students."
33. *Afro-American*, June 22, 1957, A3; "Remembering the Young King."
34. Mays, *Born to Rebel*, 265–68; Lerone Bennett Jr., *What Manner of Man: A Biography of Martin Luther King, Jr.* (Chicago: Johnson Publishing Co., Inc., 1964), 27; Eig, *King: A Life*, 60.
35. King, "Autobiography of Religious Development"; Harvard Sitkoff, *King: Pilgrimage to the Mountaintop* (New York: Hill and Wang, 2009), 12.
36. Mays, *Born to Rebel*, 265; Coretta Scott King, *My Life with Martin Luther King, Jr.* (New York: Holt, Rinehart, and Winston, 1969), 85; Martin Luther King Jr., *Stride Toward Freedom: The Montgomery Story* (New York & London: Harper & Row, 1958), 145.
37. Mays, *Born to Rebel*, 196–200.
38. Mays, *Born to Rebel*, 196–200; Herbert Homes interview with Walter McCall for the Martin Luther King, Jr. Memorial Center Oral History Project, in Taylor Branch Papers, Folder 703.
39. William Peters, "Our Weapon Is Love," *Redbook,* August 1956, 42–43, 71–73.
40. William G. Pickens in "Remembering the Young King"; interview transcript, William G. Pickens, *Connecticut Journal,* episode 126, aired on Connecticut Public Television (CPTV), May 8, 1998, transcribed by Pam McDonald, circa 2000, in Pam McDonald Collection.
41. Pickens in "Remembering the Young King"; interview transcript, William G. Pickens, *Connecticut Journal.*
42. Pickens in "Remembering the Young King"; interview transcript, William G. Pickens, *Connecticut Journal.*

26. Struggle for the Crown

1. Thurman also offers a version of this quote in his autobiography, Howard Thurman, *With Head and Heart: The Autobiography of Howard Thurman* (New York: Harcourt Brace Jovanovich, 1979), 41. See also Jacqueline Trescott, "The Men and Mystique of Morehouse," *Washington Post*, November 9, 1987, https://www.washingtonpost.com/archive/lifestyle/1987/11/09/the-men-and-mystique-of-morehouse/7761d840-5998-4957-bea0-c64bff3b185e/.
2. Martin Luther King Jr. "May 17—11 Years Later," *New York Amsterdam News,* May 22, 1965.
3. *Atlanta Daily World,* October 8, 1944, ; MLK interview with Donald H. Smith, November 29, 1963, transcript in Taylor Branch Papers Folder 701, Southern Historical Collection, Wilson Library, University on North Carolina at Chapel Hill; Smith interview with Prof. Gladstone Louis Chandler, December 4, 1963, transcript in Taylor Branch Papers Folder

701; interview with Coretta Scott King, 1968, Tape 5, Alden and Allene Hatch Papers, University of Florida, George A. Smathers Libraries.

4. Interview with Mel Kennedy, April 22, 1970, in Taylor Branch Papers Folder 701; Dennis Dickerson, "African American Religious Intellectuals and the Theological Foundations of the Civil Rights Movement, 1930–1955," *Church History* 74, no. 2 (June 2005).

5. Annie L. McPheeters, interviewed by Kathryn L. Nasstrom, June 8, 1992, P1992-09, Series J: Black and White Women in Atlanta Public Life, Georgia Government Documentation Project, Special Collections and Archives, Georgia State University Library, Atlanta, Georgia.

6. Interview with Mel Kennedy, April 22, 1970.

7. *The Morehouse Alumnus*, Fall 1965.

8. *Jet*, October 7, 1965.

9. *The Morehouse Alumnus*, Fall 1965.

10. *Jet*, October 7, 1965.

11. *Jet*, October 7, 1965.

12. Interview transcript, William G. Pickens, *Connecticut Journal*, episode 126, aired on Connecticut Public Television (CPTV), May 8, 1998, transcribed by Pam McDonald, circa 2000 in Pam McDonald Collection.

13. Donald H. Smith interview with Gladstone Louis Chandler, November 29, 1963, or December 4, 1963, Donald H. Smith Tape Recordings, State Historical Society of Wisconsin, Madison, Wis. UC344A.

14. *Jet*, October 7, 1965.

15. Smith interview with G. L. Chandler, November 29, 1963, or December 4, 1963.

16. *Jet*, October 7, 1965.

17. Smith interview with G. L. Chandler, November 29, 1963, or December 4, 1963.

18. Smith interview with G. L. Chandler, November 29, 1963, or December 4, 1963.

19. *Morehouse Alumnus*, April 1946, 13–14; MLK Papers, vol. 1; MLK interview with Donald H. Smith, November 29, 1963, transcript in MLK Papers, vol. 8; Smith interview with G. L. Chandler, November 29, 1963, or December 4, 1963; *Morehouse College Bulletin*, May 1948.

20. *Morehouse Alumnus*, April 1946, 13–14; MLK Papers, vol. 1; MLK interview with Donald H. Smith, November 29, 1963; Smith interview with G. L. Chandler, November 29, 1963, or December 4, 1963; *Morehouse College Bulletin*, May 1948.

21. Interview with Herman Bostick, April 6, 1970, transcript in Taylor Branch Papers, Folder 701; "Remembering the Young King," *Ebony*, January 1988.

22. MLK interview with Donald H. Smith, November 29, 1963.

23. MLK interview with Donald H. Smith, November 29, 1963.

24. "Remembering the Young King"; *Morehouse College Bulletin*, May 1947; "King Wins Second Prize in Oratorical Contest," https://kinginstitute.stanford.edu/king-wins-second-prize-oratorical-contest.

25. "Overcoming an Inferiority Complex," Sermon Delivered at Dexter Avenue Baptist Church, July 14, 1957, https://kinginstitute.stanford.edu/king-papers/documents/overcoming-inferiority-complex-sermon-delivered-dexter-avenue-baptist-church#fn12.

26. MLK's average is found by computing his college grades, which are found in MLK Papers, volume 1.

27. *Morehouse College Bulletin*, May 1944, 24.

28. Jonathan Eig interview with Dr. June Dobbs, phone, November 27, 2018, in possession of author, with special thanks to Jonathan Eig for sharing his interview transcripts with me.

29. Smith interview with G. L. Chandler, November 29, 1963, or December 4, 1963; see also Professor Gladstone Chandler interview in Taylor Branch Papers.

30. Interview, Edward A. Jones by Herbert Holmes.

31. Interview, Dr. Brailsford Brazeal by Judy Barton, February 16, 1972, MLK Memorial Center Oral History Project; Dr. Brailsford Brazeal to Charles E. Batten, March 23, 1948, MLK Papers, vol. 1, 156; Matthew F. Nichter, "From the Ashes of the Old: The Old Left and the Southern Christian Leadership Conference, 1957–1965," *Critical Historical Studies* 10, no. 1 (2023): 10.

32. Interview, Dr. Brailsford Brazeal by Judy Barton, February 16, 1972; interview with Herman Bostick, April 6, 1970; *Morehouse College Bulletin*, May 1944.

33. Interview with Mel Kennedy, April 22, 1970, in Taylor Branch Papers, Folder 701; interview, Melvin Kennedy with Herbert Holmes, no date, Martin Luther King, Jr. Memorial Center Oral History Project.

34. Interview, Melvin Kennedy with Herbert Holmes.

35. MLK Papers. vol. 1, 39–40.

36. Eig interview with Dr. June Dobbs, phone, November 27, 2018, in possession of author, with special thanks to Jonathan Eig for sharing his interview transcripts with me.

27. Down to Business

1. MLK Papers, vol. 1, 85; David Levering Lewis, *King: A Biography* (Urbana and Chicago: University of Illinois Press, 2013), 21. See Snipes story on the Equal Justice Initiative (EJI) History of Racial Injustice, https://calendar.eji.org/racial-injustice/jul/18.

2. Equal Justice Initiative (EJI) History of Racial Injustice, https://calendar.eji.org/racial-injustice/jul/25.

3. *Atlanta Constitution*, August 6, 1946, 6

4. *Atlanta Constitution*, August 6, 1946, 6.

5. MLK Papers, vol. 1, 121.

6. *Time*, "The South: An Attack on the Conscience," February 18, 1957.

7. George D. Kelsey, "Some Observations Regarding Martin Luther King Jr. as a College Student," no date, George D. Kelsey Papers, Box 25, Drew University Archives, Madison, New Jersey.

8. *Morehouse College Bulletin*, May 1944, May 1948; Benjamin Mays, *The Achievements of Morehouse Men in the Great Universities*, circa 1950–1951, Morehouse College Vertical Files, Morehouse College, Atlanta Georgia; *Time*, "The South: An Attack on the Conscience"; Reverend Martin Luther King Sr. with Clayton Riley, *Daddy King: An Autobiography* (Boston: Beacon Press, 1980), 124; "Remembering the Young King," *Ebony*, January 1988.

9. Martin Luther King Jr., "My Call to the Ministry," August 7, 1959, Martin Luther King, Jr. Research and Education Institute, Stanford University, https://kinginstitute.stanford.edu/king-papers/documents/my-call-ministry#:~:text=At%20first%20I%20planned

%20to,and%20humanity%20through%20the%20ministry; "Remembering the Young King"; *Morehouse College Bulletin,* May 1948.

10. George D. Kelsey, "The Present Crisis in Negro Ministerial Education," a paper prepared for the Joint Committee meeting of the Northern Baptist Convention, Southern Baptist Convention, National Baptist Convention, Inc., on Negro Ministerial Education, held on January 19, 1948, Atlanta, Georgia.

11. MLK Papers, vol. 1; "Remembering the Young King."

12. George D. Kelsey, "Protestantism and Democratic Intergroup Living," *Phylon* 8, no.1 (1947); Dennis Dickerson, "African American Religious Intellectuals and the Theological Foundations of the Civil Rights Movement, 1930–1955," *Church History* 74, no. 2 (June 2005).

13. Kelsey, "Protestantism and Democratic Intergroup Living"; Dennis Dickerson, "African American Religious Intellectuals and the Theological Foundations of the Civil Rights Movement, 1930–1955."

14. "Remembering the Young King"; Kelsey, "Protestantism and Democratic Intergroup Living"; Pickens interview on Connecticut Public Television.

15. "Remembering the Young King"; Kelsey, "Protestantism and Democratic Intergroup Living"; George Kelsey "The Nature of the Christian Ethic, *Journal of Religious Thought* 2, no. 1 (Autumn/Winter 1945).

16. Dickerson, "African American Religious Intellectuals and the Theological Foundations of the Civil Rights Movement, 1930-1955"; Martin Luther King Jr., "Martin Luther King Explains Nonviolent Resistance," in *Eyewitness: The Negro in American History,* ed., William Loren Katz, (Lanham, MD: Pitman Publishing Corp., 1967), 511–13.

17. Martin Luther King Jr., "A Legacy of Creative Protest," *Massachusetts Review* 4, no. 1 (Autumn 1962): 42–43; Martin Luther King Jr., "My Pilgrimage to Nonviolence," *Fellowship,* September 1958, Martin Luther King, Jr. Research and Education Institute, Stanford University, https://kinginstitute.stanford.edu/king-papers/documents/my-pilgrimage -nonviolence#ftnref7; Martin Luther King Jr., *Stride Toward Freedom: The Montgomery Story* (New York & London: Harper & Row, 1958), 91.

18. "Remembering the Young King"; Kelsey, "Protestantism and Democratic Intergroup Living," *Phylon.*

19. Kelsey, "Some Observations Regarding Martin Luther King Jr. as a College Student," no date; "Remembering the Young King"; Kelsey, "Protestantism and Democratic Intergroup Living"; Kelsey, "The Nature of the Christian Ethic."

20. ML Blue Book exams for Dr. Kelsey's class, March 26, 1947, December 3, 1946, circa May 1947, MLK Institute Collection.

21. ML Blue Book exam for Dr. Kelsey's class, March 26, 1946. MLK Institute, Stanford University Collection; King, "The Significant Contributions of Jeremiah to Religious Thought," MLK Papers, Box 115, folder 17, copy maintained at the MLK Institute, Stanford University.

22. Martin Luther King, "An Autobiography of Religious Development," Crozer Theological Seminary, 1950, Martin Luther King, Jr. Research and Education Institute, Stanford University, https://kinginstitute.stanford.edu/king-papers/documents/autobiography

-religious-development#fn10; Blue Book exam, March 26, 1947; See also, William Peters, "Our Weapon Is Love," *Redbook*, August 1956, 42–43, 71–73.

23. "Remembering the Young King"; *Time*, "The South: An Attack on the Conscience"; George D. Kelsey, "Some Observations Regarding Martin Luther King Jr. as a College Student."

24. *Time*, "The South: An Attack on the Conscience"; Peters, "Our Weapon Is Love," 42–43, 71–73.

25. Kelsey, "Some Observations Regarding Martin Luther King Jr. as a College Student"; Kelsey, "Martin Luther King, Jr. and His Experience of God in Christ," no date, George D. Kelsey Papers, Box 24, Drew University Archives, Madison, New Jersey.

26. Peters, "Our Weapon Is Love"; "Notes from interviews with MLK April 15–May 18, 1967," by David Halberstam, David Halberstam Collection, box 11, folder 5, Howard Gotlieb Archival Research Center, Boston University.

27. King, "An Autobiography of Religious Development"; Peters, "Our Weapon Is Love," 42–43, 71–73; "Notes from interviews with MLK."

28. "Notes from interviews with MLK."

29. "Notes from interviews with MLK"; Pickens in "Remembering the Young King"; interview transcript, William G. Pickens, *Connecticut Journal*, episode 126, aired on Connecticut Public Television (CPTV), May 8, 1998, transcribed by Pam McDonald, circa 2000 in Pam McDonald Collection; interview with Robert Williams, April 3, 1984, notes in Taylor Branch Papers, Folder 701.

30. Reverend Martin Luther King Sr. with Clayton Riley, *Daddy King*, 124–25.

31. King Sr., *Daddy King*, 124–25.

32. King Sr., *Daddy King*, 124–25.

33. King, "An Autobiography of Religious Development."

34. *Time*, "The South: An Attack on the Conscience"; *Afro-American*, June 22, 1957, A3; King, "An Autobiography of Religious Development."

35. Interview, Dr. Brailsford Brazeal by Judy Barton, February 16, 1972, MLK Memorial Center Oral History Project.

36. *Time*, "The South: An Attack on the Conscience"; MLK Papers, vol. 1, 45; King, "An Autobiography of Religious Development."

37. *Morehouse College Bulletin*, May 1944,

38. *Maroon Tiger*, Senior Edition, 1947.

39. *Maroon Tiger*, Senior Edition, 1947.

40. *Maroon Tiger*, Senior Edition, 1947; MLK Papers, vol. 1, 127–42.

41. *Maroon Tiger*, January–February, 1947, Martin Luther King Jr., "The Purpose of Education," Martin Luther King, Jr. Research and Education Institute, Stanford University, https://kinginstitute.stanford.edu/king-papers/documents/purpose-education.

42. *Maroon Tiger*, January–February 1947, King Jr., "The Purpose of Education."

43. *Maroon Tiger*, January–February 1947, King Jr., "The Purpose of Education."

44. Jonathan Eig interview with Dr. June Dobbs, phone, November 27, 2018, in possession of author, with special thanks to Jonathan Eig for sharing his interview transcripts with me.

28. The Police

1. Interview transcript, William G. Pickens, *Connecticut Journal,* episode 126, aired on Connecticut Public Television (CPTV), May 8, 1998, transcribed by Pam McDonald, circa 2000 in Pam McDonald Collection.

2. Alex Wood, "Blacks Recall Connecticut Tobacco Farms," *Journal Inquirer,* July 17, 1989.

3. *Campus Mirror,* November 1947.

4. *Chicago Defender,* August 16, 1947.

5. *Chicago Defender,* August 16, 1947.

6. *Chicago Defender,* August 16, 1947.

7. *Chicago Defender,* August 16, 1947.

8. Fay Clarke Johnson, *Soldiers of the Soil* (New York: Vantage Press, 1995), 63–65.

9. J. Edgar Hoover, "Crime-Freedom Unlimited," *Covenant Quarterly,* November 1944; *FBI Law Enforcement Bulletin,* March 1947, April 1947; *Putnam Patriot* (Putnam, CT), August 21, 1947; John G. Corey, "Police Determined to Shoot to Kill to End Itinerant Crime Wave," *We 3,* no. 19, February 25, 1947;

10. Franklin J. Watson, "A Comparison of Negro and White Populations, Connecticut: 1940–1960," *Phylon* 29, no. 2 (1968): 142–55; *Chicago Defender,* July 5, 1947, August 9, 1947.

11. *Baltimore Afro-American,* January 26, 1946; Connecticut Inter-Racial Commission, Newsletter Number 2, February 19, 1948, Pam McDonald Collection.

12. *We 3,* no. 19; Watson, "A Comparison of Negro and White Populations, Connecticut."

13. *Hartford Chronicle,* March 8, 1947.

14. *We 3,* no. 19.

15. Wood, "Blacks Recall Connecticut Tobacco Farms"; Taylor Branch, *Parting the Waters: America in the King Years, 1954–1963* (New York: Simon and Schuster, 1988), 65; Jonathan Eig, *King: A Life* (New York: Farrar, Straus and Giroux, 2023), 63.

16. All lynchings are discussed at Equal Justice Initiative, *A History of Racial Injustice,* https://calendar.eji.org/racial-injustice/.

29. Minister ML King

1. Martin Luther King Sr., "The Autobiography of Daddy King as Told to Edward A. Jones," unpublished manuscript, August 1973, 105–107.

2. Larry Williams interview, "King Stories," PRX Radio Broadcast, January 1989, https://exchange.prx.org/pieces/165027?m=false.

3. MLK Papers, vol. 1, chronology; King Sr., *The Autobiography of Daddy King,* 105–7; Martin Luther King Sr. with Clayton Riley, *Daddy King: An Autobiography* (Boston: G. K. Hall & Co., 1981), 124; Larry Williams interview, December 27, 1983, in Taylor Branch Papers, Folder 701, Southern Historical Collection, The Wilson Library, University on North Carolina at Chapel Hill; "Ebenezer Baptist Church Historic Structure Report," National Park Service, 2001; Larry Williams interview, "King Stories."

4. Jonathan Eig, *King: A Life* (New York: Farrar, Straus and Giroux, 2023), 65–68.

5. Eig, *King: A Life,* 65–68.

6. Albert Raboteau, "The Chanted Sermon," in Albert Raboteau, *A Fire in the Bones: Reflections on African-American Religious History* (Boston: Beacon Press, 1995).

7. Eig, *King: A Life*, 65–68.

8. Raboteau, "The Chanted Sermon"; Eig, *King: A Life*, 65–68.

9. King Sr., *The Autobiography of Daddy King as Told to Edward A. Jones*, 107; King Sr., *Daddy King: An Autobiography*, 127–28; Eig, *King: A Life*, 67.

30. An American Teenage Boy

1. Jonathan Eig interview with Dr. June Dobbs, phone, November 27, 2018.

2. Eig interview with Dr. June Dobbs; *Maroon Tiger*, Senior Edition, 1947.

3. Dorothy Cotton, quoted in *Biography*, "Martin Luther King, Jr.: The Man and the Dream," A&E, January 19, 1998.

4. Dorothy Cotton, quoted in *Biography*.

5. Martin Luther King Sr. with Clayton Riley, *Daddy King: An Autobiography* (Boston: G. K. Hall & Co., 1981), 133.

6. Coretta Scott King, *My Life with Martin Luther King, Jr.* (New York: Holt, Rinehart, and Winston, 1969), 68; On triangular desire see, Rene Girard, *To Double Business Bound: Essays on Literature, Mimesis and Anthropology* (Baltimore: Johns Hopkins University Press), 1988.

7. *Morehouse College Bulletin*, May 1944, 22; *Maroon Tiger*, November, 1945, February 1948; interview Dr. Herman Bostick by Herbert Holmes, April 6, 1970, MLK Memorial Center Oral History Project; "Remembering the Young King," *Ebony*, January 1988; interview with Emmett Proctor, April 15, 1970, transcript notes in Taylor Branch Papers, Folder 701, Southern Historical Collection, Wilson Library, University of North Carolina at Chapel Hill; *Atlanta Daily World*, see, June 6, 1945; April 24, 1947; June 4, 1947.

8. *Maroon Tiger*, November 1945, February 1948.

9. *Maroon Tiger*, November 1945, February 1948.

10. *Atlanta Daily World*, March 25, 1947; *Maroon Tiger*, January 1948 and February 1948.

11. *Atlanta Daily World*, March 25, 1947; *Maroon Tiger*, January 1948 and February 1948.

12. *Maroon Tiger*, November 1946; interview, Dr. Herman Bostick by Herbert Holmes, April 6, 1970, MLK Memorial Center Oral History Project.

13. *The Morehouse Companion*, 1945–1946.

14. Interview, Dr. Herman Bostick by Herbert Holmes; Herbert Homes interview with Walter McCall for the Martin Luther King, Jr. Memorial Center Oral History Project, in Taylor Branch Papers, Folder 703; interview with Emmett Proctor, April 15, 1970; interview with Edward Whitaker, July 31, 1984, notes in Taylor Branch Papers, Southern Historical Collection, Folder 703; MLK interview by Arnold Michaelis, December 1, 1965, transcript in MLK Papers, vol. 10, forthcoming; *The Maroon Tiger*, February 1948.

15. Interview, Dr. Herman Bostick by Herbert Holmes; Herbert Homes interview with Walter McCall; interview with Emmett Proctor; interview with Edward Whitaker; *The Maroon Tiger*, February 1948.

16. Interview, Dr. Herman Bostick by Herbert Holmes,; Herbert Homes interview with Walter McCall; *Billboard*, October 5, 1946, January 4, 1947.

17. Jonathan Eig, *King: A Life* (New York: Farrar, Straus, and Giroux, 2023), 69. Larry claims classmates began referring to them as "Robinson and Stevens." He fails to mention just how the name came about. See Larry Williams interview, "King Stories," PRX Radio Broadcast, January 1989, https://exchange.prx.org/pieces/165027?m=false.

18. Letter, Reverend H. Edward Whitaker to ML, October 31, 1952; telephone interview with Jimmy Jones, August 18, 1983, in Taylor Branch Papers, Folder 701; interview, Dr. Herman Bostick by Herbert Holmes; Herbert Homes interview with Walter McCall; Hallie Lieberman, "A Short History of the Condom," *The Daily JSTOR*, June 8 2017.

19. Letter, Rev. H. Edward Whitaker to ML; telephone interview with Jimmy Jones; interview, Dr. Herman Bostick by Herbert Holmes; Herbert Homes interview with Walter McCall; Eig, *King: A Life*, 69; *Billboard*, October 5, 1946, January 4, 1947,

20. Taylor Branch, *Parting the Waters: America in the King Years, 1954–1963* (New York: Simon and Schuster, 1988), 94.

21. Herbert Homes interview with Walter McCall; Sixteen '74, *Remembering Mrs. Alberta King*, video interview, WBZ-TV 4 Boston, University of Georgia Walter J. Brown Media Archives and Peabody Awards Collection, item: peabody_74055pst-arch, VHS original broadcast state aired 1974, https://bmac.libs.uga.edu/Detail/objects/514038.

22. Interview with Reverend Larry Williams, December 27, 1983, notes in Taylor Branch Papers, Folder 701.

23. Herbert Homes interview with Walter McCall.

24. *Spelman College Bulletin*, April 1945; *Campus Mirror*, January 1947, May 1948; interview with Ms. Laura Turner Williams, March 16, 1970, notes in Taylor Branch Papers, Folder 701; *Maroon Tiger*, February 1948, May-June 1948; Herbert Homes interview with Walter McCall.

25. *Billboard*, October 5, 1946, January 4, 1947; *Billboard*, January 3, 1948; Herbert Homes interview with Walter McCall.

26. Herbert Homes interview with Walter McCall.

27. Herbert Homes interview with Walter McCall.

28. "Remembering the Young King," *Ebony*, January 1988.

29. Interview with Reverend Larry Williams, December 27, 1983; David Levering Lewis, *King: A Biography* (Urbana and Chicago: University of Illinois Press, 2013), 22.

30. Interview with Reverend Larry Williams, December 27, 1983; David Levering Lewis, *King, A Biography*, 22.

31. Interview with Reverend Larry Williams, December 27, 1983, notes in Taylor Branch Papers Folder 701; Lewis, *King: A Biography*, 22.

32. Herbert Homes interview with Walter McCall; MLK Papers, vol. 1, 161; *Billboard*, October 5, 1946, January 4, 1947; Eig, *King: A Life*, 90; Lewis, *King: A Biography*, 22.

33. Herbert Homes interview with Walter McCall; MLK Papers, vol. 1, 161; *Billboard*, October 5, 1946, January 4, 1947; Eig, *King: A Life*, 90; Lewis, *King: A Biography*, 22.

34. See for example, *Maroon Tiger*, November 1945; interview with Reverend Larry Williams; Lewis, *King: A Biography*, 22.

31. Juanita

1. *Campus Mirror,* February 1947, May 1948; Obituary of Mrs. Juanita Sellers-Stone, William Gayleano Murray & Son Funeral Home, https://www.wgmurrayandson.com/obituary /MrsJuanita-Sellers-Stone.
2. *Campus Mirror,* February 1947, May 1948; Obituary of Mrs. Juanita Sellers-Stone.
3. *Campus Mirror,* February 1947, May 1948.
4. Interview with Juanita Sellers Stone, March 6, 1984, notes in Taylor Branch Papers, Folder 701, Southern Historical Collection, Wilson Library, University of North Carolina at Chapel Hill; *Campus Mirror,* November 1947, May 1948; obituary of Mrs. Juanita Sellers-Stone.
5. Interview with Juanita Sellers Stone; *Campus Mirror,* November 1947, May 1948; Juanita was a constant in the *Atlanta Daily World* "Social Swirl" section throughout her youth. See, for example, January 26,1947, 3. See also November 8, 1947, 5; obituary of Mrs. Juanita Sellers-Stone.
6. *The Maroon Tiger,* November 1943, November 1946; *Campus Mirror,* November 1947.
7. *The Maroon Tiger,* November 1946; February 1948; *Campus Mirror,* November 1947; *Atlanta Daily World,* January 26, 1945; December 22, 1946; October 18, 1947; November 4, 1947, 1; November 8, 1947, 5; November 9, 1947, 1; *Chicago Defender,* November 22, 1947, 9.
8. See for example, *Atlanta Daily World,* May 11, 1942.
9. *Atlanta Daily World,* April 3, 2008, 1.
10. Interview with Juanita Sellers Stone.
11. Interview with Juanita Sellers Stone.
12. Interview with Juanita Sellers Stone; MLK Papers, vol. 1.
13. Interview with Juanita Sellers Stone.
14. Interview with Juanita Sellers Stone.
15. *Atlanta Daily World,* April 30, 1937, 3; February 22, 1938, 3; January 22, 1941, 3; May 26, 1941, 3; March 18, 1945, 2; March 23, 1947, 3; May 7, 1948, 3; obituary of Mrs. Juanita Sellers-Stone; Coretta Scott King, *My Life with Martin Luther King, Jr.* (New York: Holt, Rinehart, and Winston, 1969), 60.
16. Jonathan Eig interview with Dr. June Dobbs, phone, November 27, 2018, in possession of author, special thanks to Jonathan Eig for sharing his interview transcripts with me; King, *My Life with Martin Luther King, Jr.,* 60.
17. Interview with Coretta Scott King, tape 5; King, *My Life with Martin Luther King, Jr.,* 68.
18. Pamphlet, "The First Annual Institute on Building for Successful Marriage and Family Living," sponsored by Morehouse and the Planned Parenthood Federation of America, April 11–13, 1946, Morehouse College Vertical Files; *The Morehouse Alumnus,* July 1946–1948.
19. "The First Annual Institute on Building for Successful Marriage and Family Living"; interview with Juanita Sellers Stone; *The Morehouse Alumnus,* July 1948. On Chivers, see, Matthew F. Nichter, "From the Ashes of the Old: The Old Left and the Southern Christian Leadership Conference, 1957–1965," *Critical Historical Studies* 10, no. 1 (Spring 2023): 10.

20. "'The First Annual Institute on Building for Successful Marriage and Family Living."

21. Martin Luther King, Jr., Papers, Boston University Box 113, folder 19, copy at MLK Institute, Stanford University.

22. Martin Luther King Jr., "Advice for Living," *Ebony*, December 1957, 120.

23. King, *My Life with Martin Luther King, Jr.*, 60–65.

24. Interview with Coretta Scott King, tape 5.

25. King, *My Life with Martin Luther King, Jr.*, 60.

26. *The Morehouse Alumnus*, July 1948; interview with Juanita Sellers Stone.

32. Reverend ML King Jr.

1. Martin Luther King Sr. and Clayton Riley, *Daddy King: An Autobiography* (Boston: G. K. Hall & Co., 1981), 127–28; "The Autobiography of Daddy King as Told to Edward A. Jones" (August 1973), 102–103.

2. Interview with Martin Luther King Sr., no date, stenographer notes, Hatch Papers Box 22, Folder 2 and Folder 3; King Sr., *Daddy King*, 127–28; "The Autobiography of Daddy King as Told to Edward A. Jones," 102–103, unpublished.

3. Interview with Martin Luther King Sr., no date; "The Autobiography of Daddy King as Told to Edward A. Jones," 102–103.

4. "The Autobiography of Daddy King as Told to Edward A. Jones," 102–103.

5. Interview with Martin Luther King Sr.; MLK Papers, vol. 1, 125.

6. MLK Papers, vol. 1, 125

7. King Sr., *Daddy King: An Autobiography*, 111.

8. MLK Papers, vol. 1, 150

9. MLK Papers, vol. 1, 142–49.

10. MLK Papers, vol. 1, 86.

33. Commencement

1. GPA in MLK Papers, vol. 1, and MLK application to Crozer.

2. Martin Luther King essay, "A Conception and Impression of Religion Drawn from Dr. Brightman's Book Entitled *A Philosophy of Religion*," March 28, 1951, in MLK Papers, vol. 2.

3. Dr. George D. Kelsey to Charles E. Batten, March 12, 1948, MLK Papers, vol. 1, 155.

4. Recommendation letters in MLK Papers, vol. 1.

5. *The Morehouse Alumnus*, July 1948.

6. *The Morehouse Alumnus*, July 1948; "Remembering the Young King," *Ebony*, January 1988.

7. "Remembering the Young King"; Samuel DuBois Cook, The HistoryMakers A2005.139, interviewed by Larry Crowe, June 20, 2005, session 1, tape 4, story 4, The HistoryMakers Digital Archive.

8. *The Morehouse Alumnus*, July 1948; *The Afro-American*, August 20, 1955, 17.

9. *Atlanta Daily World*, March 2, 1947; May 21, 1948; June 9, 1948; June 13, 1948.

10. Christine King Farris, The HistoryMakers A2010.074, interviewed by Julieanna L. Richardson, July 11, 2010, session 1, tape 3, story 6, The HistoryMakers Digital Archive; for

more on segregation scholarships, see Crystal Sanders, *A Forgotten Migration: Black South-erners, Segregation Scholarships, and the Debt Owed to Public HBCUs* (Chapel Hill: University of North Carolina Press, 2024).

11. *Atlanta Daily World*, March 2, 1947; May 21, 1948; June 9, 1948; June 13, 1948; MLK Papers, vol. 2, 163; *Campus Mirror,* May 1948; Christine King Farris, *Through It All: Reflections on My Life, My Family, and My Faith* (New York: Atria, 2010), 46–48.

12. *Atlanta Daily World*, March 2, 1947; May 21, 1948; June 9, 1948; June 13, 1948; MLK Papers, vol. 2, 163; *Campus Mirror,* May 1948; Farris, *Through It All,* 46–48.

13. *Atlanta Daily World*, June 13, 1948, 3.

14. *Atlanta Daily World*, June 13, 1948, 3.

15. *Atlanta Daily World*, May 21, 1948, June 9, 1948.

16. *Atlanta Daily World*, May 21, 1948, 1, June 9, 1948.

17. *Atlanta Daily World*, June 9, 1948.

34. Crozer

1. *Atlanta Daily World*, June 24, 1948.

2. MLK Papers, vol. 2, 1.

3. King, Class Notes, Orientation for Juniors, MLK Papers Boston University, Box 115, folder 27, copy held at MLK Institute, Stanford University.

4. "Notes from interviews with MLK, April 15–May 18, 1967," David Halberstam, David Halberstam Collection, box 11, folder 5, Howard Gotlieb Archival Research Center, Boston University.

5. Professor Smith interview with Taylor Branch, November 3, 1983, Taylor Branch Papers.

6. William Peters, "Our Weapon Is Love," *Redbook*, August 1956; interview with Reverend George Lawrence, February 24, 1984, Taylor Branch Papers, Folder 703; *Philadelphia Daily News*, January 16, 1986, K4; Taylor Branch, *Parting the Waters: America in the King Years, 1954–1963* (New York: Simon and Schuster, 1988), 74.

7. Peters, "Our Weapon Is Love."

8. Patrick Parr, *The Seminarian* (Chicago: Lawrence Hill Books, 2018), 131; Jonathan Eig, *King: A Life* (New York: Farrar, Straus and Giroux, 2023), 74–75.

9. Interview with Martin Luther King Sr., no date, stenographer notes, Hatch Papers, box 22, folder 2.

10. *The Achievements of Morehouse Men in the Great Universities*, circa 1950–1951, Morehouse College Vertical Files, Morehouse College, Atlanta Georgia; Eig, *King: A Life*, 76.

11. Marcus G. Wood, "My Life with the Late Martin Luther King," March 5, 1986, Taylor Branch Papers, folder 703; Parr, *The Seminarian*, 22–24.

12. MLK Papers, vol. 1, 329; Statement on Behalf of Ernest Nichols, *State of New Jersey v. Ernest Nichols*, by W. Thomas McGann, July 20, 1950, https://kinginstitute.stanford.edu/king-papers/documents/statement-behalf-ernest-nichols-state-new-jersey-vs-ernest-nichols-w-thomas; Parr, *The Seminarian*, 133–39; Eig, *King: A Life*, 79–80.

13. MLK Papers, vol. 1, 329; Statement on Behalf of Ernest Nichols, *State of New Jersey v. Ernest Nichols*, by W. Thomas McGann; Parr, *The Seminarian*, 133–39; Eig, *King: A Life*, 79–80.

14. MLK Papers, vol. 1, 329; Statement on Behalf of Ernest Nichols, *State of New Jersey v. Ernest Nichols*, by W. Thomas McGann; Parr, *The Seminarian*, 133–39; Eig, *King: A Life*, 79–80.

15. MLK Papers, vol. 1, 329; Statement on Behalf of Ernest Nichols, *State of New Jersey v. Ernest Nichols*, by W. Thomas McGann; Parr, *The Seminarian*, 133–39; Eig, *King: A Life*, 79–80.

16. Branch, *Parting the Waters*, 79.

17. Martin Luther King Sr. with Clayton Riley, *Daddy King: An Autobiography* (Boston: G. K. Hall & Co.), 129; interview with Reverend George Lawrence, February 24, 1984, Taylor Branch Papers, Folder 703.

18. *The Achievements of Morehouse Men in The Great Universities*; King Sr., *Daddy King*, 130.

35. Will You Marry Me?

1. Christine King Farris, The HistoryMakers A2010.074) interviewed by Julieanna L. Richardson, July 11, 2010, session 1, tape 3, story 6, The HistoryMakers Digital Archive; Christine King Farris, *Through It All: Reflections on My Life, My Family, and My Faith* (New York: Atria, 2010), 46–48.

2. *Atlanta Daily World*, January 23, 1949, 3; interview with Juanita Sellers Stone, March 6, 1984, notes in Taylor Branch Papers, Folder 701, Southern Historical Collection, Wilson Library, University of North Carolina at Chapel Hill; Christine King Farris, The HistoryMakers A2010.074; Farris, *Through It All*, 46–48.

3. MLK Papers, vol. 1; Coretta Scott King, *My Life with Martin Luther King, Jr.* (New York: Holt, Rinehart, and Winston, 1969), 53–71, 90–92; Martin Luther King Sr. with Clayton Riley, *Daddy King: An Autobiography* (Boston: G. K. Hall & Co.), 133; Patrick Parr, *The Seminarian* (Chicago: Lawrence Hill Books, 2018), 131; Taylor Branch, *Parting the Waters: America in the King Years, 1954–1963* (New York: Simon and Schuster, 1988), 78.

4. Professor Smith interview with Taylor Branch, November 3, 1983, Taylor Branch Papers; ML's grades in MLK Papers, vol. 1; Lerone Bennett Jr., *What Manner of Man: A Biography of Martin Luther King, Jr.* (Chicago: Johnson Publishing Co., Inc., 1964), 40; Parr, *The Seminarian*, 64, 143–70, 215–17; Jonathan Eig, *King: A Life* (New York: Farrar, Straus and Giroux, 2023), 81–87. See Jeff Jones and Lydia Saad, Gallup News Service, "Gallup Poll Social Series: Minority Rights and Relations," July 2013; Justin McCarthy, "US Approval of Interracial Marriage at New High," Gallup, September 10, 2021, https://news.gallup.com/poll/354638/approval-interracial-marriage-new-high.aspx.

5. Marcus G. Wood, interview with Taylor Branch, October 10, 1983; Marcus G. Wood, "My Life with the Late Martin Luther King," March 5, 1986, Taylor Branch Papers, Folder 703.

6. *Atlanta Daily World*, August 23, 1950, 3; December 27, 1951, 3.

7. Letter, Reverend H. Edward Whitaker to ML, October 31, 1952, in Taylor Branch Papers, Folder 701, Southern Historical Collection, Wilson Library, University on North Carolina at Chapel Hill.

8. Interview with Juanita Sellers Stone, March 6, 1984, notes in Taylor Branch Papers, Folder 701; *Atlanta Daily World*, August 23, 1950; Eig, *King: A Life*, 81–87.

9. Transcript of interview with Coretta Scott King, Hatch Papers, box 22, folder 4, tape 3;

Coretta Scott King, *My Life with Martin Luther King, Jr.* (New York: Holt, Rinehart, and Winston, 1969), 60; Eig, *King: A Life*, 81–87.

10. Jonathan Eig interview with Dr. June Dobbs, phone, November 27, 2018, in possession of author, special thanks to Jonathan Eig for sharing his interview transcripts with me; Jonathan Eig, *King: A Life*, 81–87.

11. June Dobbs Butts, The HistoryMakers A2006.076, interviewed by Shawn Wilson, April 13, 2006, session 1, tape 2, story 7, The HistoryMakers Digital Archive; Jonathan Eig interview with Dr. June Dobbs, phone, November 27, 2018; Eig, *King: A Life*, 89.

12. June Dobbs Butts, The HistoryMakers A2006.076.

13. Interview with Juanita Sellers Stone; June Dobbs Butts, The HistoryMakers A2006.076; Juanita Sellers Stone Obituary, *Atlanta Journal Constitution*, June 8, 2018; Jonathan Eig interview with Dr. June Dobbs, phone, November 27, 2018; Eig, *King: A Life*, 89.

14. Interview with Juanita Sellers Stone; June Dobbs Butts, The HistoryMakers A2006.076; Obituary, *Atlanta Journal Constitution*, June 8, 2018; Jonathan Eig interview with Dr. June Dobbs, phone, November 27, 2018; Eig, *King: A Life*, 89.

15. Interview with Juanita Sellers Stone; June Dobbs Butts, The HistoryMakers A2006.076; Jonathan Eig interview with Dr. June Dobbs, phone, November 27, 2018.

16. Interview with Juanita Sellers Stone.

17. *Atlanta Daily World*, December 27, 1951, 3; October 19, 1952, 3

18. Eig, *King: A Life*, 445.

19. Interview with Juanita Sellers Stone; interview with Coretta Scott King, tape 5; *Atlanta Daily World*, October 19, 1952, 2–3; Coretta Scott King, *My Life with Martin Luther King, Jr.*, 53–71; Martin Luther King Jr., *Stride Toward Freedom: The Montgomery Story* (New York & London: Harper & Row, 1958), 100–101; "Personalism" defined in *King Encyclopedia*, https://kinginstitute.stanford.edu/personalism; King Sr., *Daddy King: An Autobiography*, 131–34.

20. Letter, W. T. Handy Jr. to ML, November 18, 1952, MLK Papers, vol. 2, 160–64; Coretta Scott King, *My Life with Martin Luther King, Jr.*, 53–71; Martin Luther King Jr., *Stride Toward Freedom: The Montgomery Story*, 100–101.

36. Jewelle

1. Jewelle Taylor Gibbs, *Destiny's Child: Memoirs of a Preacher's Daughter* (North Charleston, South Carolina: CreateSpace Independent Publishing Platform, 2014), 83–96. In 1955, Gibbs would graduate and become the first Black Junior Management Analyst at the US Department of Labor. In 1956, she married Jim Gibbs, who in 1988 would become the first Martin Luther King Jr. Centennial Professor at Stanford University, the title that the author currently holds. The Kings and the Gibbs stayed in touch over the years as the Gibbs were financial supporters of the Montgomery Improvement Association and the Southern Christian Leadership Conference.

2. Gibbs, *Destiny's Child*, 83–96.

3. Gibbs, *Destiny's Child*, 83–96.

4. Gibbs, *Destiny's Child*, 83–96.

37. Coretta

1. *Baltimore Afro-American,* June 29, 1957, A3; interview with Coretta Scott King, tape 5; interview with Coretta Scott King, transcript, Hatch Papers, box 22, folder 4, tape 3; interview with Coretta Scott King by Donald H. Smith, December 7, 1963, tapes 9–10, King Institute, Stanford University; Clennon I. King, "Martin Luther King, Jr. and Coretta Scott King in Boston: A Love Story," *Boston Magazine,* January 15, 2021; Jonathan Eig, *King: A Life* (New York: Farrar, Straus and Giroux, 2023), 90.

2. *Baltimore Afro-American,* June 29, 1957, A3; interview with Coretta Scott King, tape 5; interview with Coretta, transcript, Hatch Papers, box 22, folder 4, tape 3; interview with Coretta Scott King by Donald H. Smith. Coretta Scott King, *My Life with Martin Luther King, Jr.* (New York: Holt, Rinehart, and Winston, 1969), 53–71; Martin Luther King Jr., *Stride Toward Freedom: The Montgomery Story* (New York & London: Harper & Row, 1958), 100–101; Reverend Martin Luther King Sr. with Clayton Riley, *Daddy King: An Autobiography* (Boston: G. K. Hall & Co., 131–34.

3. *Baltimore Afro-American,* June 29, 1957, A3; interview with Coretta Scott King, tape 5; interview with Coretta Scott King, transcript, Hatch Papers, box 22, folder 4, tape 3; King, *My Life with Martin Luther King, Jr.,* 53–71; King Jr., *Stride Toward Freedom,* 100–101; King Sr., *Daddy King,* 131–34.

4. William Shakespeare, Shakespeare's Sonnets, Sonnet 116; "Facing the Challenge of a New Age," Address Delivered at NAACP Emancipation Day Rally, January 1, 1957, Atlanta, Georgia.

5. Interview with Coretta Scott King, tape 5; interview with Coretta Scott King, Hatch Papers; King, *My Life with Martin Luther King, Jr.,* 53–71; King Jr., *Stride Toward Freedom,* 100–101; "The Autobiography of Daddy King as Told to Edward A. Jones," 102–3; King Sr., *Daddy King,* 131–34.

6. Interview with Coretta Scott King, tape 5; interview with Coretta Scott King, Hatch Papers; King, *My Life with Martin Luther King, Jr.,* 53–71; King Jr.; Coretta Scott King, "Up from Alabama," Address given Coppin State University, December 3, 1965, Lawrence D. Reddick papers, Sc MG 974, Box 14, Folder 1, Schomburg Center for Research in Black Culture, Manuscripts, Archives and Rare Books Division, The New York Public Library. While the transcript is dated date December 3, according to the *Baltimore Afro-American* it was given on December 17—see *Baltimore Afro-American,* December 18, 1965, 13.

7. Interview with Coretta Scott King, tape 5; King, *My Life with Martin Luther King, Jr.,* 53–71; King Jr., *Stride Toward Freedom: The Montgomery Story,* 100–101; "The Autobiography of Daddy King," 102–3; King Sr., *Daddy King,* 131–34.

8. Coretta Scott King "Up from Alabama;" *Baltimore Afro-American,* June 29, 1957, A3; interview with Coretta Scott King, tape 5; interview with Coretta Scott King, transcript, Hatch Papers; Larry Williams interview, "King Stories" PRX Radio Broadcast, January 1989, https://exchange.prx.org/pieces/165027?m=false; King, *My Life with Martin Luther King, Jr.,* 53–71; Coretta Scott King, *My Life, My Love, My Legacy* (New York: Henry Holt and Co., 2017), 31–46.

9. *Baltimore Afro-American,* June 29, 1957, A3; interview with Coretta Sott King, tape 5; interview with Coretta Scott King, transcript, Hatch Papers, box 22, folder 4, tape 3; Coretta

Scott King, *My Life with Martin Luther King, Jr.*, 53–71; Martin Luther King Jr., *Stride Toward Freedom*, 100–101; King Sr., *Daddy King*, 131–34.

10. Coretta Scott King, "The World of Coretta King: Family to Rear, Husband to Love, Home to Manage, and A Cause to Serve," *New Lady*, January, 1966, 24–37. Courtesy of The African American Museum and Library at Oakland; MLK interview by Arnold Michaelis, December 1, 1965, transcript in MLK Papers, vol. 10, forthcoming.

11. Interview with Coretta Scott King, tape 5; interview with Coretta Scott King, transcript, Hatch Papers, box 22, folder 4, tape 3; MLK interview by Arnold Michaelis; King, *My Life with Martin Luther King, Jr.*, 53–71; see also Eig, *King*, 96–97.

12. Interview with Coretta Scott King, tape 5; King, *My Life, My Love, My Legacy*, 31–46; King, *My Life with Martin Luther King, Jr.*, 53–71, 90–92.

13. King, *My Life with Martin Luther King, Jr.*, 53–71, 90–92; Coretta Scott King, "The World of Coretta King"; Coretta Scott King, "Up from Alabama."

14. King, *My Life with Martin Luther King, Jr.*, 53–71, 90–92.

15. Coretta Scott King, interview with Donald H. Smith.

16. Coretta Scott King, "Up from Alabama."

17. King, *My Life with Martin Luther King, Jr.*, 53–71, 90–92; Coretta Scott King, "The World of Coretta King"; Coretta Scott King, "Up from Alabama."

18. Coretta Scott King interview, transcript, Hatch Papers, tape 3; Coretta Scott King, "The World of Coretta King"; Jeanne Theoharis, *King of the North: Martin Luther King, Jr.'s Life of Struggle Outside the South* (New York: New Press, 2025), 37–47. Theoharis's book is a leading scholarly treatment of ML's adult ministry in the North, and also a leading examination of Coretta's significance to King's activism.

19. Coretta Scott King interview with Donald H. Smith.

20. Coretta Scott, "Why I Came to College," *Opportunity: Journal of Negro Life* (Spring 1948); John Lithgow tells this story in an interview with Jimmy Fallon, https://www.youtube .com/watch?app=desktop&v=0igAnXEby2o, accessed August 6, 2025.

21. Eig, *King*, 96.

22. Theoharis, *King of the North*, 37–47.

23. King, *My Life, My Love, My Legacy*, 31–46; King, *My Life with Martin Luther King, Jr.*, 53–71, 90–92.

24. King, *My Life with Martin Luther King, Jr.*, 53–71, 90–92. Coretta Scott King, "Up From Alabama."

25. King, *My Life with Martin Luther King, Jr.*, 53–71, 90–92.

26. Wyatt T. Walker interview by Donald H. Smith, December 1963, tape 101, side 1, Donald H. Smith Tape Recordings, State Historical Society of Wisconsin, Madison, Wis; copy at King Institute, Stanford University. On carpet, see, Eig, *King: A Life*, 444.

27. Interview with Coretta Scott King, tape 5; Coretta Scott King interview, transcript, Hatch Papers; King, *My Life with Martin Luther King, Jr.*, 53–71, 90–92.

28. Interview with Coretta Scott King, tape 5; Coretta Scott King interview, transcript, Hatch Papers; King, *My Life with Martin Luther King, Jr.*, 53–71, 90–92; Coretta Scott, "A Philosophy of Education," March 14, 1951, Antioch College, Hatch Papers box 23 Folder 4.

29. King, *My Life with Martin Luther King, Jr.*, 53–71, 90–92.

30. Coretta Scott King interview with Donald H. Smith, December 7, 1963 tape 9, side 2; tape 10, side 2.

31. Coretta Scott King interview, transcript, Hatch Papers.

32. Interview with Coretta Scott King, tape 5; King, *My Life, My Love, My Legacy*, 31–46; King, *My Life with Martin Luther King, Jr.*, 53–71, 90–92.

33. Interview with Coretta Scott King, tape 5; King, *My Life, My Love, My Legacy*, 31–46; King, *My Life with Martin Luther King, Jr.*, 53–71, 90–92.

34. *Pittsburgh Courier*, April 14, 1956, 1.

35. Coretta Scott King interview, transcript, Hatch Papers; King, *My Life, My Love, My Legacy*, 31–46.

36. Interview with Coretta Scott King, tape 5; Coretta Scott King, interview transcript, Hatch Papers; King, *My Life, My Love, My Legacy*, 31–46; King, *My Life with Martin Luther King, Jr.*, 53–71.

37. Interview with Coretta Scott King, tape 5; Coretta Scott King, interview transcript, Hatch Papers; King, *My Life, My Love, My Legacy*, 31–46; King, *My Life with Martin Luther King, Jr.*, 53–71; *Baltimore Afro-American*, June 29, 1957, A3.

38. Interview with Coretta Scott King, tape 5; Coretta Scott King, interview transcript, Hatch Papers; King, *My Life, My Love, My Legacy*, 31–46; King, *My Life with Martin Luther King, Jr.*, 53–71; *Baltimore Afro-American*, June 29, 1957, A3.

39. King, *My Life, My Love, My Legacy*, 31–46.

40. ML to Coretta, July 14, 1952, MLK Papers, Stanford University.

41. ML to Coretta, July 18, 1952, MLK Papers, https://kinginstitute.stanford.edu/king-papers/documents/coretta-scott#fn2.

42. ML to Coretta, July 18, 1952, MLK Papers.

43. ML to Coretta, July 18, 1952, MLK Papers.

44. Interview with Coretta Scott King, tape 5; King, *My Life with Martin Luther King, Jr.*, 53–71.

45. ML to Coretta, July 29, 1952.

46. Interview with MLK Sr., no date, stenographer notes, Hatch Papers.

47. See chronology in MLK Papers, vol. 2. See sermon here, https://kinginstitute.stanford.edu/king-papers/documents/communisms-challenge-christianity, accessed August 8, 2025.

48. Interview with Coretta Scott King, tape 5.

49. ML Letters to Coretta, August 13, 1952, August 20, 1952.

50. Interview with Coretta Scott King, tape 5; King Sr., *Daddy King*, 133. Also see chronology in MLK Papers, vol. 2.

51. Interview with Coretta Scott King, tape 5.

52. Interview with Coretta Scott King, tape 5.

53. Interview with Coretta Scott King, tape 5.

54. Interview with Coretta Scott King, tape 5; interview with Coretta Scott King, transcript, Hatch Papers; King, *My Life with Martin Luther King, Jr.*, 53–71.

55. Interview with Coretta Scott King, tape 5; interview with Coretta Scott King, transcript, Hatch Papers.

56. Transcript, interview with Coretta Scott King, Hatch Papers.

57. Interview with Coretta Scott King, tape 5; King, *My Life with Martin Luther King, Jr.*, 53–71, 90–92. See ML's courses in MLK Papers, vol. 2.

58. Coretta Scott, "A Philosophy of Education," March 14, 1951, Antioch College, Hatch Papers, box 23, folder 4.

59. Coretta Scott King interview with Donald H. Smith.

60. *Baltimore Afro-American,* June 29, 1957, A3; interview with Coretta Scott King, tape 5; King, *My Life with Martin Luther King, Jr.,* 53–71, 90–92.

61. *Baltimore Afro-American,* June 29, 1957, A3; interview with Coretta Scott King, tape 5; King, *My Life with Martin Luther King, Jr.,* 53–71, 90–92; letter, W. T. Handy Jr. to ML, November 18, 1952, MLK Papers, vol. 2, 160–64.

62. King, *My Life with Martin Luther King, Jr.,* 53–71, 90–92; King Sr., *Daddy King,* 133.

63. Interview with Coretta Scott King, tape 5; King, *My Life, My Love, My Legacy,* 44–45; King, *My Life with Martin Luther King, Jr.,* 53–71, 90–92.

64. Interview with Coretta Scott King, tape 5; interview with Coretta Scott King, transcript, Hatch Papers; King, *My Life, My Love, My Legacy* (New York: Henry Holt and Co., 2017), 44–45; King, *My Life with Martin Luther King, Jr.,* 53–71, 90–92.

65. Interview with Coretta Scott King, tape 5; King, *My Life with Martin Luther King, Jr.,* 53–71.

66. Interview with Coretta Scott King, tape 5; King, *My Life with Martin Luther King, Jr.,* 53–71.

67. Interview with Coretta Scott King, tape 5; interview with Coretta Scott King, transcript, Hatch Papers; King, *My Life, My Love, My Legacy,* 44–46; King, *My Life with Martin Luther King, Jr.,* 53–71; MLK Papers, vol. 2, 201.

68. Interview with Coretta Scott King, tape 5; interview with Coretta Scott King, transcript, Hatch Papers; King, *My Life, My Love, My Legacy,* 44–46; King, *My Life with Martin Luther King, Jr.,* 53–71; MLK Papers, vol. 2, 201.

69. Interview with Juanita Sellers Stone.

70. Interview with Juanita Sellers Stone; *Atlanta Daily World,* January 2, 1955, 3; August, 28,1960, 3; March 28, 1967, 5; January 21, 1968, 2; August 22, 1976, 3; April 27, 1984, 2; April 29, 1984, 2; May 5, 1987, 5; September 16, 1990, 1; February 14, 1999,4; January 9, 2000, 3; March 26, 2000, 3; October 14, 2004, 3; May 9, 2002, 6; Vernon Wayland Stone Funeral Program, October 13, 2004, Atlanta Funeral Programs Collection, Folder 128, Auburn Avenue Research Library on African-American Culture and History, Atlanta, Georgia; Juanita Sellers Stone Obituary, *Atlanta Journal Constitution,* June 8, 2018; Obituary of Mrs. Juanita Sellers-Stone, William Gayleano Murray & Son Funeral Home, Inc., https://www.wgmurrayandson.com/obituary/MrsJuanita-Sellers-Stone.

71. *Atlanta Daily World,* January 2, 1955, 3; August 28,1960, 3; March 28, 1967, 5; January 21, 1968, 2; August 22, 1976, 3; April 27, 1984, 2; April 29, 1984, 2; May 5, 1987, 5; September 16, 1990, 1; February 14, 1999,4; January 9, 2000, 3; March 26, 2000, 3; October 14, 2004, 3; May 9, 2002, 6; Obituary of Mrs. Juanita Sellers-Stone.

38. Montgomery

1. Interview with Coretta Scott King, transcript, Hatch Papers, box 22, folder 4, tape 3. On Malcolm X, see Malcom X, *Autobiography,* 226; Jeanne Theoharis, *King of the North: Martin Luther King, Jr.'s Life of Struggle Outside the South* (New York: New Press, 2025), 46.

2. Coretta Scott King, *My Life with Martin Luther King, Jr.* (New York: Holt, Rinehart, and Winston, 1969), 90–91. For a broader discussion of their relationship dynamics, see Theoharis, *King of the North*.

3. King, *My Life with Martin Luther King, Jr.*, 94; letter, W. T. Handy Jr. to ML, November 18, 1952, MLK Papers, vol. 2, 160–64; "Conversation between Cornish Rogers and David Thelen," *Journal of American History* 78, no. 1 (June 1991): 41–62.

4. King, *My Life with Martin Luther King, Jr.*, 90–93.

5. Martin Luther King Jr., *Stride Toward Freedom: The Montgomery Story* (New York & London: Harper & Row, 1958), 16–24; King, *My Life with Martin Luther King, Jr.*, 94; Benjamin E. Mays, *Born to Rebel: An Autobiography* (Athens & London: University of Georgia Press, 1971), 266; MLK Papers, vol. 2, 28.

6. King Jr., *Stride Toward Freedom: The Montgomery Story*, 16–24; King, *My Life with Martin Luther King, Jr.*, 94.

7. King Jr., *Stride Toward Freedom: The Montgomery Story*, 16–24; King, *My Life with Martin Luther King, Jr.*, 95–97.

8. King Jr., *Stride Toward Freedom: The Montgomery Story*, 16–24; King, *My Life with Martin Luther King, Jr.*, 95–97; MLK Papers, vol. 6; "The Three Dimensions of a Complete Life," Sermon Delivered at the Unitarian Church of Germantown," King Institute, https://kinginstitute.stanford.edu/king-papers/documents/three-dimensions-complete-life-sermon-delivered-unitarian-church-germantown#ftnref1.

9. King, *My Life with Martin Luther King, Jr.*, 95–97.

10. MLK Papers, vol. 2, 30.

11. Martin Luther King Jr., "Recommendations to the Dexter Avenue Baptist Church for the Fiscal Year 1954–1955," September 5, 1954, in MLK Papers, vol. 2, 287–94; Binita Mahato, Rebecca Retzlaff, and Xi Chen, "Planning, Civil Rights, and African American Voting: The Case of Montgomery, Alabama," *Journal of Planning Education and Research* 44, no. 4 (2022).

12. King Jr., "Recommendations to the Dexter Avenue Baptist Church for the Fiscal Year 1954-1955."

13. King Jr., "Recommendations to the Dexter Avenue Baptist Church for the Fiscal Year 1954–1955."

Illustration Credits

page 262: *(top photo)* "*The Maroon Tiger*, Senior Edition, May 1947." Morehouse College, *The Maroon Tiger*, 1940–1949. Morehouse College, May 1947. Morehouse College Archives; *(bottom photo)* Griffith J. Davis Photographs and Films, Duke University Libraries Repository Collections and Archives.

page 265: "*The Maroon Tiger*, December 1946." Morehouse College, *The Maroon Tiger*, 1940–1949, Morehouse College, December 1947. Morehouse College Archives.

page 272: Courtesy of the Spelman College Archives.

page 275: Courtesy of the Spelman College Archives.

page 280: "*Morehouse College Bulletin*, vol. 32, no. 102, November 1964." Morehouse College Communications: 1960–1969. Morehouse College, November 1964. Atlanta University Center Robert W. Woodruff Library.

page 292: "*The Maroon Tiger*, May–June 1948." Morehouse College, *The Maroon Tiger*, 1940–1949. Morehouse College, May 1948, Morehouse College Archives.

page 295: Richard Kaplan Collection, Wisconsin Center for Film and Theater Research, University of Wisconsin, Madison.

page 326: Photo by Axel Bahnsen. Courtesy of Antiochiana, Antioch College.

page 349: *Atlanta Daily World*. Image published with permission of ProQuest LCC. Further reproduction is prohibited without permission.

Index